Research Reports Esprit

Project 6128 · FORMAT · Volume 1

Edited in cooperation with the European Commission, DG III/F

Esprit, the Information Technology R&D Programme, was set up in 1984 as a co-operative research programme involving European IT companies, IT "user" organisations, large and small, and academic institutions. Managed by DGIII/F of the European Commission, its aim is to contribute to the development of a competitive industrial base in an area of crucial importance for the entire European economy. The current phase of the IT programme comprises the following eight domains: software technologies, technologies for components and subsystems, multimedia systems, long-term research, open microprocessor systems initiative, high-performance computing and networking, technologies for business processes, and integration in manufacturing.

The *Research Reports Esprit* series is helping to disseminate the many results – products and services, tools and methods, and international standards – arising from the hundreds of projects that have already been launched, involving thousands of researchers.

Springer
Berlin
Heidelberg
New York
Barcelona
Budapest
Hong Kong
London
Milan
Paris
Santa Clara
Singapore
Tokyo

C. Delgado Kloos   W. Damm   (Eds.)

Practical
Formal Methods
for Hardware Design

 Springer

Volume Editors

Carlos Delgado Kloos
Universidad Carlos III de Madrid
Depto. Ingeniería
C/Butarque, 15
E-28911 Leganés/Madrid, Spain

Werner Damm
Universität Oldenburg
Fachbereich Informatik, Abt. Rechnerarchitektur
Postfach 2503
D-26111 Oldenburg, Germany

Cataloging-in-Publication Data applied for

Die Deutsche Bibliothek - CIP-Einheitsaufnahme

Practical formal methods for hardware design / C. Delgado Kloos
; W. Damm (ed.). - Berlin ; Heidelberg ; New York ; Barcelona ;
Budapest ; Hong Kong ; London ; Milan ; Paris ; Santa Clara ;
Singapore ; Tokyo : Springer, 1997
  (Research reports ESPRIT : FORMAT ; Vol. 1)

CR Subject Classification (1991): B.1.2, B.4.4, B.5.2, B.6.3, F.3.1

ISBN-13: 978-3-540-62007-5   e-ISBN-13: 978-3-642-60641-0

DOI: 10.1007/ 978-3-642-60641-0

Publication No. EUR 17535 EN of the
European Commission, Dissemination of Scientific and Technical Knowledge Unit,
Directorate-General Telecommunications, Information Market and Exploitation of Research,
Luxembourg.

Typesetting: Camera-ready by the editors
SPIN: 10551972   45/3142-543210 – Printed on acid-free paper

Preface

Mike Newman

European Commission, Belgium

I am very pleased to be asked to contribute a foreword for this book. In my role as Project Officer in the European Commission as part of the Esprit Programme, I was involved with the FORMAT Project since its inception.

The use of formal methods for design verification appears to be finally entering the realm of real commercial and tangible benefits on realistically complex designs. Recent incidents, such as the famous design flaw in the processor chip from a well-known American manufacturer, have graphically illustrated the potentially enormous costs of corrective action where such a flaw is detected by customers only after sales have commenced. Since tools based on formal methods often require extensive re-training of designers, some such motivation is needed to embark on their serious use.

The FORMAT project has certainly not solved all of the problems in the use of formal methods which were identified at the start of the project, but many significant breakthroughs have been achieved. A good example is the new capability of the tools to offer counter-examples where a proof has failed. This is much more valuable to a designer than the simple knowledge that he has an error 'somewhere'. Probably the optimum verification approach will need the combined efforts of both simulation and formal verification tools for the foreseeable future, but at least they are being given a chance to work intelligently together.

In addition, the FORMAT Project was a very good example of successful application of the underlying principle of Esprit whereby several partners with complementary skills collaborate to achieve a joint goal. Thus all have equal access to exploit the common result while their costs are shared and then assisted by a contribution from the European Commission. In a successful collaboration this multiplying effect can be very beneficial and this was the case for FORMAT. Not only was the necessary mix of researchers, managers, CAD vendors and user companies involved but the indefinable spark, which is needed before such collaborations really take off, was also evident.

Valuable results have certainly flowed from the work; new and powerful CAD products were announced on the market before the project was even finished, and the user companies were also able to show important improvements in the detection of design errors in time to avoid expensive re-designs. I confidently recommend this book to any reader interested in this field.

Brussels, July 1996

Table of Contents

Part III. Technical Background

The FORMAT Model Checker
Andreas Scholz, Thomas Filkorn, Jörg Lohse, Hans-Albert Schneider,
Erik Tidén, and Peter Warkentin 175

Reasoning
Nick Chapman, Simon Finn, and Michael P. Fourman 184

VHDL Formal Modeling and Analysis
Luis Entrena, Serafín Olcoz, and Juan Goicolea 217

List of Contributors

Massimo Bombana
Italtel Sit-DRSC
I–20019 Castelletto di
Settimo Milanese (Milano)
Italy

Jörg Bormann
Siemens AG
Corp. Research and Development
Otto-Hahn-Ring 6
D–81730 München
Germany

Patrizia Cavalloro
Italtel Sit-DRSC
I–20019 Castelletto di
Settimo Milanese (Milano)
Italy

Nick Chapman
Abstract Hardware Ltd.
Brunel Science Park
GB–Uxbridge, Middlesex UB8 3PQ
United Kingdom

José Luis Conesa
Telefónica I+D
C/Emilio Vargas, 6
E–28043 Madrid
Spain

Werner Damm
Kuratorium OFFIS e.V.
Escherweg 2
D–26121 Oldenburg
Germany

Carlos Delgado Kloos
Universidad Carlos III de Madrid
Ingeniería Telemática
C/Butarque, 15
E–28911 Leganés/Madrid
Spain

Gert Döhmen
Kuratorium OFFIS e.V.
Escherweg 2
D–26121 Oldenburg
Germany

Luis Entrena Arrontes
Universidad Carlos III de Madrid
Tecnología Electrónica
C/Butarque, 15
E–28911 Leganés/Madrid
Spain

Fabrizio Ferrandi
Dipartimento di Elettronica e
Informazione
Politecnico di Milano
P.za Leonardo da Vinci, 32
I–20133 Milano
Italy

Simon Finn
Abstract Hardware Ltd.
Brunel Science Park
GB–Uxbridge, Middlesex UB8 3PQ
United Kingdom

Thomas Filkorn
Siemens AG
Corp. Research and Development
Otto-Hahn-Ring 6
D–81730 München
Germany

Michael P. Fourman
Abstract Hardware Ltd.
Brunel Science Park
GB–Uxbridge, Middlesex UB8 3PQ
United Kingdom

Juan Goicolea Ruigómez
Design Technology Department
Tecnología y Gestión de la Inno-
vación
C/Velázquez, 134 bis
E–28006 Madrid
Spain

Werner Grass
Universität Passau
Fakultät für Mathematik
und Informatik
Innstr. 33
D–94030 Passau
Germany

Christian Grobe
Universität Passau
Fakultät für Mathematik
und Informatik
Innstr. 33
D–94030 Passau
Germany

Johannes Helbig
McKinsey & Company

Hamburg
Germany

Ronald Herrmann
Siemens AG
Corp. Research and Development
Otto-Hahn-Ring 6
D–81730 München
Germany

Peter Kelb
Kuratorium OFFIS e.V.
Escherweg 2
D–26121 Oldenburg
Germany

Stephan Lenk
Universität Passau
Fakultät für Mathematik
und Informatik
Innstr. 33
D–94030 Passau
Germany

Jörg Lohse
Siemens AG
Corp. Research and Development
Otto-Hahn-Ring 6
D–81730 München
Germany

Andrés Marín López
Universidad Carlos III de Madrid
Ingeniería Telemática
C/Butarque, 15
E–28911 Leganés/Madrid
Spain

Tomás de Miguel Moro
Universidad Politécnica de Madrid
Depto. Ing. de Sistemas Telemáticos
ETSI Telecomunicación
Ciudad Universitaria
E–28040 Madrid
Spain

Heike Müller
Kuratorium OFFIS e.V.
Escherweg 2
D–26121 Oldenburg
Germany

Serafín Olcoz
Design Technology Department
Tecnología y Gestión de la Inno-
vación
C/Velázquez, 134 bis
E–28006 Madrid
Spain

Fernando Palao
Telefónica I+D
C/Emilio Vargas, 6
E–28043 Madrid
Spain

Pierre Plaza
Telefónica I+D
C/Emilio Vargas, 6
E–28043 Madrid
Spain

Tomás Robles Valladares
Universidad Politécnica de Madrid
Depto. Ing. de Sistemas Telemáticos
ETSI Telecomunicación
Ciudad Universitaria
E–28040 Madrid
Spain

Fernanda Salice
Italtel Sit-DRSC
I–20019 Castelletto di Settimo Mi-
lanese (Milano)
Italy

Rainer Schlör
Kuratorium Offis e.V.
D–26121 Oldenburg
Germany

Hans-Albert Schneider
Siemens AG
Corp. Research and Development
Otto-Hahn-Ring 6
D–81730 München
Germany

Andreas Scholz
Siemens AG
Corp. Research and Development
Otto-Hahn-Ring 6
D–81730 München
Germany

Erik Tidén
Siemens AG
Corp. Research and Development
Otto-Hahn-Ring 6
D–81730 München
Germany

Wolf-Dieter Tiedemann
Universität Passau
Fakultät für Mathematik
und Informatik
Innstr. 33
D–94030 Passau
Germany

Peter Warkentin
Siemens AG
Corp. Research and Development
Otto-Hahn-Ring 6
D–81730 München
Germany

Introduction

Carlos Delgado Kloos[1], Werner Damm[2], and Juan Goicolea[3]

[1] Universidad Carlos III de Madrid, Spain
[2] Kuratorium OFFIS e.V., Germany
[3] Tecnología y Gestión de la Innovación, Spain

1. Formal methods vs. conventional ones

If formal methods are so good, why are they not used today in industry? If they can guarantee the correctness of a design without need of extensive simulation, why are designers simulating and emulating more than ever? Is it a matter of the maturity of the theories, of the quality of the tools, of the education of the designers, of the willingness to apply new methods, or of the complexity of the formal methods per se?

Indeed designers *have been* applying formal languages and formal techniques for a long time. At the gate level, designers specify systems using the operators of Boolean Algebra and apply their formal rules transforming one description into another even without noticing. Finite State Machine descriptions belong to a well-studied part of Computer Science for which rich theories exist.

Designers have learned to appreciate the abstraction from currents and voltages to boolean values, and from gate delays and clocked designs to transition functions of finite state machines. Today eliminating this abstraction level from current design practices is not conceivable.

Boolean Algebra and the theory of finite automata are quite limited in their expressiveness. To adequately describe systems at more abstract levels –such as the system level– and verify properties requires more expressive and rich formalisms. These will be introduced into design practices if there is a need that justifies their use. If the justification is there, extensive education is needed and an adaptation of the methods to design practices.

With the introduction of VHDL as a standard hardware description language, the EDA community has already taken a step towards richer models of hardware. Designers have benefitted from powerful simulation and synthesis tools supporting VHDL, and now profit from the rich wealth of experience in modelling hardware systems in VHDL. However, the VHDL standard as it was voted did *not* come equipped with a formal model. To form a basis for formal methods, a mathematical theory supporting VHDL is required.

2. The FORMAT project

The material presented in this book shows how tools supporting correct VHDL based hardware designs can benefit from a rigorous formal model of VHDL. It builds on results of a substantial R&D effort undertaken by a consortium from EDA industry and academia, the FORMAT project, which, within a five year period, turned a firm semantical foundation of VHDL into a toolset supporting formal verification and synthesis, integrated into commercial design tools and design flows, with spin-off products available on the market today.

The technical aproach of FORMAT focused on graphical specification languages enhancing the abstraction levels offered by VHDL, model-checking based verification techniques, and formal synthesis techniques. The key technical achievements of the project, which will be extensively covered in subsequent chapters, are highlighted below.

Graphical specification formalisms were added to VHDL in a conservative style, allowing modelling of components through an extended version of *timing diagrams* and a variant of *StateCharts* designed to allow a smooth integration with the VHDL style of modelling behaviours. The designer can freely mix design-style, binding components to architectures expressed in either standard VHDL or one of several graphical specification formalisms. Designs in this extension of VHDL are compiled using an extension of a commercial VHDL analyzer from LEDA[1].

Formal Verification allows to verify whether or not a design expressed in this extension of VHDL satisfies properties expressed as timing diagrams. The underlying verification engine is a *symbolic model checker*; compilers transform VHDL designs and the properties to be analyzed into internal representations accepted by this verification engine and produce diagnostic information as a stimuli-file (accepted by VHDL simulators in case of errors being detected). To cope with complexity of larger systems, *compositional verification methods* are supported.

Formal Synthesis allows the generation of synthesizable VHDL from timing diagrams; while automatic compilation is provided, interactive use of the synthesizer allows integration of existing modules into the synthesized code.

These technical developments were complemented by substantial work on design methodology and tool evaluations using industrial case studies, including two ASIC developments for telecommunication applications, and a PCI bus controller.

The challenge undertaken by the FORMAT project to equip VHDL with such a formal design environment required a joint effort between academia and industry. Only cooperation between theory makers, tool makers and designers can provide the close feed-back loop required to achieve a balance between what is mathematically feasible and what is required in practice.

---

[1] © LEDA S.A. France

The project comprised as partners five European enterprises (Siemens, Italtel, Telefónica I+D, TGI, and AHL), the research institute OFFIS, and two universities (Madrid and Passau). The FORMAT project was funded by the European Commission from June 1992 to November 1995.

The application of formal methods has a cost: a cost in their introduction and their application. The cost will only be accepted if the techniques produce much better results than the conventional ones, they are a solution to the increased complexity of systems and/or they can prevent greater losses due to buggy designs.

Whether formal methods are cost effective or not, or whether they will be applied in the future is something the market will decide. The evaluation of the tools within the project has significantly pushed forwards the complexity of the designs that can be handled. As products come onto the market further optimizations are undertaken. The FORMAT project has paved this way for the introduction of formal design tools into the EDA market.

3. Organization of this book

This book is divided into three main parts. The first part gives an overview of the main goals and approaches of the FORMAT project. A chapter on design methodology sets the FORMAT work into the context of hardware design, its current and possible future practices. The following chapter presents the specification languages of the FORMAT project. They include both visual as well as textual languages. The visual languages are timing diagrams and a state-based formalism. The textual languages are VHDL, on which the whole project is based, and temporal logic. The following two chapters present the two main lines of investigation within the project: verification and synthesis.

Part II covers some of the experiments carried out by the industrial companies in the consortium. They have provided a very critical review of the achievements of the project from different viewpoints, especially so taking into account that the degree of familiarity of the industrial groups with formal methods varied from 'no previous experience' to high familiarity.

Part III includes the material about technical work carried out in the project, dealing in separate sections with the key technologies underlying the verification and the synthesis tools.

The FORMAT effort is a work that has extended during many years. The main lines of research were designed during 1991, when the project proposal was planned. The project itself extended from 1 June 1992 to 30 November 1995, although the cooperation among partners extended well into 1996 for the final review and the finalization of this book.

During this time, and especially after the project was finished, some of the persons moved. The authors are credited with their present affiliation, although their work might have been performed somewhere else. To reflect a fairer account of the work done, we indicate here the original affiliations:

4		C. Delgado Kloos et al.

- Ronald Herrmann moved from OFFIS to Siemens (this is also a means of technology transfer from academia to industry)
- Johannes Helbig has moved from OFFIS to McKinsey & Company
- Carlos Delgado Kloos and Andrés Marín López have moved from Universidad Politécnica de Madrid to Universidad Carlos III de Madrid
- Luis Entrena Arrontes has moved from TGI to Universidad Carlos III de Madrid

The authors would like to thank the European Commission for the support of the FORMAT project. Our Project Officer, Mike Newman, deserves particular mention and the referees Luc Claesen and Phillipe Oddo are to be thanked for their useful comments and proposals. Special thanks is to be given also to Springer Verlag, and in particular to Hans Wössner, for their understanding and patience during the finalization of the manuscript. The first editor also wishes to express his appreciation of the efforts of Peter T. Breuer and Andrés Marín in the preparation and finalization of this manuscript.

Part I

Overview

Design Methodology for Complex VLSI Devices

Massimo Bombana[1] and Fabrizio Ferrandi[2]

[1] Italtel, Italy
[2] Politecnico di Milano, Italy

1. Introduction: needs and constraints of the ESDA market

In recent years the ratio between the design time of a new microelectronic component and its mean life on the market increased constantly. This was due to the growing complexity of the devices and components required by the market for the final applications. ASICs (Application Specific Integrated Circuits) and mixed hardware/software components are more and more measured in a range exceeding the 100/200 K-equivalent gates. While adequate manufacturing technologies have been introduced, the currently available ESDA (Electronic System Design Automation) tools have not kept the pace with market requirements. Even considering the advantages introduced by the wider and wider use of hardware description languages (basically Verilog and VHDL, with a predominance of the latter) for specification and simulation purposes, the vast majority of cost-effective circuit designs being done today using efficiently ESDA tools cannot exceed the limit of 100 K-equivalent gates. Obviously the industry and users are not satisfied with such a market offer, and the pressure on the ESDA vendors to develop new and more powerful system-level tools is strong. If this demand is not successfully answered, it is expected that serious bottlenecks in the design and production of complex systems in the near future will be directly linked to the failures of the proposed design methodologies and associated design flows.

In addition to chip complexity, the next generation of ESDA tools will have also to guarantee a significant decrease of the parameter called 'time to market'. Let us consider the example of ASICs manufacturing for telecom applications. The telecom market increase is estimated in terms of a rate of growth of 7% per year. Considering Europe alone, it is expected that the telecom domain will increase from 3% to 7% of the overall gross domestic product. To keep pace with such a growth of the market, the ASIC design cycle from concept to volume production should decrease from 52 weeks in 1994 to 38 weeks (Dataquest July 1994). This goal seems difficult to satisfy, considering that this demand is overlapping with the handling of the more and more complex tasks of design and manufacturing. Such diverging requirements, coming from both the technical and economic sides, make the introduction of innovative ESDA tools and design methodologies at the same time a strategic and challenging goal.

The complexity issue is currently managed by using the features of commercially available ESDA frameworks (see chapter "Italtel Application of the FORMAT Design Flow") supported by networks of workstations. This guarantees greater computation efficiency in a multi-vendor design flow environment. Telecom companies are already fully exploiting these technological advantages. Within this perspective, the introduction of innovative design methodologies is perceived as a crucial factor to maintain or expand the market shares. Specifically, it is expected that the new design methods should lead to shorter design times through exact and rigorous design methods and to the reduction of the number of re-design loops in the implementation phase.

At this point it is necessary to look more closely at the phases of the design process. To produce manageable solutions, it is necessary to trim the goal, identifying the areas where the innovation effort should be focused. The design experience in manufacturing sites and the requirements coming from designers are the best sources of information to be merged with the market demands. A traditional analysis of the design process identifies three main critical phases: specification phase, implementation phase and validation phase. These phases are the macro-blocks of design loops, applied for error correction and improvement of the solutions. Each phase is supported by ESDA tools of different vendors and includes various specific tasks (fig. 1.1). For instance, the specification phase involves also the exploration of the design space in search of the 'best' implementation. This task is carried out applying tentatively different structural partitionings prior to the application of logic synthesis tools. Behavioral modeling of functional blocks is also a crucial task of this phase.

This level of granularity is apt to identify those critical areas of the design flow, i.e. the steps of the design process where improvements are needed to support the designers. Such critical areas tend to concentrate in the specification and validation phases. Priorities are associated with these critical areas based on the users' requirements. This fact is clearly linked with the two main factors mentioned previously: design complexity and time to market. In fact, the early stages of the design flow are unsupported in terms of automatic tools able to cope with the complexity issues. A correct approach to this phase decreases substantially the number of errors and of re-design loops, so also impacting positively the time to market. At medium and low design levels the problem has been faced and partially solved. Automatic tools, able to properly assist the designers' activity, are available on the market and used in most production sites.

As a consequence of this analysis, the FORMAT Project focused its approach on the initial and more abstract steps of the design process (namely 'capture of requirements' and 'exploration of design' in fig. 1.1). These phases still miss a sound and comprehensive semantics even if it is universally rec-

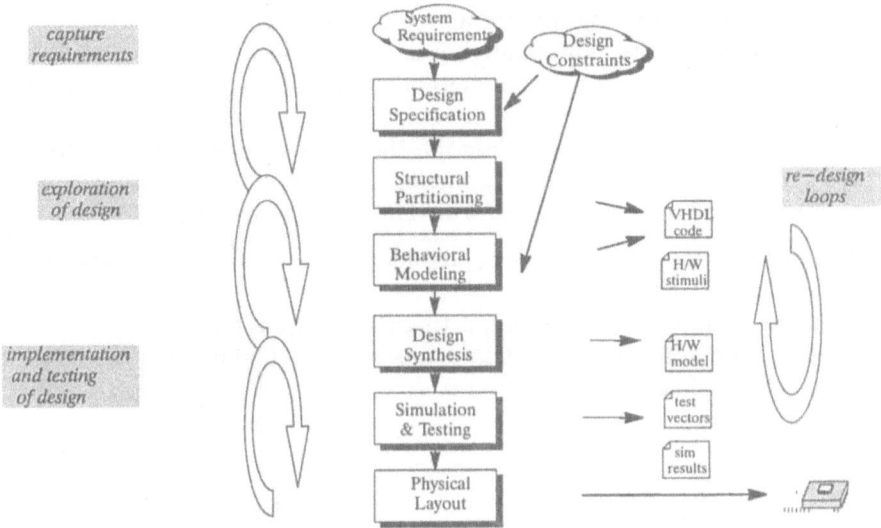

Fig. 1.1. Schematic representation of the design flow.

ognized that many choices performed at this level, i.e. design specification, architecture definition, system partitioning and so on, heavily influence the overall efficiency of the following phases of the design flow. Generally, the earlier the inconsistencies are introduced, the more difficult is the process of their identification in the subsequent phases of the design process. This is why the solution of this problem involves abstraction processes. Formal methods are potentially good candidates to solve part of the existing problems at the specification level. Formal methods guarantee the required abstract approach, the rigor of formally based proofs, and the capability of properly addressing the early design stages where no technology or even architecture commitment has yet been made.

The FORMAT Project intends to provide answers to the main existing problems:

- the complexity of designs;
- the inconsistencies of the specification languages and techniques;
- human errors;
- the resistance to the introduction of innovations;

The identified solutions involve formal methods for the correction of errors in the specifications, including partitioning strategies, transformational synthesis for control-based parts of applications, and user friendly graphical interfaces to address the last point of the list.

The condition 'sine qua non' for an effective use of these solutions is the integration of this new design phase into the consolidated design flow. This step is basic to the entire activity and is strongly required by the users. Moreover, it will guarantee users' acceptance and will help in the market exploitation of the obtained results. The final goal is to provide final users with a unified front-end supporting a design methodology from system specification to layout.

In the following sections we describe the steps covered in the FORMAT Project to develop a practical and coherent design methodology based on the ideas sketched in the previous sections. These steps include:

- the identification of the users' requirements and critical areas in the design flow for improvement;
- the implementation of tools supporting these requirements;
- the definition of a design flow based on such tools highlighting the benefits derived from their application.

2. The design flow

At a closer look, one discovers that variations of design processes and design styles in different sites are much wider than expected. A recent survey (Dataquest) shows that, in 1994, 41% of the electronic device manufacturers use up to now 'NO' automatic ESDA tools in their design flows. This piece of data is astonishing, but documents the existing resistance to the application of cost effective tools in many design environments today and testifies how large the potential market is for ESDA tools. The growth estimations of the demand for emulation and system simulation is, for instance, respectively 25% and 35% per year for the next future, while ESDA market in general will grow at the much higher rate of 100% per year.

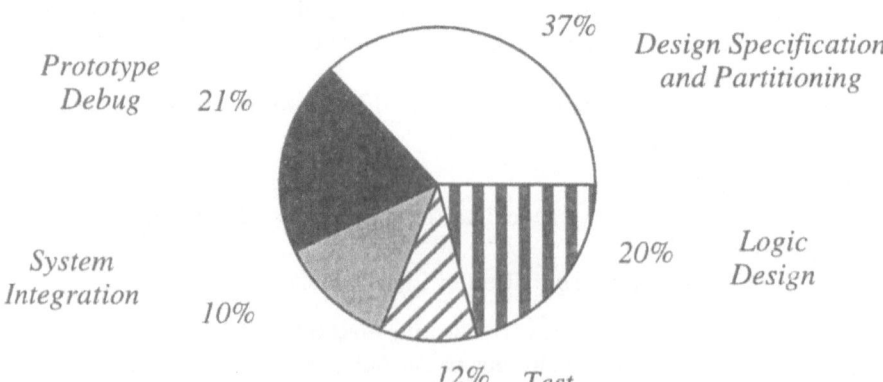

Fig. 2.1. Time splitting of design tasks.

A survey of the average time devoted to different design tasks, including specification, best system architecture partitioning, hardware and software modules cooperation, simulation and so on, can be a good indicator of the expected market needs (fig. 2.1). This data shows clearly that the specification phase, including the partitioning task, and the system integration phase, cover almost half the design time of a component. This analysis supports the feeling of the consortium of the FORMAT Project that the main effort of the ESDA developers should be devoted to provide tools supporting the designer in these two phases.

2.1 Design specification and documentation

Each manufacturing site implements different and proprietary procedures to write, prove and document initial specifications. In some cases, not even in the same site a unified approach exists or is followed strictly by all the designers. Informal strategies based on long-term experience of designers are also widely applied. Notwithstanding this variety of approaches, a few common guidelines can be identified and have a rather general validity.

As expected, natural language plays a basic role in the formalization of abstract system specifications, mainly at the initial and more abstract phases of the process. Due to the ambiguity, lack of conciseness and informality of natural language, the specifications are complemented by a series of different, more technical oriented representations. Timing properties and control based blocks are specified graphically to improve the readability of the information.

Behavioral entities and abstract functions are later described in hardware oriented languages, or in languages, such as C or C++, which allow to evaluate the computations of algorithms. Control/data flow graphs and state-based representations are used to introduce more refined descriptions of the identified functions to be performed by computation or control parts. Structural partitioning is supported by the specification of hierarchical netlists, where block types and connections are represented. Communication protocols between adjoining blocks, and between the system and the environment, are specified providing timing diagrams, which depict graphically the sequence of events on signals belonging to the interface of the cooperating modules. All these descriptions are updated by the designer during the implementation phase, according to the results obtained at levels that are closer to the final implementation, including technological parameters. At the end of this phase, this body of heterogeneous descriptions represents also the final documentation of the features and characteristics of the chip, including timing responses, latencies and so on. In this way, for instance, timing diagrams (fig. 2.2) and quantitative time annotations can be used to describe the timing behavior of the final implementation. State based charts (fig. 2.3) document the state sequence of the sequential modules, and so on.

In order to comply with the requirement of building new design features starting from the existing state of the art, the FORMAT Project proposed a new specification language, VHDL/S, based on the use of VHDL improved with the inclusion of timing diagrams and state charts.

The extensions are aimed at addressing the complex issue of hardware/software trade-off by providing VHDL with specification methods bridging the gap between hardware and the lower levels of software design. VHDL/S features a common specification interface containing timing diagrams as a graphical specification mechanism together with data type and state based specifications.

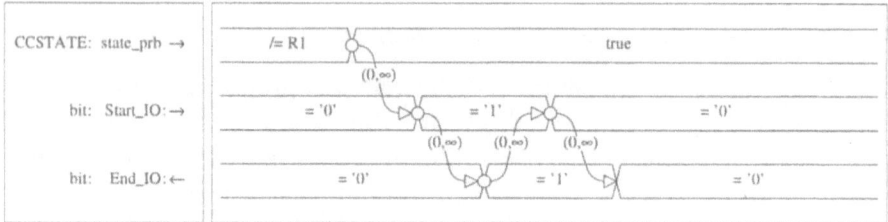

Fig. 2.2. Timing diagrams.

From the previous analysis, it is clear that designers are used to apply all these features at the specification and documentation levels. The case of VHDL will be analyzed in section 2.2, due to its wide use and fundamental importance. Timing diagrams and state charts are appreciated for their features to provide concise information about the system in a graphical and user-friendly way. In this set of representations, timing diagrams were lacking up to now a universally accepted semantics. Initially an effort has been devoted to fill this gap, allowing in this way to transform them from post-design documentation means into a real system specification language. The following chapter of this book "Specification Languages" will provide a summary of the syntax and semantics that have been defined as a task of the project for timing diagrams. Based on this formalization, two different uses of timing diagrams are foreseen:

1. they can be applied to specify general properties to be verified in VHDL behavioral models;
2. they can be used to provide the complete specification of a control-based block or protocol, to be automatically synthesized into VHDL code.

On the contrary, commercial tools applying hierarchic state-based charts as entry language for system specifications are commercially available. Some of them are very sophisticated and include tools assisting the designer in structured system descriptions. They can generate VHDL or C code associated with the nodes of the graph. Simulators and animators are linked to their internal representations of the data and provide the way to the verification phase.

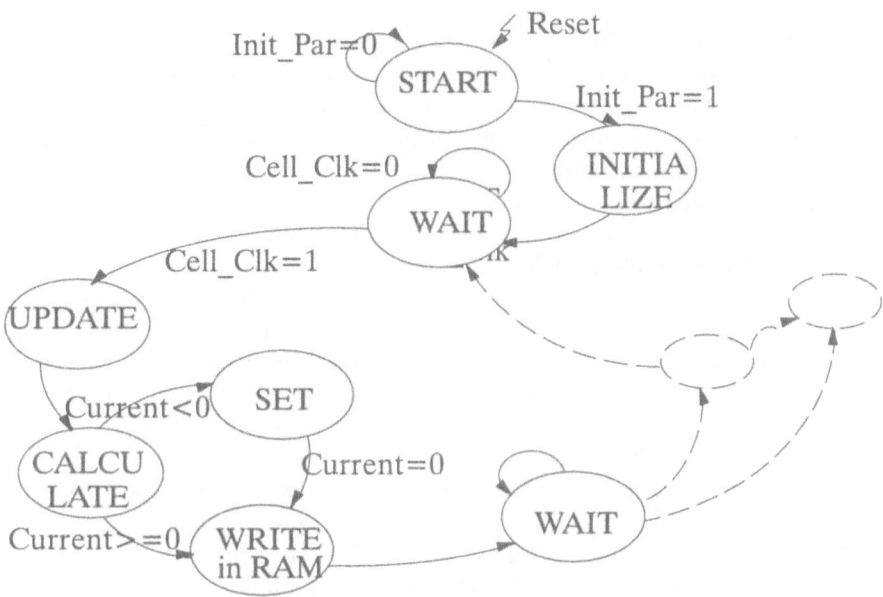

Fig. 2.3. State chart representing a phase of the control part.

From the user's point of view, there are many advantages of the specification language VHDL/S proposed in FORMAT:

- the representations are known to final users, who have been using them for a long time;
- they have the required conciseness and are able to capture a great deal of information in a simple way;
- VHDL/S allows the verification of VHDL behavioral code;
- for control-based applications the automatic generation of VHDL code is provided.

Examples of application of this new specification language will be considered in the following chapters.

2.2 VHDL for simulation and synthesis

It is widely recognized that the use of specification languages endowed with formal semantics can guarantee consistency in system definition. Moreover, validation procedures can be applied also at the specification level. The application of such methods allows an early detection of errors and minimizes the number of operating loops between specification and implementation. Hardware specification languages with a formal semantics are still missing, but VHDL has gained wide appreciation in the users' community, and has become a de-facto standard as a description language for complex systems.

Moreover, its semantics has been recently assessed by the theoretical developments in the FORMAT Project. Nowadays VHDL is the standard language used by most of the ESDA tools for hardware specifications. This makes it the ideal instrument to provide integration between different tools, and to develop portable applications.

VHDL is a powerful hardware description language to write, read and simulate hardware specifications. It approaches different levels of abstraction and different models (behavioral, structural, data-flow oriented). As a consequence it is a complex language, characterized by a great number of statements, constructs and data types. From the user's point of view this is at the same time an advantage and a drawback: the language is extremely expressive but long and expensive trainings are required before the typical designer can become acquainted with all its elements and is able to exploit efficiently all the available features.

Logic synthesis was beyond the initial scope of the language. Anyway, following its wide acceptance by users, VHDL has been selected also as entry level for many commercial synthesis tools. This step implied that a whole set of statements had to be discarded, being meaningless for synthesis. For instance, the statements involving a precise definition of quantitative time could not be included.

Basic strategies for system specification are applied when using VHDL. Structural partitioning is applied on a functional basis. Different hierarchical levels of the device are identified, and netlists are defined in terms of simpler blocks. Each block of the netlist is also described by a VHDL architectural behavior. The definition of the entity provides information on its external interface.

For simulation, synthesis and modelling purposes, VHDL has imposed itself as the most used specification language. The interfaces provided by the ESDA vendors in terms of VHDL make it also the best tool through which integration can be obtained. These facts imposed VHDL as the basic specification language to be applied in the FORMAT Project.

2.3 From specification to implementation

Implementation steps are the transformations from the abstract level of specification into the more detailed descriptions, down to the physical level. Design flows implement the selected design methodology and control and apply the required transformations. In detail, the design flow actions include the definition of the sequence of activation of ESDA tools, the number of checks and tests to be applied at each level, the overall organization and application of site dependent design rules. The characteristics of each design flow depend on the complexity of the devices, on the innovation degree of the design environment, and on the adopted ESDA framework.

ESDA frameworks constitute the backbone in which design flows are customized, and play a basic role in any industrial site. They offer the integration facilities which are essential for the implementation of a correct design flow in a multi-vendor environment. They manage the database, allowing tool developments in an integrated or encapsulated manner. Moreover, they provide support for the design process and guarantee a common user interface, increasing the designers' acceptance and the user friendliness of the design flow. The benefits associated with the multi-vendor environment are also evident: it is possible to select the best tool according to the task, it is possible to update and increase incrementally the quality and size of the environment changing the mixture of the applied ESDA tools.

Logic synthesis can potentially provide correct by construction, even if not optimized, implementations. ESDA tools applying logic synthesis are increasing their application range in industrial sites, even if it is recognized that the correctness of their algorithms, and as a consequence also of the implementations, cannot be formally guaranteed. Cases are known in which errors on synthesized netlists have been discovered by simulation or formal verification. Moreover, it is often the case that transformations and optimizations on synthesized netlists are carried out manually, thus loosing the correctness property which was preserved at the higher levels of design. Hence, a considerable effort has been recently devoted to the exploitation of the synergism between formal synthesis tools and logic synthesis tools to cover also the abstract phases of a unified standard design flow.

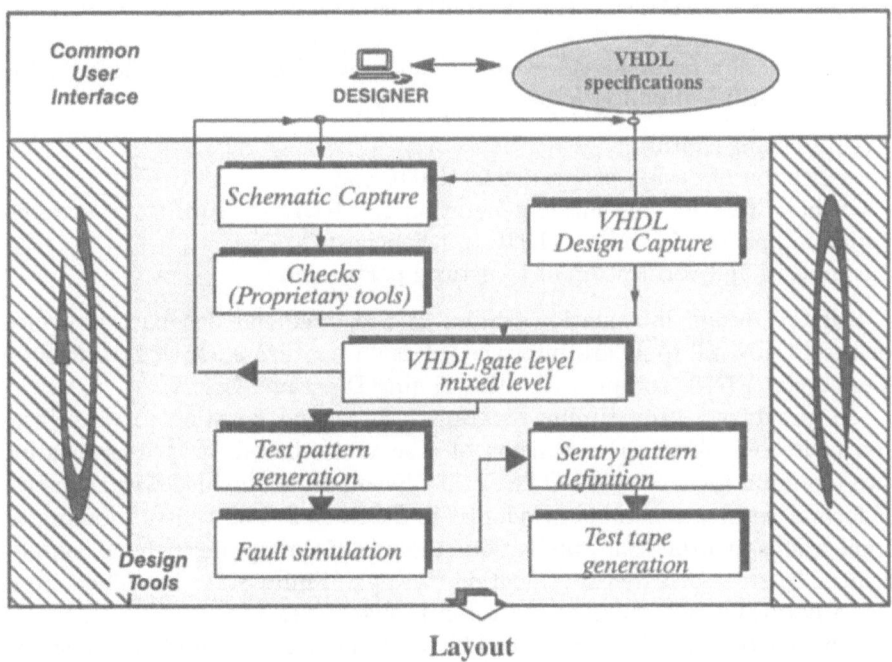

Fig. 2.4. Standard design flow encapsulated into an ESDA Framework.

Considering what we said at the beginning of section 2., it is not surprising that schematic capture is still widely used. This is due to the fact that it allows the re-use of large libraries of previously designed modules and exploits efficiently the designer's previous experience. A real design flow includes both VHDL specifications, used for the subsequent application of logic synthesis tools or for simulation, and the more traditional and error prone but efficient practice of schematic capture (figure 2.4).

Bottlenecks of this design flow include:

- the transformation from informal specification into VHDL or into schematic level specification is ambiguous;
- the verification of the equivalence between specification and implementation is done through simulation. This doesn't guarantee the exhaustive exploration of possibilities and depends on the choice of the input patterns;
- the timing simulation is cpu intensive;
- the logic synthesis process is cpu intensive and requires well defined design constraints specifications.

While the latter points are intrinsic to the methodology and can be improved only through the use of more powerful hardware platforms, the former points are suitable for improvement applying formal methods.

3. Design capture with VHDL/S

From the user's point of view, the methodological approach defined in the project identifies (fig. 3.1) four main application flows:

- requirement capture;
- verification of design properties in VHDL code;
- synthesis flow for automatic generation of VHDL descriptions of communicating protocols and of VHDL test-benches;
- compositional verification of structural partitioning.

All the design information resides in a commercial database to which all the FORMAT tools are interfaced. Design capture is carried on using a commercial VHDL compiler and the Timing Diagrams Editor.

As previously said, timing diagrams are a good notation for interfaces and protocols. With the definition of a semantic based upon a translation into temporal logic or into LOTOS, they have been embedded within the set of formal verification tools developed in FORMAT. For control-dominated applications or processor applications the use of timing diagrams is complemented by state-oriented specification concepts. Finite State Machines are in fact a natural way to specify control-intensive tasks.

The FORMAT methodology can be put to use once a complete and significant Initial Systems Requirements Specification is defined. Using the Timing Diagram Editor, temporal logic descriptions of properties and State Charts,

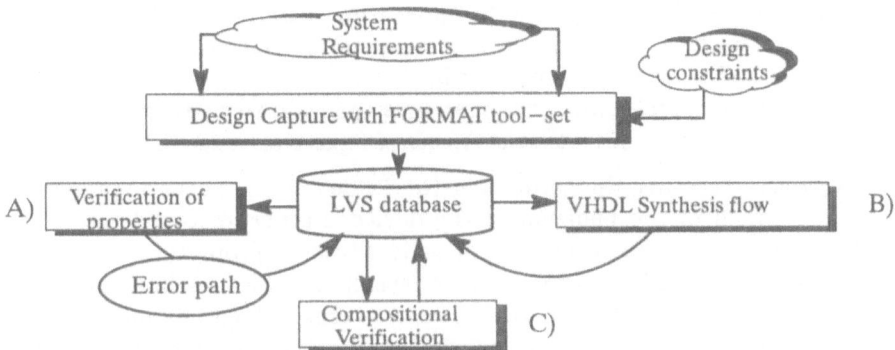

Fig. 3.1. Schematic representation of the FORMAT Design Flow.

Path A: properties verification.	Path B: synthesis.	Path C: compositional verification.
For each C_i	$S => \Sigma\ C_i$	
des_specs Temporal logic: Timing diagrams	*des_spec* Timing diagrams Annotations	*des_specs* Temporal logic: Timing diagrams
VHDL behavioral body *des_impls* VHDL configuration state−based description	*des_impls* null	VHDL entity declaration *des_impls* VHDL netlists VHDL configuration
Proof is obtained with: Symbolic model checking	Synthesis is obtained with: LOTOS−based transformational tools Structurizer	Proof is obtained with: LAMBDA + Tautology checker Proover

Fig. 3.2. FORMAT design scenarios.

the Formal Requirements Specification can be produced (see next chapter "Specification Languages"). The addition of behavioral and structural descriptions in plain VHDL will form the global system specification.

Alternatives are available to the designer. The user chooses which path to follow according to the needs and the application requirements. Specifically it is not always necessary to have a 'complete' system specification for properties verification and for compositional verification.

Figure 3.2 describes what the user must provide to activate one of the three different design paths (Paths A,B,C of figures 3.1 and 3.2):

- *design-specifications*: this term indicates the definition of general properties to be verified in the behavior of the device. Properties can describe the ability of the system to evolve correctly (liveness properties, absence of dead-locks, etc.), or conditions that the system must ensure in its functions (safe properties). Properties are expressed as timing diagrams and temporal logic formulae. They consist of assumptions, representing hypotheses on the behavior of the environment, and commitments, expressing the required properties. This information is needed for paths A and C. Activation of path B implies the specification of timing diagrams representing a complete description of the behavior required by the system;
- *design-implementations*: this term indicates the types of the device description for which properties will be checked. These can be behavioral and structural VHDL specifications or state-based charts. The activation of phase B does not require this input, because the VHDL code will be generated automatically by the tools.

A summary of the tools required in the different design scenarios is shown in fig. 3.2.

4. The Format methodology at work

The goal of the project was to design, implement and test a set of tools able to satisfy a variety of needs at the specification level. Based on the fact that different needs are satisfied by appropriate tools, and that no general solution can be provided on a monolithic basis, flexibility was enhanced designing a modular toolset, where the user could select the best tool for each need.

The verification of properties is accomplished by the use of a model checker. This tool uses BDD based model checking techniques and verifies that an implementation specified in terms of a transition system satisfies a specification given in terms of a formula in temporal logic (see next chapter "The FORMAT Model Checker"). The model checker can also prove (by a process of weak simulation) that one design entity is refined by another. A tautology checker, included in the same package, is able to determine the universal correctness of a Temporal Logic Formula. An advanced feature of this package, seldom found in similar tools, is the sophisticated error path that is produced when the property is not satisfied by the chosen implementation. This is the real important information required by the user, enabling the improvement of the implementation code. The error path consists of a simulation sequence, leading from the activation of the process till the event that contradicts the required property. An interface has been developed to allow a visualization of the sequence of patterns in the same editing tool (the Timing Diagram Editor) used to specify the properties. In this way the user is given both a simulation counter-example and a graphical representation of the found contradiction.

The compositional verification is accomplished by using the theorem prover LAMBDA, a commercial tool unique in its class of application. Previously used as a high-level formal-based synthesizer, it is at the same time a powerful interactive theorem prover which has the power to formalize all other theories within the project. A skeleton of the proofs to be accomplished is provided automatically. The user has to proceed in the proof, selecting the best strategies. This part of the methodology implies a good level of familiarity with theorem proving. This positions this part of the flow at the most advanced level of the FORMAT application.

Finally the VHDL synthesis is performed by the VHDL Synthesizer which accepts the timing diagram language annotated with a subset of VHDL and synthesizes this into working VHDL descriptions. These descriptions can then be synthesized to circuits using existing commercial tools (logic synthesizers). The intermediate format applied in the transformational tool is LOTOS. Anyway,this language is not visible to the user. It provides the semantics for Timing Diagrams and transformations, but is transparent to the final users, since a completely automatic flow has been built around it. The quality of the synthesized VHDL code, and the possible applications of this package in a development environment will be mainly covered in the sections devoted to the applications.

Graphical tools are used as support in various phases of the design flow: the Timing Diagram editor is applied to specify the design specifications as Timing diagrams, a graphical tool visualizes the obtained finite state machine generated from the timing diagrams, and supports a simplification of the representation. The Timing Diagram Editor is also applied to graphically represent the output of the error path for the verification path.

The FORMAT methodology proposes a generic design flow based around four phases (fig. 4.1):

- requirement capture;
- formal requirement specification;
- partitioning;
- implementation.

These phases are performed either manually (m), manually/automatically (m/a), or else interactive/automatically (i/a).

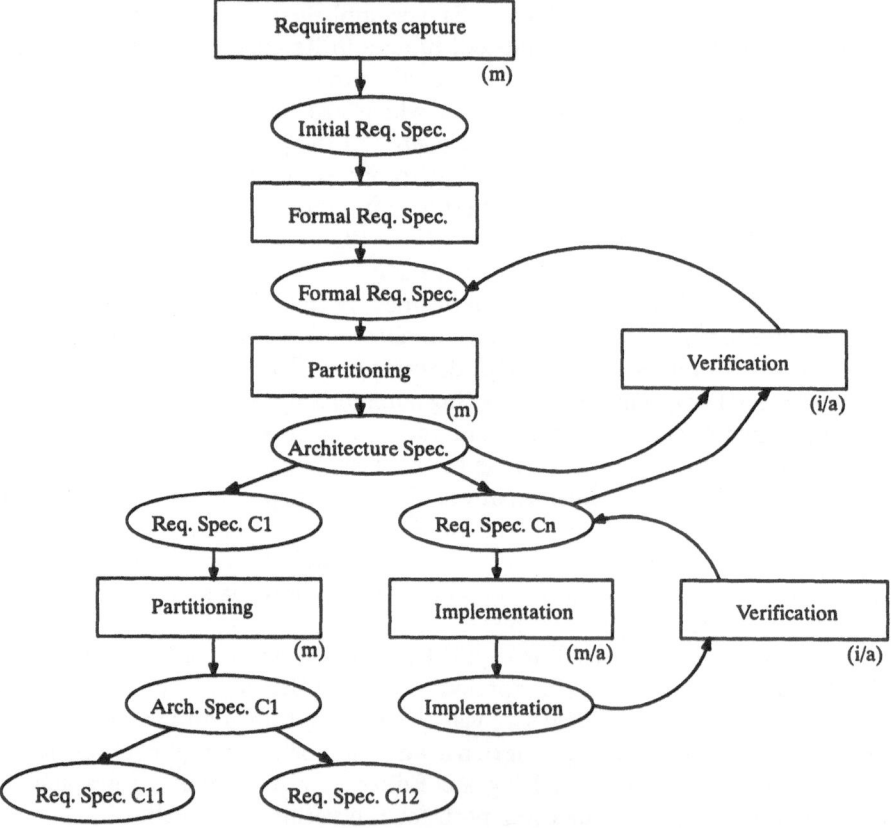

Fig. 4.1. FORMAT Design Flow.

The requirement capture phase (m) is the only informal phase of the design flow which produces the Initial Requirements Specification. This document defines the overall system requirements for the design to be produced.

The Formal Requirement Specification phase (m) takes the Initial Requirements Specification and formalizes it into VHDL/S as the System (Formal) Requirements Specification. The partitioning phase (m) takes the System Formal Requirement Specification in VHDL/S and partitions it into the modules which will together form the architecture of the design. The final phase is the implementation phase in which the modules are implemented in VHDL (either m/a and i/a). The final output of the design flow is a VHDL specification of the designed system, which can be logically synthesized to hardware using existing commercial tools. The last three phases may be iterated several times, both for the design as a whole and for the individual modules, in order to achieve the final design. The FORMAT tools will give a correct implementation of the initial system requirements specification. The problem of achieving a correct requirements specification itself falls outside the scope of the FORMAT Project. However, the limited experience of the use of formal methods to date shows that the ability to formally state and then verify general requirements (e.g. such as liveness) motivates a more through examination of the requirements which can therefore be obtained more easily.

During Structural partitioning the Formal Requirement Specification is transformed into an Architectural specification. This consists of a VHDL Architectural body with component instantiations binding components parts to their VHDL/S specifications. As the design progresses the structural partitioning may be recursively repeated for various components. The specification of components will thus move from abstract specifications as either timing diagrams or temporal logic to more concrete specifications using state charts or VHDL.

The resulting Architecture Specification is verified against the requirements specification using the LAMBDA system and the tautology checker. Eventually, provided the components are sufficiently small and sufficiently specified, components are verified using the Model Checker.

The implementation stage takes the fairly concrete specifications of the Architecture Specification, defined using timing diagrams, State Charts and VHDL and transforms this into logic synthesisable VHDL. The synthesisable VHDL can be produced either manually by step-wise refinement or by using the VHDL synthesizer.

The VHDL synthesizer can be used to produce VHDL automatically. A very high degree of design automation is possible for those components whose specifications correspond to the subset of the timing Diagram language accepted by the synthesizer. It is envisaged that this will support the I/O protocols and timing of commonly used components.

Within the FORMAT methodology the final Implementation Specification can be verified in one of three ways. The Model Checker can be used when the implementation specification (in VHDL) conforms to a timing diagram specification. In other cases the weak simulation mode of the model checker can be used (see next chapter "The FORMAT Model Checker").

Anm example of the encapsulation of the FORMAT tools into a commercial CAD framework is shown in the chapter "Italtel Application of the FORMAT Design Flow".

5. Concluding remarks

Integration links have been implemented as last goal of the FORMAT design methodology between this phase of the design flow and the lower levels, where consolidated, efficient and tested methodologies are applied down to the physical level. This step allows to fully exploit the benefits deriving from the application of formal methods to the correctness evaluation of the specifications. The adopted solution, based on the use of ESDA frameworks, makes possible the introduction and exploitation in an industrial environment of the innovative tools which have been developed. ESDA frameworks provide the most widely used environments in which a common approach to design and a common user interface can be defined and implemented. The underlying database allows designers to exploit third party tools, specialized in the solution of specific tasks. So, they are the most suitable way to fulfill the integration goal, according to the current design requirements. Moreover, standards are supported as a privileged mean to carry out the integration process, because they allow an easy and quick solution to the related problems through compatible interfaces and languages.

The implementation of this last step shows the feasibility of a design flow incorporating formal methods as a way to provide more sound and correct specifications in VHDL. A further advantage of the solution proposed here is the modularity of the toolset and the flexibility to adapt to different design sites and different application requirements. Test cases developed using this approach are described in the chapters of the book devoted to the industrial applications.

Specification Languages

Werner Damm[1], Gert Döhmen[1], Johannes Helbig[2], Peter Kelb[1], Rainer Schlör[1], Werner Grass[3], Christian Grobe[3], Stefan Lenk[3], and Wolf-Dieter Tiedemann[3]

[1] Kuratorium OFFIS e.V., Germany
[2] McKinsey & Company, Germany
[3] Universität Passau, Germany

1. VHDL/S

VHDL/S blends four different and self-contained linguistic paradigms: VHDL, state based specifications, timing diagrams, and temporal logic (figure 1.1) This is achieved by a stream based semantics that uniformly underlies all parts of the language. As a result, the designer who uses VHDL/S can switch back and forth between the paradigms without changing his pragmatic conceptual understanding of reactive behaviour in time. This approach is explained in detail in (J. Helbig et al. 1993).

	operational	declarative
textual	VHDL	Temporal Logic
visual	VHDL/S-statecharts	Timing Diagrams

Fig. 1.1. Sublanguages of VHDL/S

Syntactically, the integration is performed with the notion of a VHDL architecture serving as a common joint. To implement a component, given by its interface in form of an entity declaration, an architecture in VHDL/S can be bound to

- a VHDL structural or behavioural body,
- a timing diagram specification,
- a state based specification, or
- a temporal logic formula.

As an example, figure 1.2 may show a high-level view of a system, structurally decomposed into components, one of which is currently bound by configuration to a behavioural body, state based specification, or to a timing diagram specification. The top level environment is always VHDL. This allows existing VHDL library components to be safely incorporated into a

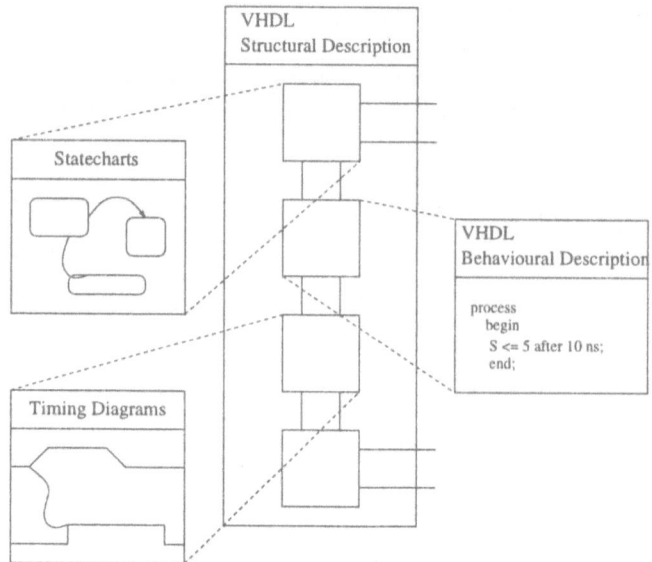

Fig. 1.2. Binding architectures to different language paradigms

VHDL/S design without modification, but broadens the expressive choices for the designer: while in plain VHDL specification the interplay between parallel and sequential behaviour is always restricted to a two-level hierarchy – a parallel composition of cyclic sequential behaviour –, which has often been felt to impair the suitability of the language on higher levels of abstraction, VHDL/S provides the designer with a way of behavioural decomposition that does not presuppose the physical structure of a preconceived implementation. Furthermore, he can do so using his two most popular graphical notations – timing and state diagrams – which maintain their suggestive reading but are supplemented with a rigorous formal meaning.

The timing diagram specification language comes in two principal *dialects*, depending on its use as requirement specification language or as specification language for high–level synthesis.

The first timing diagram dialect – referred to as *Symbolic Timing Diagrams* (STD) – can be considered as a visual form of temporal logic. STD as a requirement specification language circumvents the problem of overspecification that a specification in VHDL, as with all operational languages, would suffer from. STD distinguishes assertions about a components from those about its environment, which allows to employ a well understood proof methodology that is modular with respect to structural decomposition. This in turn is a prerequisite for the realistic application of automatic verification techniques such as model checking, owing to the limited size of models that they can handle.

The second timing diagram dialect – referred to as *Extended Timing Diagrams* (ETD) – is used in the context of synthesis, where a *complete* system description is required. Substantial for the use of timing diagrams for *complete* system specification is their inherent *cyclic* interpretation. Under this interpretation, a timing diagram reflects a recurring part of the behaviour of a system, rather than a pattern of a required behaviour.

The state based specification language of VHDL/S is based on statecharts as introduced by (D. Harel 1987)). Statecharts enhance conventional FSMs by notions of hierarchy (abstraction) and orthogonality (parallelism) to factor out common transition (sub-)structures and to avoid the problem of state explosion in the graphical representation. In VHDL/S statecharts, the action associated with a transition can consist of arbitrary sequential VHDL statements. VHDL/S statecharts are close enough to conventional statecharts to allow to build interfaces into existing commercial tools that may then utilize the services of the FORMAT system and vice versa. Although statecharts are graphical in nature, a textual version for VHDL/S statecharts has been developed that can be used as a full-fledged programming language, yet retains their structural suggestivity.

The language paradigms included in VHDL/S support two complementary, and equally important, aspects of design: While the state based specification language and VHDL define an *operational view* of a system, there is also a clear need to be able to capture *requirements*, in particular during the early stages of design. In order to state requirements of a reactive system, *declarative* specification languages are needed. One of the most popular and successful class of declarative specification languages is formed by the family of various dialects of *temporal logic* (E. M. Clarke et al. 1986, B. Josko 1993, Z. Manna and A. Pnueli 1982). Temporal logic has become famous because of the availability of powerful automatic verification techniques, which allow to prove or disprove that a given implementation (a "model") satisfies a certain requirement expressed as a temporal logic formula. Since the formulation of a desired property as a temporal logic formula becomes very often difficult to write and understand VHDL/S supports STD as graphical declarative language.

2. State based specifications

Since their introduction by (D. Harel 1987)) statecharts have gained fast and widespread recognition also in the digital design community. Statecharts enhance conventional FSMs by notion of hierarchy (abstraction) and orthogonality (parallelism) to factor out common transition (sub-)structures and to avoid the problem of state explosion in the graphical representation. Thereby, and quite apart from their visual appeal, they have proven particularly beneficial for design on the system level, where they can complement VHDL's means of behavioural abstraction, allowing the designer to specify sophisticated interplay between parallel and sequential behaviour that would be very awkward to express and very difficult to understand in plain VHDL. VHDL, on the other hand, comes with the rich set of types, operators, data- and control structures of a highly elaborate operational language, a strong concept of modularisation and reusability, and all the benefits of a worldwide accepted standard. The integration of both languages in VHDL/S allows each of them to share the virtues of the other.

Statecharts enhance state diagrams of traditional FSMs by notions of hierarchy and orthogonality. Their effect is threefold: they introduce a notion of refinement; they declutter the graphical representation of a system; and they prevent state explosion in the graphical representation of parallel behaviour. As an example, figure 2.1 shows a VHDL/S statechart for a high-level view of a SPARC CPU.

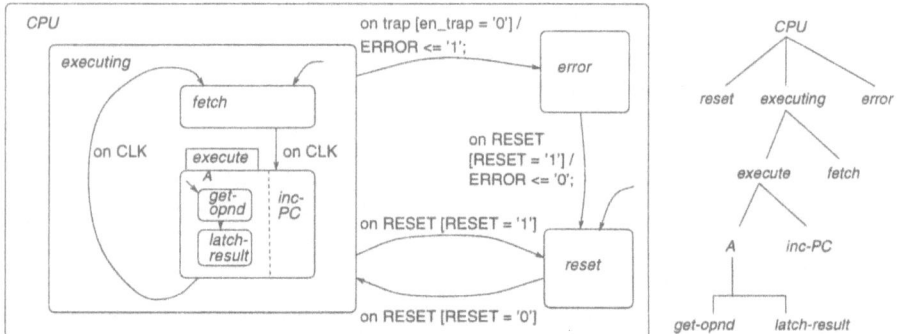

Fig. 2.1. A VHDL/S statechart and its corresponding *AND/OR*-tree

A statechart consists of a set of states, graphically represented as rectangular boxes, and a set of transitions between them, drawn as arcs. States may have substates and are either of type *AND* or *OR* to express parallel composition and sequential composition, resp.; to be in an *AND*-state – where to be in a state is the same as to say a state is *active* – implies to be in all of its substates and to be in an *OR*-state implies to be in exactly one of them (figure 2.2) The resulting overall structure of a statechart is an *AND/OR*-tree, where the leaves are called *basic* states. One substate of each *OR*-state is distinguished as *default* and is active whenever its father but none of its siblings is active.

Transitions are labelled with a label of the form *event[condition]/action*, with the implied meaning that, on occurrence of the event and provided the condition holds in the current interpretation of the data space, the source of the transition is exited, the target is entered and the action is carried out. One transition may have multiple source and target states and will in general interconnect states on different levels in the hierarchy.

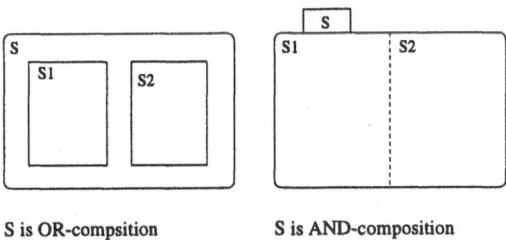

S is OR-compsition
of S1 and S2

S is AND-composition
of S1 and S2

Fig. 2.2. State constructors

In general, several transitions, i.e. those that affect only orthogonal components, are taken simultaneously, constituting a *step* of the system. Steps are always *maximal* in the sense that all transitions are included as long as they are currently enabled and not in structural conflict with another transition already in the step. If several steps can be built this way at the same time, the system chooses nondeterministically between them. A step takes a system from one *state configuration* to the next, where a configuration represents a maximal set of states that are *consistent*, i.e., can be active at the same time. The configuration reached by a step is always uniquely determined; it contains the root, with each *AND*-state all of its children, and with each *OR*-state one of them. Steps are considered instantaneous; time only elapses, in chunks of finite length, between subsequent steps, with the system sitting at a state configuration waiting for new events to occur.

2.1 Integration

The main distinction between VHDL/S statecharts and conventional statecharts is in the nature of the data space that a statechart is considered to operate upon and hence in the form of the actions that perform these operations. In VHDL/S statecharts these actions consist of sequences of sequential VHDL-statements and assign to signals and variables that behave like signals and variables of VHDL. This provides the conceptual link that integrates the behaviour of a statechart into the VHDL environment in which it is eventually meant to operate as a component; the goal was to offer to the user additional ways to construct behaviour from basic elements, but not to distract him with new basic elements, that would only subtly differ from the lot he has to master already. He may then switch smoothly between the two paradigms, applying the one that best fits his current design problem, rather than the one to which he has just adapted.

In order to achieve this, the semantics of VHDL/S statecharts have to lift this correspondence from a mere syntactic resemblance to a true conceptual analogy. The key notion providing this link is that of a *wait-configuration* of a VHDL program: according to the simulation semantics of VHDL, each process must have suspended at one of its wait-statements before time is advanced to the next scheduled transaction, which may cause new events to occur and some of the processes to proceed to their respective next wait-statement, under way carrying out as action the piece of sequential VHDL between two consecutive wait-statements. Thus the program proceeds from one wait-configuration to the next in steps that perform actions in response to events, and have to be considered instantaneous since time is only consumed at wait-configurations; hence steps are to be associated with instances on the time axis and wait-configurations with intervals between them, much the way steps and *state*-configurations are semantically treated in VHDL/S (figure 2.3). Figure 2.4 shows the resulting correspondence between basic elements of a VHDL/S statechart and a VHDL program if one leaves hierarchy out of account.

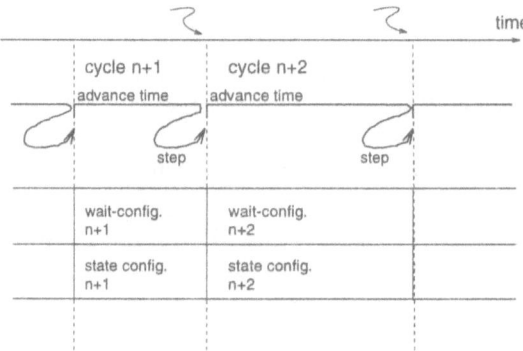

Fig. 2.3. The notion of time in VHDL/S

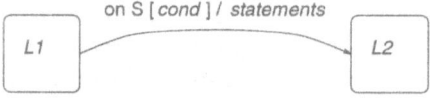

L1: wait on S until *cond*;
     statements;
L2: wait . . .

Fig. 2.4. Correspondence between basic elements of VHDL/S statecharts and VHDL

2.2 A design situation

With this correspondence in mind, one can understand more precisely what VHDL/S statecharts add – quite apart from their visual appeal – to plain

VHDL, as has been claimed in the introduction: the AND/OR–tree corresponding to a completely configured VHDL program can always be depicted as consisting of two levels only – a parallel composition of cyclic sequential behaviour (figure 2.5). Once the sequential level of description has been reached it is impossible to recur to the parallel one, so the notion of "hierarchy" in VHDL, which is obtained from component instantiation, pertains mainly to signal scope, or rather, in the context of verification, observability. This is not to be considered a flaw of VHDL, since it establishes the close correspondence to digital hardware that VHDL's contractual requirements once had called for; but while this correspondence seems adequate to *describe* hardware, practitioners have often felt that it impairs the suitability of the language to *design*, particularly at earlier stages of conceptual abstraction. The reason is that the structure of behaviour does not in general follow the structure of the physical system.

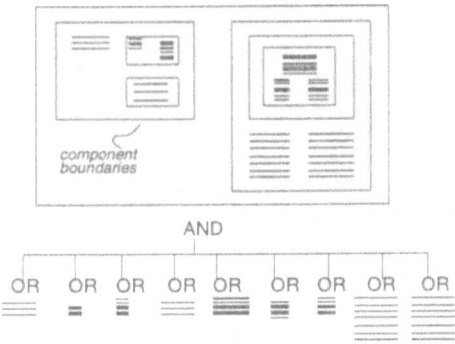

Fig. 2.5. Example of an "AND/OR-tree" of a VHDL program

As an example, consider again figure 2.1 and imagine what the corresponding specification would look like in VHDL. First assume the designer started out with a preconception of the high-level cycle betwen *run* and *stop*. A natural choice to write this in VHDL would be a process consisting of two wait-statements between two procedure calls for *run* and *stop* that can then be further refined. During refinement, however, the designer may realize that the activities for vertical movement are orthogonal to those for horizontal movement. Since VHDL cannot switch back to parallel behaviour once the sequential level has been reached, he now would convert the procedures into processes and establish explicit scheduling between them as well as artificial multiplexing of shared signals (compare, for instance, J. R. Armstrong 1988), thereby introducing many signals that won't have any counterpart in the device being modelled. Second consider the effect of hierarchy: to express the high-level aspect of the behaviour between *run* and *stop*, the triggers of the higher level transitions have to be distributed down into every wait-statement of, in general, every process corresponding to lower level states, whereupon the process has to dispatch the actual reason for resumption. So figure 2.6

sketches how, even for this small statechart with only one additional level, the corresponding VHDL program has almost completely extinguished any trace of how the designer might have had organized in his mind his knowledge about the system's behaviour. Each further refinement would again globally affect the whole specification.

```
architecture VHDL_behaviour of Sparc_Cpu is
begin
    fetch: process begin          schedule: process begin
        wait until FETCH_EN;
        . . .                     wait on CLK  ,RESET, trap;
        PC1 <= PC + 1;            if trap = '1' and en_trap ='0'
        . . .                                    then do_error
    end process;                  elsif RESET = '1' then do_reset
                                  else
    execute_a: process begin          FETCH_EN <= true;
        wait until EXEC_A_EN;     . . .
        . . .
        PC2 <= adr;               wait on CLK  ,RESET, trap;
        . . .                     if trap = '1' and en_trap ='0'
    end process;                                 then do_error
    execute_b: process begin      elsif RESET = '1' then do_reset
        wait until EXEC_B_EN;     else
        . . .                         FETCH_EN <= false;
        PC3 <= PC + 1;                EXEC_A_EN <= true;
        . . .                         EXEC_B_EN <= true;
    end process;                  . . .

                                  end process;
    procedure do_error
    . . .                         output_multiplexing: process
                                  PC <= PC1 when not PC1'quiet else
    procedure do_reset                    PC2 when not PC2'quiet else
    . . .                                 PC3 when not PC3'quiet ;
                                      . . .
                                  end process;
```

Fig. 2.6. Structure of a VHDL program for the SPARC CPU

The preceding example suggests that in certain situations a state based representation may be superiour to a VHDL description for mere structural reasons, even if it were non-graphical. We therefore developed a textual version of VHDL/S statecharts that serves as an intermediate language in the FORMAT system architecture, but can also be used as a full fledged programming language by the designer. Following the state hierarchy top-down, the language tries to keep the graphical counterpart of a program mentally present.

A textual version of the VHDL/S statechart of figure 2.1 is partly shown in figure 2.7. If this specification is to be further refined, the designer needs only locally to expand one of the basic states. The concrete syntax follows VHDL in style, flavour and construction principles, again in order to make it easier for the designer to switch back and force; in fact, the syntax has been formally defined in terms of a very narrow interface into the formal grammar for VHDL, leading to very short learning times for users familiar with VHDL.

```
state CPU is
  <local declarations>
one of
    state reset is end;
    state error is end;
    state execute is
    one of

    ...
    end state execute;

    default advance to reset;

    from reset
        when reset = '0' advance to execute;
    from execute
        when reset = '1' advance to reset;
        when trap and en_trap = '0'
          do begin ERROR <= '1'; end
        advance to error;
    ...
end state CPU;
```

Fig. 2.7. Textual version of a VHDL/S statechart for the SPARC CPU

3. Timing diagrams

Commonly, designers use timing diagrams mainly for documentation of system behaviour or for the description of stimuli in system simulation. The set of timing diagrams used for these purposes is not always suitable to represent an appropriate description of all behavioural aspects. In general, it documents a snapshot of "typical" behaviour or of some particular situations of interest. The rest of the description is mostly given in textual format, e.g. in the shape of informal explanations or by means of some description language.

However, it can be observed that there is a particular class of systems for which the description can be done by using timing diagrams nearly without any clarifying supplements. This class of systems is characterized by attributes like *open*, *reactive*, *communication-oriented*, and *control-dominated*. Quite often, such systems are components of distributed systems and communication processors.

The class of timing diagrams used in VHDL/S is derived from the notion of classical timing diagrams as used by hardware designers. They differ from traditional forms of timing diagrams in several significant points:

1. Timing Diagrams in VHDL/S have a rigorously defined semantics, given by translation into a well–defined formalism (either temporal-logic or T–LOTOS).
2. Different kinds of temporal relationships between events can be expressed by different kinds of arcs between them. Most notable is the distinction

between *presupposed* and *required* dependencies, graphically represented by dashed and solid arrows, respectively.

3. More abstract relationships between events, such as partial order and causality, can be expressed and are supported by the methodology. They lift the area of application of timing diagrams to situations that are typical for system level design.

4. A timing diagram can be used by the designer to focus on one specific aspect of the required functionality at a time; the full specification will in general comprise several diagrams with appropriate structuring mechanisms.

5. A flexible annotation language, syntactically consistent with VHDL, allows to express data dependencies between different waveform regions.

3.1 Syntax definition

The timing diagram language of VHDL/S exists in two principal dialects, due to their very different purpose either as requirement specification language (declarative) or as behavioural description language (operational).

Both dialects coincide, however, in their fundamental constituents: A timing diagram specification comprises individual diagrams, each of which consists of waveforms and temporal constraints. The main difference between both dialects is in the mechanisms (operators) provided to structure the set of diagrams, and in the type of supported temporal constraints (qualitative vs. quantitative constraints).

Syntax of STD. An STD–*specification* is, like a VHDL–architecture body, always associated with an interface declaration ("entity declaration" in the VHDL terminology). It consists of the following parts:

1. A *STD-declarative-part*, which declares one set of STD–diagrams to be used as *assumptions* of the specification (*STD-ASSM-declarative-part*), and another set of STD–diagrams to be used as *commitments* of the specification (*STD-COMM-declarative-part*). References occuring in the bodies of declared diagrams must be either to objects declared in the associated interface declaration or to local variables.

2. A *STD-specification-part*, which is a set of *specification clauses*. A specification clause has the form 'assert commitment' or 'assert commitment provided assumption-list', where *assumption-list* is a non–empty list of names of assumption diagrams, and *commitment* is the name of a commitment diagram declared in the *STD-declarative-part*. In formal derivations, a specification clause is usually denoted in the abbreviated form *commitment* (*commitment*[*assumption-list*], respectively).

Syntax of STD–diagrams. Each diagram defined in the *STD-declarative-part* of a Symbolic Timing Diagram-specification consists of the following parts:

1. A *diagram-name*, which introduces a name of the declared diagram to be used as reference in the *STD-specification-part*.
2. A *diagram-parameter-declaration*, which is a list of parameters with associated types. The scope of this declaration is the diagram.
3. A set of *symbolic waveforms*, which are linear sequences of boolean expressions (*assertions*) b_i built over objects declared in the enclosing scope of the diagram (figure 3.1). The first expression on each waveform is called

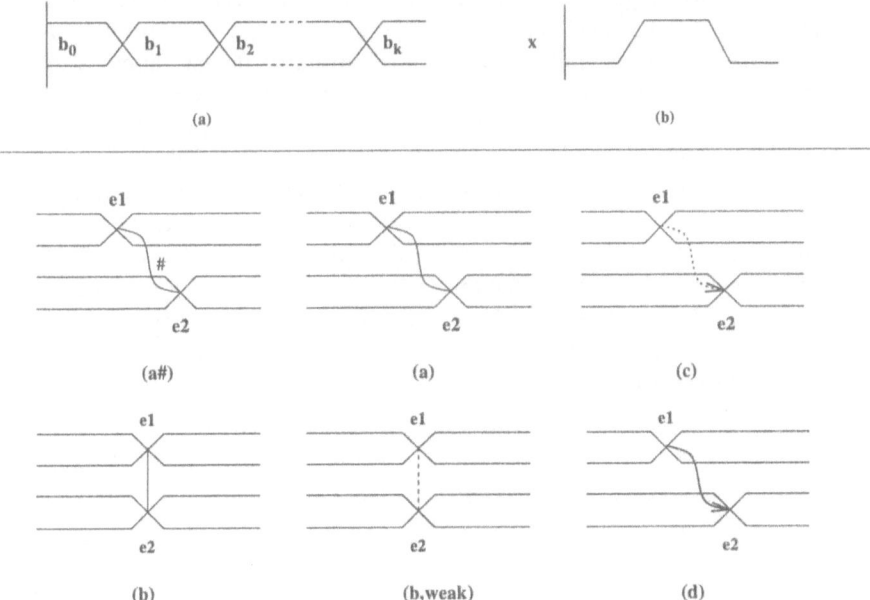

Fig. 3.1. Upper half: Symbolic waveforms. Lower half: Denotation of different types of constraints

initial assertion. It is often the case that assertions are made over the sequence of values on a particular signal x; in this case, the abbreviated form *op expr* is used in the graphical representation, where *op* is a relational operator and *expr* an expression of appropriate type (so–called *VALUE-form*). This is an abbreviation for the assertion *(x op expr)*. For a two–valued signal x (e.g. of type 'Bit'), the waveform is usually depicted as an alternating line which toggles between levels 'LOW' and 'HIGH', if the meaning of these levels is clear from the context (e.g. to represent the assertions $x = '0'$ and $x = '1'$, respectively).
4. A set of *constraints*, which are binary relations on the set of edges of the waveforms occuring in a diagram. Seven classes of relations exist, partitioned into three classes of "strong" and three classes of "weak" *partial-order constraints*, and one class of *leads-to constraints*. We illustrate the meaning of different types of constraints in figure 3.1: Precedence (a#

and a), simultaneous (b and b,weak), leads–to (c) and causality constraint (d). The constraint depicted in (a#), called *(strong) precedence#–*
constraint, denotes that edge e1 must occur before e2. The constraint depicted in (a), called *(strong) precedence*–constraint, is the same as (a#)
except that simultaneous occurrence of e1 and e2 is allowed. The constraint depicted in (b), called *(strong) simultaneous*–constraint, denotes
that edge e2 must occur simultaneously with e1. The constraint depicted
in (b,weak), called *(weak) simultaneous*–constraint, is similar to (b), but
denotes, that edge e2 *is expected* to occur simultaneously with e1, otherwise the behavioural restriction expressed by the diagram is cancelled
(preemption). Note that weak forms (denoted as dashed lines) also exist
for precedence constraints (called *weak precedence#*–constraint, respectively *weak precedence*–constraint). The constraint depicted in (c), called
leads–to–constraint, denotes that if e1 has occured and e2 has not yet
occured, then e2 is bound to occur *eventually*. The constraint depicted
in (d), called *causality*–constraint, denotes the combination of the requirements stated by (a) and (c). (The causality constraint is in fact a
superposition of a precedence and a leads-to constraint.) The constraints
a#, a, c and d are *asymmetric constraints*, denoted by curved lines. Their
orientation is always from left (source) to right (destination) w.r.t. their
horizontal position.

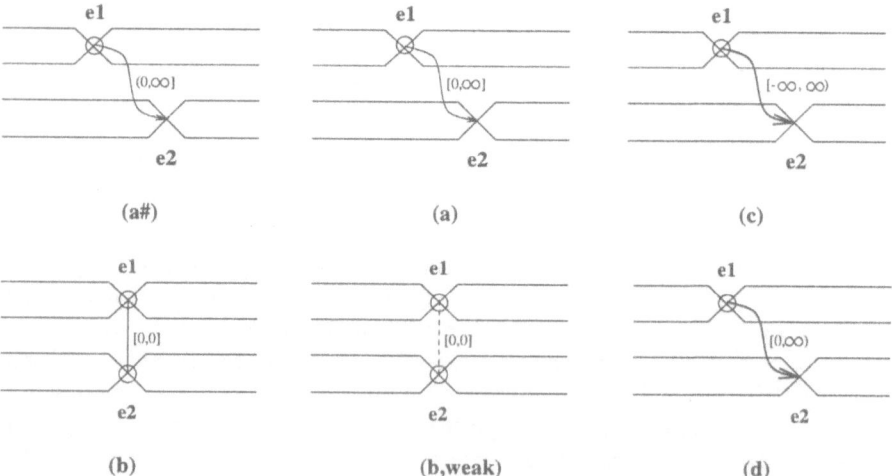

Fig. 3.2. Denotation of different types of constraints in the TDE.

It must be noted that constraints in STD only make *qualitative* assertions
on the required timing of events. On the other hand, the timing diagram
language supports also quantitative timing–constraints. The qualitative constraints used in Symbolic Timing Diagram are represented as quantitative

timing–constraints with ∞ (infinity) allowed as upper– and lower bound. The corresponding graphical syntax used in the timing diagram editor is shown in figure 3.2.

Syntax of ETD. An *ETD-specification* targeting on system synthesis consists of

1. a *system design interface* definition which specifies the *system ports* and their unique *names*. These names allow globally referencing the corresponding ports. Moreover, properties of the system ports like their direction modes (input,output) and the data-types of the values communicated on these ports are prescribed here.
2. a finite set of formal *extended timing diagrams*. Each extended timing diagram ETD specifies a certain input/output behaviour on some of the system ports.
3. a *composition expression*. The complete system behaviour is specified as a combination of invocations of ETD, given in terms of a structured composition expression. The *sequential* and the *alternative* ETD-operator are used to define this composition.

In the following the syntactical constituents of a single ETD are presented.

1. Each ETD has a unique *name* which allows invoking it within the composition expression.
2. The *ETD-interface* defines the subset of system ports considered within the ETD. The port properties are accepted as defined in the system design interface.
3. Substantial primitives of ETD are *waveforms*. Each waveform is uniquely associated with a port of the ETD-interface. It consists of a sequence of *edges*. Every waveform edge is extended by a *data annotation*. A data annotation consists of
   - a *variable declaration*, defining a local data variable associated with the related edge. The variable name has to be unique within the ETD which is at the same time the scope of the variable. Its data-type corresponds to the data-type of the port the waveform edge is related to.
   - an optional *initial constant value* for the declared variable. If no initial value is specified a default value will be assumed.
   - a *predicate* or a *computation rule*. Predicates are specified for input edges whereas for each output edge a computation rule has to be defined. Both, predicates and computation rules may reference the local data variables defined in the ETD and the global port names defined in the system design interface.

   An *annotation language* which follows an algorithmic subset of VHDL-syntax is used for the specification of data annotations.
4. A set of *constraints* interrelates the waveform edges of an ETD. *Temporal constraints* specify relations each between two different waveform edges.

- *Qualitative constraints* relate edges belonging to different waveforms. The provided qualitative constraints are the *strong constraint* and the *weak constraint*.
- The only *quantitative constraint* is the *timing constraint*. It specifies minimum and/or maximum times between arbitrary waveform edges in terms of a time interval. A time interval is defined by a lower and an upper time bound. Open or closed intervals are possible.

Enable conditions are data constraints associated with a single waveform edge. An enable condition is a predicate in terms of the annotation language which may refer to the local data variables defined in the ETD and the global port names defined in the system design interface.

In figure 3.3 the graphical appearance of the main ETD language primitives is depicted.

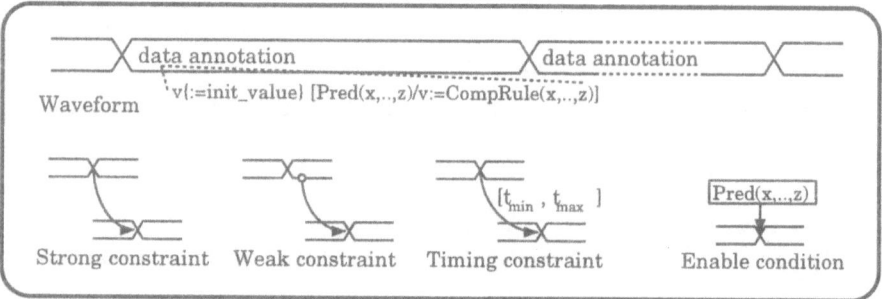

Fig. 3.3. Graphical notation of syntactical elements of ETD.

3.2 Informal semantics

Due to their different purpose as specification language, the semantics of the timing diagram language must comprise the different particularities of the two timing diagram dialects.

Semantics of STD . The most important difference of the semantics of Symbolic Timing Diagram as opposed to other formalizations of timing diagrams is its declarative nature. Each diagram appearing as commitment of an assert–clause of an *STD-specification-part* constrains the set of admissable behaviour of any associated implementation.

The second peculiarity of the semantics stems originally from the wish be able to characterize the semantics of a diagram by a temporal–logic formula. Those dialects of temporal logic which are supported by current model–checking technology do not have means to define control flow. However, a

certain idiom of the form: 'Whenever ϕ holds, then ...', can be used to simulate e.g. iteration. This idiom gave rise to the concept of activation in the
STD language.

The semantics of the language Symbolic Timing Diagram has already
been formally defined in (W. Damm et al. 1995). In this section we will give
an informal introduction to the semantics. The description will be illustrated
by an example at the end of the next chapter and should help to read the
formal semantics defined in (W. Damm et al. 1995).

The idiom 'Whenever ϕ holds, then ...' corresponds in the STD–language
to the concept of *activation*. A diagram δ is activated at time t, if the conjunction of the initial (first) assertions of each waveform of the diagram (so-
called activation condition, denoted $\phi_{\delta,act}$) holds at time t, evaluated over
the actual state (valuation) of the interface declaration associated with the
diagram. This activation is called a t–*instance* of δ and denoted as $\delta\lfloor t$. Given
a computation σ, each t–instance $\delta\lfloor t$ induces a matching process on the t–
tail of σ $(\sigma(t), \sigma(t+1), \ldots)$. *Matching* is the activity of comparing actual
values (valuations of the associated interface declaration) against diagram
annotations (boolean expressions). Changes of valuations (events) drive the
matching process.

Example 3.1. (Instantiation and matching.)
In order to illustrate the semantics of STD–diagrams, we take as illustration
the diagram sequenceoflightssafe_with_priority shown in figure 5.2 (referred
to as $\bar{\delta}$ furtheron). In figure 3.4 this diagram is shown with a numbering of its
events for further reference, with the STD–syntax for constraints shown in figure
3.1 and the following abbreviation of annotations: (HW_PRIORITY = x) is denoted
as ϕx, (FR_LIGHTS = y) as ψy, and (HW_LIGHTS = z) as ξz.

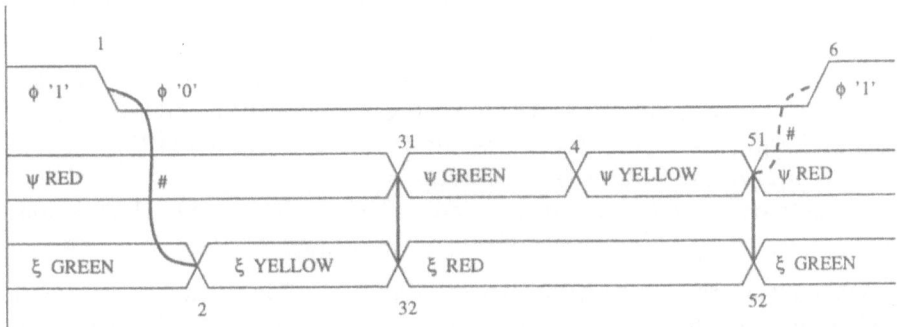

Fig. 3.4. Diagram sequenceoflightssafe_with_priority with abbreviated annotations and numbered events

Diagram $\bar{\delta}$ creates a t–instance at each time–point t, where the actual valuation
satisfies the activation condition

$$\phi_{\bar{\delta},act} \equiv (\text{HW\_PRIORITY} = \text{'1'}) \wedge (\text{FR\_LIGHTS} = RED) \wedge (\text{HW\_LIGHTS} = GREEN)$$

In this (special) case there is exactly one valuation for the ports (HW_PRIORITY, FR_LIGHTS, HW_LIGHTS), which satisfies the condition, namely (HW_PRIORITY = '1', FR_LIGHTS = RED, HW_LIGHTS = $GREEN$), which gives the match M_1 (denoted by the symbol $\models$, read 'matches' or 'satisfies')

$$M_1 : (\text{HW\_PRIORITY} = '1', \text{FR\_LIGHTS} = RED, \text{HW\_LIGHTS} = GREEN) \models \phi_{\delta,act}$$

In general, there will be a set of such matches, which cause activation.

Consider now an (arbitrary) t–instance of diagram $\bar{\delta}$. Any event on one of the ports (HW_PRIORITY, FR_LIGHTS, HW_LIGHTS) causes the current match M_1 to terminate. Assume e.g. event: (HW_PRIORITY = '1') $\rightarrow$ (HW_PRIORITY = '0'). Then the next match will be

$$M_2 : (\text{HW\_PRIORITY} = '0', \text{FR\_LIGHTS} = RED, \text{HW\_LIGHTS} = GREEN) \models \phi_{\bar{\delta},\{+1\}}$$

where $\phi_{\bar{\delta},\{+1\}}$ is the conjunction of diagram annotations after the matching of event 1,

$$\phi_{\bar{\delta},\{+1\}} \equiv (\text{HW\_PRIORITY} = '0' \wedge \text{FR\_LIGHTS} = RED \wedge \text{HW\_LIGHTS} = GREEN)$$

For a t–instance of diagram δ the matching process induced by the behaviour starting from time t determines one of three cases:

1. The actual behaviour starting from time t matches diagram δ completely and also respects its constraints. Then instance $\delta \lfloor t$ terminates normally (*completion* of $\delta \lfloor t$).
2. The actual behaviour starting from time t does not conform to the sequence of values prescribed by diagram δ or does not respect its strong constraints. Then instance $\delta \lfloor t$ terminates prior to its completion with a failure (*failure* of $\delta \lfloor t$).
3. The actual behaviour starting from time t does not respect its weak constraints. Then instance $\delta \lfloor t$ terminates prior to its completion with an exit (*exit* or *deactivation* of $\delta \lfloor t$).

From these cases, only the second (fail–case) has the effect of rejecting the computation which induced it; the other two cases let the computation analysed so far pass. A computation σ is rejected by a diagram δ iff there is a t–instance $\delta \lfloor t$ which rejects σ. The existence of liveness–constraints (causality- or leads–to constraints) in a diagram adds the following case to the previous ones:

4. Assume that the actual behaviour starting from time t matches diagram δ partially such that the source of a liveness constraint has been matched, but its destination has not been matched. This means that the actual behaviour must eventually contain new valuations which cause further matching of instance $\delta \lfloor t$ (*propagation state* of $\delta \lfloor t$).

An (infinite) computation, for which the matching process stops in a propagation state, is also rejected by t–instance $\delta \lfloor t$.

Example 3.2. (completion, failure and exit of diagram instances)

We continue the example of diagram `sequenceoflightssafe_with_priority` (denoted as $\bar{\delta}$). Table 3.1 shows sample computations and the response from the specification. Between time 0 and 5 a complete cycle of the traffic light controller is performed. Note however that at time 5 diagram instance $\bar{\delta}\lfloor 0$ still has an unmatched event (event 6) and is not yet completed. However, it is *effectively completed* (denoted as $[\bar{\delta}\lfloor 0 \downarrow]$) , which means that all events connected to a strong constraint have been matched and no rejection can come from this instance anymore. At time 6 another instance $\bar{\delta}\lfloor 6$ of diagram $\bar{\delta}$ is created. At the same time, instance $\bar{\delta}\lfloor 0$ is completed (all events have been matched).

t	(ϕ '#1') as #1, RED as R	(ψ #2) as #2, YELLOW as Y	(ξ #3) as #3, GREEN as G	creation (↑) and termination (↓) of $\bar{\delta}$–instances
0	1	R	G	$\delta\lfloor 0 \uparrow$
1	0	R	G	
2	0	R	Y	
3	0	G	R	
4	0	Y	R	
5	0	R	G	$[\delta\lfloor 0 \downarrow]$
6	1	R	G	$\delta\lfloor 6 \uparrow$ $\delta\lfloor 0 \downarrow$
7^1	1	R	Y	$\delta\lfloor 6$ fails
7^2	0	R	G	
8^2	1	R	G	$\delta\lfloor 6$ exits $\delta\lfloor 8 \uparrow$
9^2	0	R	Y	
10^2	0	G	Y	$\delta\lfloor 8$ fails

Table 3.1. Example traces and responses of diagram $\bar{\delta}$.

Example 3.3. (failure and exit of diagram instances .)

In table 3.1 two possible continuations of the computation prefix discussed so far are considered. At time 7^1, an event on signal HW_LIGHTS caused a match of event 2, before event 1 has ocurred, which means that the traffic–controller starts to withdraw the passing allowance (GREEN–light) from the highway road, although the signal HW_PRIORITY is asserted. With respect to the diagram, this is a violation of the strong precedence(sp)–constraint $1 \xrightarrow{sp} 2$, hence instance $\bar{\delta}\lfloor 6$ fails at this point. This computation is therefore rejected.

Another possible continuation is shown at time 7^2, where the signal HW_PRIORITY has been deasserted. Immediately after that event, at time 8^2 the signal is again asserted.

First consider instance $\bar{\delta}\lfloor 6$: The deassertion of signal HW_PRIORITY matches event 6, while event 51 has as yet not been matched. With respect to the diagram, this is a violation of the *weak* precedence(wp)–constraint $51 \xrightarrow{wp} 6$, hence instance $\bar{\delta}\lfloor 6$ *exits* at this point. Note that this is not a rejection of the computation; it simply means that instance $\bar{\delta}\lfloor 6$ does not 'observe' (i.e., restrict) the behaviour any longer.

At the same time (8^2), a new diagram–instance $\bar{\delta}\lfloor 8$ is created. The computation then continues two steps. At time 10^2, an event on signal FR_LIGHTS causes a match of event 31, before event 32 has ocurred. Such a behaviour would mean an insecure state of the road crossing. With respect to the diagram, this is a violation of the strong simulaneous(ss)–constraint 31—32; hence this computation is also rejected.

Semantics of ETD. In the following the interpretation of ETD-specifications as used in the synthesis process will be briefly explained.

Each single ETD reflects some aspects of a system's input/output behaviour describing events observable on some of the system ports.

Basic elements of ETD are *waveforms*. Each waveform is uniquely associated with a system port. It consists of a sequence of *edges* specifying a recurring succession of system events on the related port. This interpretation of waveforms implies the *cyclic* view of ETD. The inherent cyclic interpretation of ETD is substantial for a a *complete* specification of system behaviour. Thus, an ETD reflects a recurring part of the behaviour of a system rather than merely a behavioural requirement.

Every waveform edge has to be supplemented by a *data annotation*. It textually describes requirements on the data value(s) the system exchanges with its environment. Basically each data annotation consists of a *variable declaration*. This declaration relates a uniquely named variable to a waveform edge. Every data value received or transmitted by a corresponding system event will be assigned to this variable. A particular initial value (differing from the default value) may be specified for each variable.

Additionally, a *predicate* is associated with every input waveform edge. Such a predicate serves to restrict the data values that can be received with corresponding system events. A *computation rule* associated to every output waveform edge specifies the data value the system actually has to communicate with corresponding events. Predicates and computation rules may reference the current values of the local variables declared at waveform edges within a ETD as well as the current values of the signals on the system ports. Accordingly, variable references imply data dependencies between different waveform edges.

However, it is substantial to notice that there is no implicit temporal relation between events specified by *different* waveforms in a ETD. The arbitrarily chosen graphical position of the waveform edges does not imply any order among the events on different system ports. Therefore such an ETD is a precise and clear *abbreviation* for all the different possible orders of those events.

In general the events on the different ports of a system are not completely independent. *Qualitative constraints* impose a temporal order on the events underlying the related source and target edge. Strong constraints specify a *strict alternating sequence* of these events starting with a "source event". Weak constraints specify a *condition* for occurrences of target events. The condition is defined by the data annotation of the source edge. Whenever the value of the signal of the source edge port equals the current value of the local variable declared at the source edge, target events are possible. The occurrence of a source event is not restricted.

Further on, communication-oriented systems often have to meet rigid absolute timing constraints. This means that events are not simply ordered but they additionally have to occur within certain time frames. A timing constraint specifies a minimum and/or maximum time to pass between the related events in terms of a time interval. After the occurrence of a source event the corresponding target event has to occur within this time interval.

Finally the occurrence of system events can also depend on the current data configuration. Therefore, an *enable condition* can be related to each waveform edge in order to reflect *conditional* behaviour. The enable condition *predicate* specifies the data condition for the occurrence of corresponding events.

Concluding, already a single ETD is a compact *representative* for a possibly very complex behaviour. It implicitly represents the finest granularity of *parallelism* of the described system events complying with the prescribed constraints. Therefore, it retains most freedom for a subsequent synthesis process offering a variety of possible implementations.

However, a single ETD in general will not be sufficient to give an appropriate and complete specification of a system behaviour. Such an ETD would soon get very large, forfeiting its advantageous clearness. Moreover, especially alternative system behaviours cannot be described conveniently using only a single ETD. Therefore a concept for the *composition* of ETD by operators is provided. These composition operators permit constructing a ETD-specification from single ETD of reasonable size.

The *alternative operator* is used to specify a set of different possible system behaviours. Alternatively composed ETD reflect a collection of different functionalities of the specified system. Therefore, this operator can be used for an iterative extension of a system specification. The composed ETD are not simply interpreted as strict choices between the specified behaviours rather every alternatively composed ETD enriches the system behaviour in a very flexible way. Alternative behaviours will be exclusive if the same set of ports is concerned or they may occur (partially) in parallel as long as they do not interfere each other. In addition, any common subbehaviour, specified in different alternative ETD is united.

Finally, the *sequential operator* is used to split large ETD into several smaller ones. This allows structuring and even condensing an ETD-specification since e.g. common behaviours can be extracted into a single ETD.

This compositional approach considerably eases a clear specification process. It allows a stepwise construction of a system specification by iteratively enhancing the specification functionalities.

4. Example: a traffic light system

In this part we describe a traffic light system and illustrate the various specification languages of VHDL/S applied to the example.

4.1 Structure of the traffic light system

In a top level view, the traffic light system controls the traffic lights at a highway which has a finite number of intersections with farm roads (cf. figure 4.1).

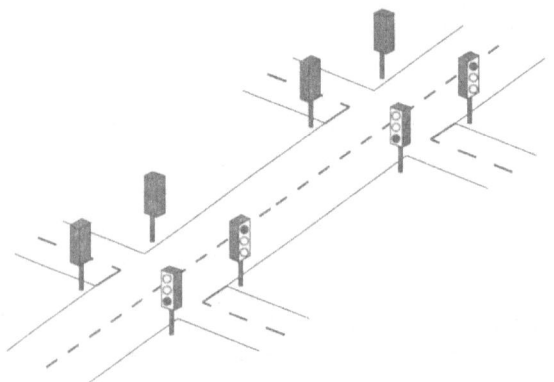

Fig. 4.1. The traffic light system

Each intersection is controlled locally by a traffic light controller which turns the highway lights to red when a car is detected on the farm road. The highway lights are eventually turned back to green and remain green as long as no car is detected. Privileged cars on the highway can raise a priority signal which is forwarded to all traffic light controller and keeps the highway lights green even if there are cars waiting on farmroads.

The package TRAFF (figure 4.2) defines, beside general types, subtypes and a resolution function, the three components from which the traffic light system is composed. DETECTOR and LIGHTS shall represent the physical detectors and the physical lights. CONTROLLER denotes the component for the traffic light controller of a single intersection. Its input port CARS_DETECTED, which will in the composed system be wired to a DETECTOR instance, signals that a car is waiting on the farmroad. Its input port HW_PRIORITY signals that a privileged car is on the highway. It controls the lights at the corresponding farmroad and highway through its output ports FR_LIGHTS and HW_LIGHTS. The HW_GREEN_ACTLOW output port signals with its LOW value that the highway lights output port has value green. In the composed system all those signals are connected with a "wired or" function which indicates with its LOW value that all highway lights show green.

```
package TRAFF is
  type THREE_COLORS is ( GREEN, YELLOW, RED );
  type bit_array is array ( POSITIVE range <> ) of BIT;
  function wired_or ( x : bit_array ) return BIT;
  subtype resolved_wire is wired_or BIT;
  component DETECTOR
    port ( cars_detected : out BIT);
  end component;
  component LIGHTS
    port ( COLOR : in THREE_COLORS);
  end component;
  component CONTROLLER
    port ( CARS_DETECTED   : in BIT;
           HW_PRIORITY     : in BIT;
           HW_GREEN_ACTLOW : out BIT;
           FR_LIGHTS       : out THREE_COLORS;
           HW_LIGHTS       : out THREE_COLORS);
  end component;
end TRAFF;
```

Fig. 4.2. Package for traffic light system

```
use WORK.TRAFF.all;
entity TRAFFIC_SYSTEM is
  generic ( Number_of_intersections : POSITIVE );
  port ( PRIORITY            : in BIT;
         hw_all_green_actlow : out resolved_wire);
end TRAFFIC_SYSTEM;
```

Fig. 4.3. Entity for traffic light system

```
architecture SYSTEM_BODY of TRAFFIC_SYSTEM is
  type Color_array is array ( POSITIVE range <> ) of THREE_COLORS;
  signal detect : BIT_VECTOR (1 to Number_of_intersections);
  signal fr_light : Color_array (1 to Number_of_intersections);
  signal hw_light : Color_array (1 to Number_of_intersections);
begin
  SYSTEM : for I in 1 to Number_of_intersections generate
    DET : DETECTOR port map (detect(I));
    FR : LIGHTS port map (fr_light(I));
    HW : LIGHTS port map (hw_light(I));
    TRAFF1 : CONTROLLER
      port map (detect(I),PRIORITY,hw_all_green_actlow,
                fr_light(I),hw_light(I));
  end generate;
end SYSTEM_BODY;
```

Fig. 4.4. Architecture for traffic light system

The TRAFFIC_SYSTEM determines the traffic light system with several intersections. Their number is given as generic. The SYSTEM_BODY generates for each intersection the corresponding components. The global PRIORITY input is distributed to all the HW_PRIORITY inputs of CONTROLLER instances. The global hw_all_green_actlow output is determined via a wired or on all hw_all_green_actlow outputs from CONTROLLER components.

4.2 Behavioural description of the traffic light system

The components of the traffic light system can in a later step be configured with concrete entities and architectures. As shown in figure 1.2 the concrete architectures can use different language paradigms. The following entity declaration TRAFFIC_CONTROLLER defines the same ports as the CONTROLLER and allows therefore to configurate it to this components.

```
use WORK.TRAFF.all;
entity TRAFFIC_CONTROLLER is
  port ( CARS_DETECTED : in BIT;
         HW_PRIORITY : in BIT;
         HW_GREEN_ACTLOW : out BIT;
         FR_LIGHTS : out THREE_COLORS := RED;
         HW_LIGHTS : out THREE_COLORS);
end TRAFFIC_CONTROLLER;
```

Fig. 4.5. Entity for traffic light controller

We provide two descriptions of the TRAFFIC_CONTROLLER entity, one as VHDL behavioural description and the other as Statechart description.

VHDL description of the TRAFFIC_CONTROLLER. The architecture VHDL_BODY of figure 4.6 implements the traffic light controller as a finite state machine in VHDL notation. The states are defined through the type CONTROLLER_STATES. The variable CURR_STATE determines the actual state and is used in the case statement to perform the step to the sucessor state. The local TIMER_OUT signal is used to ensure minimum times for different phases of the traffic light controller. The traffic light controller stays in its current state and does not change the lights as long as TIMER_OUT is not raised.

Statechart description of the TRAFFIC_CONTROLLER. An implementation can alternatively be given as a Statechart description. The architecture SC_BODY of figure 4.7 shows how the same functionality as VHDL_BODY can described with a Statechart.

```
architecture VHDL_BODY of TRAFFIC_CONTROLLER is
  type CONTROLLER_STATES is ( WAIT_LONG_TIMEOUT, SWITCH_FR,
                              WAIT_MEDIUM_TIMEOUT, SWITCH_HW );
  signal TIMER_OUT : BIT := '1';
begin
  main : process ( TIMER_OUT, CARS_DETECTED, HW_PRIORITY )
  variable CURR_STATE : CONTROLLER_STATES := SWITCH_HW;
  begin
    case CURR_STATE is
    when WAIT_LONG_TIMEOUT =>
      if CARS_DETECTED = '1' and TIMER_OUT = '1'
                                 and HW_PRIORITY = '0'
      then
        HW_LIGHTS <= YELLOW;
        HW_GREEN_ACTLOW <= '1';
        TIMER_OUT <= '0', '1' after 1 sec;
        CURR_STATE := SWITCH_FR;
      end if;
    when SWITCH_FR =>
      if TIMER_OUT = '1' and HW_PRIORITY = '0' then
        HW_LIGHTS <= RED;
        FR_LIGHTS <= GREEN;
        TIMER_OUT <= '0', '1' after 2 sec;
        CURR_STATE := WAIT_MEDIUM_TIMEOUT;
      elsif TIMER_OUT = '1' and HW_PRIORITY = '1' then
        HW_LIGHTS <= GREEN;
        HW_GREEN_ACTLOW <= '0';
        CURR_STATE := WAIT_LONG_TIMEOUT;
      end if;
    when WAIT_MEDIUM_TIMEOUT =>
      if CARS_DETECTED = '0' or TIMER_OUT = '1' then
        FR_LIGHTS <= RED;
        TIMER_OUT <= '0', '1' after 1 sec;
        CURR_STATE := SWITCH_HW;
      end if;
    when SWITCH_HW =>
      if TIMER_OUT = '1' then
        HW_LIGHTS <= GREEN;
        HW_GREEN_ACTLOW <= '0';
        TIMER_OUT <= '0', '1' after 3 sec;
        CURR_STATE := WAIT_LONG_TIMEOUT;
      end if;
    end case;
  end process;
end VHDL_BODY;
```

Fig. 4.6. VHDL implementation for traffic light controller

```
architecture SC_BODY of TRAFFIC_CONTROLLER is
begin
        state TLC is
                signal TIMER_OUT : BIT := '1';
        one of

                state WAIT_LONG_TIMEOUT is end;
                state SWITCH_FR is end;
                state WAIT_MEDIUM_TIMEOUT is end;
                state SWITCH_HW is end;

                default advance to SWITCH_HW;

                from WAIT_LONG_TIMEOUT
                when CARS_DETECTED = '1' and TIMER_OUT = '1'
                                        and HW_PRIORITY = '0'
                do begin
                        HW_LIGHTS <= YELLOW;
                        HW_GREEN_ACTLOW <= '1';
                        TIMER_OUT <= '0', '1' after 1 sec;
                end
                advance to SWITCH_FR;

                from SWITCH_FR
                when TIMER_OUT = '1' and HW_PRIORITY = '0'
                do begin
                        HW_LIGHTS <= RED;
                        FR_LIGHTS <= GREEN;
                        TIMER_OUT <= '0', '1' after 2 sec;
                end
                advance to WAIT_MEDIUM_TIMEOUT;
                when TIMER_OUT = '1' and HW_PRIORITY = '1'
                do begin
                        HW_LIGHTS <= GREEN;
                        HW_GREEN_ACTLOW <= '0';
                end
                advance to WAIT_LONG_TIMEOUT;

                ...

        end
end SC_BODY;
```

Fig. 4.7. Statechart implementation for traffic light controller

5. Timing diagram description

In this section we illustrate the use of the timing diagram language applied to the traffic light system–example.

STD–specification of the the traffic light controller. In the context of verification we are interested in the formal verification of selected system properties. The compositional approach underlying VHDL/S supports a two–step methodology, which can be explained to the designer as follows: (1) Find *local* STD–specifications of system components and verify them using model–checking, and (2) establish the selected system properties from the locally established component properties by interactive verification.

First, we consider the specification of the traffic light controller. In general, such a specification is designed using a graphical tool, called the timing–diagram–manager (TDM). The TDM displays STD-specifications as shown in figure 5.1. The *STD-declarative-part* is an implicit part of the *STD-specification-part*: Those diagrams which are linked to other diagrams are declarations of commitments, the other ones are declarations of assumptions. The declarations of commitments also define the *STD-specification-part*. E.g., commitment diagram **sequenceoflights** depends on the assumption diagrams ENV_DELAY_LIVE, **cars_come** and **cars_stay_until_green**.

As can be seen in figure 5.1, there is usually a set of several local component properties which have been verified by model–checking. In general, in order to derive a particular system property, only selected local properties will be need.

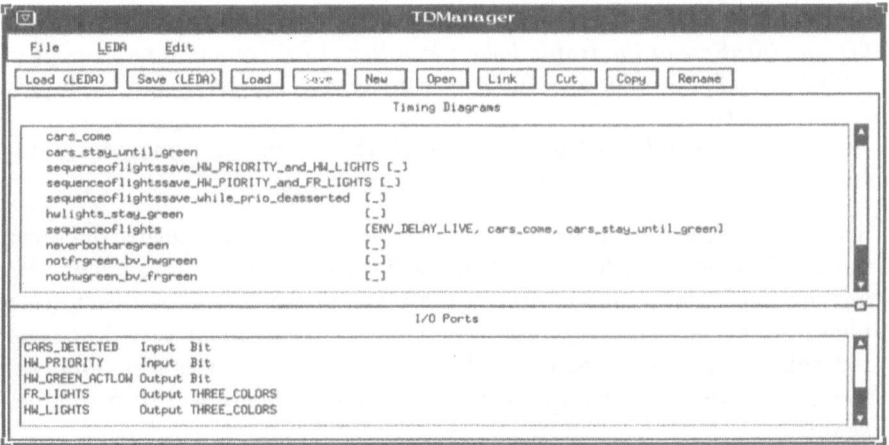

Fig. 5.1. Representation of Symbolic Timing Diagram-specification in the TDM

As an example of an STD–diagram, figure 5.2 shows a local property, which expresses the behaviour of the ports FR_LIGHTS and HW_LIGHTS

dependent of the behaviour of the input port HW_PRIORITY as STD–
diagram named `sequenceoflightssafe_with_priority`. This diagram has
three symbolic waveforms, two strong simultaneous–constraints, and two
precedence#–constraints, one strong and one weak. Note in particular the
weak constraint at the end of the diagram, which expresses that the component only has to follow the specified behaviour provided signal HW_PRIORI-
TY is kept low.

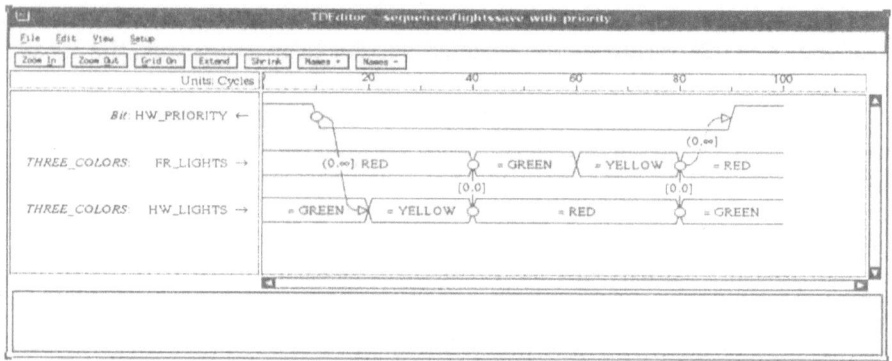

Fig. 5.2. Diagram `sequenceoflightssafe_with_priority`

Note that diagram `sequenceoflightssafe_with_priority` becomes invalid for the suggested behaviour VHDL–description if the weak constraint
pointing to the event '0' → '1' on input signal HW_PRIORITY is omitted (see
chapter 'Verification flow').

ETD–specification of the traffic light controller. In this section an excerpt of
the ETD-specification for a traffic light controller component shall exemplify
the use of ETD.

Analyzing the informal specification of the traffic light component the
following three major functionalities can be distinguished.

[CarDetect-TimeOut] If a car is *detected* on the farmroad during the green
period of the highway lights the lights will turn to amber and to red observing the *minimum period of time* of the green phase. The subsequent green
phase of the farmroad lights is restricted to a *maximum period of time*,
regardless of any detected cars. After the expiration of this time limit the
farmroad lights will turn to red and the highway lights will turn to green
again.

[CarDetect-NoCar] This functionality resembles the one before. However,
the green phase of the farmroad lights is prematurely finished due to the
absence of cars.

[CarDetector] The state of the car detector signal is permanently *monitored*.

Considering the commonly strict ordering green, amber, red, aso. of traffic light colours and some security aspects one can easily find the ETD depicted in figure 5.3 specifying these functionalities.

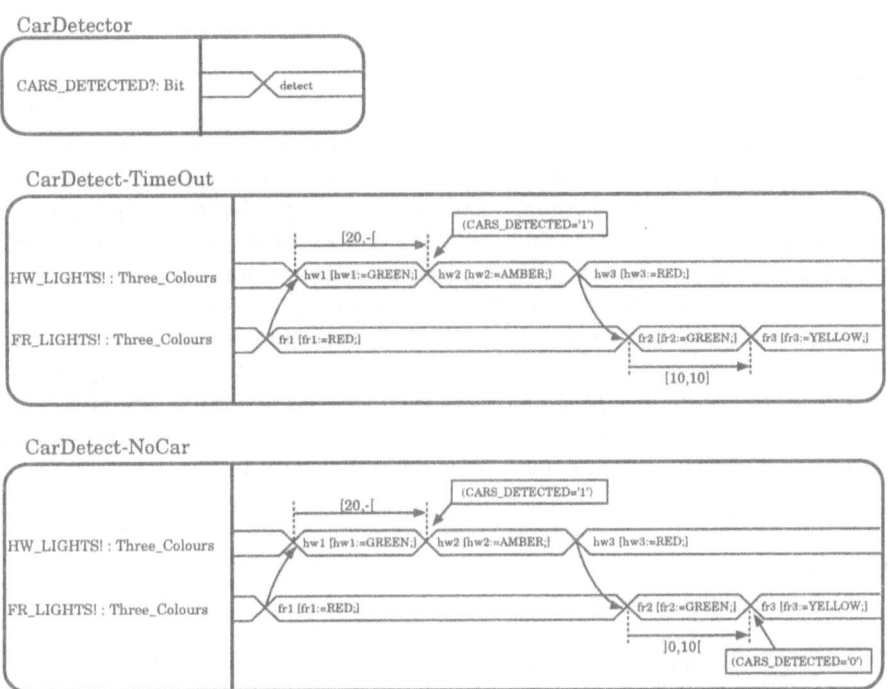

Fig. 5.3. Excerpt of ETD-specification for the Traffic Light Controller.

The ETD specifying the [CarDetector] function is very simple since neither temporal nor data constraints apply to this signal. A waveform consisting of a single edge without restricting data predicate specifies arbitrary successions of events on the CARS-DETECTED port.

The ETD describing the [CarDetect-TimeOut] behaviour considers the output ports HW-LIGHTS and FR-LIGHTS. For both ports a waveform with appropriate data annotations describes the recurring sequences of traffic light colours. Since the traffic lights should not act independantly, temporal constraints have been introduced. Two strong constraints specify that the lights on the one road always have to turn red before the lights on the other road turn to green. The minimum time period for the green phase on the highway is reflected by a timing constraint. However, even after this minimum time period the highway lights will only change if a car is detected on the farmroad. A data constraint on the "amber" event of the highway lights expresses this conditional behaviour. The time limit for the green phase on the farmroad is again specified by a timing constraint.

The ETD for the [CarDetect-NoCar] behaviour is similar to the previous one and will not be discussed any further.

Finally, the alternative composition of these three ETD reflects the complete input/output behaviour of a traffic light controller component.

6. Summary

VHDL/S allows the designer to cover both operational specification of systems and declarative specification of requirements in a single language framework. The design of this language has always been guided by the pragmatics of its use: Timing diagrams and state based specifications are offered, with their familiar graphical suggestivity; existing VHDL library components may be arbitrarily incorporated, since they will find their expected environment; a compositional proof methodology allows to employ automated verification at the limit of the current state of the art; the semantics of timing diagrams as well as state based specifications encourage an incremental design style; and syntax as well as conceptual background have been unified across paradigms so one may switch between them with ease.

References

J. Helbig, R. Schlör, W. Damm, G. Döhmen, and P. Kelb. (1993): VHDL/S - integrating statecharts, timing diagrams, and VHDL. *Microprocessing and Microprogramming 38*, pages 571–580.

D. Harel (1987): StateCharts: A Visual Formalism for Complex Systems. *Science of Computer Programming 8*.

E.M. Clarke, E.A. Emerson, and A.P. Sistla (1986): Automatic verification of finite-state concurrent systems using temporal logic. *ACM Trans. on Programming Languages and Systems*, 8:244–263.

B. Josko (1993): *Modular specification and verification of reactive systems*. Habilitationsschrift, University of Oldenburg.

Z. Manna and A. Pnueli (1982): Verification of concurrent programs: The temporal framework. In R. S. Boyer and J. S. Moore, editors, *Correctness Problems in Computer Science*, chapter 5, pages 215–273. Academic Press.

J.R. Burch, E.M. Clarke, K.L. McMillan, D.L. Dill, and J. Hwang (1990): Symbolic model checking: 10^{20} states and beyond. In *Proceedings of the Fifth Annual Symposium on Logics in Computer Science*, pages 428–439, June.

J. R. Armstrong (1988): *Chip-level Modeling with VHDL*. Prentice-Hall, New York.

W. Damm, B. Josko, and R. Schlör (1995): Specification and verification of VHDL-based system-level hardware designs. In E. Börger, editor, *Specification and validation methods*. Oxford University Press, pages 331 – 41.

M. Fujita and H. Fujisawa (1990): Specification, verification and synthesis of control circuits with propositional temporal logic. In J.A.Darringer and F.J.Rammig, editors, *Computer Hardware Description Languages and their Applications*, pages 265–279. Elsevier Science Publishers B.V..

G. Boriello (1992): Formalized timing diagrams. In *Proceedings, The European Conference on Design Automation*, pages 372–377, Brussels, Belgium, March.

Ph. Moeschler, H.P. Amann, and F. Pellandini (1993): High-level modelling using extended timing diagrams. In *proceedings of EURO-DAC'93*, pages 494–499,September.

K. Khordoc, M. Dufresne, E. Cerny, P. Babkine, and A. Silburt (1993): Integrating behavior and timing in executable specifications. In *Conference on Hardware Description Languages and their Applications*, pages 385 – 402. OCRI Publications, April.

G. v. Bochmann (1993): Specification languages for communication protocols. In *Conference on Hardware Description Languages and their Applications*, pages 365 – 382. OCRI Publications, April.

Verification Flow

Werner Damm[1], Gert Döhmen[1], Ronald Herrmann[2], Peter Kelb[1], Hergen Pargmann[3], and Rainer Schlör[1]

[1] Kuratorium OFFIS e.V., Germany
[2] Siemens AG, Germany
[3] Carl-von-Ossietzky-Universität Oldenburg, Germany

1. Verification tools

The FORMAT-project aims at a verification environment for VHDL-based hardware design, employing two major state-of-the-art verification methods: (1) (compositional) symbolic model checking (SMC), and (2) interactive theorem proving, supported by automatic verification tools for finite-state subtasks.

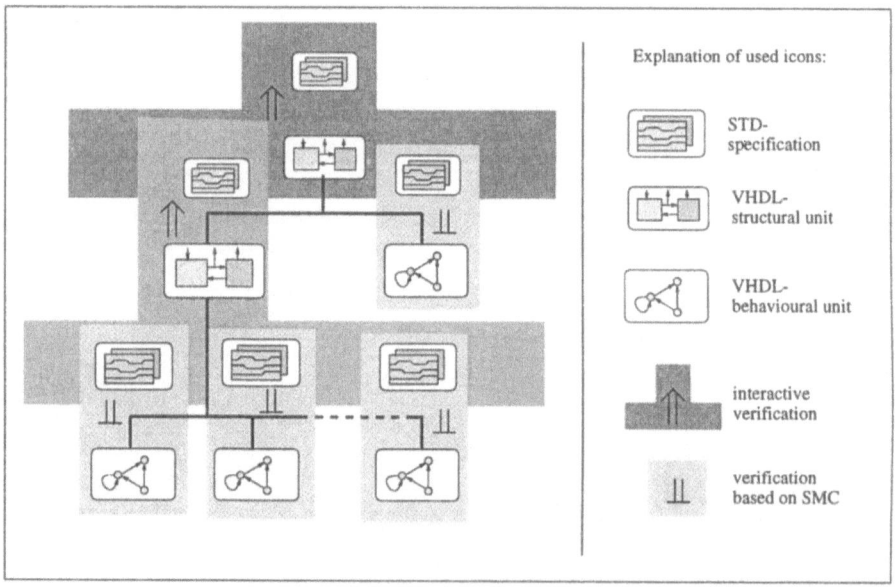

Fig. 1.1. Verification of an hierarchically structured VHDL-design

The basic idea is to verify a complex, hierarchically structured VHDL-design (cf. figure 1.1) in a sequence of verification steps, inferring at each level of the design relevant properties at that level from the specification of its sub-components. The leafs of such a tree-structured design are VHDL-behavioural bodies, whose finite-state machine representation is verified against the specification of that component using SMC. The derivation of relevant properties of an inner node of the design (which must be a structural description) is performed by an interactive prover.

Specifications as VHDL, Statechart or Symbolic Timing Diagrams reside in a central database. Editors as well as verification tools store and extract objects in this database. Derived objects which are Temporal logic specifications (TLS) as well as symbolic transition systems (STS) are stored externally in ASCII files. Figure 1.2 depicts the dataflow between verification tools.

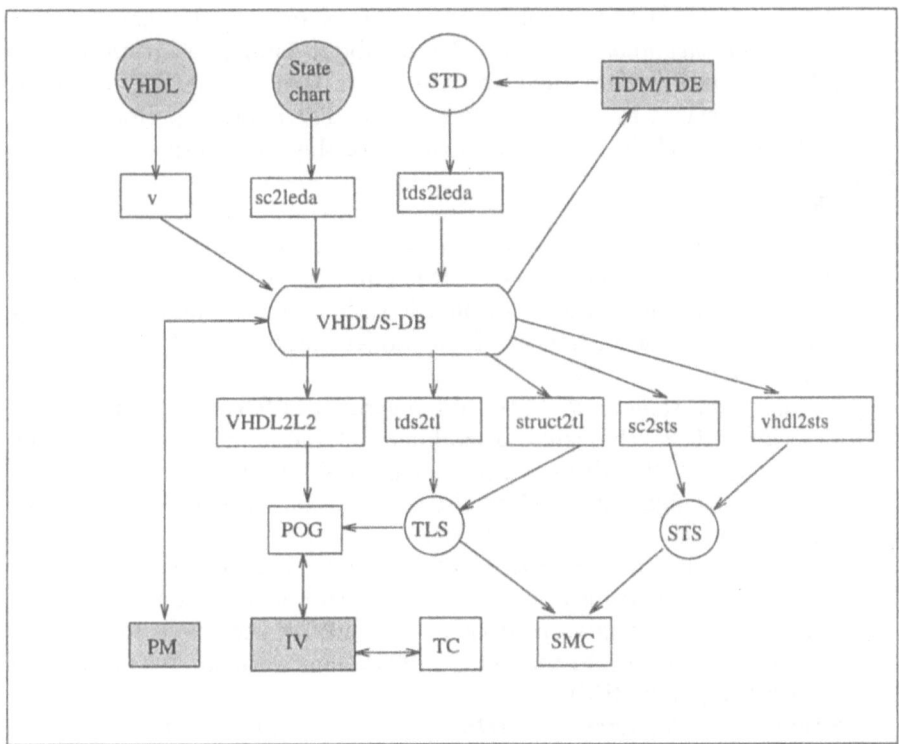

Fig. 1.2. Interaction of verification tools

In figure 1.2, dataformats and tools which are directly handled by the user are shaded. Three classes of tools can be identified:

1. **Support of specification language.**

   VHDL-to-database analyzer (v): A VHDL source code description (as ASCII file) is analysed and put as design unit in the database. This tool is a commercially available analyser from the LEDA VHDL SYSTEM (© LEDA S.A. France).

   Statechart-to-database analyzer (sc2leda): A textual Statechart specification (as ASCII file) is analysed and put as architecture body in the database. An architecture body is always bound to an VHDL entity declared by an entity declaration. Thus it can be used in design hierarchies like any other VHDL architecture body.

Timing-Diagram Manager/Editor (TDM/TDE): The specification language Symbolic Timing Diagram is supported by a graphical editor to draw and modify diagrams (© Abstract Hardware Limited UK). In general, a Symbolic Timing Diagram-*specification* consists of a collection of diagrams, which is handled by the TD-Manager. Created/modified specifications are stored to an intermediate file, or into the database.

STD-to-database analyzer (tds2leda): Symbolic Timing Diagrams can be analysed and stored in the database where they are always bound to an entity declared by an entity declaration. The analysis performs a full static semantic check for well-formedness of the specification.

2. **Compiler.**

Compiler from Symbolic Timing Diagram to temporal logic (tds2tl): Symbolic Timing Diagrams can be characterized by (linear-time) first-order temporal logic (FoTL) formulae. The compiler tds2tl performs this translation, building the bridge to automatic verification techniques operating with temporal logic such as symbolic model checking (SMC) and tautology checking (TC).

Compiler from structural VHDL to temporal logic (struct2tl): VHDL provides elaborate mechanisms to modularize large hardware designs. The compiler STRUCT2TL derives from a structural VHDL unit a characterizing FoTL-specification based on the compositional semantics for VHDL described in (W. Damm et al. 1995).

Compiler for VHDL declarations (VHDL2L2): The prover makes use of a compiler, which translates (a significant subset of) VHDL–functions, –constants and –type declarations to L2, which is the native logic of the LAMBDA system (M. Francis et al. 1993). This work has been described in (Nick Chapman 1994).

Compiler from behavioural VHDL to symbolic transition systems (vhdl2-sts): This compiler works on the analysed VHDL from the database. It elaborates the VHDL and generates a highly optimized finite-state BDD-based model which is used by the symbolic model checker (cf. (G. Döhmen and R. Herrmann 1995) and (G. Döhmen et al. 1995)).

Compiler from Statecharts to symbolic transition systems (sc2sts): This compiler produces a highly optimized finite-state BDD-based model for a Statechart description. As for behavioural VHDL, this is used by the model checker.

3. **Verification tools.**

Proof manager (PM): All proofs are executed and controlled via a common tool, the proof manager, which keeps track of the completed proofs, identifies missing sub-proofs and controls the consistency of proofs. Existing proofs may be invalidated by changing (incidentally or deliberately) parts of the specification of the design which is to be verified. The PM automatically detects, which (sub-)proofs are invalidated by the change and have to be either re-run or built completely new in order to establish the proof again. Details can be found in section 2..

Proof obligation generator (POG): The POG is an interactive tool. It is invoked by the PM in order to derive properties of a structural design from properties of its sub-components. It appears to the user like a browser on the sub-design to be verified, allowing the selection of relevant sub-components with according relevant parts of their specifications necessary to derive the properties. It then calls the according compilers for all referenced Symbolic Timing Diagram specifications, VHDL declarations and the structural unit and produces a *proof-obligation* to be verified by the interactive verifier.

Interactive verifier (IV): A general theorem prover[1], enhanced by an implementation of the FoTL with various proof-systems and tactics to manage large proof obligations. All datatypes supported by L2 (LAMBDA's native logic) can be referenced in the logic; in this context, they are used to represent VHDL dataypes as transformed by the compiler VHDL2L2. Yet another proof-subsystem with an own set of temporal operators representing graphical "fragments" of the specifications allows to reason directly over the (special) class of TL obtained from STD-specifications, aiming at *semi–graphical* proof rules at the textual level provided by the IV. These semi–graphical operators encapsulate the native "low-level" TL-operators into more powerful idioms, yet retaining the full flexibility of the basic logic.

Tautology checker (TC): For those parts of a proof-obligation, which can be expressed by PTL, an external TC is connected to the IV. The TC has a graphical error-path diagnosis, which facilitates the detection of errors in the design to be verified (or in the specification!) by comparison with the graphical specification.

Symbolic model checker (SMC): The model checker is used to check a Symbolic Timing Diagram specification against a finite-state model which represents a behavioural description either as VHDL or Statechart specification. This is explained in detail in section 5..

2. Proof manager

2.1 Purpose of the proof manager

The verification of VHDL/S designs often leads to complex proof states. Parts of the design have already been proved, other parts still have to be verified.

---

[1] Within the FORMAT project the LAMBDA-prover (© Abstract Hardware Limited UK) is used.

During the various iteration phases of the design flow, parts of the design which have been proved correct may be changed by the designer. The changed parts have to be verified again. Since a complex design will be developed by a group of designers it is very difficult to get an overview, which parts of the design are proved and which ones are not, because they have been changed or the corresponding proof have never been validated.

The proof manager supports the designer in getting an overview of the current proof state and performing appropiate proofs to verify parts of the design. It is the central tool in the verification flow of VHDL/S designs. Although no parts of the design will be proved by the proof manager, every proof will be initiated by it. Since the proof manager has a complete overview of the proof state it can compute which proofs have to be rerun if parts of the design are changed or which parts have never been proved correct.

Besides the administration of the proof structure the proof manager recognizes the proof method by which certain parts of the design should be verified. For example if the user wants to check whether a VHDL behavioural body satisfies a timing diagram specification the proof manager initiates a model checker session by calling the corresponding FORMAT tools.

2.2 Verification of behavioural descriptions

The general strategy in the FORMAT context is that all proofs have to be handled by the proof manager. The tool offers the user a graphical frontend which allows to initiate new proofs and to get a fast overview about the current proof state of the design. In most cases proofs of parts of the design are composed by basic proof tasks. These basic proof tasks can be handled by the FORMAT verification tools. For example the verification task that a VHDL behavioural body meets a timing diagram specification will be broken up into several subproofs. Each subproof checks whether the VHDL behavioural body meets one single timing diagram of the timing diagram specification. Initiating the proof by the proof manager the subproofs are **not** executed directly. The proof manager first only constructs a proof dependency graph which shows the user, what subproofs have to be proved. The user has to start the execution of the proofs manually. This allows the designer to delay the achievement of time intensive proofs.

Both specifications and implementations are VHDL architectures in the FORMAT context. It is necessary that the specification and the implementation of a proof have the same VHDL entity. Thus the proof manager associates with an entity the proofs of this entity.

Figure 2.1 shows the top window of the proof manager for the VHDL/S design introduced in the chapter on specification languages. The window indicates all entities of the design library. By selecting one entity the user can open a window containing all architectures of the selected entity (Figure 2.2). The example consists of four entities. The entity *TRAFFIC_CONTROLLER*

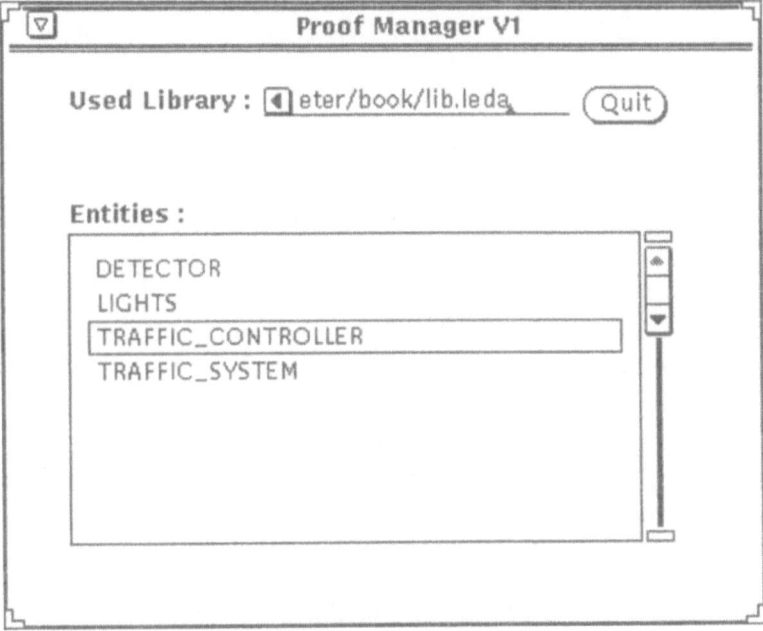

Fig. 2.1. Top window of the proof manager

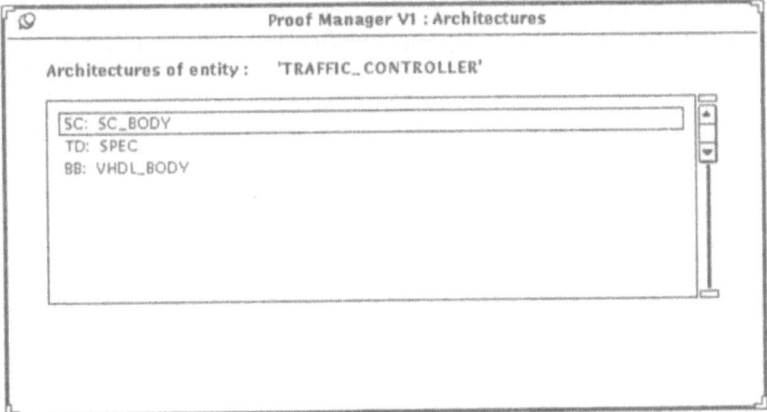

Fig. 2.2. Overview of the architectures

has three architectures. The architecture *SPEC* is a timing diagram specification, *VHDL_BODY* is a VHDL behavioural body and *SC_BODY* is a
VHDL/S Statechart implementation. The proof manager recognizes the type
of the different architectures. Four types can be distinguished. The type *TD*
indicates a timing diagram specification, *BB* a VHDL behavioural body, *SC*
a VHDL/S Statechart specification and *SB* a VHDL structural body (see
below).

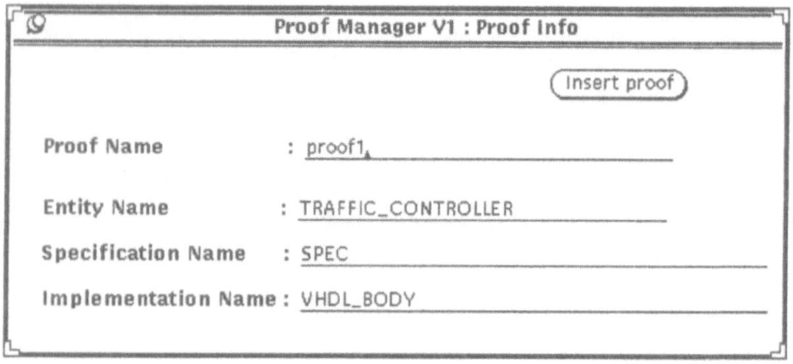

Fig. 2.3. Initiating a new proof

By selecting an entity a new proof for this entity can be initiated. Figure 2.3 shows the corresponding window. The user has to specify a specification and an implementation from the set of architectures by selecting them in the architecture window (Figure 2.2). In the example the user wants to prove that the implementation *VHDL_BODY* meets the timing diagram specification *SPEC*. Each proof has to be named – in this case the proof is named *proof1*. The proof manager inserts the proof into the VHDL/S database and determines the proof method which has to be used for the proof task. In the example the proof manager recognizes that the VHDL behavioural body will be checked against the timing diagram specification by calling the model checker.

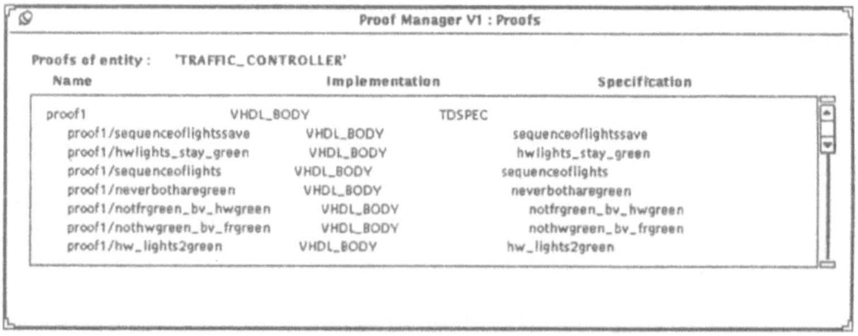

Fig. 2.4. Proofs of the selected entity

Figure 2.4 displays all proofs associated with the selected entity. One can see that the proof *proof1* has been inserted into the design database. The proof *proof1* is not a basic proof task which can be handled by a single verification tool. The proof depends on several subproofs. These are listed below the proof, e.g. *proof1/sequenceoflightssave*. If all subproofs are valid the proof *proof1* is verified. In this case the timing diagram specification consists of eight single timing diagrams. Thus the proof depends on eight subproofs.

The user has to execute each of the subproofs. This kind of partitioning allows a flexible rerun strategy of (sub-) proofs depending on modified design parts. For example if the single timing diagram *sequenceoflightssave* will be modified, only the subproof *proof1/sequenceoflightssave* has to be rerun.

By selecting a proof the proof manager first checks whether the proof is valid or not, depending on the states of subproofs. If parts of the design have been changed the proof manager recognizes which proofs have to be rerun and which are still valid. In order to verify proof *proof1* all subproofs have to be executed. The current proof state can be displayed in a separate window.

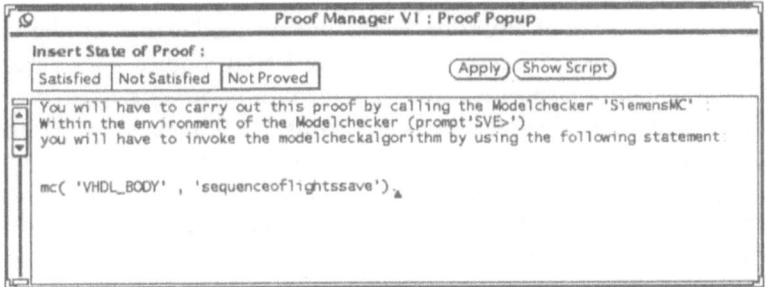

Fig. 2.5. The state of a proof

Figure 2.5 depicts the proof state of the first subproof. The state can be one of the three *satisfied, not satisfied* or *not proved*. The first two distinguish whether a proof is satisfied or not. The third state indicates that the proof is in execution but not terminated. In the example the proof *proof1/sequenceoflightssave* has not been executed, indicated by the state *not proved*. Furthermore, the text in the window informs the user about the next steps in the verification flow. In this case a model will be generated, the timing diagram will be translated into temporal logic, and the model checker will check the model against the specification. Pressing the *Execute Proof* button the verification process will be started. In this case the proof manager checks whether the model has to be generated, because no one exists or the VHDL behavioural body has been recompiled. The same happens for the timing diagram. If the model checker will be called the user has the possibility to change the flags in an additional window. The flags will be discussed in section 5.2.1.

During execution of the proof, the proof manager informs the user about the current status of the proof. This information may confuse the unpracticed user, but can be very useful for the practiced one. He can see whether a model checker run will not terminate because of space complexity problems. In this case the information can help to find the correct model checker flags (see section 5.2.1). The messages generated by the tools, e.g. the model checker or the LAMBDA system, can be stored into the VHDL/S database. They will be associated with the proof and can be displayed later on in order to document how the proof has been performed. The user gets the messages by pressing the *script* button.

Since executing the single tasks of a proof can take a very long time the proof manager doesn't wait on the termination of the whole proof. Thus the proof manager only initiates the proof and takes the result over after termination. This allows the designer to use the proof manager although one or more proofs are running. For example the user can still navigate through the design and generate new proof tasks.

2.3 Handling hierarchical structures

The most complex proof situation arises during verification of hierarchical designs. In the context of FORMAT structural VHDL bodies can be validated against timing diagram specifications. These kinds of proofs require two steps. In the first step a so-called *abstract configuration* will be checked against the timing diagram specification, in the second step a proof of this abstract configuration and a so-called *concrete configuration* will be performed. An abstract configuration is a configuration binding all components to timing diagram specifications. If not all components are bound to timing diagram specifications but to VHDL structural or behavioural bodies or VHDL/S Statechart specifications the configuration is called concrete. The first step of the proof has to be done by the proof system based on the LAMBDA theorem prover. In some cases even this task can be done fully automatic using a tautology checker for the calculus of timing diagrams (see section 4.). After proving that the abstract configuration meets the timing diagram specification the user can prove that the concrete configuration is a correct implementation of the abstract one. This task consists of several single subtasks, each checking a component of the concrete configuration against the timing diagram specification of the corresponding component of the abstract configuration. The proof manager generates all necessary proofs and subproofs and stores them into the VHDL/S database. The following pictures will explain these steps of proving a hierarchical design.

Figure 2.6 shows the three architectures of the entity *TRAFFIC_SYSTEM* named *TDSPEC*, *A_IMPL* and *IMPL*. The first architecture is a timing diagram specification, both other are configurations. The proof manager recognizes that *A_IMPL* is an abstract configuration, i.e. all components are bound to timing diagram specifications. The architecture *IMPL* is a concrete configuration.

To prove that *IMPL* meets *TDSPEC*, first the user has to show that the abstract configuration *A_SPEC* satisfies the timing diagram specification. For this task a new proof named *proof2* will be initiated and inserted into the VHDL/S database (see Figure 2.7).

This proof will be validated interactively using the LAMBDA-based prover. Similar to the model checker call described above, a proof obligation generator will be executed by pressing the *Execute Proof* button. The proof obligation

```
┌─────────────────────────────────────────────────────────────┐
│ Ⓠ                Proof Manager V1 : Architectures             │
│                                                               │
│  Architectures of entity :   'TRAFFIC_SYSTEM'                 │
│  ┌──────────────────────────────────────────────────────┐ ▲ │
│  │ SB: SYSTEM_BODY                                        │   │
│  │     CONF(abstract) : A_IMPL                            │ ▼ │
│  │     CONF(concrete) : IMPL                              │   │
│  │ TD: TDSPEC                                             │   │
│  │                                                        │   │
│  │                                                        │   │
│  │                                                        │   │
│  └──────────────────────────────────────────────────────┘   │
└─────────────────────────────────────────────────────────────┘
```

Fig. 2.6. Architectures of the entity *TRAFFIC_SYSTEM*

```
┌─────────────────────────────────────────────────────────────┐
│ Ⓠ                   Proof Manager V1 : Proofs                 │
│                                                               │
│  Proofs of entity :   'TRAFFIC_SYSTEM'                        │
│    Name                    Implementation       Specification │
│                                                            ▲  │
│   proof2          A_IMPL            TDSPEC                  ▼  │
│                                                               │
│                                                               │
│                                                               │
└─────────────────────────────────────────────────────────────┘
```

Fig. 2.7. Proof: *A_IMPL* meets *TDSPEC*

generator translates the structural VHDL body into proof obligations the user has to verify by the LAMBDA system.

This verification task is described in detail in section 4. When the task has been completed, then the abstract configuration can be checked against the concrete one. A new proof *proof3* will be instantiated and inserted into the VHDL/S database (see Figure 2.8).

```
┌─────────────────────────────────────────────────────────────┐
│ Ⓠ                Proof Manager V1 : Proof Info                │
│                                                               │
│                                              ( Insert proof ) │
│                                                               │
│   Proof Name           : proof3_____   │
│                                                               │
│   Entity Name          : TRAFFIC_SYSTEM_____   │
│                                                               │
│   Specification Name   : A_IMPL_____   │
│                                                               │
│   Implementation Name : IMPL_____   │
└─────────────────────────────────────────────────────────────┘
```

Fig. 2.8. Initiating the proof: *IMPL* meets *A_IMPL*

Figure 2.9 shows the two proofs *proof2* and *proof3* associated with the entity *TRAFFIC_SYSTEM*. The last one depends on four subproofs – for each component one subproof. In order to execute the subproofs the user has to switch to the corresponding entities.

Proof Manager V1 : Proofs		
Proofs of entity : 'TRAFFIC_SYSTEM'		
Name	Implementation	Specification
proof2	A_IMPL	TDSPEC
proof3	IMPL	A_IMPL
proof3/DET	VHDL_BODY	TDSPEC
proof3/FR	VHDL_BODY	TDSPEC
proof3/HW	VHDL_BODY	TDSPEC
proof3/TRAFF1	VHDL_BODY	TDSPEC

Fig. 2.9. The proofs of the entity *TRAFFIC_SYSTEM*

Proof Manager V1 : Proofs		
Proofs of entity : 'TRAFFIC_CONTROLLER'		
Name	Implementation	Specification
proof3/TRAFF1	VHDL_BODY	TDSPEC
proof3/TRAFF1/sequenceoflightssave	VHDL_BODY	sequenceoflightssave
proof3/TRAFF1/hwlights_stay_green	VHDL_BODY	hwlights_stay_green
proof3/TRAFF1/sequenceoflights	VHDL_BODY	sequenceoflights
proof3/TRAFF1/neverbotharegreen	VHDL_BODY	neverbotharegreen
proof3/TRAFF1/notfrgreen_bv_hwgreen	VHDL_BODY	notfrgreen_bv_hwgreen
proof3/TRAFF1/nothwgreen_bv_frgreen	VHDL_BODY	nothwgreen_bv_frgreen
proof3/TRAFF1/hw_lights2green	VHDL_BODY	hw_lights2green

Fig. 2.10. Generated proofs of the entity *TRAFFIC_CONTROLLER*

Figure 2.10 depicts the generated proofs for the traffic light controller. These proofs are identical to the ones, which were generated in the previous section manually. The verification of the VHDL behavioural body *VHDL_BODY* against the timing diagram specification *TDSPEC* depends on several subproofs. Each of them will be verified using the model checker.

One can see that the structure of the proof of a structural design leads to complex situation. In general the user will have problems to see which parts are already proved and which ones still have be validated. To get a fast overview about the current proof state the user has to select the proof he is interested in and the proof manager shows which subproofs have been evaluated. For example consider that the subproof *proof3/DET* has been proved successfully. In Figure 2.11 one can see that the proof *proof3* still depends on the subproof *proof3/DET* but to validate proof *proof3* only the three other subproofs – *proof3/FR*, *proof3/HW* and *proof3/TRAFF1* – have to be checked.

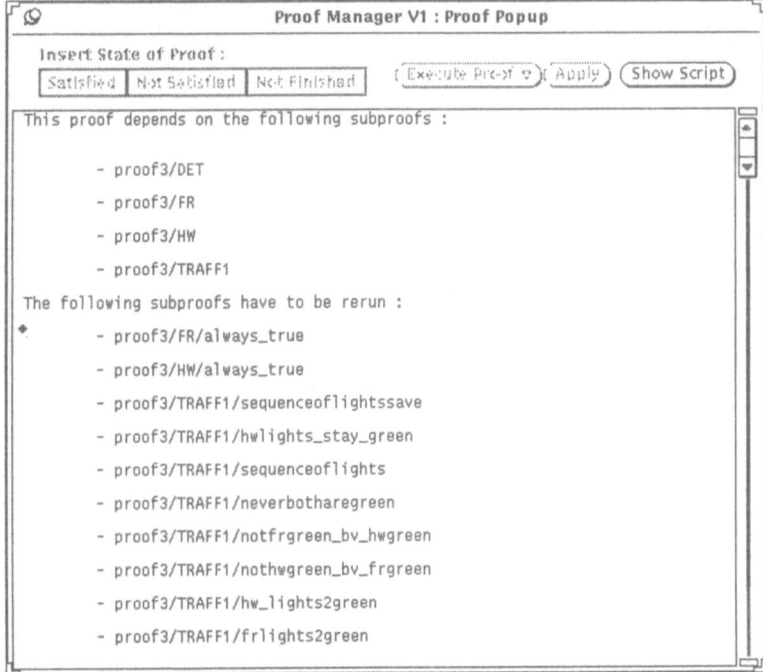

Fig. 2.11. Unevaluated subproofs of proof *proof3*

3. Proof steps for the traffic light system

The diagram shown in figure 3.1 defines the global goal that we want to prove for the traffic light system which components are configured with VHDL_BODY architectures. Informally it specifies that whenever a privileged car is on the highway keeping the PRIORITY signal high then *all* highway signals stay GREEN in order to let this priviledged car pass. This goal states a safety aspect – it does not mean that all the highway lights will eventually switch to GREEN. They will be kept GREEN if they are already GREEN.

The proof is done in several steps. First we have to find local STD specifications for all the components of the structured design SYSTEM_BODY which are sufficient enough to derive the global goal from.

The compositional proof – depicted in figure 3.2 – is done purely on the basis of this local properties. Section 4. shows this proof where the STD specification with the single diagram HW_GREEN_ACTLOW_lasts_while_priority_is-_asserted (cf. figure 4.1) is used as local property for each C1 component. No STD specifications have to be given for the other components since they are not relevant for the global goal. The binding is done by an abstract configuration which instantiates all C1 components of SYSTEM_BODY with this STD specification.

64   W. Damm et al.

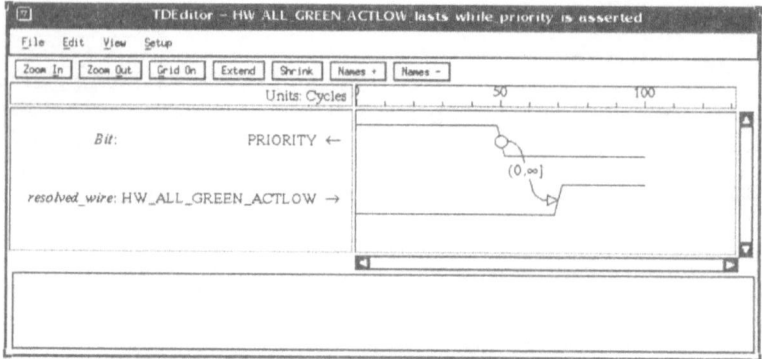

Fig. 3.1. Diagram stating the global property

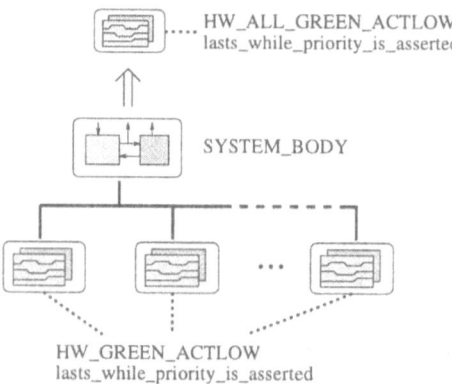

HW_GREEN_ACTLOW
lasts_while_priority_is_asserted

Fig. 3.2. Proof of the abstract configuration

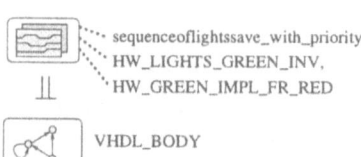

Fig. 3.3. Local component verification

The second step shown in figure 3.3 proves the validity of an STD specification comprising the timing diagram of figure 5.2 in the chapter on specification languages and two invariants named HW_LIGHTS_GREEN_INV and HW_GREEN_IMPL_FR_RED. The first states that always

$$\text{HW\_GREEN\_ACT\_LOW} = \text{'0'} \text{ iff } \text{HW\_LIGHTS} = \text{GREEN}$$

and the second that always

$$\text{HW\_LIGHTS} = \text{GREEN} \rightarrow \text{FR\_LIGHTS} = \text{RED}$$

Section 5. shows how this proof can be performed.

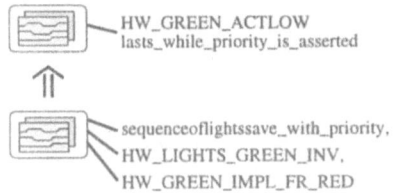

HW_GREEN_ACTLOW
lasts_while_priority_is_asserted

sequenceoflightssave_with_priority,
HW_LIGHTS_GREEN_INV,
HW_GREEN_IMPL_FR_RED

Fig. 3.4. Weakening of the Symbolic Timing Diagram Specification

The third step – shown in figure 3.4 has now to prove that our local STD specification used in step one derives from the STD specification we have proved in step two. Such a proof can be performed with the interactive verifier as explained in section 4.. This verifier has the option to deliver subproofs to an external tautologychecker which will perform the subproof automatically. Note that this can only be done if we need not to reason about infinite or generic structures. The weakening of the two Timing Diagram Specifications of figure 3.4 can be done automatically by the external tautologychecker.

All three proofs together will (by transitivity) ensure that the SYSTEM_BODY architecture where all components are configured with VHDL-_BODY architectures fulfills the global property of figure 3.2.

4. Compositional verification

In this section we want to illustrate the complete sequence of steps necessary to perform a proof in the interactive verifier.

The global property. As global property we take the one shown in the STD of figure 3.1, named

HW_ALL_GREEN_ACTLOW_lasts_while_priority_is_asserted

(abbreviated ϕ_G). We wish to derive that *whenever* the signal PRIORITY is asserted (= '1') and the flag HW_ALL_GREEN_ACTLOW is asserted (= '1') (recall that it has been asserted in reaction to the assertion of signal PRIORITY), then flag HW_ALL_GREEN_ACTLOW will be kept asserted while signal PRIORITY is asserted.

The local property. We recognize a property (very similar to the global one), which each of the components of the system should satisfy, and suppose that these local properties will be sufficient to ensure the global one. This property, HW_GREEN_ACTLOW_lasts_while_priority_is_asserted (abbreviated ϕ_C), states that *whenever* the component signal HW_PRIORITY is asserted (= '1') and the component flag HW_GREEN_ACTLOW is asserted (= '1') , then flag HW_ALL_GREEN_ACTLOW will be kept asserted while signal PRIORITY is asserted.

The diagram shown in figure 4.1 is the local property as stated in STD.

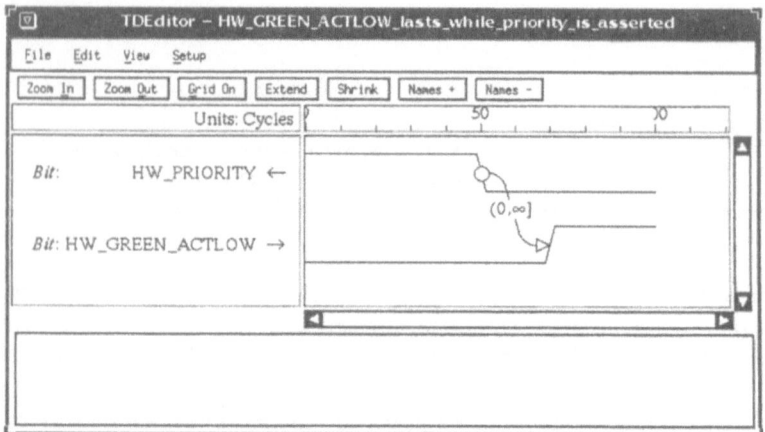

Fig. 4.1. Diagram stating property ϕ_C

This property can be derived *automatically* from the property shown in figure 5.2 of the chapter specification languages and two invariants named HW_LIGHTS_GREEN_INV and HW_GREEN_IMPL_FR_RED, which can be verified (also automatically) using model–checking (cf. section 5.).

Construction of the proof-obligation. Since the global property should hold for an arbitrary number of components, an automatic derivation as provided by the tautology checker is not possible. Instead, the interactive prover must be used. The proof–manager (PM) calls the proof–obligation–generator (POG), which guides the user through an interactive dialog, where he/she selects the global property to be established against an *abstract* configuration of the system, where component C1:CONTROLLER has been bound to a specification containing the local property explained above.

The result is a file which contains a number of L2–items (L2 is the name of LAMBDA's native logic) corresponding to the following VHDL–items:

– **VHDL–type declarations.** All referenced type and subtype–declarations are translated. E.g. the VHDL-type declaration:
type BIT is ('0', '1');
generates an according L2–declaration:
datatype BIT = c'0' | c'1';
– **Encapsulation of diagram annotations.** All VHDL–annotations occurring in the diagrams involved in the verification task are translated in according function (relations). E.g., diagram ϕ_G has the VHDL–annotation:
PRIORITY = '1' ,
which generates an L2–relation:
fun ϕ_G_0_ANN (PRIORITY,ret) =
is_BIT#(PRIORITY) − >>
is_BOOLEAN#(ret) /\ ret == PRIORITY = ord_BIT c'1';

– **Translation of diagrams.** Each diagram involved in the verification task is traslated into a formula in the embedded temporal logic.

– **Translation of expressions.** Further VHDL–expressions occur, in this example, in the port–maps of the component–instantiation–statements of the VHDL–architecture SYSTEM_BODY of TRAFFIC_SYSTEM. These are encapsulated into according functions which have the free variables of the expression as parameters.

E.g. the expression FR_LIGHT(I) in the association–element:

FR_LIGHTS => FR_LIGHT(I),

in the (generic) instantiation of the CONTROLLER–component induces an according L2–relation:

```
fun α_C1_PORT_MAP_FR_LIGHTS_TIME_rel (I,FR_LIGHT,ret) =
is_INTEGER#(I) /\ is_COLOR_ARRAY#(FR_LIGHT) - >>
is_THREE_COLORS#(ret) /\ INDEX (FR_LIGHT,I,ret);
```

(where α is a unique identifier prefix)

– **The proof–obligation.**
This is a logical implication (formulated in temporal logic), which has to be established as a tautolgy.

Carrying out the proof. Once the proof–obligation has been generated, the main task of the proof–engineer begins (this level of verification will usually be done by a specialist). The LAMBDA–theorem–prover (TP) is invoked and the generated proof–obligation is pushed onto LAMBDA's so–called goal–stack. The proof starts from the trivial conclusion:

```
*******   LEVEL 1.1   *******
1: G // H |- PROOFOBLIGATION
   ------------------------
   G // H |- PROOFOBLIGATION
```

The task is now to evaluate and discharge premise 1. Applying a predefined expansion–tactic (yet retaining the abbreviations of the property–formulas) yields:

```
*******   LEVEL 1.2   *******
1:G // H
  |- +1 <<= NUMBER_OF_DEVICES' == true
     /\ HW_ALL_GREEN_ACTLOW' == wired_or_TIME HW_ALL_GREEN_ACTLOW_IN'
     ->>
     (fn t =>
      forall I.
        (+0 <<= I) && (I <<= NUMBER_OF_DEVICES') == true
        ->>
        P_SYSTEM_C1_HW_GREEN_ACTLOW_lasts_while_priority_is_asserted#(
                        PRIORITY',
                        el_val#(HW_ALL_GREEN_ACTLOW_IN',I)) t)
```

```
Imp
G_HW_ALL_GREEN_ACTLOW_lasts_while_priority_is_asserted#(
                         PRIORITY',
                            wired_or_TIME HW_ALL_GREEN_ACTLOW_IN')
== tt
-------------------------------------------------------------------
G // H |- PROOFOBLIGATION
```

The first line to the right of the turnstile (|-) accounts for the fact that
NUMBER_OF_DEVICES is of type POSITIV, i.e. $\geq +1$. The next line is derived
from the fact that the value of port HW_ALL_GREEN_ACTLOW is a resolved value
determined by the values HW_GREEN_ACTLOW^I driven by the (generated) component C1^I:CONTROLLER (for $I = +1 \ldots$ NUMBER_OF_DEVICES). These values
are collected in the array HW_ALL_GREEN_ACTLOW_IN. The resolution function
wired_or has been compiled into the according L2–function wired_or_TIME
(the postfix TIME stems from the fact that signals are in the prover represented as *time sequences*, i.e.as mappings from the domain TIME (isomorphic
to the set of natural numbers) to according type–domains).

The abbreviation el_val#(x,i) denotes the value of the (unbounded)
array x at index i. The temporal–logic equivalents of the properties are encapsulated into abbreviations with respective names.

The next step is to inspect and simplify the generated temporal–logic
formulas of the properties. Unwinding and subsequent simplification using a
predefined expansion tactic yields:

```
*******    LEVEL 1.3    *******
1:G // H
  |- +1 <<= NUMBER_OF_DEVICES' == true
    /\ HW_ALL_GREEN_ACTLOW' ==
        (fn t => any ret. wired_or (HW_ALL_GREEN_ACTLOW_IN' t,ret))
    ->>
    (fn t1 =>
    forall I.
       (+0 <<= I) && (I <<= NUMBER_OF_DEVICES') == true
       ->>
Alw#((fn t => el_val#(HW_ALL_GREEN_ACTLOW_IN',I) t = ord_BIT c'0' ==
       true) And (fn t => PRIORITY' t = ord_BIT c'1' == true) Imp
     ((fn t => el_val#(HW_ALL_GREEN_ACTLOW_IN',I) t = ord_BIT c'0' ==
       true) And (fn t => PRIORITY' t = ord_BIT c'1' == true)) Unless
     ((fn t => el_val#(HW_ALL_GREEN_ACTLOW_IN',I) t = ord_BIT c'0' ==
       true) And (fn t => PRIORITY' t = ord_BIT c'0' == true))) t1)
Imp
Alw#((fn t =>
     (any ret. wired_or(HW_ALL_GREEN_ACTLOW_IN' t,ret)) = ord_BIT c'0'
     == true) And (fn t => PRIORITY' t = ord_BIT c'1' == true) Imp
```

```
((fn t =>
 (any ret. wired_or (HW_ALL_GREEN_ACTLOW_IN' t,ret)) =
  ord_BIT c'0' == true) And
 (fn t => PRIORITY' t = ord_BIT c'1' == true)) Unless
((fn t =>
 (any ret. wired_or (HW_ALL_GREEN_ACTLOW_IN' t,ret)) =
  ord_BIT c'0' == true) And
 (fn t => PRIORITY' t = ord_BIT c'0' == true))) == tt
```

```
G // H |- PROOFOBLIGATION
```

On this expansion level, annotations of the original diagram are unrevealed. Note that '0' is represented as ord_BIT c'0' and '1' is represented as ord_BIT c'1'. The used temporal operators are: And, Or, Imp and Not# as Boolean connective, and Alw# (always), Unless and Until as temporal operators. It turns out that both properties are of the form Alw#(P Imp (P Unless Q))) (*), for which a special operator UNLESS inspired by the UNITY–logic exists. Rewriting the form (*) into the (equivalent) abbreviation (P UNLESS Q) yields:

```
*******   LEVEL 1.5   *******
1:G // H
|- +1 <<= NUMBER_OF_DEVICES' == true
   /\ HW_ALL_GREEN_ACTLOW' ==
      (fn t => any ret. wired_or (HW_ALL_GREEN_ACTLOW_IN' t,ret))
->>
(fn t1 =>
 forall I.
  (+0 <<= I) && (I <<= NUMBER_OF_DEVICES') == true
  ->>
  ((fn t => el_val#(HW_ALL_GREEN_ACTLOW_IN',I) t = ord_BIT c'0' ==true
   ) And (fn t => PRIORITY' t = ord_BIT c'1' == true) UNLESS
   (fn t => el_val#(HW_ALL_GREEN_ACTLOW_IN',I) t = ord_BIT c'0' ==true
   ) And (fn t => PRIORITY' t = ord_BIT c'0' == true)) t1) Imp
((fn t =>
  (any ret. wired_or (HW_ALL_GREEN_ACTLOW_IN' t,ret)) = ord_BIT c'0'
  == true) And (fn t => PRIORITY' t = ord_BIT c'1' == true) UNLESS
 (fn t =>
  (any ret. wired_or (HW_ALL_GREEN_ACTLOW_IN' t,ret)) = ord_BIT c'0'
  == true) And (fn t => PRIORITY' t = ord_BIT c'0' == true)) == tt
```

```
G // H |- PROOFOBLIGATION
```

Separating temporal– and time–independent reasoning. Typically the prover-task arrives eventually at a point, where temporal– and time–independent assertions can be separated. In our example, the proof–obligation can be established from two independent facts:

1. (**reasoning about the resolution function.**) From the recursive definition of the resolution function, we have to establish that

```
...  |- (any ret. wired_or (HW_ALL_GREEN_ACTLOW_IN' x',ret))
        = ord_BIT c'0' ==
     true ==
     forall I.
       (+0 <<= I) && (I <<= NUMBER_OF_DEVICES') == true
       ->>
       (fn t => el_val#(HW_ALL_GREEN_ACTLOW_IN',I) t
        = ord_BIT c'0' == true)
       x'
```

i.e.that the result (`ret`) of the (L2 equivalent of the) resolution function `wired_or` applied to the array of driving values `HW_ALL_GREEN_ACTLOW_IN'` *at an arbitrary point* `x'` *in time* is '0' (represented as `ord_BIT c'0'`) **iff** each of its elements has the value representing '0'.

2. (**UNLESS-conjunction rule.**) The time-dependent part or the proof–task can be handled by a rule (rule–schema) called 'UNLESS-conjunction rule', which is:

```
|- forall n.
     +0 <<= n == true
     ->>
     (fn t1 =>
      forall I.
        (+0 <<= I) && (I <<= n) == true
        ->> (P#(I) And Q UNLESS P#(I) And R) t1) Imp
   ((fn t => forall I. (+0 <<= I) && (I <<= n) == true
                                      ->> P#(I) t) And Q
      UNLESS
      (fn t => forall I. (+0 <<= I) && (I <<= n) == true
                                      ->> P#(I) t) And R
    ) == tt
```

This rule is contained in a *rule–library* which is part of the prover. LAMBDA greatly facilitated the search for an appropriate rule by means of a sophisticated rule–browser.

Finally, application of the results of these two sub–proof–tasks discharges the premises of the goal and establishes the proof.

5. Component verification

5.1 Introduction

The proof of a complex design can be divided into two parts: the verification of single components and the structural verification. In this section we give a survey on the verification of system components based on Symbolic Model Checking.

It is a full automatic method to check whether a finite system, e.g. a VHDL or VHDL/S StateChart implementation, satisfies a temporal logic specification. In our approach we use the temporal logic CTL as specification of the behaviour of system components. On the one hand this logic is expressive enough to describe most of the interesting temporal logic properties of the implementation of the given design. On the other hand this logic can be checked very efficiently, i.e. the time and space complexity to check a given CTL formula is linear in the size of the formula and the size of the transition system of the design to be checked. Although model checking has this convenient property, non-trivial examples are in general to large to be represented in an explicit structure. This problem is known as the so-called state-explosion problem. A technique to overcome this problem is the representation of the system by its characteristic functions. These functions will be represented by ROBDDs, a canonical graph structure for boolean functions. Therefore the model checking algorithm performs no graph traversal, but a symbolic computation of fixed-points of the related boolean functions. It is well known that the performance of ROBDD-operations extremely depend on the choose variable ordering encoding the symbolic transition system. Because it is unknown which functions have to be represented during model checking the ordering of the set of variables relies on heuristics which can be influenced by a few parameters.

The specification of the temporal behaviour of the system is given in terms of symbolic timing diagrams. We use an assumption/commitment style symbolic model checker, where assumptions as well as commitments are derived from symbolic timing diagrams. The main difference is that assumptions are transformed into a linear time logic which is used to build a tableau and the commitments are transformed into a branching time logic. Section 6. describes the construction of temporal logic formulae out of symbolic timing diagrams.

A Petri net semantics of VHDL, which is the foundation for our approach, is given in (W. Damm et al. 1993). A more implementation oriented Petri net   model is introduced in (G. Döhmen 1994). A characterization of VHDL as deterministic finite-state models is given in (G. Döhmen and R. Herrmann 1995) and (G. Döhmen et al. 1995) where the second paper shows also the construction of BDD-based models. This BDD-based model will be used by the symbolic model checker. (R. Herrmann and H. Pargmann 1994) presents the coding of VHDL datatypes in the symbolic model whereas (H. Pargmann and R. Herrmann 1995) shows reduction techniques for the models.

5.2 Verification of the traffic light controller

5.2.1 Safety properties. The timing diagram as shown in figure 5.2 describes a safety property which should hold for the VHDL-implementation of the traffic light controller as shown in figure 4.6. We expect this safety property to hold under all possible behaviours of the environment and thus we do not state any assumption to hold.

The verification of the property *sequenceoflightssave_with_priority* for the VHDL-implementation *VHDL_BODY* of the entity *TRAFFIC_CONTRO-LLER* is performed using the FORMAT proof manager. The chosen timing diagrams specification *SPEC* consists of several properties including the selected one. The proof of this property can now be invoked as described in section 2.. The starting window of the component verification (figure 5.1) gives an overview about the current state of the ongoing proof. The user is now able to configure the symbolic model checker.

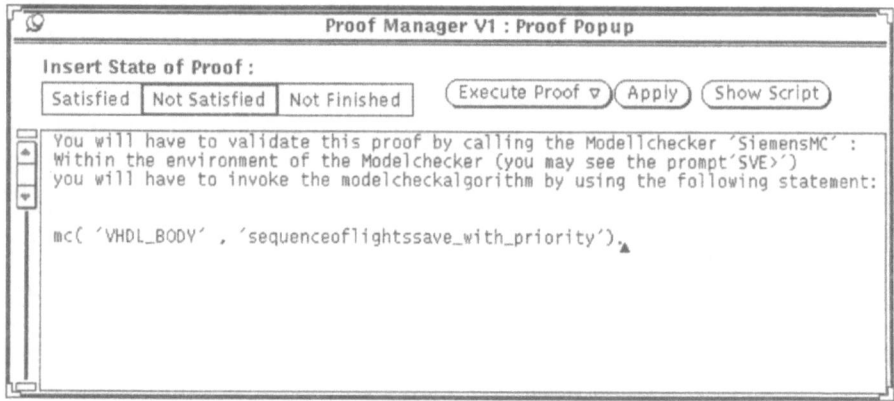

Fig. 5.1. Proof properties

The symbolic model checker provided by SIEMENS can be influenced by several flags. We will now introduce the most important flags for optimizing the run-time of the model checker. The representation of the next step relation can be given in functional or relational manner. If the representation is functional, e.g. this is the case for a transition system derived from VHDL, the user can choose whether the model checker uses the functional representation directly or transforms it into a relational one. The computation of a reachability set indicates the complexity of the search space for symbolic model checking and can also be used to influence the effect of dynamic variable reordering. Dynamic variable reordering is done also in the phase of computing the reachable set of states. The user can choose whether this set is computed on the model itself or the model combined with the tableau derived from the assumptions. If the user is sure that the complexity can be handled he can switch off dynamic reordering to speed up the model checking. The proof can be started by activating *Execute Proof*. Now the tool

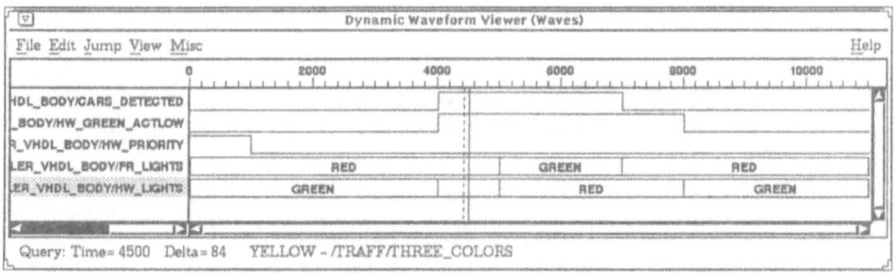

Modelcheckerflags	
partitionSize :	30000
predEvalFkt :	fkt | rel
modelReachability :	Yes | No
reachability :	Yes | No
reorder :	Yes | No
reorderLimit :	(1000 + 2 * X , X)
fairnessReorder :	Yes | No
fairnessConstraints :	modelR | tabR | fairOld
predDontCare :	intersection | restriction
sucDontCare :	intersection | restriction
mcMode :	backward | forward
	(Apply)

Fig. 5.2. Flags of the symbolic model checker

checks, if there is already a finite state machine representation for the VHDL implementation *VHDL_BODY*. If not it will be generated automatically. The execution of the proof will be monitored in a separate window.

First the full timing diagram specification *SPEC* will be checked and inserted into the design database. Next the timing diagrams are compiled into temporal logic. After this stage the model generation is started. The user can control the output of the model checker in a separate window and has the ability to change the model checking flags to optimize the model checking run.

Fig. 5.3. Synopsys representation of Error Path

Model checking the property *sequenceoflightssave_with_priority* against the symbolic model of *VHDL_BODY* results to *NOT true*. If the symbolic model checker has evaluated a proof to *NOT true*, the integrated debugger computes a counterexample which shows the violation of the checked property. To debug an error situation for a VHDL proof, a VHDL-test-bench is generated by the model checker, which can be used to simulate the VHDL

implementation together with the test-bench in the SYNOPSYS CAE framework for VHDL (© SYNOPSYS Inc.). Thus the full flexibility of a VHDL
simulation environment can be used to locate and to eliminate the error.

Figure 5.3 shows the output of a Synopsys simulator driven by a stimuli file which has been automatically produced by the debugger. The timing
diagram is activated directly after the first step, so that the user has to
compare the timing diagram with the waveforms of the specifications in the
dynamic waveform viewer. The symbolic timing diagram is activated with
HW_PRIORITY = '1', FR_LIGHTS = RED and *HW_LIGHTS = GREEN*.
After a car has been detected *HW_LIGHTS* switched to *YELLOW*, after
a certain amount of time has been elapsed, the highway lights switched to
RED and simultaneously the farm road light switched to *GREEN*. Now the
error occurs in the following way: No more cars are detected, hence the farm
road switched to *RED*, but it was expected by the timing diagram specification to switch to *YELLOW*. After modifying the VHDL implementation
as shown in figure 5.4, we can redo the proof and verify that the property
sequenceoflightssave_with_priority is valid.

```
architecture VHDL_BODY of TRAFFIC_CONTROLLER is
...
   when WAIT_MEDIUM_TIMEOUT =>
      if CARS_DETECTED = '0' or TIMER_OUT = '1' then
         FR_LIGHTS <= YELLOW; -- changed from RED
         TIMER_OUT <= '0', '1' after 1 sec;
         CURR_STATE := SWITCH_HW;
      end if;
   when SWITCH_HW =>
      if TIMER_OUT = '1' then
         FR_LIGHTS <= RED; -- inserted
         HW_LIGHTS <= GREEN;
         HW_GREEN_ACTLOW <= '0';
         TIMER_OUT <= '0', '1' after 3 sec;
         CURR_STATE := WAIT_LONG_TIMEOUT;
      end if;
...
```

Fig. 5.4. Correct VHDL-implementation

Two invariants named HW_LIGHTS_GREEN_INV and HW_GREEN-
_IMPL_FR_RED which are necessary for the proof in section 4. can be proved
by model checking in the same way as the property above.

5.2.2 Liveness property. To check the liveness property of figure 5.5 we
need to state assumptions about the behaviour of the environment of the
VHDL-module. Timing diagrams are also used to specify assumptions which
are part of a symbolic timing diagram specification (refer to section 4.). We
modify the timing diagram of figure 5.2 by introducing an arc from the upper

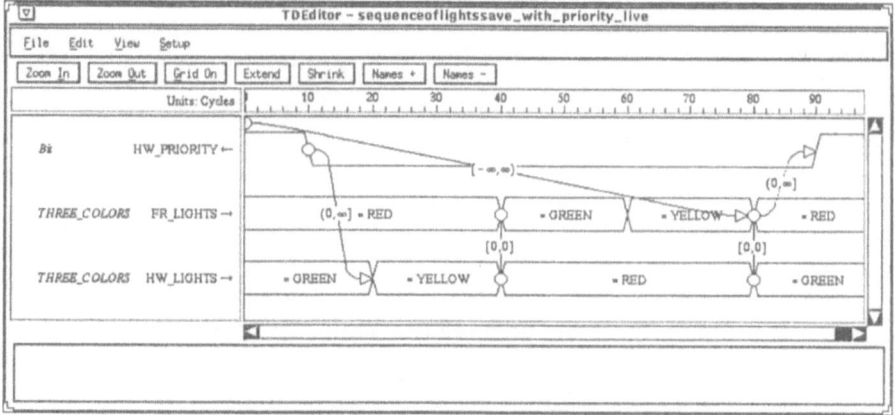

Fig. 5.5. Liveness property of the light-cycle

left corner to the event where FR_LIGHTS switches from YELLOW to RED.
This indicates that whenever the farm road light becomes GREEN and YEL-
LOW we require that light finally has to become RED again. This property
is expressed by figure 5.5.

To verify this property we need the following assumptions:

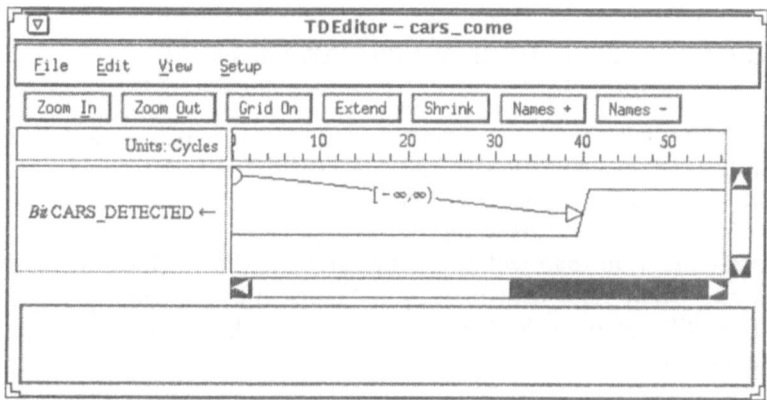

Fig. 5.6. Assumption: Cars will come

– **CarsWillCome** (cf. figure 5.6)
   This property indicates that finally there will be car detected on the farm
   road in front of the traffic light whenever CARS_DETECTED was set to
   low.
– **CarsWillStayUntilGreen** (cf. figure 5.7)
   This timing diagram expresses the fact that a car that has been detected
   by the sensor of the traffic light will stay until the farm road traffic light

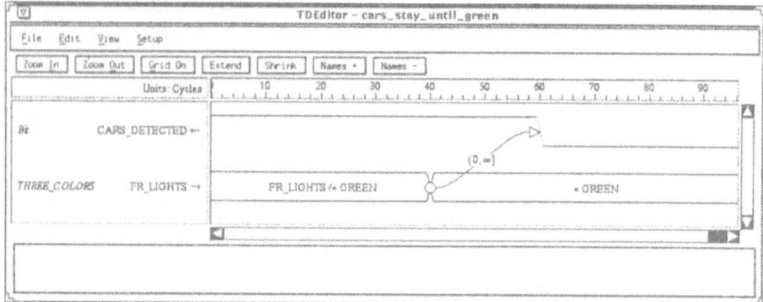

Fig. 5.7. Assumption: Cars will stay until GREEN traffic light

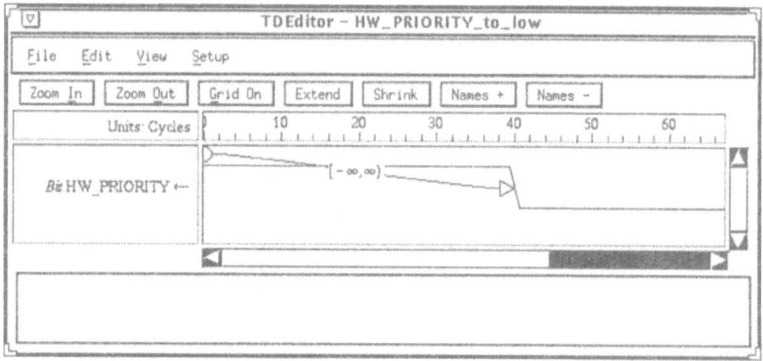

Fig. 5.8. Assumption: HIGHWAY_PRIORITY to low

has switched to GREEN. This property is important, because the traffic light controller checks again whether there is a car in front of the farm road traffic light before switching to GREEN.

– **HIGHWAY_PRIORITY2low** (cf. figure 5.8)
 To verify that the farm road will finally become GREEN we have to guarantee that the traffic light controller is not blocked by the signal HIGHWAY_PRIORITY set to to high which prevent the highway traffic light from switching to RED.

If the model checker is started to perform the proof he has first to compute the tableau for the assumptions. Next he has to combine the tableau with the symbolic model. During the generation of the tableau it may be necessary to introduce additional fairness constraints which have to be evaluated on the combined model. Now the model checker can start to verify the commitment. To speed up model checking we have set the flags *modelReachability* and *reachability*:

subtask	time in seconds
reachability	6.83
tableau construction	4.43
reachability on tableau and model	7.02
fairness	1.95
CTL model checking	29.91
CTL Debugger	-

This section has shown how properties specified using symbolic timing diagrams can be verified against a model generated out of VHDL-implementations. In VHDL/S, also state charts can be used to implement the behaviour of a module. If the proof manager detects that an implementation is given as a StateChart, then the StateChart will also be translated into a symbolic finite state machine which can be used to perform model checking. The main differences are that the representation of the model is a relation and that no VHDL-test-bench can be generated. The model checker computes a trace which represents the simulated error situation.

6. Generation of temporal logic

Automatic verification methods like modelchecking, as well as tautology-checking and interactive methods like compositional reasoning in a theorem prover, operate on temporal–logic representations of Symbolic Timing Diagram–specifications. For the automatic verification methods, the user never needs to inspect the temporal–logic representations. Only when working in the interactive prover the temporal–logic representations becomes visible. A more ambitious aim would be to allow the process of interactive reasoning to operate directly on the graphical language. Such approaches have already been investigated, see e.g.(G. Kutty et al. 1993).

The goal of this section is to explain the generation of the temporal-logic formula in an informal way (which suffices to understand the generated formula in the interactive prover). For a strict formal semantics definition of the language Symbolic Timing Diagram, the interested reader is referred to (W. Damm et al. 1995).

For the explanation, we use diagram

```
sequenceoflightssafe_with_priority
```

shown in figure 5.2 of the chapter of specification languages as 'running example'.

Generation of simulation graph. The first step in the generation of the temporal logic formula is to build a so–called *simulation graph* (SG), which represents all unwindings of the diagram corresponding to valid matching–runs.

Figure 6.1 shows a version of the original diagram, where the events have been numbered and the event–annotations (assertions) have been abbreviated as follows: (HW_PRIORITY = x) is ϕx, (FR_LIGHTS = y) is ψy, and (HW_LIGHTS = z) is ξz. Note that the simplified notation of constraints shown in figure 3.1 has been used.

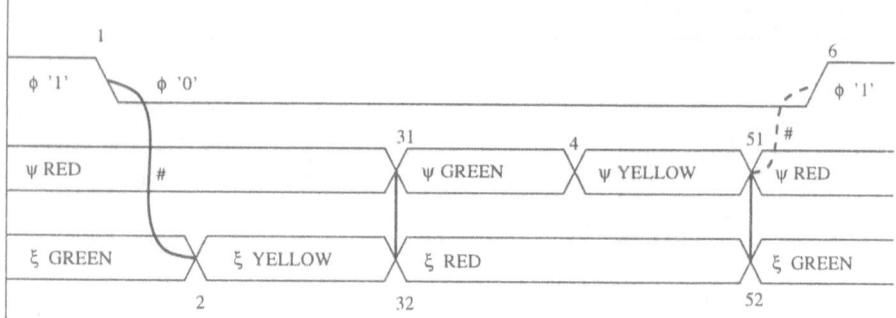

Fig. 6.1. Diagram `sequenceoflightssafe_with_priority` with abbreviated annotations and numbered events

The simulation graph is built by unwinding the diagram from left to right, taking the constraints into account. Figure 6.2 shows the result of this unwinding process. Edges are labeled with the number of the events which have been matched. Those events which are connected by simultaneous constraints (i.e. between events 31 and 32 as well as events 51 and 52) can only be matched simultaneously. Note that after event 1 has been matched, deactivation occurs when signal HW_PRIORITY changes from '0' → '1'. This is reflected by according transitions to the so–called *deactivation state* of the simulation graph.

Note the self–loops at all inner states of the SG, which indicate possible saturation points. For invalid saturation points, these loops are associated with a *fairness condition* which states that eventually the state must be left. For our example, all states are valid saturation points.

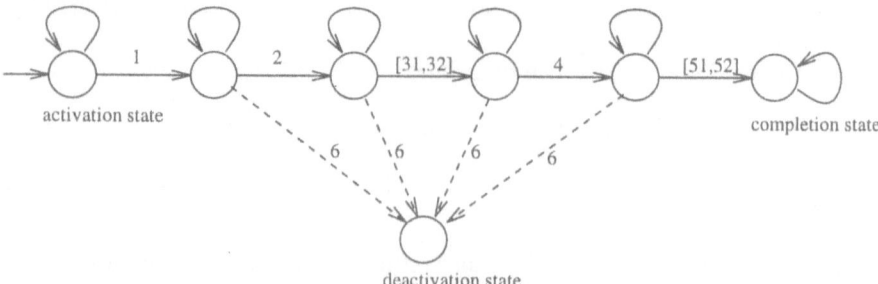

Fig. 6.2. Simulation graph of diagram `sequenceoflightssafe_with_priority`

Generation of characterizing temporal logic formula. From the simulation graph, the characterizing temporal logic formula is obtained. First, the transitions of the simulation graph are annotated with state–assertions (formulae) characterizing the condition when an according match in the diagram occurs. Figure 6.3 shows the result of this annotation.

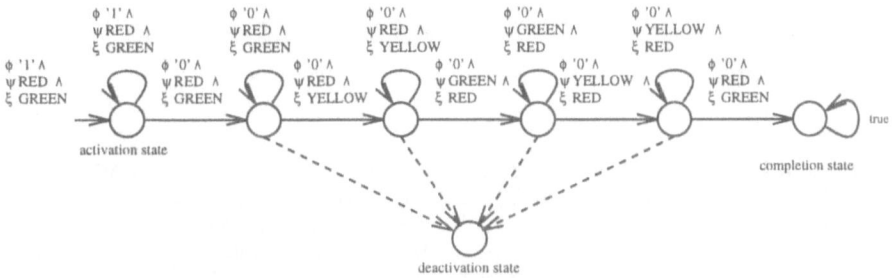

Fig. 6.3. Annotated simulation graph of diagram
`sequenceoflightssafe_with_priority`

Given these annotations, the formula is generated by combining the transition formulas with appropriate temporal logic operator which characterize the transition relation. Also, the activation condition is represented by a special temporal operator ($\Box$, read as 'always'). Again, for a formal treatment of formula generation the interested reader should see (W. Damm et al. 1995).

For our example, the following formula is generated:

$$\Box((\phi'1' \wedge \psi\text{RED} \wedge \xi\text{GREEN}) \quad \rightarrow \quad (\phi'1' \wedge \psi\text{RED} \wedge \xi\text{GREEN}) \textbf{ unless}$$
$$((\phi'0' \wedge \psi\text{RED} \wedge \xi\text{GREEN}) \wedge$$
$$(\phi'0' \wedge \psi\text{RED} \wedge \xi\text{GREEN}) \textbf{ unless}$$
$$((\phi'0' \wedge \psi\text{RED} \wedge \xi\text{YELLOW}) \wedge$$
$$(\phi'0' \wedge \psi\text{RED} \wedge \xi\text{YELLOW}) \textbf{ unless}$$
$$((\phi'0' \wedge \psi\text{GREEN} \wedge \xi\text{RED}) \wedge$$
$$(\phi'0' \wedge \psi\text{GREEN} \wedge \xi\text{RED}) \textbf{ unless}$$
$$((\phi'0' \wedge \psi\text{YELLOW} \wedge \xi\text{RED}) \wedge$$
$$(\phi'0' \wedge \psi\text{YELLOW} \wedge \xi\text{RED}) \textbf{ unless}$$
$$(\phi'0' \wedge \psi\text{RED} \wedge \xi\text{GREEN})$$
$$\vee\phi'1')$$
$$\vee\phi'1')$$
$$\vee\phi'1')$$
$$\vee\phi'1')$$
$$)$$

It can be seen that already for this simple example, the generated formula becomes large and, in more difficult cases, difficult to write and understand, while the original diagram states the required property in a fairly natural way.

7. Summary

The FORMAT-project has developed a verification environment for VHDL-based hardware design, employing two major state-of-the-art verification methods, viz. (compositional) symbolic model checking and interactive theorem proving.

References

W. Damm, B. Josko, and R. Schlör (1993): A net-based semantics for VHDL. In *EURO-DAC'93/EURO-VHDL'93*. IEEE CS Press, pages 514–519.

W. Damm, B. Josko, and R. Schlör (1995): Specification and verification of VHDL-based system-level hardware designs. In E. Börger, editor, *Specification and validation methods*. Oxford University Press, pages 331–410.

M. Francis, S. Finn, E. Mayger, and R.B. Hughes (1993): Reference manual for the LAMBDA system, Version 4.2. Technical report, Abstract Hardware Limited.

Nick Chapman (1994): Translating VHDL into L2. Technical report, Abstract Hardware Limited.

G. Döhmen and R. Herrmann (1995): A deterministic finite-state model for VHDL. In *Formal Semantics for VHDL*. Kluwer Academic Publisher.

G. Döhmen, R. Herrmann, and H. Pargmann (1995): Translating VHDL into functional symbolic finite-state models. *Formal Methods in System Design*, 7:125–148.

W. Damm, B. Josko, and R. Schlör (1993): A net-based semantics for VHDL. In *EURO-DAC'93/EURO-VHDL'93*. IEEE CS Press, pages 514–519.

G. Döhmen (1994): Petri nets as intermediate representation beween VHDL and symbolic transition systems. In *EURO-VHDL'94*, Grenoble, France, September.

R. Herrmann and H. Pargmann (1994): Compiling VHDL data types into BDDs. *Technical Report*, OFFIS, Germany.

H. Pargmann and R. Herrmann (1995): Reduced Symbolic Transition Systems for VHDL. In *Proceedings GI/ITG Workshop*, Passau.

G. Kutty, Y.S. Ramakrishna, L.E. Moser, L.K. Dillon, and P.M Melliar-Smith (1993): A graphical interval logic toolset for verifying concurrent systems. In *5th International Conference on Computer Aided Verification*, pages 123–137, June 1993.

Synthesis Flow

Werner Grass[1], Wolf-Dieter Tiedemann[1], Carlos Delgado Kloos[2], and Andrés Marín López[2]

[1] Universität Passau, Germany
[2] Universidad Carlos III de Madrid, Spain

1. Introduction

Synthesis denotes the refinement process from a more abstract specification to a more detailed implementation. Since this activity includes the creativity of the designer it is inherently difficult to automate. In order to obtain a reasonable computer aid nevertheless, there are different approaches along two directions: the *automatic top-down* synthesis and the *interactive bottom-up* synthesis.

An automatic synthesis, if aimed at producing practically acceptable results, needs to concentrate on selected architectural models, design styles and/or technologies. For instance, *High level* synthesis commonly uses the model of a synchronous digital machine that consists of a data path and a single controller. The data path is composed from functional units, like ALUs, registers, etc., while the controller is realized as a finite state machine or by micro-programming.

Interactive synthesis is not subject to these restrictions. However, it does not work automatically but provides only a support of the exploratory activity of the designer. It is strongly related to verification. The main difference consists in its ability to provide a proposition about the correctness of a design already for a *partial* solution instead of just for a complete solution, as verification usually does. Interactive synthesis is particularly useful for designing the top-most levels of the design hierarchy.

Within FORMAT we aim at *Very High Level* synthesis that refines from system level to the algorithmic level. The input on system level is given in the form of timing diagrams, while the output is in terms of the hardware description language VHDL and, thus, can be further input to High level synthesis tools (eg. Synopsys). We support both synthesis approaches, the automatic and the interactive way. This opens the benefits of both worlds, depending on the designer's choice. For instance, he could follow a meet-in-the-middle strategy, construct a top level design structure interactively and then synthesize each particular structural block automatically.

Moreover, our synthesis system founds on a rigorous formal basis. From the modelling of timing diagrams to the verification of design decisions, all processing is based on a real time process algebra semantics. Hence, we are in a position not only to reason about control sequences but also about time and data domains. Our system is therefore more universal than other systems with similar application areas. A prototype has been used in real applications designing integrated telecommunication circuits. It has also been used successfully in the development of interface circuits based on off-the-shelf modules for the AT bus. But there are also other possible applications. Designers can use the system to transform timing diagram documentations from data sheets into VHDL code in order to simulate and to better understand what has been documented. Also the production of VHDL code from timing diagrams that represent just simulation stimuli is a very promising approach.

In this chapter, we will give an overview of our methodology, the languages involved and the prime issues. For details please refer to the chapters **Specification Languages** (beginning p. 22), **Synthesis Techniques** (beginning p. 228), and **Generating VHDL** (beginning p. 265).

2. Design flow

Today's hardware systems are usually implemented as a composition of communicating subsystems. In order to support their design on this (system) level it is consistent to focus on the communication behaviour (input/output behaviour) of the system components. Often, such behaviour is described by means of timing diagrams. For this reason we took the approach to use timing diagrams as a vehicle for specification. From that it followed the necessity to provide a formal semantics for timing diagrams. Having this, we can consider timing diagrams a *formal* specification that can be refined through the use of formal transformation methods. The result of the refinement process is an *implementation description* that is (wrt. to its specification) correct by construction.

The whole synthesis path is illustrated in figure 2.1. Design specifications are given exclusively as graphical timing diagrams, sometimes supplemented with textual annotations. Their formalization is done in terms of the formal description technique T-LOTOS, which bases on a timed process algebra. This supplies a pure behavioural T-LOTOS description of the design. Such a behavioural representation can be translated directly and automatically into VHDL code. However, since the model that is used for this translation is a finite state machine model, the size and the readability of the generated code is improvable. Hence, we support optionally an interactive synthesis technique that is suitable to introduce structure into the resulting code.

Such a technique (P. Michel et al. 1992) organizes a design session as a user-guided sequence of formal transformations, where the user is iteratively requested to name always one module, which he wants to see as part of an implementation. Provided a library of predefined module descriptions, the synthesis tool checks, whether the behaviour of the selected module matches with the specified design behaviour. Only if this condition holds, the module is considered to be a part of the implementation. Thus, step by step a netlist of modules arises. In each intermediate step all the modules in the present netlist describe a partial behaviour of the specified design behaviour. From this partial behaviour it is possible to derive automatically a description of the supplementary remainder behaviour.

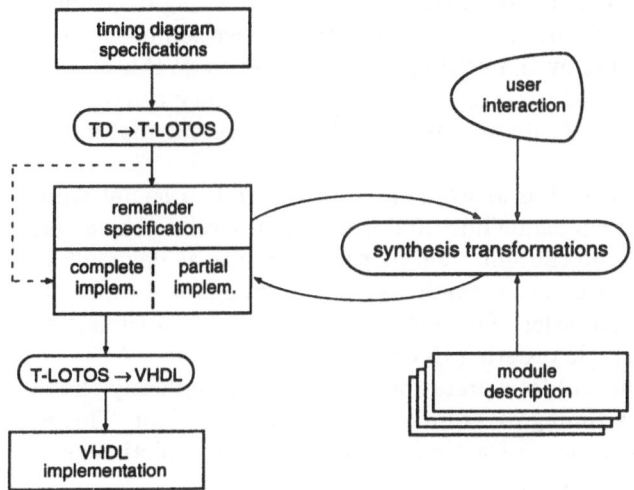

Fig. 2.1. The FORMAT synthesis path

Interactive synthesis enables the user to perform a *bottom-up* style system design. The main advantage of interactive synthesis, however, in comparison with usual formal hardware verification, where specification and implementation are checked for consistency not before the complete implementation is present, is that this approach allows the designer to get fast advice just at that time, when each individual submodule becomes integrated.

The following sections will go into the various key items in more detail.

3. Timing diagrams as specifications

Commonly, designers use timing diagrams prevailingly for documentation of system behaviour or for the description of stimuli in system simulation. The set of timing diagrams used for these purposes is not always at the same time suitable to represent a complete description of every behavioural aspect. In general, it just documents a snapshot of "typical" behaviour or of some particular situations of interest. The "rest" of the description is mostly given in some textual format, eg. in the shape of informal explanations or some description languages. However, it can be observed that there is some kind

of system behaviour for which the description can be done nearly without
any clarifying supplements, just by using timing diagrams. Systems showing this property are mostly qualified also by attributes like *open, reactive,
communication-oriented,* and *control-dominated.* Quite often, such systems
are components of distributed systems, and communication processors. It is
a short step to suppose that this class of systems can nicely, appropriately,
and conveniently be described exclusively by timing diagrams.

Moreover, we argue that a *complete* specification of the system behaviour
can be done just by timing diagrams. In order to do this easily it is necessary
to resolve the tight interpretation of documentary timing diagrams a little.
The practical advantage is to be able to represent multiple alternatives in
one shot.

For instance, it is reasonable to consider two signal transitions, which
occur on different signal lines and which are not related by any kind of explicit
constraint, ie. no causality and no time distance, as being allowed to occur in
arbitrary order or even simultaneously, although the timing diagram shows
them in a fixed order. This helps to save versions of timing diagrams which
depict each single ordering in detail.

Another useful interpretation is to assume implicitly that the behaviour
specified by a timing diagram is a repetitive behaviour. This meets the common comprehension of a timing diagram as a depiction of *one cycle* of a
protocol, a processor, etc.

Other important issues that have to be made precise in order to conceive
timing diagrams of being a formal specification language for synthesis concern
the facilities

- to express data manipulations and
- to structure one single (extensive) behavioural specification into a combination of several small and plain timing diagrams.

In chapter **Specification Languages** (beginning p. 22) the syntax of
the graphical specification language "Extended Timing Diagrams (ETD)"
is presented in summary. That chapter contains also an example, namely
the *traffic light controller* taken from (C. Mead and L. Conway 1980). The
following section 4. sketches how to introduce a formal semantics for this
language in terms of the timed process calculus of T-LOTOS. Later in this
book, chapter **Synthesis Techniques** (beginning p. 228) resumes this topic
in more detail.

4. T-LOTOS semantics of timing diagrams

The formal semantics of an extended timing diagram specification is defined
by a transformation into processes described in terms of the formal specification language T-LOTOS.

T-LOTOS (J. Quemada and A. Fernandez 1987) is an extension of LO-TOS which includes the possibility of expressing quantitative time. LOTOS is a language based on a process algebra. It was developed within ISO (International Organization for Standardization) for the formal specification of open distributed systems (ISO 1989), and in particular for the OSI (Open Systems Interconnection) computer network architecture. LOTOS supports the specification of systems at different levels of abstraction ranging from the capture of requirements to implementation-oriented specifications. Today, there are powerful tools for supporting the different phases of specifying, like proof-generators, compilers and simulators.

Chapter **Synthesis Techniques** (beginning p. 228) on Synthesis Techniques gives an overview of this language.

4.1 Formalization of timing diagram specifications

Just like a timing diagram is an assembly of graphical constituents such as waveforms, precedence arrows, timing constraints etc., which all have their isolated meaning, we propose to pursue a similar, compositional approach for giving a formal representation of the associated behaviour.

Therefore, at first we define for each graphical language element a generic recursive T-LOTOS process. This process is considered as a model that mimics the behaviour of the corresponding language element. As an example think of a precedence arrow between two events s_0, s_1 within a timing diagram. Such a graphical stroke symbolizes that a s_0 event has to occur in advance of a s_1 event each time when a situation like the one depicted in the timing diagram appears. In terms of T-LOTOS an equivalent statement reads as

```
process PRECEDENCE[s0, s1] :noexit :=
    s0; s1; PRECEDENCE[s0, s1]
endproc
```

The behaviour of the entire timing diagram is described simply by composing all instantiated processes in parallel. Finally, we treat even compositions of multiple timing diagrams in the same way, since both, the *alternative* operator $\oplus$ and the *sequential* operator $\triangleright$ can also be modeled by T-LOTOS process equivalents.

In summary, a complete timing diagram behaviour *ETDSPEC* can be described as a parallel composition

```
process ETDSPEC[Act] :noexit :=
    (((Waveforms[Act₁] |[S₁]|
        Constraints[Act₂]) |[S₂]|
      ETDOps[Act₃]) |[S₃]|
    Timing[Act₄]) |[S₄]|
  Data[Act₅](initvalues)
endproc
```

where $Act, Act_i, i = 1, \ldots, 5$ are the sets of event names the corresponding processes participate in. $S_i, i = 1, \ldots, 4$ are appropriate sets of those events, which are shared by the parallel processes. Waveforms is the process which results from the parallel composition of the waveform translations, Constraints is the resulting process from all temporal constraints, ETDOps is the result from the parallel composition of the translations of the combination operators for single timing diagrams, Timing results from the translation of all timing annotations, and Data describes the translation of all data annotations.

For an example of a timing diagram formalization please refer to chapter **Synthesis Techniques** (beginning p. 228) where this topic is dealt with in more detail.

4.2 Timed graphs as internal representation

The immediate formalization of timing diagrams leads to a parallel composition of T-LOTOS processes, which is a rather concise representation. However, in order to determine some important relations between processes, like their equivalence or some refinement preorder, it has to be computed the operational model of the description, ie. a timed transitional system. Unfortunately, the transitional graphs of timed processes grow, depending on the time domain, to tremendous size or (for dense time domains) even to infinite size. In order to condense this representation, we use "Timed Graphs", also known as "Timed Automata", a representation that has been introduced in (R. Alur et al. 1990), (R. Alur et al. 1992) for describing a model for model-checking of real time CTL formulae. In (X. Nicollin et al. 1992) it has been demonstrated, how timed process algebra expressions can be translated into Timed Graph representations.

A Timed Graph resembles the graph of a finite state machine. In addition, it is characterized by a set of *timers*. A timer can be understood as a stop watch, which displays always the time that has elapsed since its last reset. A reset appears instantaneously, ie. it does not affect the continuous flow of time.

Timers are used in predicates, which are attached to the edges of a timed graph and describe a timing condition that has to hold in order to allow the corresponding transition to take place.

Simultaneously with the occurrence of a transition it is possible to reset the values of some timers. Those timers that are supposed to be reset on the event of a transition have to be listed in a set that is also attached to the corresponding edge.

Altogether, a sample edge of a timed graph might look as follows:

$$s \xrightarrow{a, t_1 < 25 \land t_2 > 6, \{t_0\}} s'$$

This says that a system being in state s moves to state s' whenever timer t_1 displays a value less than 25, timer t_2 displays a value greater than 6, *and* an event a occurs. Immediately with the occurrence of a the value of timer t_0 becomes reset.

T-LOTOS allows to model timed graphs directly, simply by committing to a particular style of writing T-LOTOS descriptions. Chapter **Synthesis Techniques** (beginning p. 228) explains how this can be done.

After having the timing diagram specification translated into T-LOTOS, the next step consists in transforming this description into some refined description that corresponds to an implementation description. This transformation shall be performed on the formal T-LOTOS level in order to be able to guarantee the correctness of the result. Within FORMAT we provide two ways for transformation that differ in their degree of automation and wrt. their suitability for being translated into different VHDL views.

5. The different ways of producing T-LOTOS implementation descriptions

5.1 Automatic transformation

As it has been sketched in section 4.1, timing diagrams are translated into a parallel composition of appropriate T-LOTOS processes. By applying the so-called *expansion law* it is possible to transform this composition into an equivalent T-LOTOS expression without any parallelism operator. Moreover, the expanded representation can be understood directly as a timed graph. In this respect it describes the complete system's behaviour "operationally", ie. every possible system state is explicitly known together with all of its legal outgoing transitions and their corresponding enabling conditions. Of course, this model is a rather expensive one, since all parallelism has been resolved into an explicit sequential representation.

However, the expanded representation can already be translated into VHDL code. Key idea is just to map the timed graph into a VHDL finite state machine-like description (see section 6.). Although it is evident that this direct translation brings along some limitations wrt. the quality of the generated code, it is rather useful for rapid prototyping purposes, or early generation of simulation models.

5.2 Interactive transformation

Applying the automatic transformation approach leads to behavioural VHDL. In order to achieve some structural VHDL code we propose to apply optionally an interactive bottom-up approach for synthesis (P. Michel et al. 1992).

The principle of such an interactive synthesis approach consists in

1. asking the user for a proposal of a module that promises to be an integral part of a potential implementation,
2. verifying automatically that the corresponding module behaviour actually does not violate the timing diagram specification (here it is assumed that the module's behaviour is known and can for instance be retrieved from a module library),
3. checking whether the integration of this module updates the previous (partial) implementation in a way that it now satisfies the complete specification.

Technically, the background of the transformation procedure can be understood best by taking the so-called *protocol viewpoint*. Assume, any system is given by a specification of its externally visible I/O behaviour. Any implementation that satisfies this specification can be thought of as being a parallel composition of modules that, entirely, exposes a behaviour that meets the specified behaviour. Uniformly, each module's description is again a description of an externally visible I/O behaviour. A slight graphical manipulation, as it is suggested in figure 5.1, reveals, that this situation can be interpreted in a special way, notably to view the remainder implementation, ie. the overall implementation without this one module, as a protocol converter, that adapts the whole system's behaviour to the module's behaviour. The importance of this viewpoint comes with two facts: first the implementation "black box" is reduced by one component and, clearly, could be reduced by more components in the same way (this is equivalent to a reduction of the design problem) and, second, a converter can be generated automatically, provided the both involved behaviours are known (this makes the whole procedure automatable).

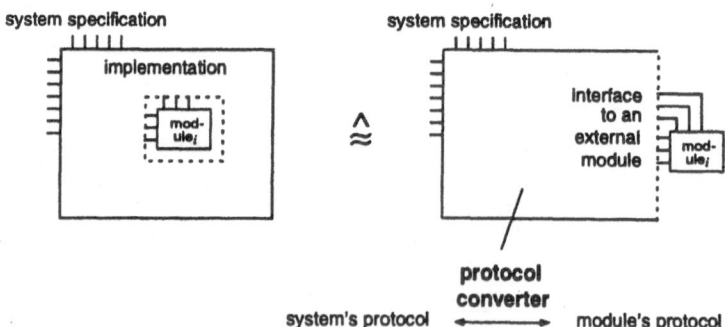

Fig. 5.1. Protocol viewpoint

In order to realize this idea, there has to be dealt at first with two preliminary points,

– the implementation relation and
– the converter generation.

The *implementation relation* **sat** denotes a preorder that relates pairs of Timed Graphs $(I, S) \in$ **sat**, where I is regarded as being an implementation that satisfies the specification S. Usually, I is a more detailed behaviour, ie. it describes events that do not occur at all within the specification graph and are therefore called (implementation-) internal events. Furthermore, an implementation might sometimes select one from several specified alternatives or expose a behaviour that goes beyond the specified behaviour. The general idea of such an implementation relation shall be sketched informally as follows:

An implementation I satisfies its specification S (written I **sat** S) says that

- whenever an *input* event is specified ($S \xrightarrow{i,t} S'$) this event must be accepted from the implementation ($I \xrightarrow{i,t} I'$) and I' **sat** S', except that
- I is able to escape ($I \xrightarrow{e,u} I'$) by performing an output or internal action at time $u \leq t$ and I' **sat** $Age(u, S)$, ie. the time-shifted specification,
- whenever an output event is implemented ($I \xrightarrow{o,t} I'$) this event must be specifed ($S \xrightarrow{o,t} S'$) and I' **sat** S'.

If the application of this definition holds recursively for all referenced follow-up behaviours, we say that the timed implementation graph satisfies the timed specification graph.

By *converter generation* we understand an automatic derivation of a so-called "converter". The task of a converter consists in converting one communication protocol, or communicating behaviour, into another. In our context, two modules follow different protocols, if they do not perform a closed communication with each other or if they mutually violate timing constraints. In terms of T-LOTOS this means, that a parallel composition of both equal-sorted entity behaviours A and B, restricted to their common sort G, written $(A|G|B\backslash G)$, equals a process that is free from deadlocks and produces only internal actions. If they do not communicate in this way, there is need for a third module X, which supplements both modules in such a way, that each module together with X can perform a closed communication with always the other satisfying all timing constraints. In terms of T-LOTOS this can be expressed by an equation

$$A|G_{A,X}|X \approx X|G_{B,X}|B. \tag{5.1}$$

Note that equation 5.1 holds also for some undesired X, eg. a converter that produces an initial deadlock (**stop**) on both sides or that participates in irrelevant communications. To ensure, that X neither imposes restrictions on A or B, nor dissipates with superfluous communications, we require the *neutrality* of X. Expressed in terms of T-LOTOS this leads to an equation

$$AB|G_X|X \approx AB \quad \text{where} \quad AB = A|G_{A,B}|B. \tag{5.2}$$

A solution X for equations 5.1 and 5.2 can be derived automatically. The procedure that performs this task is related to methods, which can be referred to as "equation solvers" (J. Parrow 1987), (K. G. Larsen, L. Xinxin 1990), (W. D. Tiedemann 1992). Our equation solver operates on deterministic timed graphs, ie. graphs, where each state possesses at most one transition for each action.

Having an impression of the meaning and the operation of **sat** and *convert*, we can state the interactive bottom-up synthesis procedure more formally: it consists in each iteration i of an automatic verification whether

$$\text{partial\_impl}_i \; |G_i| \; \text{remainder}_i \; \textbf{sat} \; \text{spec}_0$$

where

$$\text{partial\_impl}_i \; \approx \; \text{partial\_impl}_{i-1} \; |H_i| \; \text{module}_i,$$

$$\text{remainder}_i \; \approx \; convert(\text{partial\_impl}_i, \; \text{spec}_0),$$

module_i represents the behaviour of the user's interactively proposed module that should be integrated next, and G_i, H_i are appropriate gate sets used for synchronization.

The proposition "$\text{partial\_impl}_i \; |G_i| \; \text{remainder}_i \; \textbf{sat} \; \text{spec}_0$" states that the composition of the partial implementation, which includes the proposed module, together with the current specification of the unknown remainder satisfies the original specification. Initially, there is no partial implementation, a fact that is described by the inactive behaviour

$$\text{partial\_impl}_0 \; \approx \; \textbf{stop}$$

and an unknown remainder that equals the complete specification

$$\text{remainder}_0 \; \approx \; \text{spec}_0.$$

After selecting one after the other module, we finish with a (partial) implementation, that satisfies the original specification, ie.

$$\text{partial\_impl}_n \; \textbf{sat} \; \text{spec}_0.$$

partial_impl_n is equivalent to a parallel composition of n user-selected module behaviour descriptions and, thus, can be interpreted as a netlist of an implementation.

6. Translation from T-LOTOS to VHDL

6.1 Translation process

This section explains the translation of the T-LOTOS originating from the synthesis transformations sketched in section 5. to VHDL. At first, we describe how the T-LOTOS provided by the previous transformation steps looks like. After that, we show how we translate it to VHDL.

See chapter **Generating VHDL** (beginning p. 265) for more details and optimizations on the translation process.

6.1.1 Characterization of the input. The input to this phase of the synthesis line within the FORMAT project is a FSM-like description in T-LOTOS. It consists of one specification (T-LOTOS top-most behaviour unit) where a process is instantiated.

This process contains the behaviour defined in the original timing diagram specification. The constraint arcs, the timing and the data annotations described in the timing diagram specifications are described by this process. The data types used in the specification are referenced to a library. An equivalent VHDL package exists and it is a cardinal point for the translation tool. All the data types are translated based on the data types defined in package STD_LOGIC_1164[1]. The external interface is preserved, thus the names of the gates of the process are equal one to one to the names of the ports in the timing diagram specification.

The behaviour described in the specification is contained inside the body of the process. In our case, the behaviour of the process is a choice expression among several behaviours. The behaviours inside the choice expression can be again choice expressions, or external offers. Choice expressions are in general non-deterministic, as sometimes occurs in the inner choices. The outermost choice is always deterministic as it represents the choice among the different states of the specification. The store of the state is a variable present in the instantiation list of the process.

The possible behaviours in a choice expression are subject to be preceded by a guard. A guard contains some operations on expressions (as defined in T-LOTOS) which are evaluated to decide whether the process can or cannot evolve like the guarded behaviour. The most common guards we find in the T-LOTOS provided by the timing diagram translation are operations on the state variable, especially comparisons with constant values.

The communication in T-LOTOS is performed by means of the so called external offers which express the synchronization that take place in a gate. The type of offers we deal with in this project implies a data interchange. External offers may have predicates, which express the set of values that may

---

[1] developed by the IEEE Model Standards Group (PAR 1164). This package defines a standard to be used by designers for describing the interconnection data types used in VHDL modeling.

be accepted in the synchronization. For the moment we have restricted ourselves to translate unidirectional gates, though it is planned to change this
with the aid of the data types of the mentioned package STD_LOGIC_1164.
An example of external offer may be gate_outdata_val for a gate which
only accepts to synchronize with the value data_val. This is interpreted as
an output, while gate_in?x: data[(x>lbound)and(x<rbound)] is interpreted as an input, where every value of sort data satisfying the predicate
[(x>lbound)and(x<rbound)] is accepted in gate_in to synchronize.

Time annotations define the time when the synchronizations may occur. The semantic interpretation is similar to the predicates over the
values, but checking for the age of the offers instead of the values offered (J. Quemada and A. Fernandez 1987), (J. Quemada et al. 1990).

The behaviour that follows an external offer can be any, but the most
frequent is a self instantiation with a new value for the state variable.

6.1.2 Translation to VHDL. In section 6.1.1 we have illustrated how
the behaviour of the main process resembles a FSM. Thus we translate
the behaviour of the process in a similar FSM in VHDL. The FSMs
we use have an asynchronous common **reset** for initialization purposes.
They also have an **enable input** to make it easier to translate the instantiation, enable and disable operators. FSMs are composed of two
processes: a sequential and a combinational one. Several descriptions have
been made about the modeling of FSMs in VHDL (R. Airiau et al. 1994),
(D. E. Ott and T. J. Wilderotter 1994).

The implementation of a T-LOTOS operator can require one or more of
the FSM states.

A non-deterministic choice of behaviours must be mapped to a deterministic selection in VHDL, due to the fact that VHDL is deterministic. There are
several possibilities for expressing alternative sequential behaviour in VHDL.
In our translation process we use the **if then else** statement.

The algorithm used for the translation of a choice among several offers is
the following:

1. A list is built with the different alternatives. Each element in the list
   contains a reference to the guard condition, gate identifier, values and
   variables, predicates and timing annotations involved in the offer.
2. The list is ordered. At the head of the list, the output offers are placed,
   while the input offers are placed at the end of the list. Offers at the same
   gate are placed together in the list.
3. A **when** clause is used to enable the synchronizations if the guards allow
   it.
4. The next **when** clause, also common for all the alternatives in the choice,
   checks in all the allowed gates for the progress of the synchronization.
   The translation for output gates and input gates is different:
   − if an output gate has successfully sent the value and it has been ac-
     cepted, the synchronization is allowed to commit, whenever the time

condition is accomplished. The next state of the FSM is the one corresponding to the following behaviour unit in T-LOTOS.

– if an input gate has received a value which satisfies its predicate and timing condition, the following state will be one in which it is checked whether the sender commits the synchronization or aborts it. The first will correspond to a successful new value of the state, whereas the second would imply to go back to the first **when** clause of the translation of the choice.

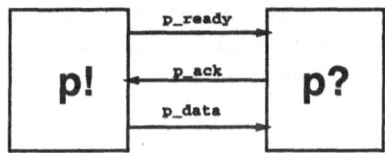

Fig. 6.1. Synchronization protocol

The algorithm deals with beginning synchronizations, checking values received and committing or checking for commitment of the synchronizations. This is implemented by means of a protocol. Figure 6.1 illustrates the VHDL point of view of a T-LOTOS synchronization between one receiver (p?) and one emitter (p!). The protocol has three phases that have to be satisfactory fulfilled in order to commit the protocol: *agreement on beginning, passing of values, and agreement on finishing*. The protocol itself is not a crucial point, since the specifications that are derived from the timing diagram translation do not use parallel operators and so the communication is performed in a one to one basis with the environment. Nevertheless our translation scheme permits a broader subset of T-LOTOS as input.

The protocol is placed inside standard components of a predefined library. They are responsible for direct communication with the environment. The control of these components is done with several signals assigned and read in the combinatorial process of the FSM.

This division makes it possible to evaluate different synchronizations that may happen at different gates. So initially, all the synchronizations are fired in parallel, and the first possible one is committed.

The reinstantiation of a process in T-LOTOS is easily translated by changing the state variable to the first value and giving appropriate values to the variables the process is instantiated with. This scheme has to be enriched with additional mechanisms in order to translate all the possible instantiations in T-LOTOS, such as multiplexers in the **enable input** of the FSM.

6.2 VHDL produced

The code we produce consists of a main entity, which maintains the same interface of the T-LOTOS specification. Three signals (clock, enable, and reset) are added to deal with the synchronous FSMs.

The architecture of this entity consists of several instances (one per gate) of standard components of a predefined library, which changes the interface from the three wires (needed to perform the protocol that implements the T-LOTOS synchronization) to one. A separate entity instantiated as a component in the top unit, has a main process comprises the behaviour specified in the TDS. It describes a FSM which controls the instances of the library components mentioned in section 6.1.2, which contain the protocol that implements T-LOTOS synchronization.

6.2.1 Some of the VHDL Code for the traffic light controller.

```
ENTITY test_shell IS
   PORT( clk:  IN std_ulogic;
         CStest_shell:  IN std_logic;
         Reset:  IN std_logic;
         HL:    OUT integer;
         FL:    OUT integer;
         D:     IN  Boolean);
END test_shell;
ARCHITECTURE beh OF test_shell IS
BEGIN  -- signal declarations deleted
  TrafficLightController1 : TrafficLightController
  PORT MAP(clk=> clk,
           CSTrafficLightController=> CStest_shell,
           Reset=> Reset,HL_a=> HL1_a,HL=> HL1,HL_r=> HL1_r,
           FL_a=> FL1_a,FL=> FL1,FL_r=> FL1_r,D_a=> D1_a,
           D=> D1,D_r=> D1_r);
  gate1: gate_in_Boolean_logic
  PORT MAP(Reset=> Reset,clk=> clk,gate_a=> D1_a,
           gate_i=> D1,gate_r=> D1_r,gate_o=> D);
-- component instantiations deleted
END beh;
ENTITY TrafficLightController IS
   PORT( clk:  IN std_ulogic;
         D_r:  IN  std_logic_vector(1 downto 0)
      ); -- ports deleted
-- colours are mapped to std_logic_vector (...)
END TrafficLightController;
ARCHITECTURE beh OF TrafficLightController IS
BEGIN
  Gate_Val_2: Synch_Val_logic
```

```
     PORT MAP(
             clk=> clk,Reset=> Reset_FL,
             tin=> tin_FL,val=> Val_FL,
             gt_a=> FL_a,Ok=> Ok_FL,gt=> FL,
             gt_r=> FL_r,nack=> Nack_FL,ack=> Ack_FL);
      -- component instantiations deleted
COM: PROCESS(clk)-- variable declarations deleted
BEGIN -- default variable assignments deleted
 IF CS = '1' and clk = '1' THEN
     CASE state IS
      . WHEN 0=> next_state <=1;
                 CS1 <= '0';
        WHEN 1=> vReset_FL:= '0';
                 vVal_FL:=  To_StdlogicVector(1);
                 next_state <= 2;
        WHEN 2=> IF Ack_FL='1' THEN
                    ASSERT (Now-Ttime)= Tlong
                    REPORT "Time assertion failed"
                    SEVERITY FAILURE;
                    vOk_FL:= '1';
                    next_state<=3;
                 END IF;
        WHEN 3=> vReset_HL:= '0';
                 vVal_HL:=  To_StdlogicVector(2);
                 next_state <= 4;
        WHEN 4=> IF Ack_HL='1' THEN
                    ASSERT (Now-Ttime)=Tlong
                    REPORT "Time assertion failed"
                    SEVERITY FAILURE;
                    vOk_HL:= '1';
                    next_state<=5;
                 END IF;
        WHEN 5=> next_state <= 0; vlast_state:= '1';
                 sState_931 <= To_StdlogicVector(1);
                 sCarsInFR_941 <= To_StdlogicVector(false);
                 CS1 <= '1'; Ttime:= Now;
     END CASE;
 END IF; -- signal assignments deleted
END PROCESS;
END beh;
```

7. Conclusion

In this chapter we have only seen an overview of the FORMAT synthesis design flow. It will be detailed in two further chapters: chapter **Synthesis Techniques** (beginning p. 228) presents the applied synthesis techniques with more technical detail, while chapter **Generating VHDL** (beginning p. 265) focusses on the process of generating VHDL code from T-LOTOS descriptions.

References

R. Airiau, J. M. Bergé, and V. Olive (1994): *Circuit Synthesis with VHDL*, Kluwer.

R. Alur, C. Courcoubetis, D. L. Dill (1990): Model Checking for Real-Time Systems; *Proc. 5th IEEE Symposium on Logic in Computer Science LICS'90*, 414–425.

R. Alur and D. L. Dill (1992): The Theory of Timed Automata; *Proc. REX'91 Workshop on Real Time: Theory in Practice*, LNCS 600, Springer, 45–73.

ISO (1989): *Information Processing Systems — Open Systems Interconnection — LOTOS: A Formal Description Technique Based on the Temporal Ordering of Observational Behaviour.* IS-8807. International Standards Organization. Published 15 Feb. 1989

K. G. Larsen, L. Xinxin (1990): Equation Solving Using Modal Transition Systems; *Proc. IEEE Symp. on Logic in Computer Science LICS'90* 108–117.

C. Mead, L. Conway (1980): *Introduction to VLSI Systems*, Addison-Wesley.

P. Michel, U. Lauther, P. Duzy (eds.) (1992): The Synthesis Approach to Digital System Design; *Int. Series in Eng. and Computer Science; VLSI, computer architecture and DSP*, Kluwer.

X. Nicollin, J. Sifakis, S. Yovine (1992): Compiling Real-Time Specificatuions into Extended Automata; *IEEE Transactions on Software Engineering* 18 9, 794–804.

D. E. Ott, T. J. Wilderotter (1994): *A designer's guide to VHDL Synthesis*, Kluwer.

J. Parrow (1987): Submodule Construction as Equation Solving in CCS; *Proc. Foundations of Software Technology and Theoretical Computer Science*, LNCS 287, Springer, 103–123.

J. Quemada, A. Azcorra, D. Frutos (1990): TIC – A Timed Calculus for LOTOS; *Proc. 2nd IFIP Int. Conference on Formal Description Techniques FORTE'89*, North-Holland, 195–209.

J. Quemada, A. Fernández (1987): Introduction of Quantitative Relative Time into LOTOS; *IFIP Workshop on Protocol Specification, Testing and Verification VII*, North Holland.

J. Quemada, S. Pavón, A. Fernández (1989): State Exploration by Transformation with LOLA; *Workshop on Automatic Verification Methods for Finite State Systems*, Grenoble, June 1989.

W. D. Tiedemann (1992): An Approach to Multi-paradigm Controller Synthesis from Timing Diagram Specifications; *Proc. EURO-DAC'92*, 522–527.

Part II

Industrial Experience

Application of a Formal Verification Toolset to the Design of Integrated Circuits in an Industrial Environment

Pierre Plaza, José Luis Conesa, and Fernando Palao

Telefónica Investigación y Desarrollo, Spain

1. Introduction

This chapter describes the application of a formal verification toolset to the high level design of telecom ICs. The tools have been developed in ESPRIT project number 6128 (FORMAT). An explanation will be given of how these tools have been integrated into the current Telefónica I+D IC design flow and the benefits will be analysed in terms of the time and effort required to check the correctness of a design against its specification. The advantage of using formal verification methods is that a more complete specification capture may be achieved and the formal verification of important system properties simpler and not as time consuming as it is in a standard simulation-based design process. The new design tools and methods have been applied to a real example: an HDLC frame assembler/disassembler (the DEPTH IC).

Nowadays, IC designers face very difficult challenges when trying to cram millions of devices onto a single component. This degree of complexity is becoming very hard to handle with current design techniques. The EDA companies are now having to adapt their existing software in order to handle the new deep-submicron designs. While simulation is still the most important verification method applied in the industry, run times are increasing exponentially. High level design tools have been coming onto the market in the last couple of years because of the lack of aids to design at this level. They provide flexibility and descriptive power when specifying and defining the architecture of a system. Formal verification tools are emerging into this environment. They allow the early detection of mistakes in the design and specification of circuits.

TI+D has realised the need to define a new design methodology that can cope with the above mentioned challenges. In this chapter the integration of formal verification tools from FORMAT into the existing CAD suite of tools will be described. An outline description of the DEPTH circuit will be presented as an example of the kind of application the FORMAT tools are capable of handling. Finally practical results will be summarized together with some conclusions on advantages, disadvantages, limitations of the tools and possible improvements for the future.

2. Description of the DEPTH circuit

The DEPTH circuit is a digital device whose functions are:

1. To receive and extract incoming HDLC frames from logical channels established in a PCM primary digital link.
2. To assemble and transmit HDLC frames through the dynamically configured logical channels.

The PCM primary link is divided into 32 channels of 64Kb/s each. Figure 2.1 shows the structure of the PCM link.

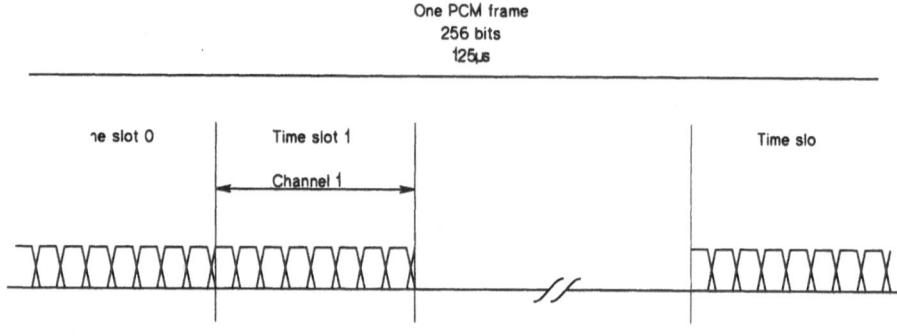

Fig. 2.1. 12048 Kb/s PCM format (CCITT Rec. G732).

HDLC is a data transmission protocol for the bit oriented part of OSI level 2 (link level). A HDLC frame is composed of different fields: address, control, optional, information, CRC and FLAG. Its structure can be seen in Figure 2.2.

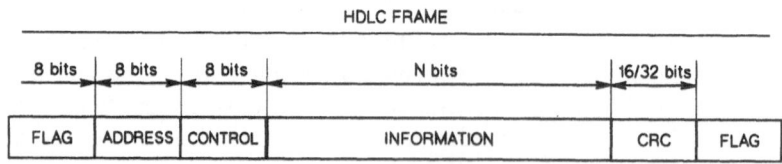

Fig. 2.2. HDLC frame structure.

One DEPTH circuit can handle up to 32 HDLC logical channels. The channel configuration is programmable by the user. The information for the logical channels is extracted from the PCM link. Every logical channel will have assigned one or several PCM channels on every frame (see Figure 2.1) depending on the programmed configuration. Therefore a DEPTH circuit can drive between one and 32 logical channels, respectively functioning at

2Mb/s and at 64 Kb/s in these cases. This circuit is included in the EDPN64 system (primary data link on N 64 Kb/s channels) which is part of a packet switching node (TESYS-B) designed at Telefónica I+D. The main functions and characteristics of the DEPTH design are:

1. dynamic assignment of physical slots to logical channels;
2. HDLC frames transmission and reception;
3. programmable CRC (16/32 bits);
4. automatic stuffing signalling units transmission and filtering (number 7 system signal);
5. line activity monitoring;
6. error control and statistical measures;
7. the 2 input/output serial lines can be programmed to function either for reception or transmission dynamically;
8. an internal loop can be created for testing purposes.

2.1 DEPTH interface with the environment

The DEPTH communicates with its environment (HOST) in the following ways:

1. with two serial bi-directional PCM lines at 2.048 Mb/s and related control signals;
2. through the use of messages queued in a common memory area (parallel interface).

Memory can be accessed in DMA mode by the DEPTH circuit. The mechanism of communication through common memory areas allows a totally asynchronous protocol to be used, in which HOST and DEPTH are completely decoupled (no interrupts). The message queues can be classified into the following categories:

– HOST commands;
– DEPTH responses;
– transmission channels configuration and data (32 message queues);
– reception channels configuration and data (32 message queues);
– free data buffers and
– initialization table.

The type of memory used is FIFO. The communication structure is depicted in Figure 2.3.

2.2 Architecture

The DEPTH circuit design is divided into the following sub-blocks (see Figure 2.4):

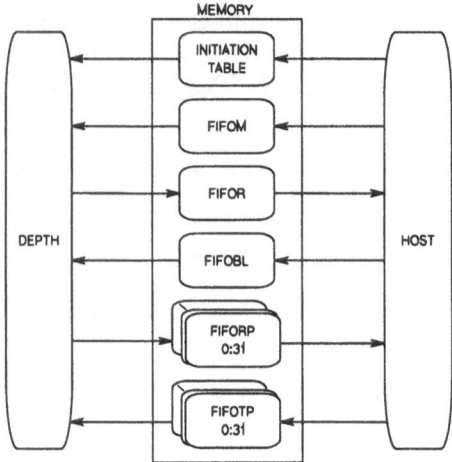

Fig. 2.3. DEPTH-HOST communication structure.

1. Initialization block (CI): the starting up procedure of the circuit is handled inside this block;
2. Central Control block (CC): here the overall communication protocols between the different blocks are handled;
3. Transmitter (TX): this assembles HDLC frames and transmit them;
4. Receiver (RX): this receives HDLC frames and dis-assembles them;
5. Motorola Bus Interface (IABM): this handles the communication between a Motorola microprocessor and the DEPTH circuit;
6. Bus Access Control (CAB): prevents bus contention and deadlocks between the IABM and the rest of the blocks;
7. Serial line control (CLS): this manipulates the PCM serial lines and generates the synchronization control signals.

The CI block is responsible for the initialization of the DEPTH circuit. After the reset signal is activated, this block handles a procedure in which the HOST has to write four addresses in four CI registers. The latter are used by the circuit to point to the data tables on the main memory.

The CI block is responsible for the operations that have to be carried out during initialization. It will generate an internal reset until the initialization table has been read completely.

The internal memories contents will also be initialized to 0 during this phase.

The CI block will maintain the rest of the circuit under rest until the four write cycles from the HOST are finished.

After initialization, the logical channel organization (dynamic assignment of PCM slots to given HDLC logical channels) is programmed and this status is maintained in memory. The transmitter and receiver work as finite state machines which will read and save the status of a logical channel at every working time slot. The Serial Line Control (CLS) block will contain the nec-

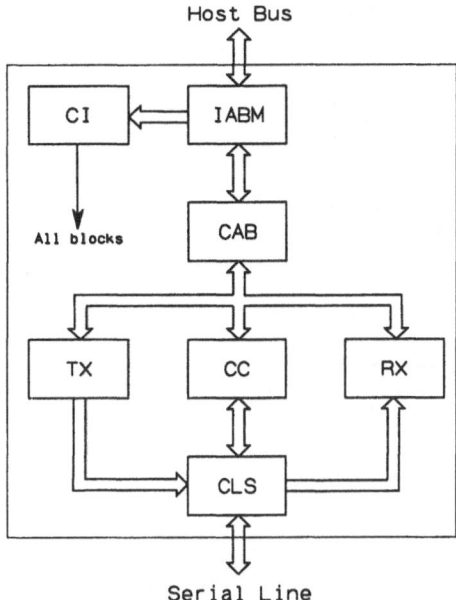

Fig. 2.4. DEPTH architecture.

essary information for the operation of every logical channel for either of the two transmission directions (relation between physical slots and logical channels). It will inform the transmitter and the receiver when to modify their status (context). The transmitter and receiver can be seen as two independent finite state machines, but, through the context mechanism, they will each function as N independent machines, where N is the number of enabled logical channels.

The status mentioned above consists of the following types of information:

1. dynamic information administered by the finite state machines;
2. logical channel Configuration which is programmed by the Central Control block (CC) and consists on: enabled/disabled status, CRC type, etc.

The configuration memories reside in the CC block. The reading control signals are generated by the CLS block. And the signals containing the information go to the TX and RX blocks.

All internal asynchronous communication mechanisms (configuration programming through the CC, statistical measures, etc) are implemented with memories or FIFOs. Data collisions are avoided by multiplexing in time the access to the memory buses.

CLS indicates to the TX and RX blocks in which logical channels they should operate, with 2 independent signals (cl_tx and cl_rx). This signals are accompanied with 2 extra signals (asig_tx, asig_rx) which determine if the physical PCM slot is or not assigned to the given logical channel. The basic CLS signal timing is shown in Figure 2.5.

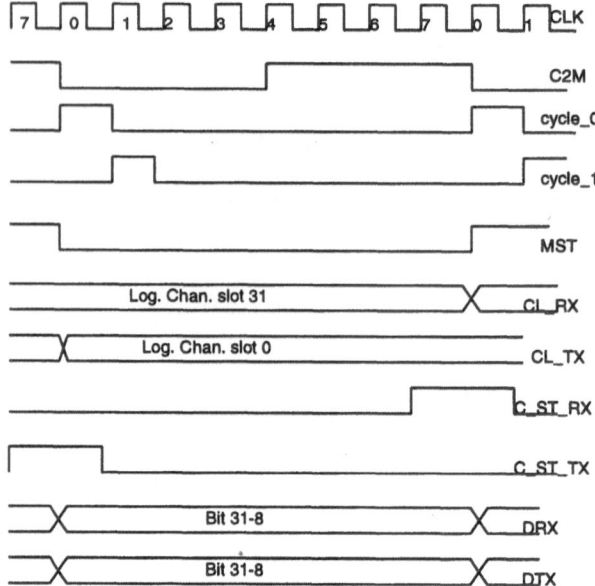

Fig. 2.5. Basic DEPTH timing.

The CLS takes care of this task, generating the synchronization signals used by the rest of the blocks. The main timing control signals are cycle¡0:7¿ which distinguish every clock cycle. This block will also count the necessary slots and bits for every data frame.

We can consider four different processes trying to access the Bus Access Control block (CAB): ATX, ARX, ARX2 and ACC.

1. ATX: process which manages the administration of the FIFOTP_xx queues;
2. ARX: process which manages the administration of the FIFORP_xx queues;
3. ARX2: process which manages the administration of the FIFOBL queue;
4. ACC: process which manages the administration of the FIFOM and FIFOR queues.

In the CAB there is only one FIFO. Incoming data should be retrieved by the block which has requested the data when the CAB acknowledges the reception of data with a signal (cab_data_ready). Access to the FIFO is performed by multiplexing in time (TDM) the incoming data from every block. Every process has a given period to access the CAB. There is an overflow signal when the FIFO is full. Figure 2.6 clarifies the concepts explained above.

The Central Control block handles the commands stored on the FIFOM queue by the HOST. The CC modifies the configuration memories of the related blocks. The commands are executed as a consequence of the modification on the block configurations, and at the time the logic channels refresh their context.

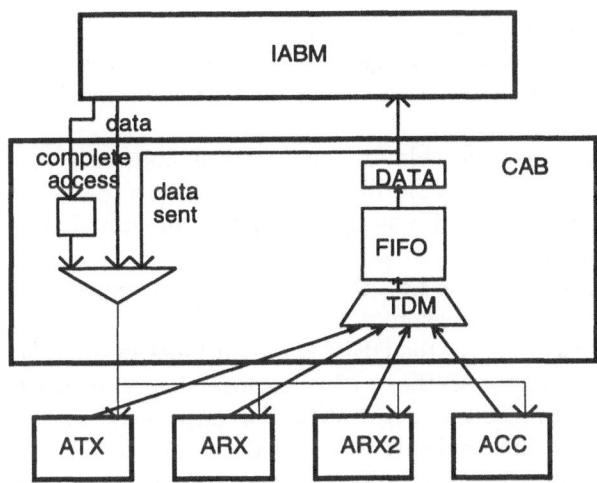

Fig. 2.6. Memory access control.

The commands related to statistical measures, logic channel assignment and internal feedback loop setting, are executed immediately by the CC and then they are acknowledged via the FIOFOM and FIFOR queues.

The signal timing is insured by explicitly acknowledging the command or by timing considerations for responses.

Every communication queue between the HOST and the DEPTH circuit needs a polling policy (FIFOM, FIFOTP, FIFOR, FIFORP, FIFOBL).

The CLS block generates signals that indicate to the FIFOBL, FIFOM and the FIFOR if it is their turn to be read for example.

The TX and RX blocks implement the polling policy for the 32 FIFOTP_xx and 32 FIFORP_xx queues respectively. Every independent finite state machine will control the polling process per queue.

2.3 Considerations and decisions regarding FORMAT

The DEPTH circuit is a very large and complex application, that indeed covers a wide range of processing algorithms very suitable as a test bench for the FORMAT tools. But since the objective of the work was to evaluate and explore formal methods and not the implementation of the whole DEPTH circuit, it was decided to withdraw several DEPTH blocks from the FORMAT testbench that would not contribute to the verification or synthesis approaches with different characteristics that could be interesting to explore with the FORMAT tools.

Therefore the Receiver (RX) and the transmitter (TX) blocks were not considered in the scope of the application work of Telefónica I+D.

One important conclusion we can draw from what has been explained above is that Telefónica I+D did not target the verification of the DEPTH circuit as a whole but the efforts were focused in the synthesis and verification of smaller and more manageable blocks: CI, IABM, CAB, CLS and CC (they are referenced in the previous section). In general Formal verification and synthesis with the FORMAT tools should focus on medium scale blocks at the most to obtain good results.

Moreover the blocks that were suitable for the synthesis approach were identified, selecting: the CI, CLS and IABM blocks. This decisions was taken on the basis that the synthesis approach is suitable basically for communication protocol handling circuits.

In the following Section we describe how the FORMAT tools have been incorporated into the design flow of Telefónica I+D.

The complete VHDL descriptions of the DEPTH circuit blocks were written at the beginning of the project, together with their formal specifications. Simulations were carried out to insure that the VHDL descriptions were correct and to pave the way for the application descriptions and correctness proofs and also for the identification of problems in, strengths of and possible improvements to the FORMAT tools.

3. Integration of the FORMAT tools into the Telefónica I+D design process

Exploitation of the FORMAT results is a key issue. In the case of Telefónica I+D, the tools are to be applied in the design of ASICs. Therefore the existing tool framework has to be extended to accommodate the FORMAT tools. This section shows and explains how this integration has been performed.

The current Telefónica I+D design flow at the system level is shown in Figure 3.1.

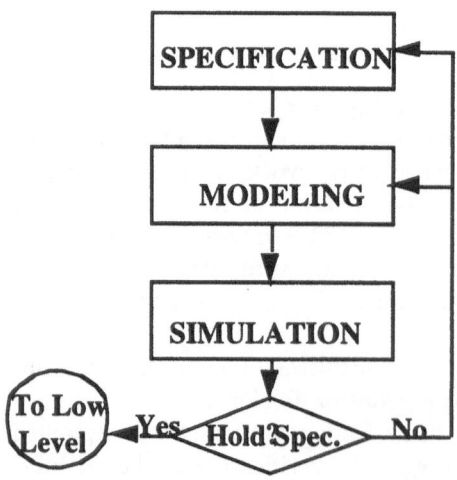

Fig. 3.1. High level design flow.

FORMAT has designed tools that impact the major three design steps displayed in Figure 3.1. In the circuit specification the timing diagram editor (TDE) permits the graphical representation of the signals behaviour or the conditions and restrictions the designed system has to comply with. Moreover, finite state machines can be conveniently written in a FORMAT proprietary state chart language.

The modelling phase, which includes steps such as architecture studies and possible implementation evaluation, can be drastically simplified by using a synthesis path which generates synthesizable VHDL code from a description couched in terms of timing diagrams. The state chart language provides a very powerful and user friendly way of designing finite state machines, incorporating interesting concepts such as granularity of the design plus hierarchical decomposition of an automaton.

The simulation process duration can be also considerably decreased by proving system properties fast and reliably coming out of the specification process in a straight forward fashion from timing diagrams. In Figure 3.2 the relationship between the FORMAT tools and the design flow is represented.

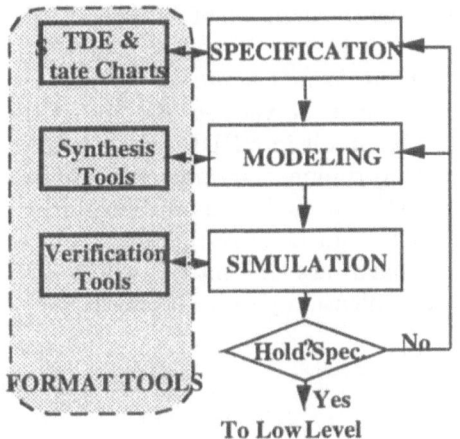

Fig. 3.2. Impact of the FORMAT tools on the design flow.

The tools have a common database (LVS from Leda) where all descriptions are stored, from specifications down to VHDL code. This is very convenient since version control is much easier in such a way. The tools will be probably interfaced in the future with the CADENCE framework, which is already in use by TI+D.

3.1 System specification

The specification of circuits that can be integrated through the actual silicon technologies has become very complex in the telecommunications area. Traditionally the specifications were generated after several meetings between system engineers and IC designers, in the form of documentation written in an informal and textual way. Only relevant stimuli-reaction dependencies were highlighted in such documents, leaving several details of the solution to be adopted for the implementation in the designers hands.

Sometimes the inherent complexity of the algorithms is such that natural language is not sufficient for the purposes of arriving at a comprehensive and readable specification. This leads to misinterpretations in the behavioural description phase which are practically impossible to identify during the design cycle since the system will be conceived and thus tested in the wrong manner. These kind of errors are very difficult to detect before fabrication, leading to very costly loops. All this can be translated to a need in the industry for tools that could improve the quality and reliability of the system level design phase. At Telefónica I+D, until now only HDL was used for capturing system descriptions, with only textual input. With the FORMAT approach, timing diagrams can now help to express a complex system functionality. In fact these descriptions will be integrated in the same database as the VHDL descriptions, namely LVS. Something very similar occurs with the state chart language. It provides to the system designer the possibility of writing control procedures in a systematic way, thus avoiding the creation of individual HDL conventions to describe an FSM.

The state chart language provides a more formal approach to the writing of control circuit. The descriptions can then be verified directly by the FORMAT tools without having to code the circuit in VHDL.

Through the synthesis tools the existing timing diagrams have a direct translation, therefore an equivalent, in VHDL. Not only can implementations be obtained straight away from specifications, but also testbenches can be so obtained. The former will not be perhaps hardware efficient but will be very rapidly "coded". In Figure 3.3 the new specification process is shown.

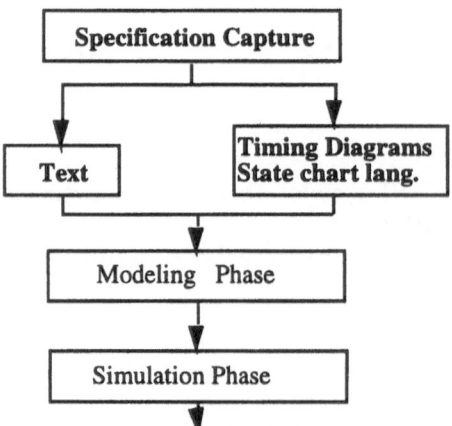

Fig. 3.3. Integration of the timing diagrams and state charts into the specification process.

3.2 Synthesis tools

The high level synthesis approach in FORMAT is very much related to the modelling phase. In fact it can be seen as a rapid prototyping tool for VHDL. From a timing diagram or a collection of them, a VHDL description is being generated. The code structure is scalable, maintaining always the same foundations and appearance.

The output of the timing diagram editor is taken as input for the synthesis tools and no user interaction is needed. Nevertheless a third party public domain tool can be used, GraphEd, to analyse the finite state machine generated in LOTOS and deduce if further refinement of the timing diagram specification is needed to reduce the complexity and amount of states. The key issue to get a manageable number of states is to reduce as much as possible parallel behaviour, introducing constraint arcs to insure signal dependencies and restrict possible system transitions.

Integration into the design flow has been very straightforward since programs are called as standard Unix commands. In Figure 3.4 the synthesis toolset integration into the modelling flow is sketched.

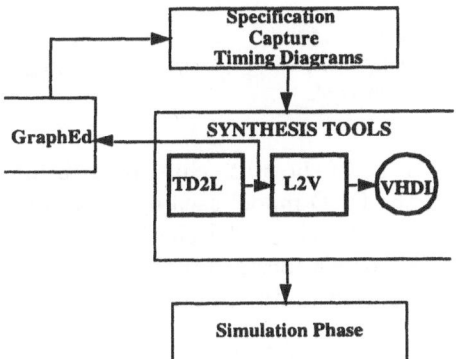

Fig. 3.4. Integration of the synthesis line into the modelling process.

3.3 Verification tools

What was called the simulation phase before now has a broader meaning, and should be called the Verification phase where simulation is just another tool which is, for the moment, very difficult to replace completely. The problem with simulation is certainly the time consumed to perform exhaustive checks to prove and validate a given design. Moreover certain properties related to real life are very difficult to recreate via a testbench.

Application of formal methods to the high level design verification phase can increase productivity a lot by relieving the simulation task of part of its job. With these new tools verification starts at the specification phase because the designer will have to think already then about important signal relationships which can be easily expressed with simple timing diagrams. Moreover, the granularity of this approach makes its application quite easy since properties can be defined in a modular fashion taking into account a small set of ports for each instance of a given entity, leading to easy to read and comprehensible timing diagrams.

The verification tools integration work at Telefónica I+D is exclusively focused on the model checking verification process. The results of this work are shown in Figure 3.5.

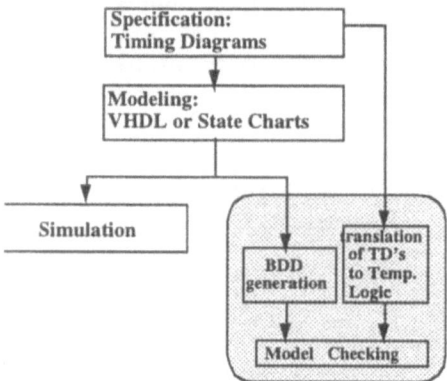

Fig. 3.5. Integration of the verification tools.

After modelling a given block in VHDL or in the state chart description language, a tool (FSM) is run that builds the BDD model used by the model checker. The assumptions and commitments to be model checked are described with the timing diagram editor and post-processed with translation tools to get the correct formula format processed by the model checker.

4. Working methodology and results

4.1 The synthesis line

The synthesis tools designed in the FORMAT project give to the user the capacity to describe circuits within a language that is well known and, indeed, classical in the definition of circuits: timing diagrams. These diagrams have to comply with certain syntactic rules but are very much like the ones you may find in any documentation. In order to do so, a user friendly timing diagram editor has been designed that produces text as well as PostScript files, a feature that is very handy for documentation.

The toolset produces VHDL code which will always have a very similar structure. This toolset is suited for interfacing-circuitry types of applications since it is not easy to express complex processing units with timing diagrams alone. The code is synthesizable by commercial tools such as SYNOPSYS. Another application of this toolset is to rapidly produce VHDL testbenches from timing diagrams. Command options are available for this purpose.

The user can also view the transition system that will be translated to VHDL, in order to check the correctness of the timing diagram descriptions. Although an optional feature, it has shown itself to be of great help since it provides another representation of the circuit behaviour that is very convenient for checking the control process. Some examples are shown later on.

The synthesis of some selected blocks of the DEPTH circuit was carried through completely, as described above. These blocks perform, among other functions, interfacing operations and could be described easily with timing diagrams. The selected blocks are:

1. CI (Initialization Circuit);
2. CAB (Bus Access Controller);
3. CLS (Serial Communications Controller);
4. IABM (Motorola Bus Interface).

The design steps are listed below:

1. Use the timing diagram editor in order to draw the specifications. A specification file can be composed of several timing diagrams which could be linked using an "EXOR" or an "OR" operator meaning an alternative or a parallel composition respectively. The timing diagrams have to be saved in an ASCII file which will be then taken as the input for the synthesis tools.
2. Pre-process the timing diagrams in order to generate the GraphEd representation (<filename>.ged) in order to check the correctness of the timing diagrams. Moreover if several timing diagrams are being used for a specification, the only way to obtain an immediate overview of the system behaviour is via GraphEd. In fact GraphEd is very suitable when defining decision trees.
3. Timing diagrams for synthesis should use only "mandatory" type of constraints. The "possible" constraints produce unexpected results on the decision tree.
4. It is necessary to generate alternative timing diagrams in order to obtain a new branch on the decision tree in GraphEd. The alternative timing diagram should be identical to the original one up to the point where the decision is to be made. Each alternative timing diagram is meant for a given branch on the graph.
5. The decision making process should be controlled always by changes on a given input only (not on outputs).
6. It is convenient to always start a specification with a given signal transition which should appear in every alternative timing diagram.
7. Once the timing diagrams and graph meet the user specification requirements, the VHDL generation process can be started. This process

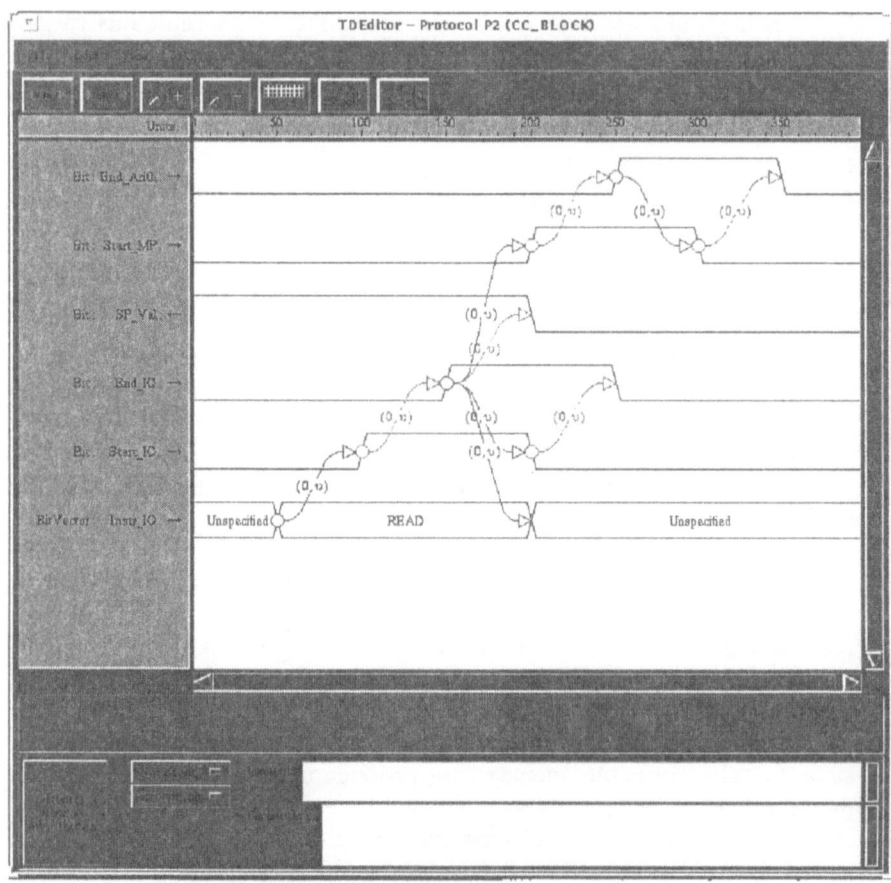

Fig. 4.1. Example of a Timing Diagram Editor window.

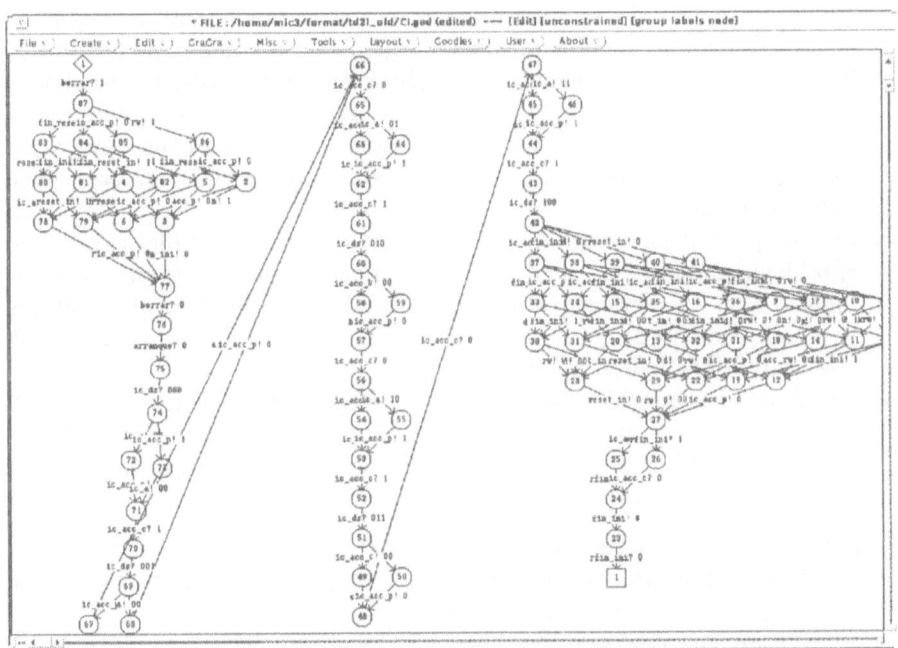

Fig. 4.2. Example of a GraphEd window.

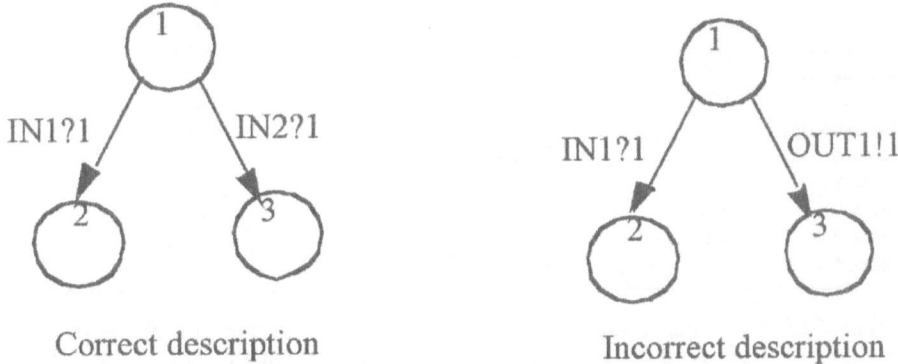

Correct description   Incorrect description

Fig. 4.3. Descriptions of an alternative path.

translates a LOTOS description obtained from the timing diagrams into VHDL code. The generated VHDL code is synthesizable and implements the graph decision tree algorithm as a typical finite state machine. In order to simulate the model, some delays between transitions have to be introduced in the test bench, to let the internal controlling flow signals reach a steady value. In principle, the user does not have to care about the latter signals. The delays are introduced in terms of the finite state machine master clock cycles: the input are to be modified after a given number of clock cycles.

8. For complex blocks it is possible for the user to introduce hierarchy: each sub-block could be specified with independent timing diagrams, and the highest level of hierarchy (the interconnection of those sub-blocks) has to be implemented by hand (coded in VHDL). In fact the IABM block has been implemented in such a way.

9. The finite state machine can be set to its initial state by generating stimuli on the general signals RESET and CSxx (these signals will appear always in any example). The problem is that the outputs will remain on the same state they were before the reset.

The timing diagrams specifications that are presented in this work had to be conceived with a tool version that did not support yet complex assertions, only constant values were accepted on the waveforms. Therefore we had to introduce some simplification but the main behaviour has been captured on the timing diagrams of every block. Some statistics are included in a table below in order to have an idea of the complexity of every circuit and the performance of the synthesis tools.

Table 4.1. Practical results: statistics for all examples.

Block Name	No. of states	Orig. VHDL lines	Final VHDL lines	Simulation discrepancies
Entrada_cab	31	107	163	None
Salida_cab	29	129	159	None
CI	67	359	305	None
CLS_assig	55	*	412	None
CLS_CC	62	Total 132	353	None
Iabm_1	125	**	496	None
Iabm_2	125	**	496	None
Iabm_3	132	**	615	None
Iabm_4	132	Total 224	615	None

* The CLS block has been divided into two timing diagram specifications. The original description consisted of one VHDL description with a total of 132 VHDL lines of code.

** The IABM had to be divided into four different timing diagram specifications. Originally there was only one VHDL description of 224 lines of code.

The results of the synthesis were simulated with the QuicksimII Mentor simulator and the results were compared with those from the blocks described by hand in VHDL. Basically no problems were found and the results were satisfactory.

The synthesis run is not very long at least for the Telefónica I+D test benches. It can vary from seconds to an hour of CPU time depending on the complexity of the specification. From the point of view of computing resources, no serious limitations were found since the tools could run in any almost SPARC workstation with more than 16 MB of RAM.

The critical points to be drawn from the FORMAT synthesis approach are:

1. The complexity of the results seems to be very high if counting lines of code. This factor is a bit tricky, but has to be definitely taken into account if the result is to be synthesized into gates (real hardware). The main problem lies on the fact that the generated finite state machines normally have a very high number of states. Therefore care should be taken in choosing for synthesis blocks that have a level of complexity that really would benefit from such a short design cycle in spite of the extra hardware that is to be generated.

2. The generated finite state machine will always have three extra signals on the interface: Reset, Chip select (CSxx) and clock (clk).

3. The control of the output signal delay is not evident and for some applications the solution will be too slow.

Below the specifications of two different blocks (the CI and the CAB) are appended together with the graph of the resulting finite state machine in order to give to the reader an idea of the complexity of the specifications that were handled for this work.

The timing diagram specification for the CI block consists of only one diagram. The specification and the decision tree representations are shown in Figure 4.4 and Figure 4.5 below.

The functionality of this block is to control the start of operation of the DEPTH circuit. After receiving an external reset, the block has to reset the whole circuit and perform 4 different reading cycles in order to program 4 initialization registers. After the fourth access, the block waits for a signal that indicates the end of initialization. The block responds by taking out of reset the whole circuit. In the timing diagram, the handshake of every operation can be withdrawn.

The synthesized VHDL code length is 305 lines of code. The complexity of the code is not very easy to measure using this tool since even for a very small example a given number of VHDL lines of code is generated in order to define variables and blocks. The finite state machine generated by the synthesis is not a direct translation of the decision tree shown. It goes through several optimization steps. The result has been simulated with the Mentor QuicksimII simulator in a few seconds. In order to drive a synthesized

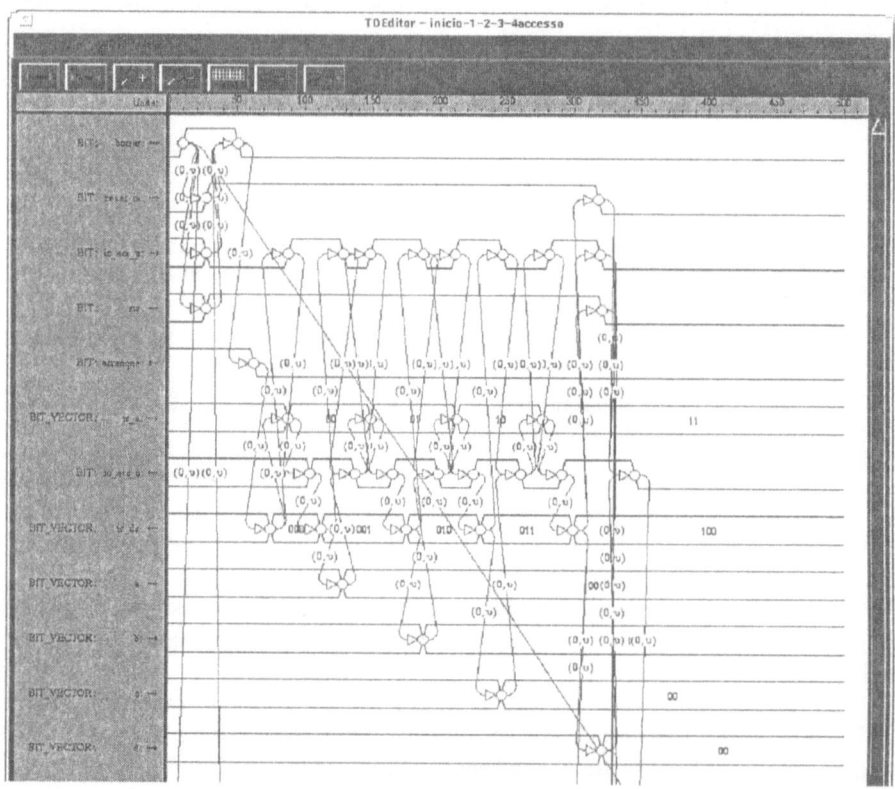

Fig. 4.4. Snap-shot of the CI timing diagram Specification.

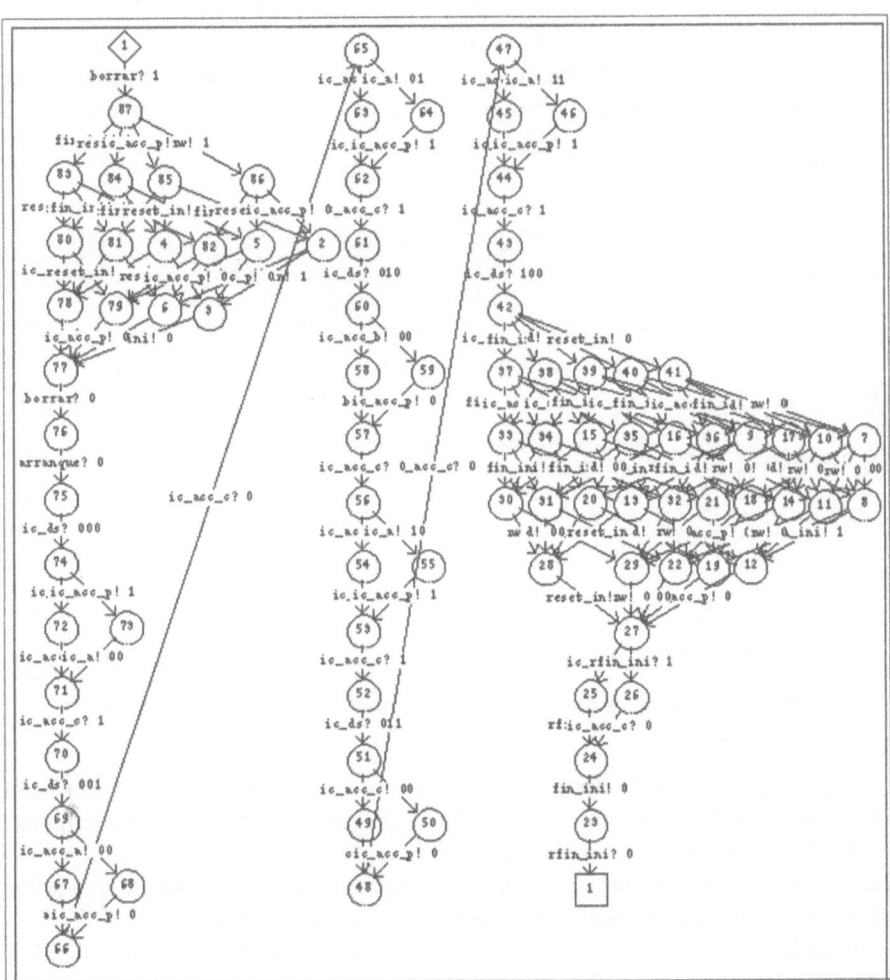

Fig. 4.5. CI decision tree.

block for simulation, it is necessary to write stimuli basically for three control signals added by the tool: The Finite State Machine clock ("clk"), a reset signal ("Reset") and an enable ("CSTest_shell"). Moreover the block input sequence has to be provided.

The CAB block controls the access to and from the internal bus of the DEPTH circuit. For the purpose of synthesis, only the input and output processes were considered. The input process consists of the time multiplexing of four sources that access a common FIFO. These four sources are connected to the same bus. Their data is written to a FIFO in a time slot assigned to every source. The timing diagram of the input block is shown in Figure 4.6 below.

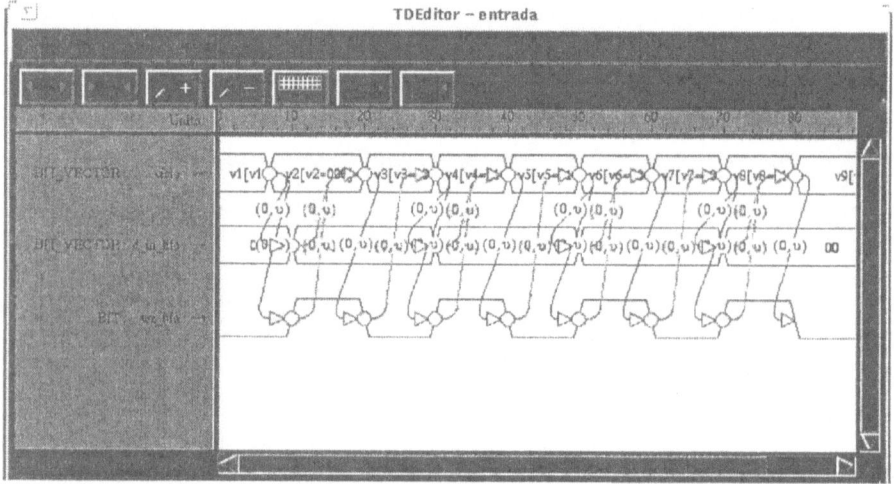

Fig. 4.6. Timing diagram of the input part of the CAB circuit

The output block of the CAB basically controls the reading of the same FIFO that holds all the accesses on the CAB mentioned for the input block. When the block detects data on the FIFO, it flags to the external world that data is available and performs the reading access to the memory. Its specification timing diagram is also shown in Figure 4.7 below.

Finally, the decision trees generated from the two descriptions are included below. This time the finite state machines can be understood easily, and the synthesized VHDL was the smallest for these two blocks from all the testbenches that were chosen. They both have around 500 lines of code. The synthesized code was also simulated with QuicksimII from Mentor.

4.2 The verification line

The FORMAT verification tools provide a very powerful method for checking block properties from a VHDL description. The main goal of this approach,

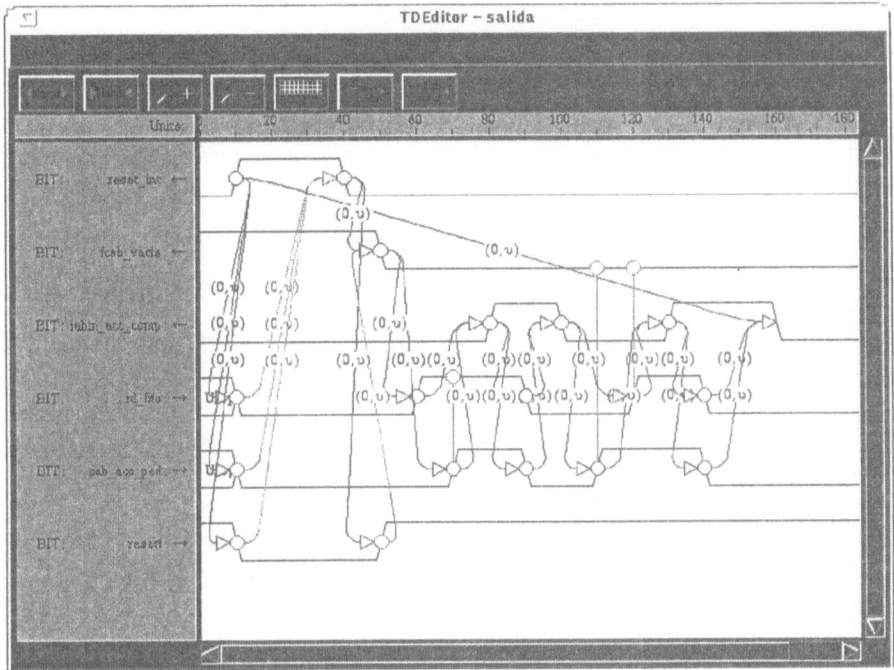

Fig. 4.7. Timing diagram of the output part of the CAB circuit

from the Telefónica I+D perspective, is to reduce simulation time as much as possible by moving some functionality checks to the verification process. The inputs to the verification tools are from one side the VHDL code of the block itself, and from another, the timing diagrams where properties (signal sequences) are defined in an assumption-commitment style. Instead of the VHDL input, a FORMAT state chart language may be used to write a block behaviour.

Normally the timing diagrams will be very simple. They do not follow the same syntax as the ones studied earlier for the synthesis approach. It is crucial for the user, to understand perfectly how a given property is to be expressed with the timing diagrams, otherwise the results from the verification may be misleading. To understand better the output of the verification when the property is found to be untrue, some useful feedback can be obtained in the form of a simulation test-bench or a timing diagram. The verified property is expressed as a sequence of stimuli producing an output that is different from the one expressed on the property.

The result of this approach is simple and straightforward: the model checker simply returns with an "ok" or "not ok" answer. Nevertheless the steps to get to the result can be analysed, seeing how the model checker has driven the BDD in order to check the properties.

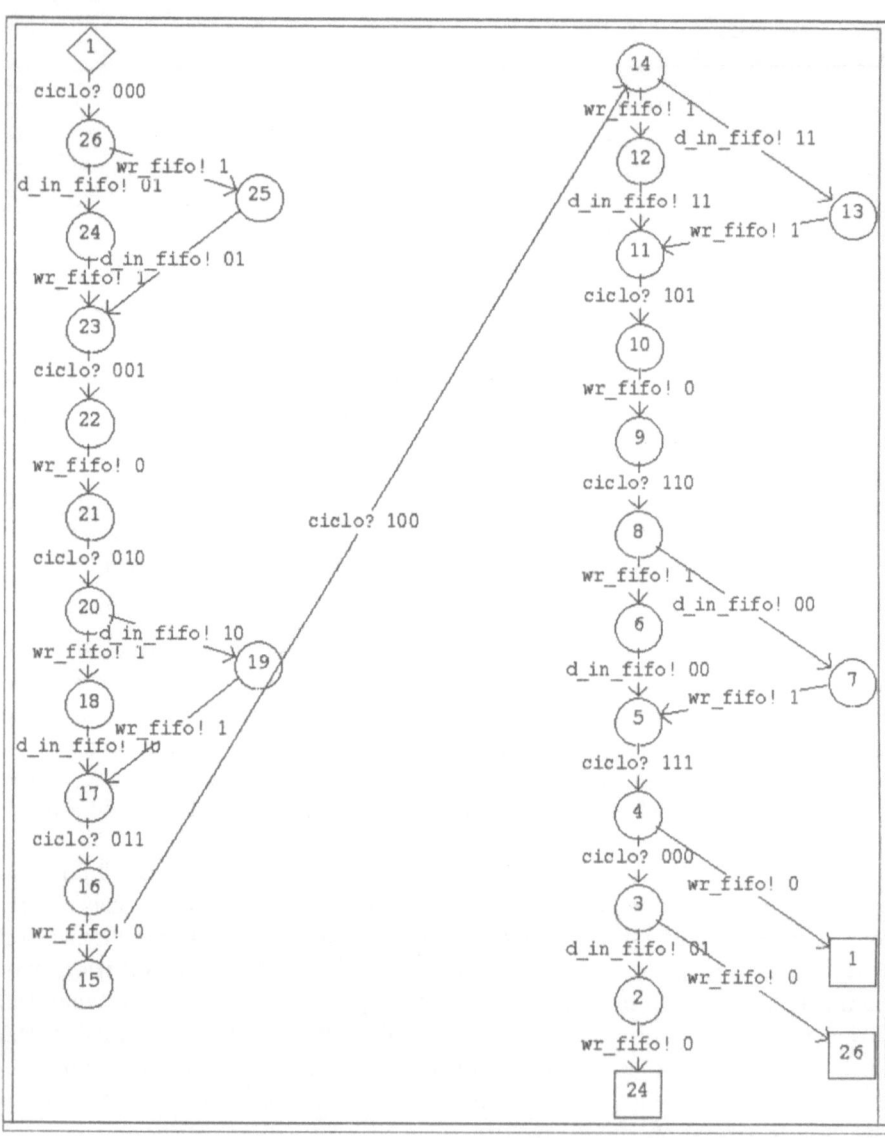

Fig. 4.8. Decision tree of the input part of the CAB

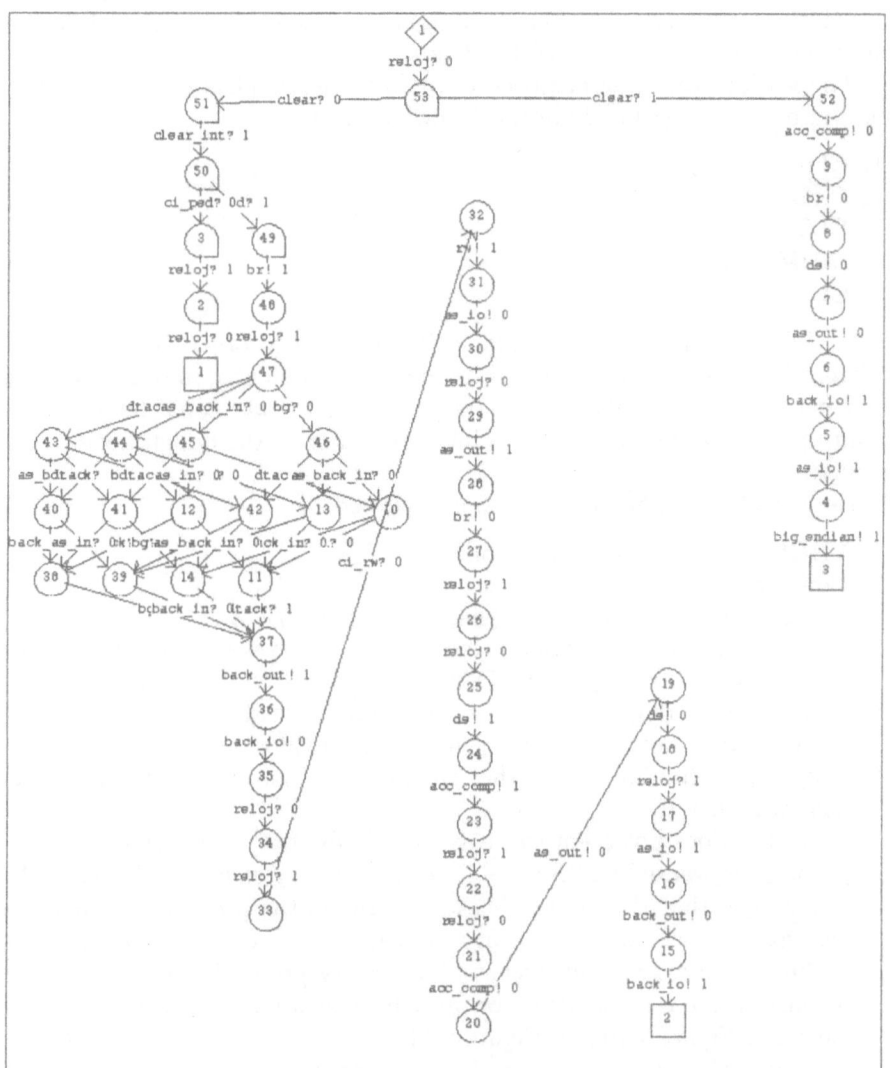

Fig. 4.9. Decision tree of the output part of the CAB

The main restriction of the FORMAT verification tools is the subset of VHDL that can be translated to the BDD that is handled by the model checker, and state explosion. At the moment, the major VHDL statements are supported. Complexity problems appear when wide buses or a lot of I/Os appear in a description. One simple solution to the latter problem is to reduce the width of the buses that handle data and not control signals. In this way the functionality of the verified block is preserved.

The work in this area has been devoted to the verification of the VHDL and state chart descriptions of the following blocks:

1. CI
2. CAB
3. CLS
4. IABM
5. CC

State chart descriptions are available for the control oriented parts of the different blocks only. All the VHDL models were simulated in order to assess their correct functionality so that the verification trials would be more oriented to the learning of the methodology and not to the design itself of the circuits.

Here are the design steps that were followed:

1. VHDL coding or state chart coding.
2. Compilation.
3. Translation to a BDD model (use of the tool FSM 3.1).
   This process may take a long time and it can be seen as the bottleneck of the verification approach. This is the crucial point for any approach that considers BDDs, since the translation can lead to a huge amount of branches that become unmanageable (state explosion).
4. Property definition with the timing diagram editor (assumption-commitment).
   This step does not seem to be very difficult, but it is fundamental for getting the wanted and profitable results. A very strict syntax has to be followed so that the model checker interprets the property in the same way as the user does. There are basically 2 sets of properties that are mainly used: safety and liveness. The safety properties help to express for instance initial conditions or probable transitions. Some examples are shown in Figure 4.10 and Figure 4.11.
   The liveness properties state that a given sequence of transitions will eventually occur. Some examples are shown in Figure 4.12 and Figure 4.13.
   What is important is to understand the meaning of the intervals on the constraint arrows. Here below the more commonly used are explained:
   a) $[-\infty, \infty)$ means that the second event will eventually happen. There is no specification being made on the order;

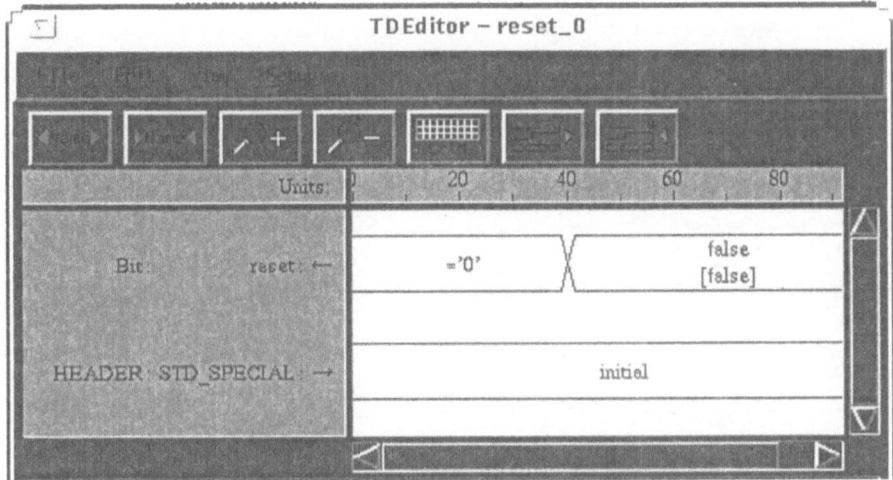

Fig. 4.10. Safety, initial property

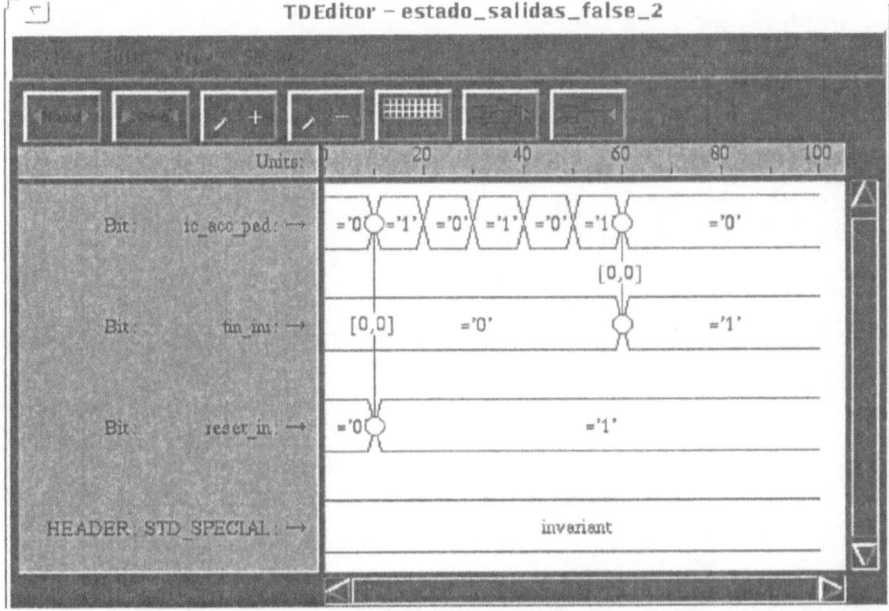

Fig. 4.11. Safety property with simultaneous constraints

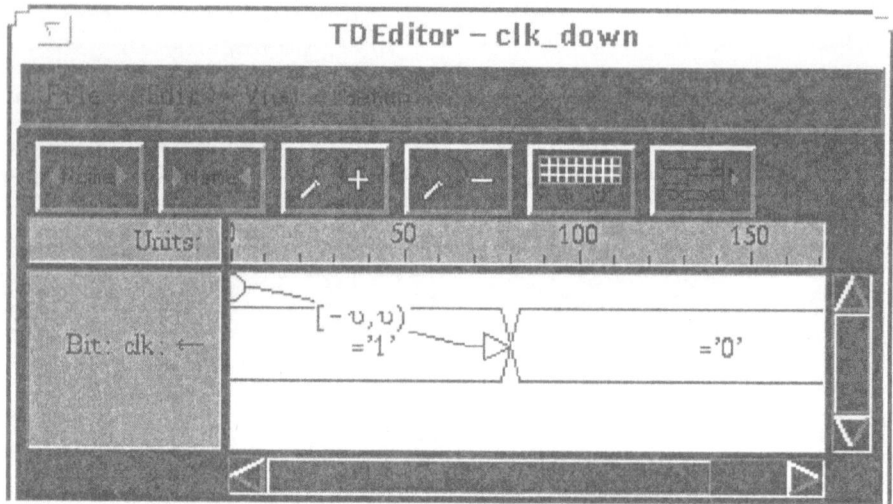

Fig. 4.12. Liveness property and ...

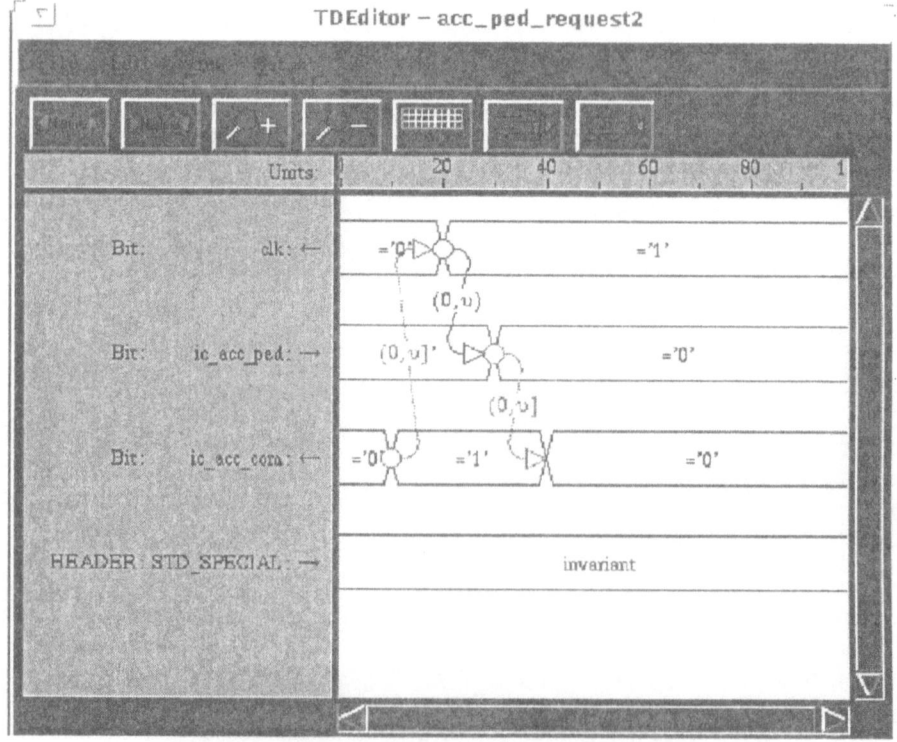

Fig. 4.13. ... A more complex property.

b) $(0, \infty)$ means that the second event has to occur after the first one, whilst $(0, \infty]$ means it may occur;

c) $[0, 0]$ and $(0, 0)$ are simultaneous constraints, the first one states that the events have to occur at the same time or never, the second one states that the events occur at different times or never;

d) $(0, 0]$ and $[0, 0)$, $(-\infty, \infty)$, $[-\infty, \infty]$, $(-\infty, \infty]$, $[\infty, 0]$, $(\infty, 0]$, $[\infty, 0)$, $(\infty, 0]$ are never used;

e) all other combinations can be deduced.

5. Translation from timing diagrams to temporal logic formulae.

These formulae are the ones that are in fact understood by the model checker. This is a simple translation step.

6. Finally the model checker has to be run in order to check the properties that were previously translated.

It is important to get to know the different modes of operation and start conditions for the model checker in order to get the best out of it. But it is easy to use.

In this chapter the results obtained with one of the testbenches, the CI block, will be discussed. As mentioned previously, the original CI description had to be simplified because the BDD generation could not handle the amount of bits at the interface (buses up to 32 bits). The simplified version contains only buses with at the most 10 bits. Some probes have been included: probes are extra signals introduced by the user in order to get access to internal variables and check their values.

The BDD generation of the CI takes about one hour CPU time. In Table 4.2 a list of all properties that were model-checked is appended:

Table 4.2. Summary of all checked properties for the CI Block

commitment	assumptions
outputs_state_false_2	reset_0,clk_down,clk_up,acc_comp_comes_up, acc_comp_comes_down,arr_comes
outputs_state_false_1	reset_0,clk_down,clk_up,acc_comp_comes_up, acc_comp_comes_down,arr_comes
acc_request2	reset_0,clk_down,clk_up,acc_comp_comes_up, acc_comp_comes_down,arr_comes
output_status	reset_0,clk_down,clk_up,acc_comp_comes_up, acc_comp_comes_down,arr_comes
end_init	reset_0,clk_down,clk_up
acc_request1	end_ini_0,reset_0,clk_down,clk_up,arr_down, arr_down
begin_init	reset_comes
outputs_states_3	reset_0,clk_down,clk_up,acc_comp_comes_up, acc_comp_comes_down,arr_comes

To show how a property can be expressed, the "end_init" commitment from the above table is explained together with its related assumptions.

The commitment timing diagram is shown in Figure 4.14.

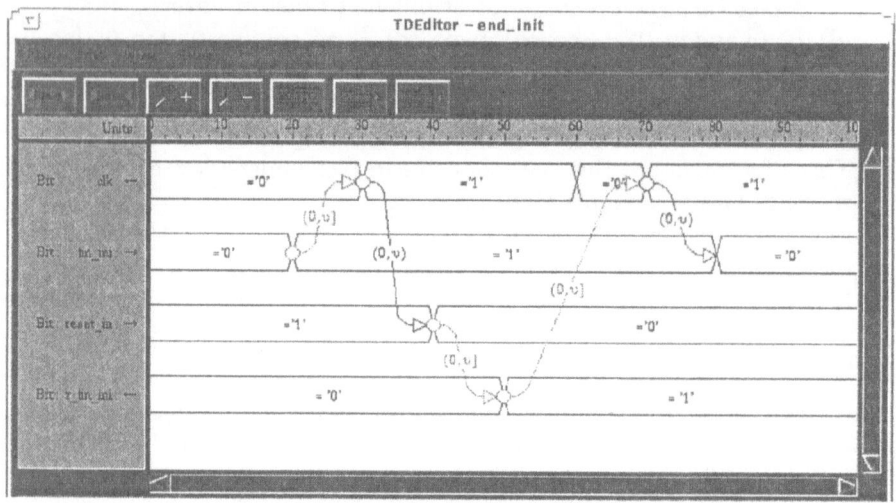

Fig. 4.14. END_INIT commitment

This property is intended for checking the end of the initialization process handled by the CI circuit. This property can be understood in the following way: when the block has finished the four accesses to the a, b, c and d registers (in state 2 of the VHDL code), the CI generates an end of initialization signal (fin_ini=1 on the timing diagram). With the rising edge of the clock the CI will deactivate the internal reset of the circuit (reset_in=0 in the timing diagram). As soon as the acknowledge of the end of initialization is received (r_fini_in=1) the end of initialization (fin_ini) signal will be set to "0" with the rising edge of the clock.

This commitment is valid under the assumptions shown in Figure 4.15.

The assumption in Figure 4.16 states that the reset signal will remain always inactive (reset=0).

The assumption in Figure 4.17 expresses the fact that the clock will eventually have a falling edge.

This assumption is very similar to the previous one but this time it says that the clock will eventually go from "0" to "1". In other words, the above assumptions state that the block will receive a valid clock and that the block will not be put under a reset condition. The results of the verification of the 8 commitments listed on table 2, are summarized in Table 4.2:

Within the specification languages, a state chart description can be employed to describe Finite State Machines in a very convenient and simple way. The state chart description of the CI block control process is shown in

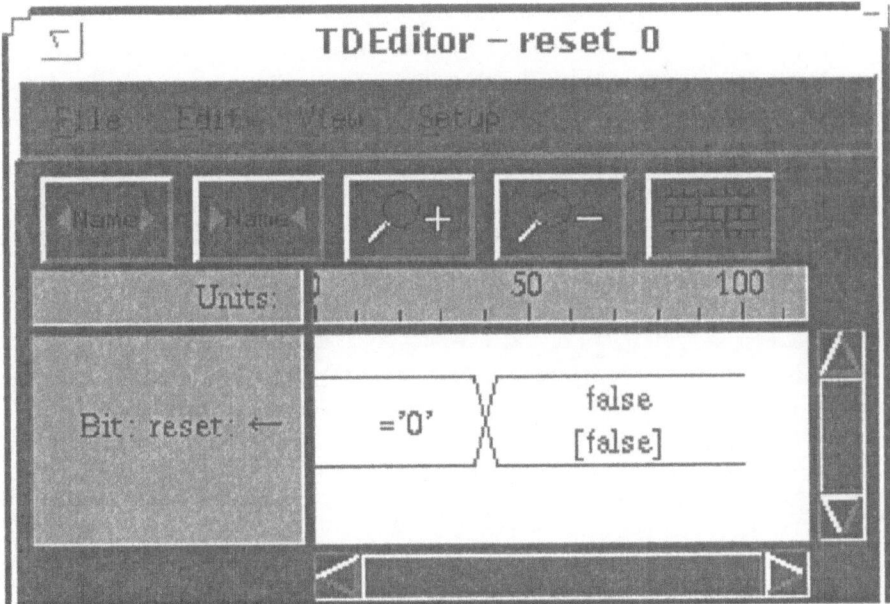

Fig. 4.15. RESET_0 assumption

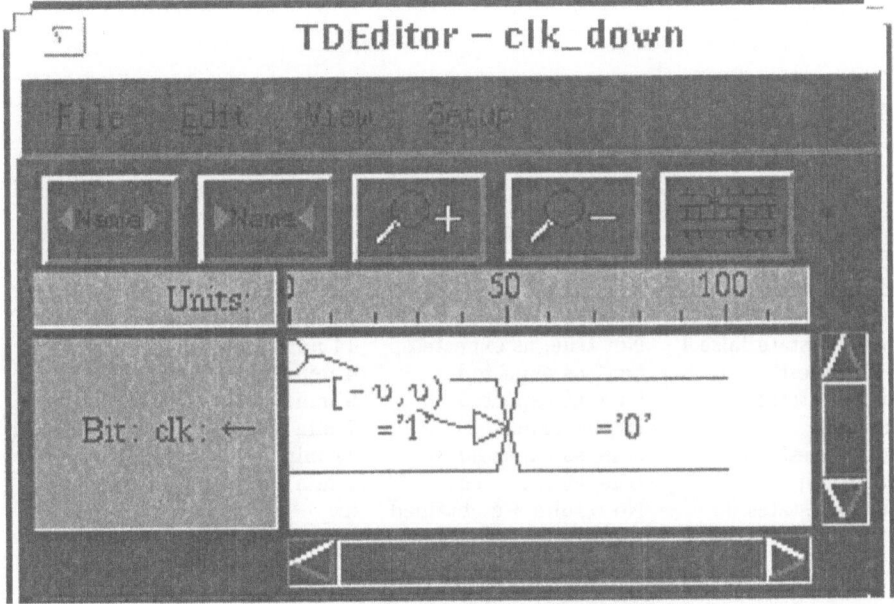

Fig. 4.16. CLK_DOWN assumption

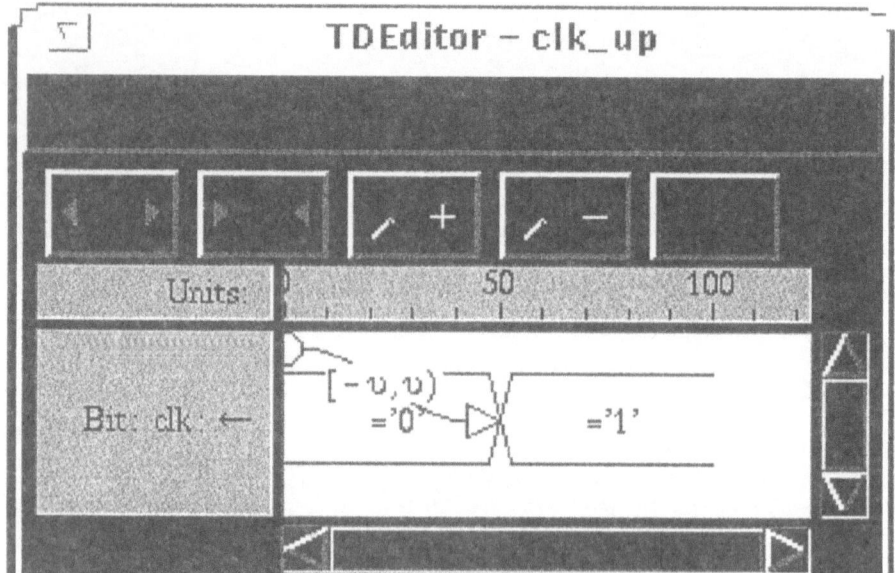

Fig. 4.17. CLK_UP assumption

Table 4.3. Results of the verification

commitments	verification results	Time elapsed
outputs_state_false_2	Not true, as expected	13 min
outputs_state_false_1	Not true, as expected	14 min
acc_request2	true, as expected	4 min
output_status	true, as expected	9 min
end_init	true,as expected	7 min
acc_request1	true, as expected	11 min
begin_init	true, as expected	5 min
outputs_states_3	No results are obtained	xx

Figure 4.18. The verification process was followed in exactly the same way as for the VHDL description. This time the BDD used by the model checker is generated with a different tool capable of handling state chart descriptions.

```
architecture state_ci of ci is
begin
state status_ci is
  SIGNAL di: integer range 0 to 3;
  SIGNAL ped: bit;
  one of
    state d0 is end;
    state d1 is end;
    state d2 is end;
    state d3 is end;

  default advance to d0;

  from d0
    when (arr='1') do
    begin
      di <= 0;
      ic_acc_ped <='1';
      ped <= '1';
      reset_in <= '1';
    end
    advance to d1;

  from d1
    when ((ic_acc_com='0') and
(ped='0')) do
    begin
      ic_acc_ped<='1';
      ped <='1';
      di<= (di+1);
    end
    advance to d1;

  when ((ic_acc_com='1') and
    (di/=3)) do
    begin
      ic_acc_ped<='0';
      ped <= '0';
    end
    advance to d1;
  when ((ic_acc_com='1') and
(di=3)) do
    begin
      ic_acc_ped<='0';
      ped <= '0';
      fin_ini<='1';
    end
    advance to d2;

  from d2
    when (true) do
    begin
      reset_in<='0';
    end
    advance to d3;
  from d3
    when ((r_fin_ini='1')) do
    begin
      fin_ini<='0';
    end
    advance to d0;

end status_ci;
end state_ci;
```

Fig. 4.18. The FORMAT state chart description of the process "MAQUINA" on the VHDL code of the CI block.

It is important to mention that in the description only the basic control flow is described, the data assignments are not yet handled efficiently. This code can be then translated to the BDD format that is handled by the model checker.

The critical points of the FORMAT verification approach are:

1. The limited VHDL subset that can be processed by the tools.
2. State explosion when handling big I/O interfaces or buses that have widths of more than 10 bits.

3. Clear error reporting pointing where the critical points are when having trouble with a VHDL translation to a BDD.

4. The writing of commitments and assumptions is not an easy task if good results are to be obtained. A deep knowledge of the circuit is required and of the basic vocabulary of the constraints.

5. Conclusions

Formal methods provide a body of techniques that are gaining more and more acceptance for the design of hardware, due to the high level of complexity that is being now reached with deep submicron technologies. Simulation is not enough as the only means for verifying the correctness of circuits due to the large time required to check all the different algorithms processed on a system.

The FORMAT tools provide very innovative concepts and interesting solutions for the validation and synthesis at the high level design phase. Today they can handle relatively small sub-blocks, so they can be only applied in up-to-date designs after having refined the design hierarchically: the circuit should already have a clear structure and a well-defined function performed by every block. Tools have recently been provided in order to check hierarchical decompositions, but unfortunately these tools could not be tested for the purposes of this book.

Basically Telefónica I+D could test the synthesis and the model checker based tools.

In the synthesis line encouraging results were obtained. VHDL descriptions can be obtained from timing diagrams in a very short time (less than an hour). These VHDL descriptions are synthesizable by SYNOPSYS. They have been proved to run as specified on the timing diagrams. If the user wants to use the result of synthesis as a real hardware implementation, the following considerations are to be taken into account:

1. the implementation is a finite state machine where a control clock, reset and enable (CSxx) signals are needed and thus they will have to be generated somewhere else;

2. for small examples the complexity of the implementation is too high in terms of size/area;

3. whether or not strict timing requirements are needed for the signals at the interface.

It is possible to work with a state chart representation in parallel with the timing diagrams, in order to verify the user's specification. Parallel and serial composition of timing diagrams is possible and handy in the case of defining several decision branches (parallel composition).

In the verification field, tool improvements are needed in order to get results that could help in the design of up to date circuits and systems. Nevertheless the approach is really a breakthrough on the way of providing a tool that could be used together with simulation in order to decrease validation times exponentially.

The FORMAT tools are capable of checking system properties defined with timing diagrams against the system's behaviour described in VHDL or in a proprietary state chart language. The syntax of timing diagrams is not complex but the user has to have a great deal of expertise to be able to express a property as he really intended, otherwise contradictory results are obtained.

Another important issue is that a complete subset of VHDL is not supported, so care should be taken when writing a block that is to be validated with this set of tools.

Finally the complexity factor that appears to be formost in this area is the bus width and the interface size of the block to be model-checked.

Italtel Application of the FORMAT Design Flow

Massimo Bombana, Patrizia Cavalloro, Fabrizio Ferrandi, and Fernanda Salice

Italtel, Italy

1. Introduction

The design approach developed in the FORMAT Project provides the user with modular, configurable design toolsets (figure 1.1). Each homogeneous toolset addresses a specific need in the ESDA domain, and provides solutions to some of the open problems in today's design environments. The development of the toolsets has been conducted in parallel with the evaluation of their features. The evaluation has been performed by selected designers on a part time basis. They re-designed a selected application among those recently developed in the SM (Tools and Methodology) Laboratory of the Central D&R Dept. of Italtel adopting the style proposed by the FORMAT Project.

A set of 'key' criteria has been established to measure quantitatively the applicability and market potentialities of the results of the project. Such criteria focus mainly on the technical profile of the tools, and include:

1. the ability to cope with the average complexity of industrial applications;
2. the degree of integration into proprietary CAD design flows;
3. the user-friendliness of the interfaces, conditioning users' acceptance;
4. compliance with the market or de-facto standards of CAD design;
5. benefits (or, possibly drawbacks) in comparison with competitive approaches, regarding design time, design quality, quality of results, reduced time-to-market.

Obviously the list is not complete, and it could include many other criteria, for instance more economic oriented parameters such as the expected return of investments and so on. Anyway the compliance with the previous five technical points is considered fundamental for the introduction of any innovative tool into the ESDA market. Compliance to points 1 and 2 is mandatory for the presentation to technical management, compliance to points 3 and 4 greatly increases the acceptance of final users (designers usually are the 'decision makers'), the last point increases the competitive profile.

In the following sections the results of our beta-test evaluation are discussed. At first we give a short description of the selected device. Design capture of the specification of the device is realized using the FORMAT

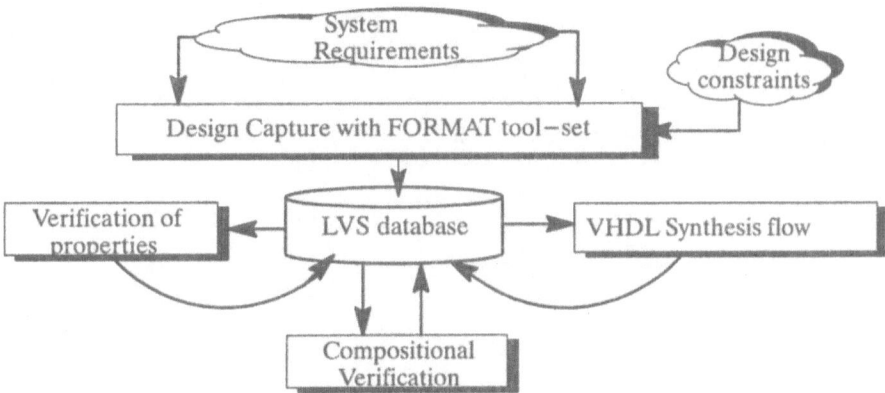

Fig. 1.1. Schematic representation of the FORMAT design flow.

toolset, consisting of the usual VHDL entry features of the selected data-base increased by the application of the Timing Diagram Editor (TDE) for the definition of properties and sub-modules in the form of timing diagrams. The adopted strategy concerning the verification path is described afterwards. Alternative descriptions are developed for the control-oriented modules of the component, and consistency is verified, against the global properties required by the behavior of the system. Compositional verification extends this line of reasoning, with the inclusion of structural descriptions in the task of properties checking. Finally, a similar strategy is presented for the synthesis path, whose goal is the automatic generation of VHDL code for control modules and related communication protocols. In both cases, some emphasis is given to the structural partitioning of the device as a strategy to cope with complexity. The same partitioning has been applied in all the cases.

2. Device specification in VHDL/S

The device selected as test-bench belongs to the telecom domain. Telecom devices are expected to gain a larger and larger share in the Application Specific Integrated Circuits (ASICs) domain. Their complexity is a good challenge for the ESDA tools of the next generation. For these reasons these applications provide good examples to verify the expressive power and user friendliness of VHDL/S and the associated interfaces and also for the subsequent application of the toolsets for verification and synthesis. The device is designed to monitor the run-time behavior (incoming rate) of the Asynchronous Transfer Mode (ATM) connections, acting as a filter when they do not comply to specifications. The module is part of a large board (figure 1.2) composed of several ASICs, memories, busses and a micro-processor. The unit operates as an arithmetic co-processor of a more complex ASIC devoted to data packages analysis and translation. The behavior of the device implements a modified

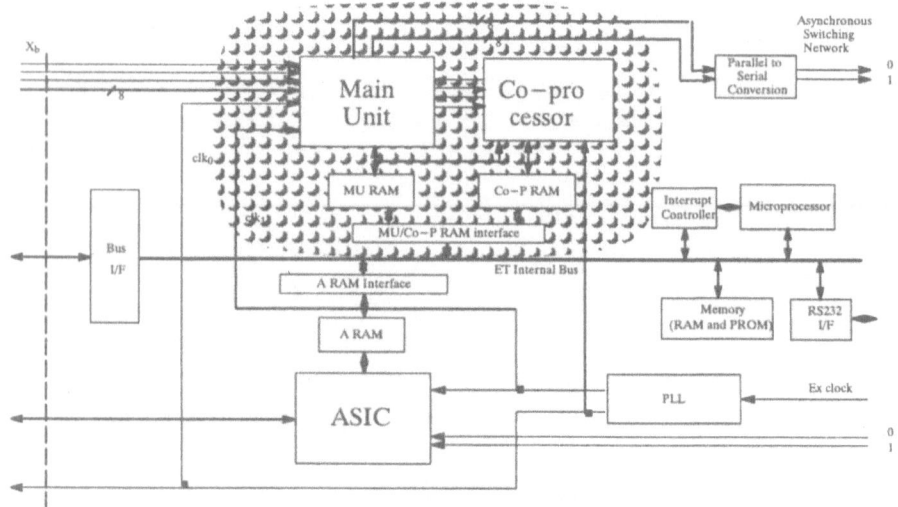

Fig. 1.2. An overview of the board where the PU is sitting.

"leaky-bucket" algorithm. The modification from the classical algorithm involves the addition of a computing part aiming to avoid data overflow. The computation of the algorithm is parameterized by values characterizing different users. Such data are stored in a register file upon the initialization phase. In the selected implementation, four classes of users are considered. During the computation of the algorithm, each user class manages a particular set of parameters.

The following sections describe how the device is specified in VHDL/S.

2.1 Design capture

The task of providing complete and coherent system specification is very complex. The FORMAT design flow introduces a set of complementary tools interfaced to the LVS data-base. The main goal of the toolset is to provide user-friendly interfaces and facilities to describe the behavior, the interconnections among the sub-components, and the properties to be satisfied by the final implementation. Modularity is applied to solve specific tasks.

The initial phase of the design process (design capture, figure 2.1) involves the application of a 'divide and conquer' strategy to decrease the behavioral complexity of the system, and to increase the content of implementation details. The result of this task is the definition of a hierarchical partitioning. The task is accomplished by identifying different functional entities inside the global specification and associating them with specific modules. Memories, control blocks, data-paths are among the most commonly used sub-parts. An abstract view of the structure of the specification is given in figure 2.1. Each module is defined as an entity, to which different architectures are associated.

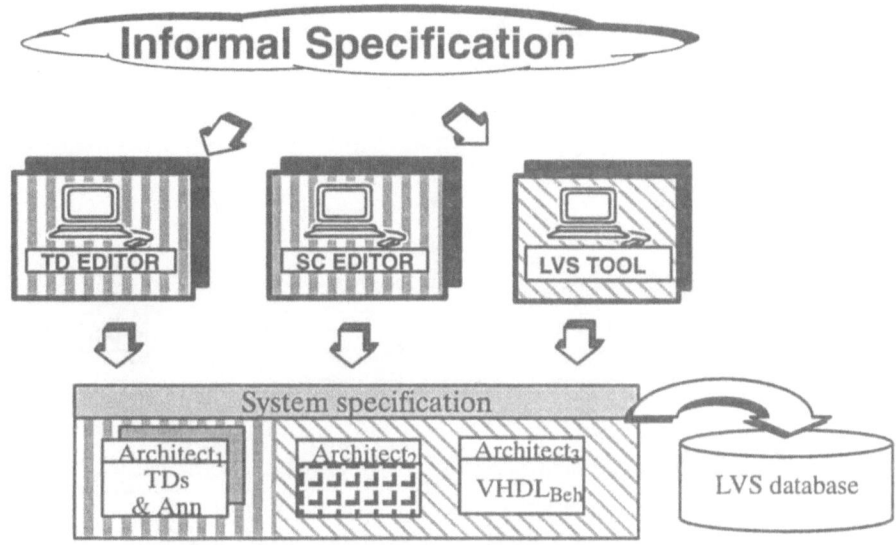

Fig. 2.1. Design capture in the FORMAT Design Flow.

In addition to the traditional structural and behavioral descriptions in VHDL, new architectures including timing diagrams (TDs) and state-based specifications (SCs) are incorporated. TD descriptions can be exhaustive when the synthesis path is considered or partial when they describe particular properties to be checked during the verification path. The 'design capture' phase is considered complete when the instantiation of the complementary architectures, i.e. filling the boxes with the specific pieces of information in figure 2.2, has been accomplished.

In figure 2.2 a rather detailed specification of the device is shown. It includes different types of memory elements (REGISTER_FILE, RAM_REG, RF_REG and the specific RAM), a control block for the computation of the algorithm and a computational block to execute it. A second control block is devoted to the management of the I/O operations between the computation module and the RAM. Simpler supporting modules, such as counters and random logic, are also included. Each of these modules is still very complex and the strategy is again applied, producing further structural decompositions into simpler elements at a later stage. In this way it is natural to include also design constraints and implementation details, like word length, data handling in records, memory elements initialization, available RAM components, testability issues and so on. The process of partitioning ends when all the blocks of all the levels are defined in forms suitable for logic synthesis or specified as netlists of components belonging to a reference CAD library.

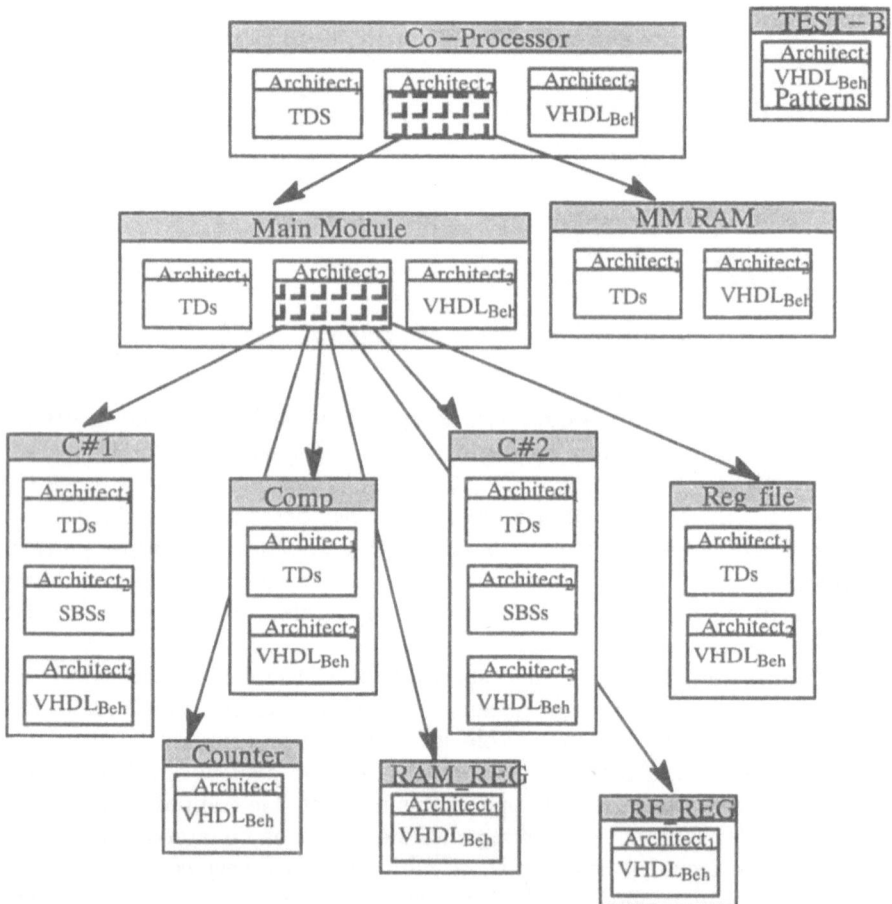

Fig. 2.2. Abstract specification structure in VHDL/S of the device under test.

Following the market and de-facto standard, the larger part of any specification is composed by plain VHDL code. LVS performs syntax checking and compiles the code into its proprietary data-base.

A block diagram of the netlist corresponding to the abstract specification is given in figure 2.3. This representation is closer to the implementation level. It highlights internal connections and support logic. At this stage all the architectural decisions have been taken and the solution provided is considered the optimal in terms of partitioning.

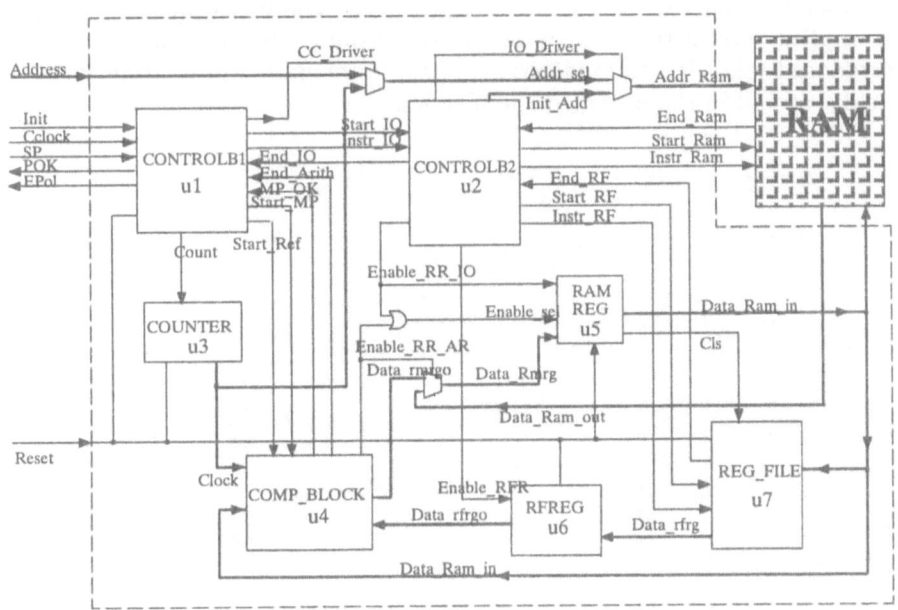

Fig. 2.3. Adopted partitioning of the system.

3. The verification flow

The toolset devoted to the application of the verification path (figure 3.1), includes:

– the Timing Diagram Editor;
– the VHDL analyzer;
– the compiler from VHDL into Binary Decision Diagrams (BDDs);
– the compiler from Timing Diagrams to Temporal Logic;
– the use of the Model Checker.

Applying the toolset involves the verification of the full compatibility and good integrability of the single tools into a unique design flow. The

Timing Diagram Editor provides the starting data for the properties. The VHDL description of the behavioral code in terms of a finite state machine for the control modules has been written, simulated and compiled into the LVS data-base. In this way the VHDL/S database is defined. An alternative description in terms of state-charts is also provided for completeness' sake. The features of the VHDL analyzer are applied by the other tools and this makes it transparent to the user.

The entire path is characterized by a high degree of user interaction: both the compiler into BDDs and the Model Checker require the insertion of some parameters, which cannot be made automatic. The entire line is meant to be applied several times, in a design loop fashion. In fact, corrections are introduced following the indications of the error path when inconsistencies are discovered in the provided specifications.

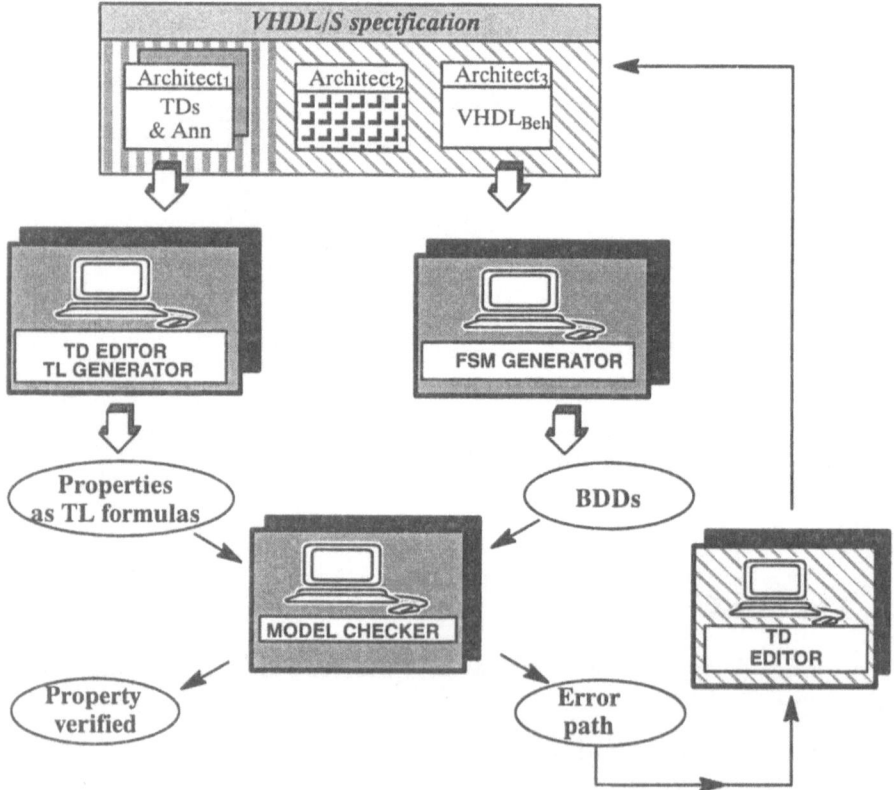

Fig. 3.1. Verification Flow for design properties through model-checking.

After the selection of a few parameters, the VHDL code is compiled automatically and the functional symbolic transition system is extracted. Average execution times for simple behaviors span from a few seconds to half a minute on a Sparc 10 with 32 Mb of RAM. Statistics related to the size of BDDs are also generated for user documentation. From these numbers the user can get an idea of the complexity of the generated BDDs (see tables 3.1 and 3.2).

Table 3.1. Parameters of the analyzed modules (delta par = 0,0).

Parameters	Main Module	Control Block #1	Control Block #2	Computation Block
States [a]	226	155	73	63
Transitions [a]	319	214	94	75
Input variables [b]	21	15	9	19
Local variables [b]	89	60	52	64
Input bits [c]	39	15	10	46
State bits [c]	255	81	69	182

[a] Control Automaton parameters.
[b] VHDL parameters.
[c] FSM parameters.

Table 3.2. Parameters characterizing the next step BDD generated for the different modules.

Parameters	Main Module	Control Block #1	Control Block #2	Computation Block
Amount [a]	8	8	7	6
Minimum [a]	52	53	14	662
Maximum [a]	745	155	75	762
Average [a]	328	110	53	711
Amount [b]	247	73	62	176
Minimum [b]	3	3	3	3
Maximum [b]	71	57	33	58
Average [b]	21	23	17	16
Amount [c]	255	81	69	182
Minimum [c]	3	3	3	3
Maximum [c]	745	155	75	762
Average [c]	31	31	20	39

[a] Next step BDDs for the Control Automaton.
[b] Next step BDDs for the VHDL State Space.
[c] Next step BDDs for the combination of the previous two cases.

3.1 Design properties

The definition of properties to be verified in the code is a more complex task. Properties consist of assumptions and commitments. Assumptions are very few in this example. They concern the activation of the algorithm, which is constrained by two edges: the Reset signal must go down (after having gone high, meaning that the reset phase is terminated) and the Clock signal must go high (meaning that a ATM call has arrived and the algorithm should be activated). On the contrary commitments are numerous. The best way to approach the task of their definition is to define some general functional classes (taxonomy) in which the properties can be grouped. For a control-dominated application, we identified six main groups:

1. required sequences of events or states;
2. prohibited conditions involving multiple signals;
3. requirements of the behavior on reset;
4. general requirements on behavior;
5. actions performed in a state of the FSM;
6. stability in basic states.

Each group includes both liveness and safety properties. This taxonomy helps the user in the definition of the properties, and provides a better framework to support the decision phase on which properties to select. Some examples for each of them is given in the following. The names associated with the properties intend to be self documenting, in terms of signals involved and interaction between them.

Group 1

A) *ReadtoWriteseq*. This property expresses the requirement for the signal Instr_I0 to assume the sequence of values READ and WRITE, and to become WRITE on the falling edge of the signal End_Arith. This is a liveness property, because it is required that the transition on Instr_I0 will occur in a finite time. This property is based on two assumptions (in addition to the standard ones): that a cell arrives and the algorithm is activated (CellClockUpLive).

B) *ReadtoWriteseqsafe*. This property expresses the fact that the Instr_I0 signal assumes the sequence of values READ and WRITE, and it becomes WRITE on the falling edge of the signal End_Arith. It differs from the previous one because no liveness arc is specified. It is a safeness property, no liveness is implied.

C) *StateR1toI0*. This property expresses the requirement that from state R1 the system evolves into state I0 (correct sequence of the states should be from R1 to I0). It's a liveness property based on the assumption (in addition to the standard ones) that the reset goes down after a finite time.

D) *StateR1toI0onReset0*. This property expresses the same requirement as
   C), but in this case the assumption on the reset is explicitly introduced
   into the same TD. In this case the property must be verified using the
   standard assumptions.

Group 2

A) *NeverEnd_ArithandInstrIOeqwrite*. This property expresses the requirement that a WRITE value on `InstrI0` must never occur when the signal
   `End_Arith` is high. This condition is expressed using a probe in which
   the boolean expression `not(End_Arith = '1' and Instr_I0 = WRITE)`
   is always set to true.

Group 3

A) *GoingtoR1onReset1*. This property expresses the fact that from any state,
   the occurrence of the reset signal will bring the system to R1. This property is rather important, even if it did not take long to verify. It is related to the presence of an asynchronous reset signal. Briefly the property
   states that, independently of the state in which the FSM is, it will jump
   to state R1 on reset high.

Group 4

A) *Cell_accepted*. This property expresses the requirement for the signal POK
   (connection arrived and accepted) to go high after `mp_ok` and `end_io`
   go high. This property is based on the assumption (in addition to the
   standard ones) that a cell arrives and the algorithm is activated (*Cell-
   Clockuplive*).

Group 5

A) *EventsfromI0*. This property expresses the requirements on the behavior
   specified in the corresponding FSM when the system is in state I0 and
   evolves to state I1. Only the standard assumptions are necessary. Similar
   services are requested for the other states of the FSM.

Group 6

A) *GoingtoRR1onInitdown*. This property expresses the requirement for the
   system to go back to fundamental state RR1 when the signal `Init` goes
   down. Only the standard assumptions are necessary.

The translation of assumptions and commitments described through Timing Diagrams into Temporal Logic Formula is automatic. An example of the
resulting code for the assumption CellClockuplive follows:

```
'CellClockuplive':=
        let( [ sXX := ( true ) ] ,
        let( [
          sX0 := until((((vhdl('Cell_Clock = '0''))),
            (
            ((vhdl('Cell_Clock = '1''')) /\ sXX) \/
            (((((vhdl('Cell_Clock = '0''')) \/
              (vhdl('Cell_Clock = '1'' \/
                  (vhdl('false')))) /\
              ((( ~(vhdl('Cell_Clock = '0''')) \/
                  ~(vhdl('Cell_Clock = '1'' \/
                  (vhdl('false'))))
            ))) ],
          g(((vhdl('true')) /\
            (vhdl('Cell_Clock = '0''')))  ==> sX0 )
          )
        ).
```

It is evident that timing diagrams are more user friendly than the representation of the logic formula. This is the main advantage of the current approach. A set of properties has been verified and the obtained results are reported in the following table.

Table 3.3. Model checking times for properties evaluation on Control Block #1.

Property	Assumptions	Result	Execution time [a] minutes
ReadToWriteSeq	CellClockUpLive	FALSE	12
ReadToWriteSeqWithStartIO	CellClockUpLive	FALSE	71
ReadToWriteSeqSafe	-	FALSE	71
StateR1ToI0	ResetDownLive	TRUE	13
StateR1ToI0OnReset0	-	TRUE	1
NeverEndArithAndInstrIOEqWrite	-	FALSE	39
NeverCountAndInstrIOEqWrite	-	TRUE	1
NeverStart_refAndStart_mpEq1	-	TRUE	2
GoingToR1OnReset1	-	TRUE	8
End_pollFollowsInit	-	FALSE	14
CellAcceptedReadToWriteSeq	CellClockUpLive	FALSE	106
CellRejected	CellClockUpLive	FALSE	74
EventsfromI0	ResetDownLive	FALSE	85
StayingRR1UntilCellClockUp	-	FALSE	29
GoingToRR1OnInitDown	-	FALSE	21

[a] Timing measured on a Sparc 10.

Two points are worth considering in table 3.3. First, the execution times are quite reasonable and acceptable in most cases. Second, the percentage of properties which result false, is very high. It is expected from a real design that many errors are introduced in the specification and in the implementation. Moreover, the interesting cases are those in which errors are made. Even so the number of failures is higher than expected. A closer analysis of these cases must be accomplished to really understand how to manage correctly the task of properties definition.

NeverEnd_ArithandInstrIOeqwrite has been proved FALSE. A counter-example has been generated by the system in which the signal End_Arith switches to '1' and Instr_IO switches to WRITE. The sequence involves 142 steps from the initial state to the state that contradicts the commitment. This result depends on the fact that the designer imposed a relationship between an input signal and an output signal. This is not correct because, while the output signals are defined by the behavior under test, the input signals are allowed to cover exhaustively the range of values allowed by their type definition. From this example the following rule can be assessed: it is good practice to state a relationship between output signals only, and to impose assumptions on the values of the input signals.

EventsfromIO has been proved FALSE. The execution time is large because the timing diagram is rather complex. From this example the following rule can be assessed: it is good practice to split a complex property into several simpler ones (in this case three) and evaluate them separately. A counter-example has been generated by the system in which the signal Start_IO switches to '1' without an event on the signal Init. In this case the sequence involves 27 steps from the initial state to the state that contradicts the commitment. Anyway, this result doesn't impose a modification of the specification (VHDL code). In fact, the signal Start_IO can switch to '1' also in states different from the considered Start_IO and so independently from signal Init. So, the property can be verified as a sufficient condition, but not as a necessary one. From this example another design rule can be assessed: it is good practice to state relationships holding in general, otherwise the property will be proved false.

ReadtoWriteseqsafe has been proved FALSE. A counter-example has been generated by the system in which the signal End_Arith switches to '0' without Instr_IO switching to WRITE. This happens when Instr_IO switches from INITT to READ. Also in this case the property has been stated in a too restricted fashion. In this case the sequence of the counter-example involves 106 steps from the initial state to the state that contradicts the commitment.

The analysis of these test cases introduces the following comments. Execution times are not too large and in average comparable with simulation times for the same models. The advantage of the approach lies in the automatic definition of the debugging sequence. Properties to be verified must be selected with care. Only the most meaningful and general should be applied. Execution times strongly depend on the type of properties, so these should be kept as simple as possible. For the same property, the execution time depends on the size of the model, i.e. the number and range of IO ports and the number of the internal states of the finite state machine. The model of the previous example is manageable because all the IO ports are bits.

Some of the properties can be compared with the simulation of the model obtained using Mentor Graphics QuicksimII. Observing the simulation results, the local relationships between the various signals are clearly identified. On the contrary, properties express global relationships, i.e. a relationships which are proved correct over the whole behavior of the model. Another difference from simulation, lies in the fact that the simulation results are strongly dependent on the correct sequence of the input signals given by the designers but are not exhaustive. As a consequence it is not possible to guarantee that an unexpected but possible sequence of events may generate a misbehavior. On the contrary, when a property has been proved TRUE by the model checking technique, it is so for all the possible sequences of input events.

3.2 Users' feedback

Experiments conducted on other modules of the application have shown similar results to the ones presented for the case of the control module. Some more general comments are derived from the more extensive use of the technique. These points have a general validity and will be considered in the following.

Local variables and states are almost always present in the behavioral code representing the model to be verified. Properties are very often dependent on these internal signals (local variables) and states. In order to verify properties addressing this kind of signals, they must be explicitly defined in the VHDL entity of the model. Practically they must be declared as output ports, in order to be observable. This implies that the VHDL code, describing the specification of the device, must be changed in order to accommodate this feature.

For example some modifications on the VHDL description of the Control Block #1 has been performed:

```
ENTITY Controlblock#1 IS
  PORT (
  Reset : IN bit ;
  Init : IN bit ;
  Cell_Clock : IN bit ;
  End_IO : IN bit ;
  :
  :
  :
  state_probe : OUT CCSTATE -- This signal has been added
                            -- to make the state visible
  ) ;  END Controlblock#1 ;
```

```
ARCHITECTURE arch of Controlblock#1 is
BEGIN
PROCESS (Reset, Init, Cell_Clock, End_IO, End_Arith, SP_Val)
  VARIABLE state : CCSTATE; -- local variable for the state

  BEGIN
  :
  :
  CASE state IS
  :
    WHEN R1 =>
      IF (reset = '0' )  AND (Reset'EVENT) THEN
        Start_IO <= '0' ;
        state := IO ;
        state_probe <= state; -- this line must be added
                              -- to make visible the
                              -- value of the state
      END IF;
  :
```

As one can see, the changes to the code are not dramatic. Anyway the designers pointed out that inserting them prior to the verification phase, and deleting them afterwards implies a manipulation of the specification which is not guaranteed to be error free.

The execution times, quite acceptable for the control based module, increase considerably when the computation module is involved, or when the top entity definition is verified. This observation proves that the model checking technique is suitable for control-dominated applications, but has limitations when the data path is involved. In fact, all the functions performed in the data path (arithmetic operations including multiplication) have to cope with wide range of data. The top level architecture presents many local variables with wide range of data. In this situation the generation of the BDD representation is unmanageable, because of sizing problem. So, the module cannot be verified, unless the range of the data is artificially reduced. Only in this case one can verify many properties on the behavior, because of the smaller range of involved data. Designers criticized this step for two reasons: first, also in this case one has to manually modify the specification twice, so increasing the possibility of making errors; second, the specification with decreased values of the range is similar to the initial one, but not exactly the same. So, one looses the soundness claimed by the proof. Of course, for control-dominated applications this is not the case. Unluckily in the telecom domain, almost all the applications involve data path, unless one arbitrarily isolates the control modules alone, as it has been done in the partitioning phase described in the previous section.

A very positive comment involved the information provided by the debugger of the model checker. In fact, the sequence of events can be so long that the designers admitted that it would have been almost impossible for them to conceive such a sequence to identify the error. Moreover, the debugger is extremely user friendly because the simulation sequence is visualized into the TD Editor. This also improves the documentation phase of the design.

4. The synthesis flow

This chapter describes the application of the toolset following the VHDL synthesis flow (figure 4.1), that includes:

- the Timing Diagram Editor;
- the compiler from Timing Diagrams into LOTOS;
- the compiler from LOTOS into VHDL;
- the Structurizer.

Testing the whole line involves also the verification of the full compatibility and good integrability of these tools into a unique toolset. The Timing Diagrams describing the protocol to be synthesized represent the user defined input to the toolset. The VHDL code representing the implementation of the protocol is the final output. The comparison between the automatically generated representation with the hand-coded one by the designer is useful only on a very limited basis. Commercial tools for simulation and logic synthesis may follow this path, using the generated VHDL code as input.

The invocation of the toolset is controlled by a shell script, provided that one is interested in the entire design flow, i.e. from the definition of the timing diagrams down to the generated VHDL code.

The availability of the Structurizer has been introduced to allow a hierarchical partitioning of the specification, and the isolation of simpler modules to be used in the synthesis flow.

4.1 From timing diagrams to VHDL

To clarify the designer activity in this design flow, we consider as example the module Control Block #1, which has been used for the same purpose in the previous section. This module performs pure control, and involves only signals of type bit with the exception of Instr_IO that is an enumerative type with three possible values (bitvector of range 2). The starting point for this path is the definition of the functionality in terms of the protocols with the other modules belonging to the same partitioning level and with the environment. Abstracting from the FSM representation, one can see that its functionality is rather complex and includes four different phases and an

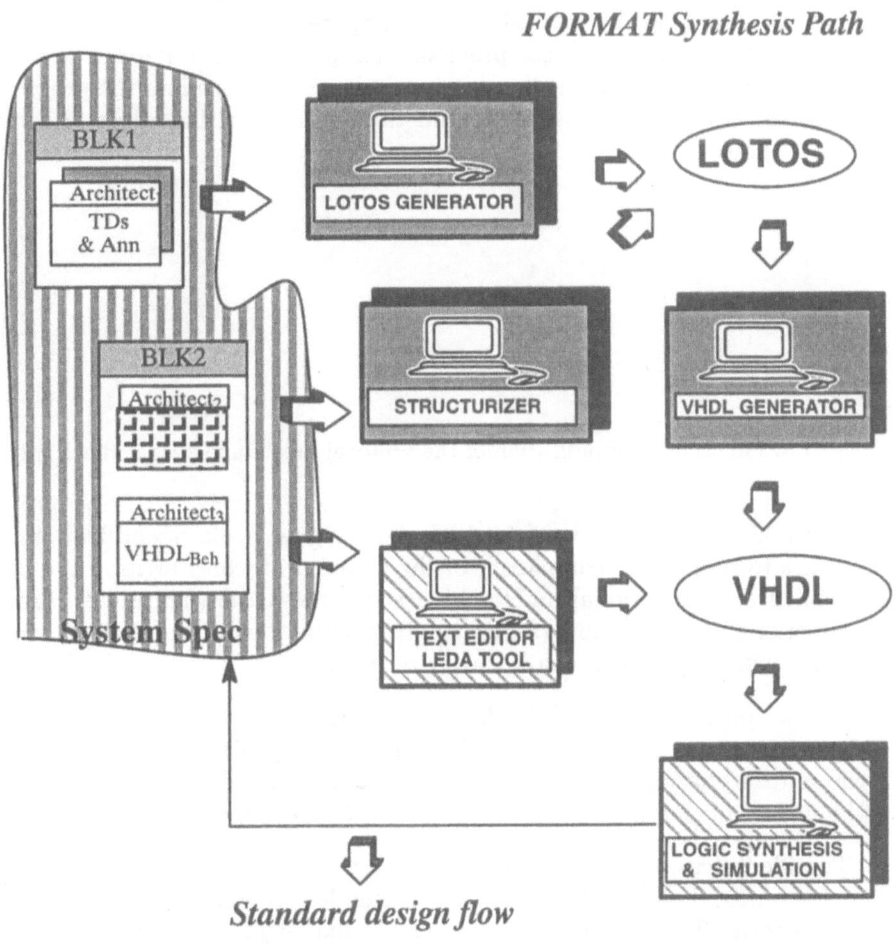

FORMAT Synthesis Path

Fig. 4.1. Synthesis Flow: automatic generation of VHDL.

1. U1, *Control_Block #1*: generates control signals for the computation of the algorithm, acting as an interface between the environment and the computational block. Moreover it communicates with the second control block, managing the data exchange between with the RAM and the register file.

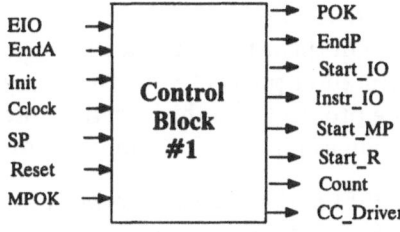

Fig. 4.2. Entity definition.

asynchronous signal (reset). The interface and the behavior of the module are expressed graphically and informally in figure 4.2.

The VHDL code used in the previous example involves a limited number of states. The state in which the machine finds itself determines the progress towards the subsequent state in conjunction with the rising edges of some control signals.

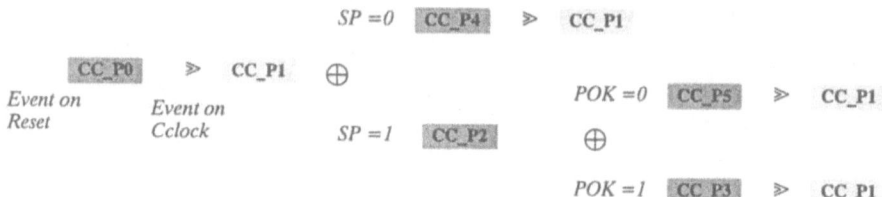

Fig. 4.3. Functional simplification of the protocol involving Control Block #1.

The main problem to be solved by the designer is the identification of strategies to reduce the complexity of the global protocol. Partitionings can be applied on a functional and/or on a structural basis (figure 4.3). From the functional point of view (following strictly the previous approach), four different operating phases can be easily recognized:

– the reset phase (controlled by the **reset** signal);
– the initialization phase (controlled by the **init** signal);
– the refresh phase (controlled by the **cell_clock** signal);
– the make-policing phase (controlled by the **SP_val** signal).

The identification of these phases allows the simplification of the global complex protocol partitioning into a set of simpler protocols based on a functional criteria. The sub-protocols are connected together by the operators of sequentiality ≫ and alternative ⊕ provided in the specification language implemented in the TDE. The global 'cyclical' property is represented by the fact that all the final protocols are sequentially connected to CC_P1. A special role is played in the TDs by the asynchronous signal **reset**, which starts the first protocol.

On the other hand, a simplification of the protocol is also possible from a structural point of view (figure 4.4). In this case the partitioning criteria of the protocol into three distinct protocols is based on the identification of the modules directly and uniquely involved in the sub-protocol:

– PC1 is the protocol between the Control Block #1 and the environment;
– PC2 is the protocol between the Control Block #1 and the Computation module;
– PC3 is the protocol between the Control Block #1 and the other control module.

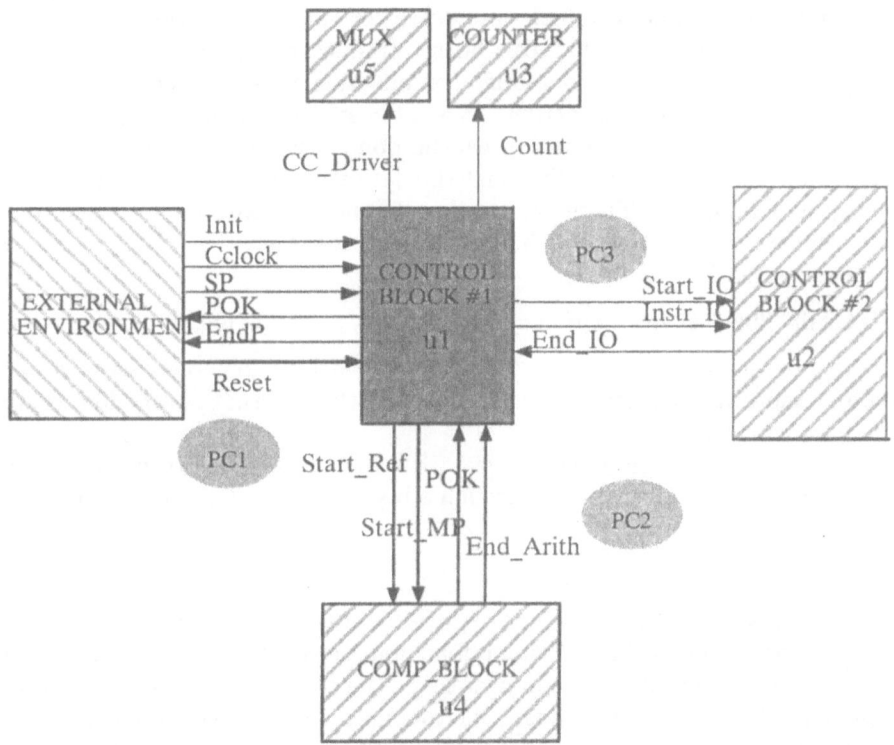

Fig. 4.4. Structural simplification of the protocol involving Control Block #1.

This is clearly an over-simplification, since interactions exist between signals belonging to the different structural sub-protocols. Anyway, this is a convenient starting point for the present analysis. The functional and structural partitionings are not mutually exclusive, but can be combined to further reduce the complexity of the representation.

Timing Diagrams have been defined to describe the various protocols of the Control Block #1.

One particular aspect of TD is worth commenting: data annotation of some signals. Data annotation are related to edges of a waveform in a timing diagram and they may be used to define data constraints on edges. Two types of data annotation are available: predicates or value declaration. Predicates restrict the data values that can be received with the action denoted by an edge. Value declarations specify computation rules for the data values managed during an output actions. When the synthesis is performed without the Structurizer, data annotation can be done either by specifying a single constant value, either by stating that the data is valid, or using the so called anonymous functions. These are merely references to external functions that are assumed to be correctly defined in an external file.

The syntax is:

`(ANONYMOUS (type) functname (p1, ..., pn) LIBREF libname)`

where *functname* is the name of the referenced function, *type* is the result type of the function, *libname* is the name of the external library file where the function is defined.

When the synthesis is concerned with the use of the Structurizer, the data annotation is given either through a boolean expression either using the following syntax:

`[ v := expression ; ]`

where *expression* is a structurized expression of the same type as variable v.

The application of GraphEd, a public domain tool for graphical display of transitional graphs, also helps in decreasing the complexity of the representation generated by the TDs. In fact the tool graphically depicts the states and the transitions generated by constraining arcs in the TD. A simplification in the representation can be obtained by increasing the number of constraints in the TD. The designer usually does not include such constraints because they are taken for granted. In this way, it is easy to identify these cases and to correct the representation accordingly. Using the TDE and GraphEd in a sort of design loop, before generating the VHDL code, gave reductions of 60% or more on the initial representation, so considerably decreasing the complexity of the generated VHDL code.

The following step towards the synthesis is the translation of the timing diagrams into T-LOTOS, producing the related FSM. This phase has been accomplished for the Control Block #1, and a report on the compilation statistics has been produced. That report says that only strong constraints exist (252), and the number of alternative composition processes is 686. The total number of generated T-LOTOS processes is 1037. Initially the number of generated states for the FSM is 174, but after the optimization phase, it is reduced to 72.

The generation of the VHDL code for both simulation and synthesis is derived from the representations of the protocols of the module. The VHDL behavioral architectures representing the protocols *CC_P0-5* are considered separately in order to allow an easier analysis of the generated code.

The protocol *CC_P0* represents the reset phase and the initialization phase that always follows it. The first part of this protocol involves all the output signals of PC1,2,3 and the Init and Reset signals of PC1. The second part of the protocol represents the initialization phase, and involves a section of PC3 combined with a section of PC1, that is the signals Init and End_Pol. The meaning of *CC_P1* in words is the following: "the Init signal triggers the activation of PC3 setting Instr_I0 = INITT (value = 01) and End_Pol to HIGH; after PC3 is terminated, End_Pol goes again to LOW". The two sub-protocols are combined together using the operator ≫ of sequentiality between protocols (this level of granularity is not visible in figure 4.3).

The generated VHDL code has the following characteristics:

- The synchronization code is placed in two library components called Gate_Val and Gate_Var. This leads to a much cleaner code, as the user has to deal only with the control of these components instead of dealing with the whole synchronizations;
- The number of states is large due to the LOTOS semantics applied in the transformations not visible to the users. This number cannot be put in direct comparison with the number of states of the corresponding VHDL specification;
- It is possible to have an higher degree of parallelism, as several synchronization components can be activated in parallel (even if only one of them is allowed to successfully commit the synchronization);
- The data types are defined in the ieee package std_ulogic_1164;
- Configurations and test shells are produced automatically, and they contain the special components converting from the ports present in the entity definition and the number of ports required by the LOTOS internal process;
- The number of internal variables is large;
- The arrangement of components and functions in separate libraries (H_IEEE and HARPO), also leads to a cleaner code.

4.2 Using the structurizer

The Structurizer is the tool organizer for the interactive synthesis of control-dominated applications in the synthesis path of the FORMAT project. It supports the designer with a graphical interface that consists of an organizer menu and the DIALOG interface of AHL. Structurizing is a refinement process where the designer tries to find an implementation for his specification by selecting modules from a library, complete the specification and connect them and complete them among each other. Each design step is checked by system with respect to the completeness of the current implementation and the validity of the new added modules. The final result is a structural VHDL netlist.

Using the Structurizer implies following a bottom-up approach. A library is assumed to consist of some predefined modules to be selected step by step by the user to build up the implementation for the specification. These modules can be, and in our test-case are, Timing Diagrams.

Again, the Policing Unit has been used to test the tool. The device has been partitioned and the sub-blocks have been used as modules of the library of the Structurizer. The adopted partitioning is the one previously described in section 2.1 of this chapter. Also in this case, the block RAM has been excluded. The dashed polygon contains the main subdivision. You may recognize the two control blocks (Control Block #1 and Control Block #2), a data path, a counter and two registers.

First, the top level of the device is considered. A number of timing diagrams has been defined to describe the protocols of the Policing Unit.

The following step towards the synthesis is the translation of the timing diagrams into T-LOTOS, producing the related FSM. This phase has been accomplished for the Policing Unit , and a report on the compilation statistics has been produced. That report says that only strong constraints exist (211), and the number of alternative composition processes is 156. The total number of generated T-LOTOS processes is 392. Initially the number of generated states for the FSM is 123, but after the optimization phase, it is reduced to 78.

Figure 4.5 shows the graph created by the GraphED tool for the Policing Unit. You can note that the init phase and the normal phase appear in two branches and are considered as two separate processes.

Once the top level has been analyzed, the second level is taken into consideration, and in particular the two control blocks are studied. The Control Block #1 has been described in detail in the previous section.

Similarly, the Control Block #2 has been described. Compared with the Control Block #1, its functionality is less complex.

Figure 4.6 shows one of the five Timing Diagrams that have been produced to describe the Control Block #2.

Note that the initial assertions of all the signals are set to "Unspecified" or True. In fact, initial assertions are ignored, so any value can be set to the signal.

Figure 4.6 shows the existence of an arc connecting an edge at the beginning of the protocol and an edge at the end of it. For instance, the Int_state switching edge is connected to the Start_IO falling edge. Its meaning is

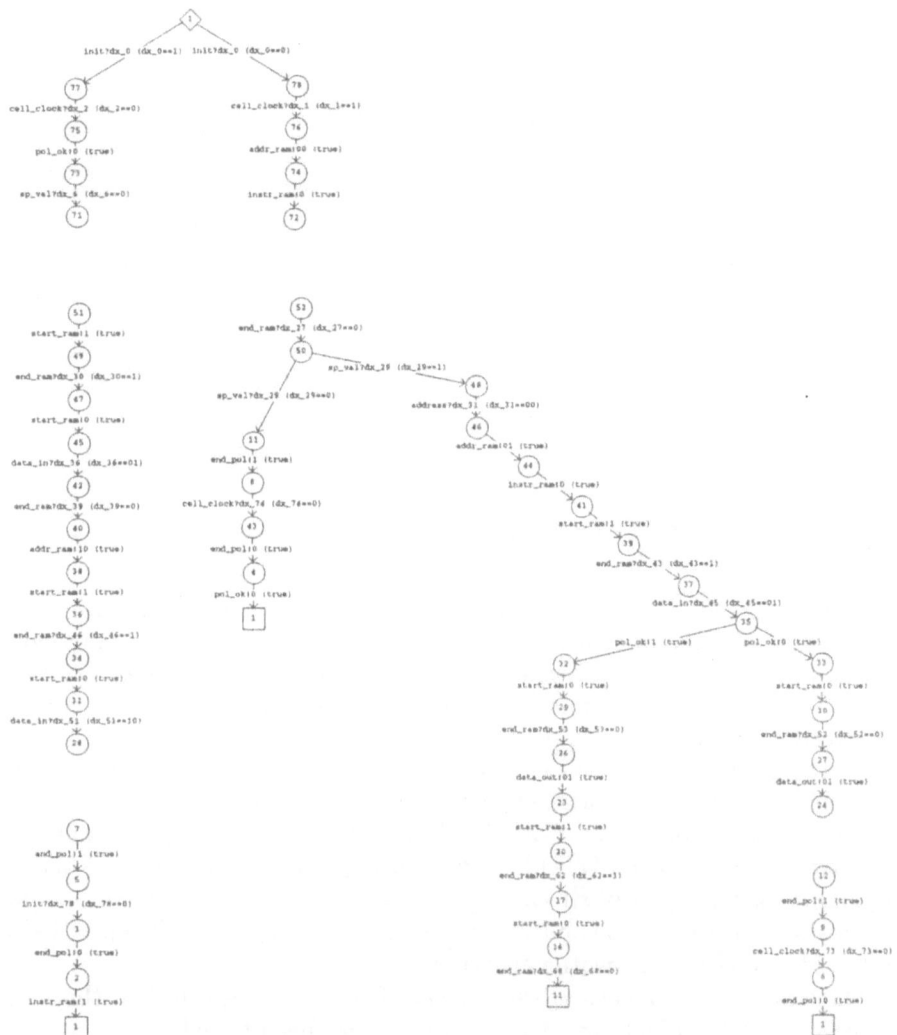

Fig. 4.5. Graph generated with GraphED for the PU

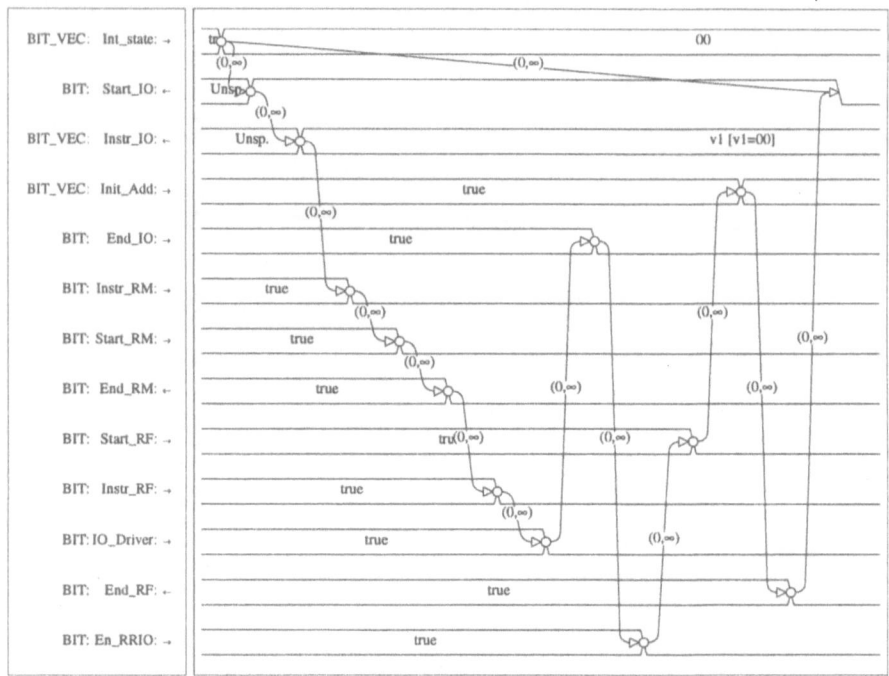

Fig. 4.6. TD for one protocol of the Control Block #2

twofold: first, the Start_IO can fall only after the Int_state switches, and second, the Int_state cannot switch again before the end of the protocol, that is the Int_state is prevented to switch continuously. This arc, and in general arcs of this kind connecting edges at the beginning and at the end of the protocol, prevent the FSM to have a very large number of states. Obviously, the only case in which it is not necessary to set this arc is when the protocol starts and ends on an edge on the same signal.

The specification of the Control Block #2 through timing diagrams is then translated into T-LOTOS. The report on the compilation statistics highlighted the number of strong constraints (79), the number of alternative composition processes (99) and the number of generated T-LOTOS processes (189). The generated transitional system has 50 states.

Once all the sub-blocks of the Policing Unit have been defined through the related timing diagrams, the Structurizer has been tested.

The use of this new tool, brings up the following observations. From the user's point of view, the way of connecting the various blocks through their pins is not straightforward. Problems can rise either in user's mistakes in selecting the various pins, or in the high number of pins of a block. This problem can be overcome either by using a VHDL configuration file, either by opening textual windows in which it is possible to connect pins through text using a VHDL syntax.

One very interesting feature of the Structurizer is the Error path, which allows the identification of mismatches among high-level descriptions and corresponding low-level ones on the signals behavior. In the Policing Unit, one error has been detected that has not been highlighted in the simulation phase.

A final comment: the Structurizer can be used only to verify the control path of a device. Concerning the data path, they are assumed to be valid, without verifying the computation that produced them.

5. Example of FORMAT tools encapsulation into a framework

An example of the encapsulation of the Format tool set has been performed in Italtel. The Format Tools were integrated into ITALTEL proprietary ASIC design flow, called ICDE (Integrated Circuit Design Environment), that is based on Mentor Graphics Falcon Framework environment.

The encapsulation was performed into the Falcon Framework registering a new icon (Format) and developing the dialog boxes (figure 5.1).

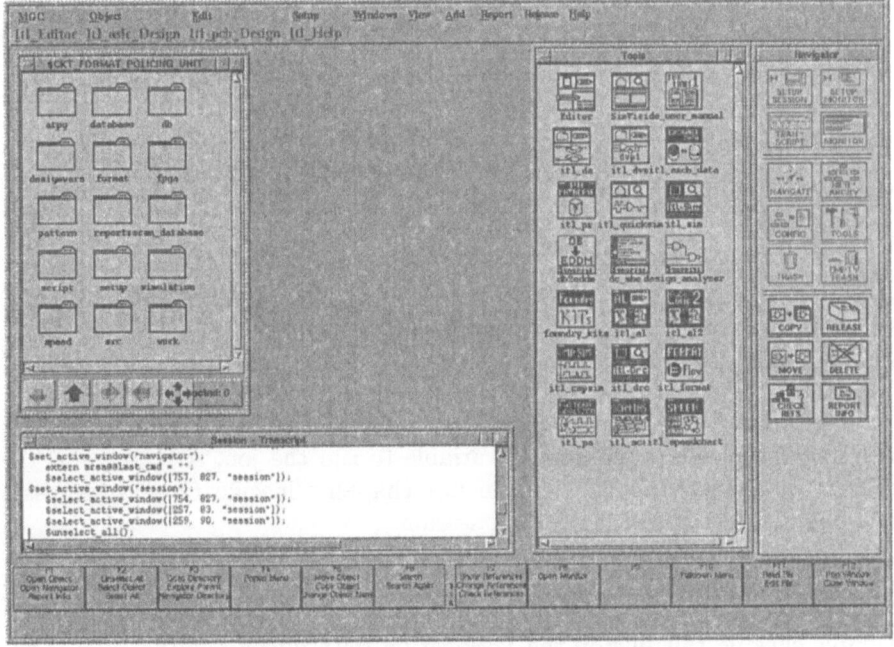

Fig. 5.1. Itl_dmgr starts showing these windows

Basically, to the Format icon is connected one dialog box that let the user to choose which path to follow. The dialog boxes drive the user to run the Format Tools on the proper design database with the user selected options.

Working with ICDE, the designer can start Format Synthesis/Verification Paths double clicking on the FORMAT icon. This action opens the dialog box "FORMAT TOOLS SETUP" (figure 5.2) in which is already visible the default project previously selected and the three possible selections:

- Timing Diagram Editor (starts the TDE directly)
- Verification Path (opens a new dialog box to run the steps of the formal verification)
- Synthesis Path (opens a new dialog box to run the steps of the formal synthesis)

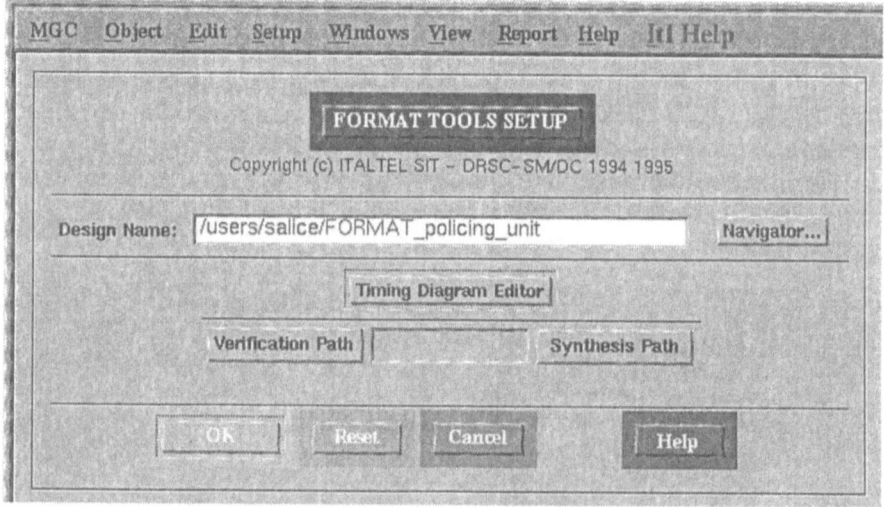

Fig. 5.2. Format Tools starting dialog box

Timing Diagram Editor

Double clicking this button the TDE starts directly opening a new shell, defining the proper environment variable to run the job. At this point the editing windows of the TDE appear (see chapter "Specification Languages") and the designer starts the editing session.

Verification Path

Double clicking this button the Verification Path dialog box (figure 5.3) appears and the designer can choose the action to do among the following:

- Compile VHDL or SC code of the circuit/block into LEDA database
- Create the FSM from Leda description of the circuit/block
- Compile assertions (timing diagrams) into LEDA database
- Convert Leda assertions into temporal logic
- Submit to the Model Checker the defined assertion in order to verify if they are true or false
- View the false assertion (through the TDE)

These actions can be selected together or one by one, depending on the task to be performed by the designer.

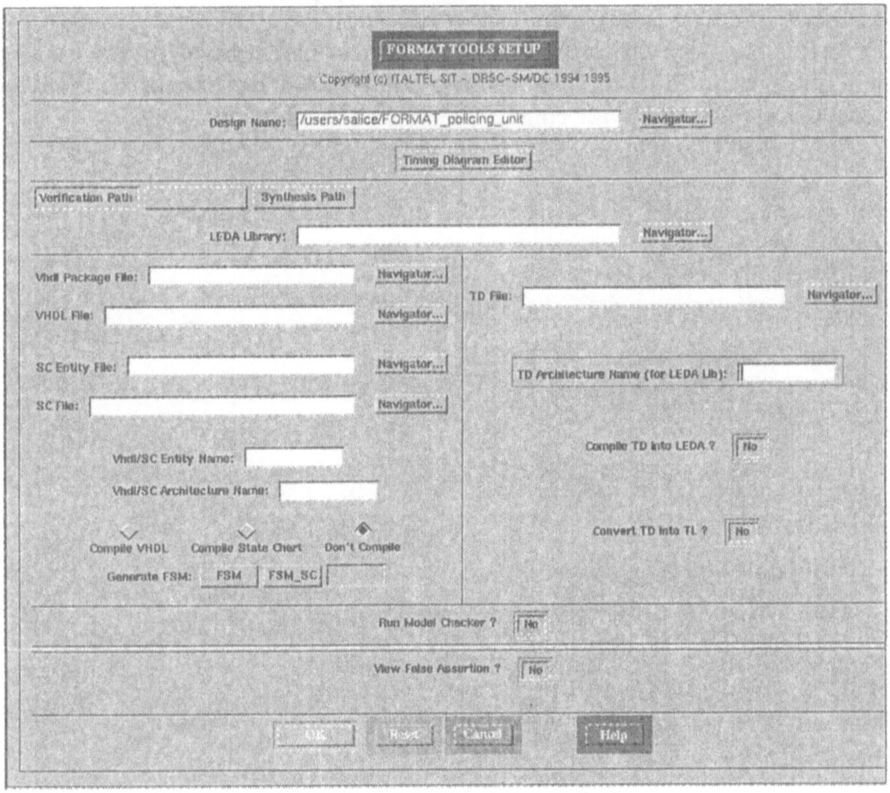

Fig. 5.3. Verification path dialog box

Synthesis Path

Double clicking this button the Synthesis Path dialog box appears and the designer can select the formal synthesis steps, like he did for the formal verification through, the Verification Path dialog box.

6. Conclusion

The verification methodology has been applied to a set of industrial bench-marks. From the designer point of view, the methodology has been evaluated positively. In fact, it allows the solution of several problems in the first phase of the design flow. Furthermore, the set of tools provides a lot of information useful (e.g. debugging sequence) during the verification flow. For the integration of the methodology in an industrial environment a team of experts in design verification is necessary. In fact, the average knowledge of the designers is not sufficient for the analyzed methodology.

The toolset evaluated is yet in a preliminary phase with the exclusion of the model checker. In fact, the execution times are quite high. In any case, the execution times are acceptable and comparable with the corresponding simulation times. Finally, the analysis of the test-benches has shown that the methodology is suitable for control-dominated applications.

Siemens Industrial Experience

Ronald Herrmann, Jörg Bormann, Thomas Filkorn, Jörg Lohse, and Hans-Albert Schneider

Siemens AG, Germany

This chapter presents a summary of the application results obtained by using automatic verification tools in practice. Therefore a summary of the design and verification methodology and a walk through several different applications, which have been treated with formal verifications tools at several different sites of the Siemens AG, is given. For each application we describe the basic functionality and how formal verification technique was used during the design process.

The use of formal verification allows early and fast detection of logical errors during the design process. Formal verification enables us to detect errors which cannot be found easily by standard simulation. The main advantage is that we can now verify not only static behavior but also the dynamic behavior, e.g., the absence of deadlocks. Since we are dealing with reactive systems, the main task is to verify that the system reacts as expected on arbitrary input sequences. Input stimuli can be restricted to their expected behavior. This kind of verification is referred to as Model Checking.

Using formal verification helps to reduce simulation time and reduces the risks of late design or reengeneering changes. This is very important to achieve faster time-to-market goals and to manage reengineering changes without risks.

1. Design flow and verification methodology

In practice we find two different verifications tasks which are sub-summarized by horizontal or design verification and vertical verification or implementation verification.

- During the early design phases the designer has to prove whether his design fulfills a given specification, i.e., the designer has to check whether his VHDL implementation guarantees the specified properties.
- When the design process has reached a stage in which a consistent VHDL implementation is available for simulation, the design is refined and optimized. In order to retain the specified and proven properties it is necessary to use a tool to check the equivalence between the original design and the the modified (more optimized) design.

Formal verification is applicable if there is a precise and clear semantics for its input languages and if the tools are able to cope with a realistic amount of complexity. Today it is not possible to cope with full designs without any user interaction, but components of full designs are in the range where automatic verification tools are applicable.

In order to integrate formal verification tools into the design process, they must be

- nearly full automatic,
- able to handle at least the leaf components of a complex design without forcing the designer to perform major changes in order to reduce the complexity.

Today most design processes at Siemens are based on synthesis. VHDL code is used as the input of synthesis. The designs are using standard VHDL libraries and packages, predefined by vendors or by design projects. Therefore the formal verification tools must be able to handle these libraries.

The model checker is used to automatically check systems described in VHDL or VHDL/S state charts against properties expressed as temporal logic formulae. The temporal logic formulae are either generated from timing diagram specifications or specified directly by the user. The last option seems to be uncomfortable, but the experiences show that very often a small set of standard temporal formulae can be reused by just changing the atomic conditions about the signals.

In the FORMAT framework *Finite State Machines* (FSMs for short) are used to represent behavioral descriptions. VHDL components are translated by the front-end tools into this FSM representation. The most remarkable aspect about the FSM format is the use of BDDs (binary decision diagrams (R. E. Bryant 1986)) to represent sets, relations and functions. This is the basic data structure used in FORMAT to tackle the well known *state explosion problem*.

The complexity of BDD-based representations is very sensitive to the underlying variable order. Recently automatic techniques for improving the size of BDD-representations by *reordering of variables* were published (R. Rudell 1993), (E. Felt et al. 1993). The integration and further development of these important algorithms into the BDD-package underlying the FORMAT verification tools has opened the way to integrate several optimizations into the verification tools.

It is very important that the translation step from VHDL code to FSMs is manageable. The size of the resultant FSM gives a hint on the complexity of the following verification steps. Unfortunately, there is no way to predict the complexity of verification runs. Theoretical results about upper bounds are so bad, that even the verification of very small designs cannot be guaranteed. So verification tools, like other CAD tools, have to use several heuristics to cope with the complexity and the actual complexity is far less than the theoretical upper bounds. The success of a verification step strongly depends on the applicability of these heuristics.

Model Checking has one important aspect, which is often pointed out to be a drawback, but which is not in our experience: The writing of precise specifications using timing diagrams or temporal logic. The designer has an intuition of circuit properties and in many cases a lengthy design documentation manual containing the design specification. It is an essential and typically not easy task to specify assumptions and commitments for formal verification based on the existing design documentation. We recommend to write STD and TL specifications first and to integrate them into the design documentation in such a way, that they can be used directly for verification.

From our point of view, formal verification is more general than simulation and can be used in addition to simulation. Today it cannot replace simulation, because the tools are yet not powerful enough to handle full designs.

2. Application reports

In the following subsections we will provide an overview about some selected case studies in which formal verification based on VHDL descriptions and model checking has been applied. Some of these case studies have been performed with the support from our group at central research and development labs. Others have been done by the designers themself.

2.1 Verification of a token ring controller

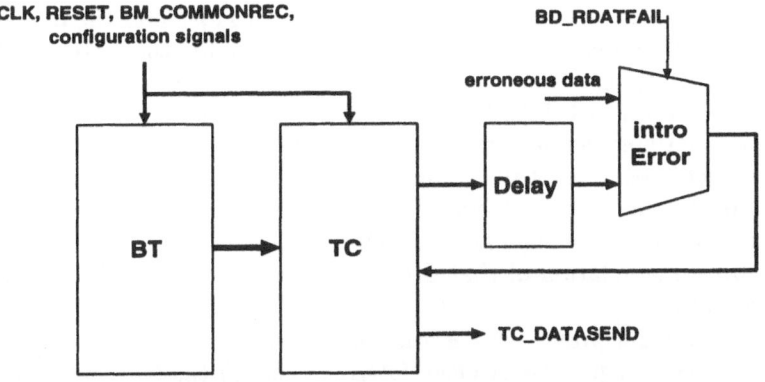

Fig. 2.1. Minimal configuration of a bus system with TC

The Token Ring Controller has been developed as a part of a base station for a cellular mobile communication network in GSM standard. The design of the base station is modular. It can be configured with several different kinds and numbers of sub-boards. These sub-boards interchange data packages via a bus system. These data packages (referred to as bursts) can be divided into two subclasses:

1. timing-oriented bursts for data transmission of user data,
2. event-driven bursts for intercommunication between different boards (COMMON bursts).

The bus access is organized by a token ring protocol. To allow these different data transmission schemes on one bus, bursts are combined into periodic frames. A single frame needs 7500 bus cycles. The bus protocol is realized through a Bus Access Circuit (BAC) which is the interface between bus and micro processor. The token ring protocol is automatically configured in the start up phase and reconfigured in inconsistent situations. The timing for a TC is provided by one timing generator (BT) for each TC. The BTs are globally synchronized.

The designers of the TC had to cope with problems that arise from the complexity of the distributed control. Moreover the BAC unit delays transmission and reception of data by several clock cycles. This additionally increases the logical complexity. Therefore, the validation by simulation took three times more effort than the development of the blocks.

Starting from the existing VHDL description used as input to synthesis, we had to examine a minimal configuration where the bus is used by only one client (see figure 2.1). The corresponding model consists of one TC, one BT, an abstraction of the bus interface unit in the form of a delay block, and a multiplexor to model bus errors. This configuration was considered to be sufficient, because the important functionality can be verified with it. It was also used during extensive simulation.

After translating the given VHDL code into a FSM description, a computation of the set of reachable states was performed to optimize the model checking process by determining a good variable order for the BDDs and reducing the search space. This reachability analysis took 4 days on a SUN-SPARC 10 workstation with 128 MByte of main memory, but after this effort important properties could be verified very quickly. We checked properties about the correct execution of the configuration procedure and token passing within 1 to 2 hours. 4 days are a lot of time but the verification results correspond to an exhaustive simulation which is impossible in practice. Even for the incomplete simulation of that design, several weeks have been used by the design group.

The most important properties describe the bus access: If data should be send to the bus (i.e., signal BM_COMMONREC active) the TC will allow the bus access (i.e., signal TC_DATASEND active), provided that there is a point of time after which no more bus errors occur. Figure 2.2 shows the corresponding timing diagram. The verification of this property needed 4.5 hours, but this short property examines the following operations:

– Detection that no token is present,
– Configuration procedure,
– Detection, that no partner TC is in the bus system,
– Creation of the token,

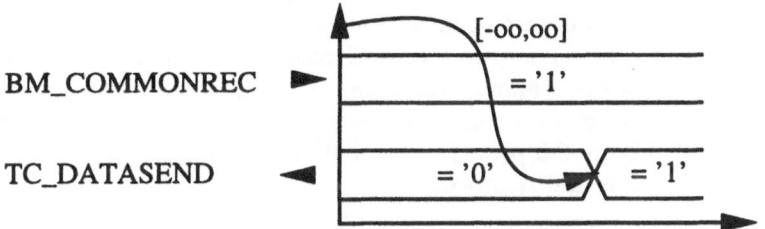

Fig. 2.2. Commitment: TC will grant bus access

– Passing to the token,

with the guarantee, that bus errors occurring at arbitrary points of time cannot drive the TC into a deadlock situation. This example demonstrates, that complex industrial designs can be verified with symbolic model checking techniques.

2.2 Verification of an arbiter

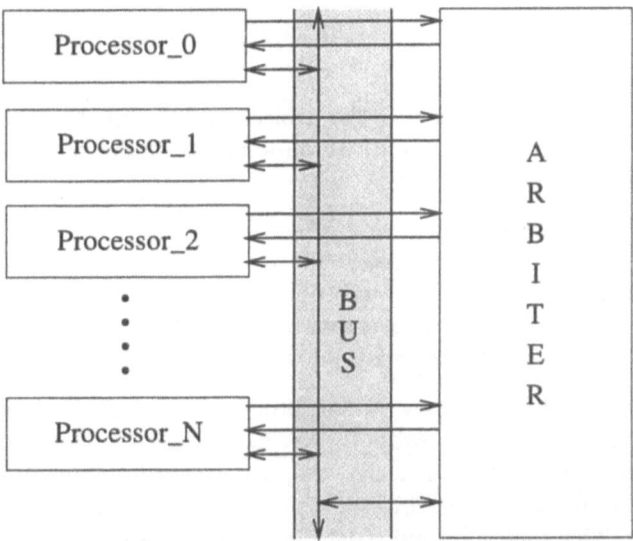

Fig. 2.3. The arbiter manages the bus access of N processors

SNI MR PD 151 works on the development of components for multiprocessor computers. For several applications environments have to be designed in which a configurable number of standard high speed processors can work together. Such a multiprocessor environment consists of busses and interface circuits like I/O components, bridges between different bus systems or arbiter components. An arbiter is used to control the bus access of several processors. Due to the fact that busses are a critical resource in a multiprocessor environment, maximum performance with safe and fair bus arbitration is essential for the performance of an multi processor system with a high amount of data throughput. Figure 2.3 provides a global view about the interaction between an arbiter, a bus and N processors.

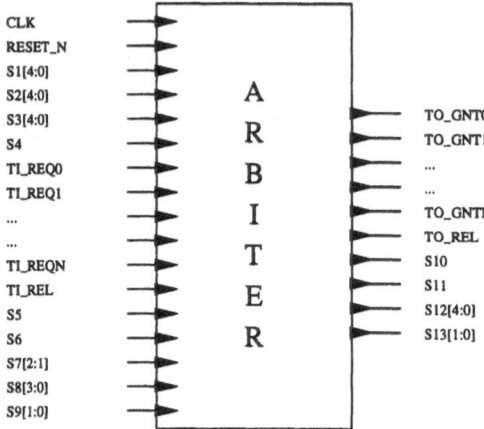

Fig. 2.4. Arbiter Interface

Figure 2.4 shows part of the interface of the arbiter component. For the verification with model checking we concentrate on a subset of the original interface with the following signals:

- ReqJ : Bus request from processor J,
- GntJ : Processor J has exclusive bus access,
- Priority : With the priority vector, the round robin bus arbitration scheme can be influenced in such a way that processors with a higher priority will have earlier bus access than processors with a lower priority.

The bus protocol is roughly as follows. One processor indicates a bus request by setting the signal ReqJ and waits for the GrantJ signal from the arbiter. If all processors have the same priority, the bus arbitration follows a round robin algorithm. Otherwise, the arbiter has to grant the bus according to the priority ordering. There are a lot more details in the protocol, e.g., the arbiter itself can own the bus or one processor does not need to release the bus until another processor has indicated a request.

The verification of deadlock freedom and of correct priority handling were the main tasks. Figure 2.5 shows a timing diagram for the property, that for a processor every request leads to a grant under the assumption, that the priority was set low for all processors. Dynamic priority changes leads to more difficult situations, which were treated separatly. The timing diagram in figure 2.6 describes the situation, in which:

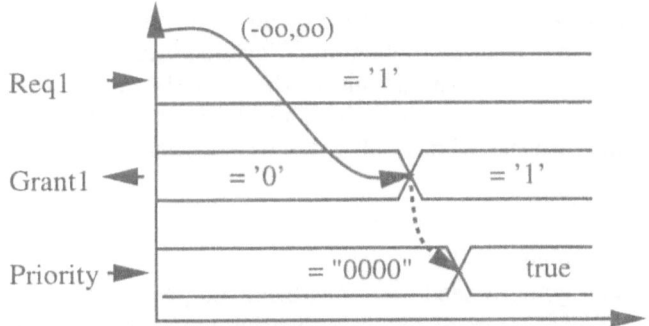

Fig. 2.5. Every request signal leads to a grant from the arbiter.

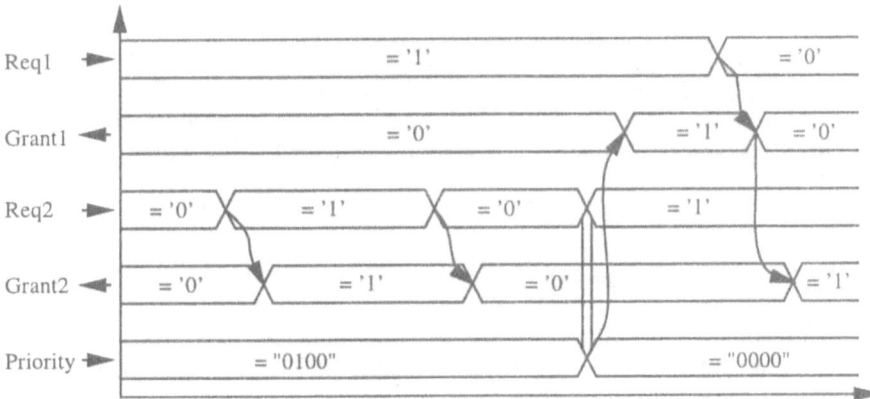

Fig. 2.6. Correct bus arbitration with respect to priority changes.

1. the processor with higher priority gets bus access before the processor with the lower priority,
2. if the priority changes the arbiter will immediately obey the new priority.

Table 2.1. FSM-Generation for module arbiter

	time (min.)	memory MByte	inputs bits	states bits	outputs bits	BDD-size nodes	VHDL lines[a]
arbiter	50	25	34	62	15	95115	752
reqhdlr	60	40	136	224	127	75271	616
mux	40	20	307	195	86	3808	294

[a]Lines of VHDL does not include packages.

At SNI the VHDL design of the arbiter was used as input for synthesis, which produced the actual gate level representation. Table 2.1 shows the generation results for module arbiter. Table 2.2 provides a global overview on the runtime for different verification runs. All specified properties were

expressed as TDs or temporal logic. In the case of an error situation, the
model checker needs additional time for debugging. Several error situations
occurred due to missing or incorrect assumptions. In that way the verification
clarified some assumptions at the interface which must be obeyed by the
environment, because otherwise the arbiter will not work correctly. Examples
of assumptions are:

- stability of input values,
- correct clock design and behavior,
- the arbiter expects exact synchronized reactions from the processors,
- correct notification of all processors during initialization of the bus system.

Table 2.2. Verification results for module arbiter

commitment	verification (time)	simulation
bus arbitration is deadlocks-free	12 sec per processor	validation is
bus arbitration is exclusive	280 sec per processor	possible only for
handling of dynamic priorities	120 sec per processor	finite prefixes

2.3 Verification of a serial V24 interface controller

A V24-Interface is used for serial data transmission. The controller transforms
the serial data into blocks of one byte each, so a CPU can handle the information. The main advantage is that the CPU is relieved of this transformation
and used only when necessary.

Model checking was used by a design group at Siemens public communication networks to figure out, where the main advantages and disadvantages of
the application of formal verification techniques are. The design was already
finished, but an earlier error situation was reintroduced into the design to
find out, whether it could have been found by formal verification. This error
was crucial, because it was found with great luck during a later code-review
and the designers said, that it is unlikely to find this error with standard simulation, since it was caused only in situations where an interrupt occurred in
a certain state of the V24 controller. This error forced an expensive redesign.

To allow efficient model checking the example was modified : A slide register was removed to decrease the sequential complexity and with an additional
input signal, a part of the design could be deactivated by setting this signal
to a constant value. The modified example could be translated into an FSM
without any complexity problems. The specification of the properties required
some training, but after a while the designer got used to it. Furthermore the
specification of assumptions required an exact analysis of the environment
in which the controler will be operated. Using Model Checking the designer
was able to prove the correctness of a read/send cycle as shown in figure
2.7. Therefore an exact formal specification of the procedures INIT, ISR and

SEND_BYTE was prepared. These specifications were verified against the VHDL implementation. The specification expressed for example that position 1 is executed only once after initialization and that the procedures ISR and SEND_BYTE are executed in an loop.

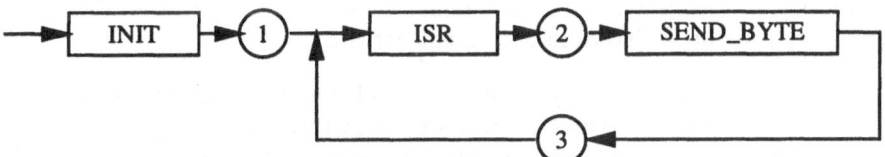

Fig. 2.7. After initialization, the procedures ISR and SEND_BYTE will be executed in a loop.

Formal verification of subcomponents increases the quality of a whole design. An early usage of formal verification will not lead to a higher expense, because it can shorten simulation time and covers more of the possible input patterns. For the V24 controller it was possible to detect the mentioned error with a single model checking run. The check of a global lifeness property produced a counter example showing a deadlock situation caused by an internal reset-operation.

The response from this case study was very positive, because it was done by designers at the Siemens business unit public communications networks without any further support from the tool developers. It demonstrated that model checking is manageable and useful from the designers point of view. Even if no errors are detected the specification and verification of properties helps the designer to get a deeper understanding of his design. More detailed information about this case study can be found in J. Lattermann 1995).

2.4 Verification of an ATM component

The development of ATM components (Asynchronous Transfer Mode) is a very important field for the Public Communications Networks department of Siemens. ATM standards are now sufficiently well defined to allow a useful degree of interworking between systems. Essential characteristics of ATM technology are:

– The basic information transfer unit in ATM is a small fixed-size packet called cell. This concept permits the information transfer rate to adapt to the actual service requirement and limits set by the physical transfer medium.
– Multiplexing and cross-connect/switching capabilities: ATM cells are identified and routed by information contained in the header. The main routing information is the virtual path identifier (VP).

168   R. Herrmann et al.

- The 'core-and-edge' principle: Actions between the user layer (UL) and the ATM transport network is done through the service dependent ATM adaption layer AAL. The transport of the cells will thus be service independent and different services can dynamically share the transport network.
- Two important characteristics of ATM management capabilities are the supervision and maintenance mechanisms and the ability of the ATM network to provide a virtual management network.

To receive a maximum throughput most of the algorithms have been implemented directly in hardware. Because ATM technology requires a lot of different components, it is very important to receive a high degree of reusability for already designed reliable subcomponents.

With model checking, we have treated two components of an actual design:

- A cell rejecting component (CRC), which is responsible for accepting or rejecting cells arriving via different input channels.
- A queue controller for a configurable number of cells.

It was the verification task, to check, whether the cell accepting algorithm works correctly or not. Due to the fact that the component reads the input cells byte sequential from several input channels, the CRC has to store these cells in order to validate them. To decrease complexity, these buffers have been removed from the component and replaced by smaller registers keeping only the necessary header and status information of the cells. After that step we were able to compute an FSM from the VHDL description.

Unfortunately, the handling of the full component required so many assumptions, so that we verified only some local properties referring to components. We decided to continue with the subcomponents which all represent state machines. The five subcomponents have the size listed in Table 2.3.

Table 2.3. FSM-Generation for CRC and subcomponents

Component	Inputs (bits)	State Variables (bits)	Outputs (bits)	total Size BDD nodes	VHDL lines[a]
CRC	212	301	202	64478	3575
algorithm	43	10	18	395	
condition1	24	0	6	212	
condition2	16	0	6	45	
arithmetic	33	0	2	158	
register	233	276	277	3557	

[a]Lines of VHDL does not include packages.

These components represented state machines where three of them are combinational. We checked the following properties:

– All states are reachable,
– every state can be reached infinitely often,
– all states can be reached in the specified order,
– certain input stimuli forces these controllers to react in the expected way i.e., producing the expected outputs and continuing in the expected way

Several small differences between the documentation and the VHDL implementation have been detected using formal verification tools.

2.5 Verification of a FIFO buffer component

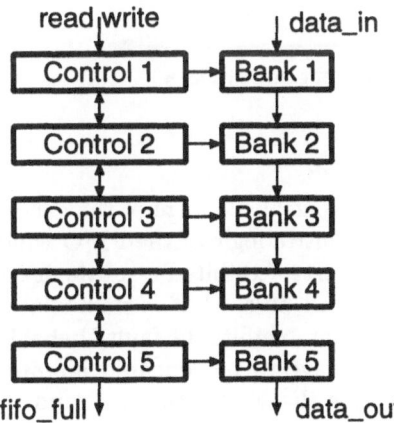

Fig. 2.8. Implementation of a 4x5 FIFO

The FIFO is a generic VHDL description that is used in different designs. It is scalable in size and optimized to reduce the area consumption of the synthesized circuits. It is implemented by banks of latches (see figure 2.8). Data is moving from the first bank to the last. A control mechanism is associated with each bank and determines whether the bank contains valid data or not. If the bank is empty and the previous bank contains valid data, the data is shifted down one bank.

Instances of the generic description were compiled into FSMs. We have checked the commitment 'noLostData' represented by the timing diagram in figure 2.9 for different instances of the generic description. The timing diagram specifies that if the data "1010" was read in at some point of time, it will eventually show up at the output port.

Additional assumptions describe the environment of the FIFO. They assure that

– consecutive write pulses are separated by 2 clock cycles,
– no writes will occur, if the FIFO is full,
– consecutive read pulses are separated by 2 clock cycles, and

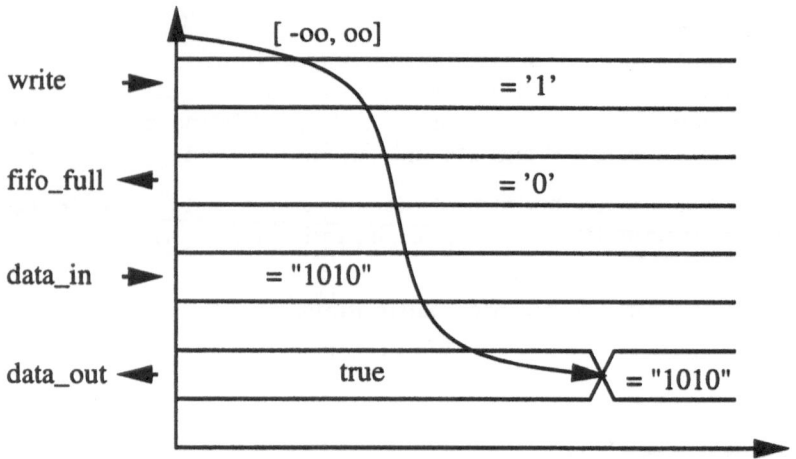

Fig. 2.9. TD specifying commitment noLostData.

– infinitely many reads will happen.

The property is natural for a FIFO. It is a specialized form of the general property that no data is lost and it tests the control logic of the FIFO which is its critical part. The verification of this property, exhibited a subtle design error that occurs, if a full FIFO receives a read pulse that is immediately followed by a write pulse. The input sequence that exhibits the faulty behavior consists of 26 steps, where the last 10 steps have to be repeated infinitely often. Table 2.4 shows the execution times for the verification run and the computation of a contradictory input sequence.

Table 2.4. Execution times[a] for FIFO memory

width	depth					
	5		10		15	
	mc	debug	mc	debug	mc	debug
4	69.3	17.6	323.9	44.4	602.6	69.0
8	37.4	17.0	852.5	104.3	1336.7	142.1
12	373.3	66.3	711.0	98.0	6908.5	618.3
16	208.0	49.8	2953.0	315.0	11436.6	986.3

[a]All times in seconds on a SPARC 10 with 128 MB.
mc: Time to detect the error.
debug: Time to construct the counter example.

This example shows how model checking can be used successfully. Since it requires almost no effort to start the model checker, parts of a design can be checked at very early stages where a bug is quickly located and fixed. Note that small scale instances of designs are very often sufficient to detect even subtle errors in the control logic.

3. Conclusion

In the last sections we have shown, that at different Siemens sites formal verification has been successfully applied to parts of actual designs. The best experiences have been made with the model checker and its facility to perform a proof under a set of nontrivial assumptions (assumption-commitment style model checking). Basis for the verification was in all cases a VHDL description of the designs from which the gate level design is synthesized. There is a request for graphical specification languages at Siemens departments but especially state charts are so far not very well established and the problem is that state charts are not a standard so that they cannot be used by different development tools without changes at least in syntactical writing.

The major problems and experiences encountered during the case studies carried out at Siemens where:

- The time-to-market pressure is so hard that designer often have no time to learn the handling of new complex tools. Very often the use of formal verification tools is restricted to certain people working in support groups.
- New tools have to be fully automatic and easy to handle so that they can be used off the peg. They have to be adapted to the specific applications at least by setting (a lot of) parameters correctly. Additionaly it is very important that the designer gets an intuition for the complexity in order to abort runs of the tools which will not terminate in reasonable time or with realistic memory consumption. If such a situation occurs, the designer has in may cases the chance to continue the proof after some changes, e.g., weakening the proof goal a little bit or adding more assumptions to the proof.
- The counter example facility is a major step to a better acceptance, because it enables the designer to use formal verification in early design phase in which he knows that the design has bugs. The generation of VHDL test benches helps him to tackle the problem systematically by using his standard simulation environment without writing stimuli files. The same is during the end of the design validation just before sign off. The verification tools would be useful, if it would guarantee that the design is totally correct. But due to incomplete specifications of the requirements, is is very unlikely to have 100 percent coverage. On the other hand, if the formal verification tool has detected an error, an exact error diagnose is necessary. Without the automatic generation of test-benches, the designer would have to generate lots of stimuli files to find the error.
- During the practical use of the formal verification tools some subtle errors have been found but in total not a huge amount of errors. This is caused by the fact, that all of the design have been simulated a lot and reached nearly final status before the designer started with formal verification. We expect an increase in the number of detected errors, if the use of the tools is integrated also in earlier phases of the designs flow.

Today formal verification is on its way to be integrated in the standard EDA design environment. The designers are observing that they are no longer able to establish the correctness of a design just by running simulations either on VHDL level or with prototypes in special test environments. On the other hand there are limits which have to be overcame, e.g., the use of BDD based representations is critical and maybe some verification algorithms have to be adopted to more complex data structures.

Acknowledgements We would like to thank F. Korf, J. Lattermann, H. Vogt and D. Werth for their support of this work and their departments for supplying the designs and applying formal verification techniques.

References

J. Bormann (1993a): CVE deckt Fehler im Entwurf eines FiFo-Speichers auf. Siemens Bericht ZFE BT SE 1-93/94-JB-2.

J. Bormann (1993b): Formale Verifikation eines Token Ring Controllers mit CVE. Siemens Bericht ZFE BT SE 1-93/94-JB-1.

J. Bormann, J. Lohse, M. Payer, G. Venzl (1995). Model Checking in Industrial Hardware Design. In Proceedings *32nd DAC*, San Francisco, CA.

R. E. Bryant (1986): Graph-based algorithms for boolean function manipulation. *IEEE Transactions on Computers*, C-35(8):677–691, August.

J. R. Burch, E. M. Clarke, K. L. McMillan, D. L. Dill, L. J. Hwang (1992): Symbolic Model Checking: 10^{20} States and beyond. Inf. Comput. (USA), vol. 98, no. 2, p. 142-170.

E.M. Clarke, J.R. Burch, O. Grumberg, D.E. Long, K.L. McMillan (1992): Automatic Verification of Sequential Circuit Designs. Philos. Tran. R. Tran. R. Soc. A, Phys. Sci. Eng (UK), vol. 339, no. 1652, page 105-120, April.

J. Lattermann (1995): Model Checking eines V24-Controllers mit CVE Siemens Bericht ÖN TN EC B32, September.

E. Felt, R. Brayton, A. Sangio-Vincentelli, and G. York (1993): Dynamic variable ordering for BDD minimization. In *Proc. of the European Design Automation Conference (EURO-DAC'93)*, September.

R. Herrmann and F. Korf (1995): Formale Verifikation eines Arbiters mit CVE2. Siemens Bericht ZFE T SE 1-94/95-RH-1, ZFE T SE 1, SNI MR PD 151.

R. Rudell (1993): Dynamic variable ordering for ordered binary decision diagrams. In *Proc. of the 9th Int. Conference on Computer Aided Design (ICCAD'93)*, November.

Part III

Technical Background

The FORMAT Model Checker

Andreas Scholz, Thomas Filkorn, Jörg Lohse, Hans-Albert Schneider, Erik Tidén, and Peter Warkentin

Siemens AG, Germany

1. Introduction

This chapter describes the tools used for automatic verification within the FORMAT project. The *FORMAT model checker* is the core of this tool set. Figure 1.1 gives an overview on the various languages and tools used on the verification path of FORMAT. Following some short explanations on the overview, the remaining sections of this chapter will give an overview of the architecture of the model checker and each of its components.

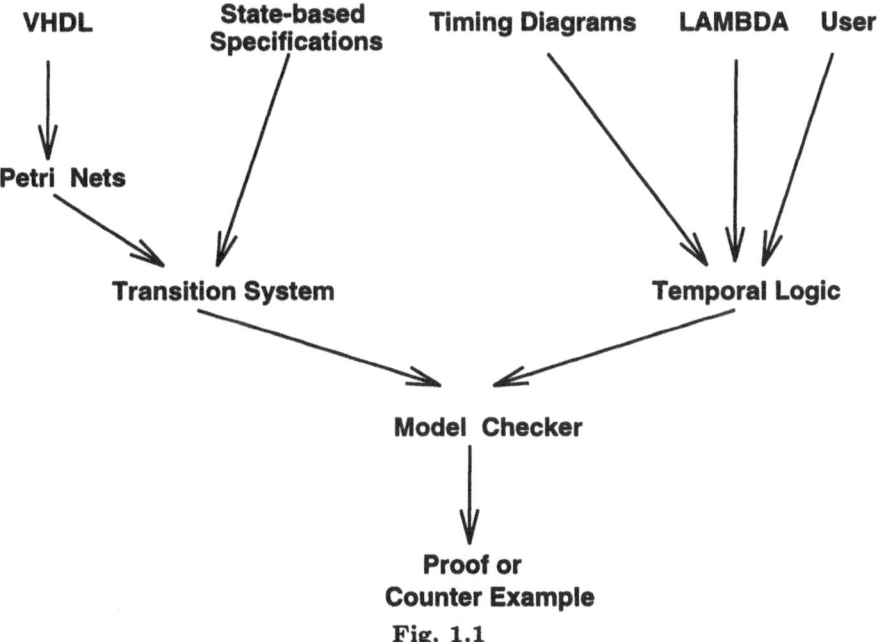

Fig. 1.1

The model checker will be used to automatically check systems described in VHDL or the state-based specification language against properties expressed as temporal logic formulae. The temporal logic formulae are either generated from timing diagram specifications or by the interactive theorem prover LAMBDA as a proof goal during the compositional correctness proof of a composed system. Furthermore the user may enter temporal logic formulae directly if a property can not be expressed using a timing diagram.

The use of transition systems and temporal logic formulae provides a uniform interface to all other FORMAT tools. A system can be described using VHDL or a state based description technique. One might think of other description techniques which appear convenient from the users point of view. As long as there is a way to translate descriptions to transition systems, the tools of the FORMAT verification path (e.g. timing diagram editor, model checker) can still be used.

2. Architecture

The software architecture of the model checker developed within FORMAT is shown in figure 2.

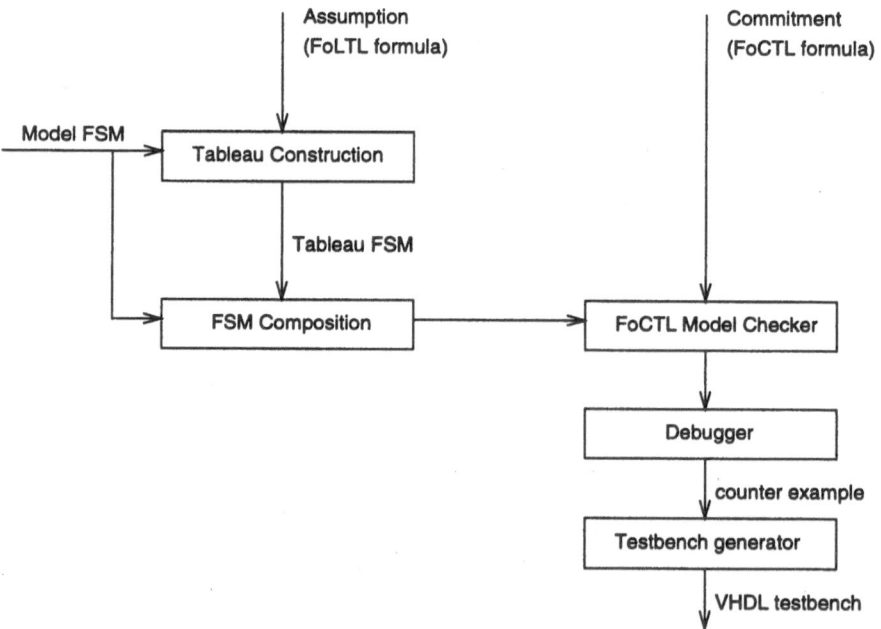

Fig. 2.1. Architecture of the Model Checker

2.1 Interfaces

The interface which connects the model checker and rest of the tools developed in FORMAT consists of two parts. The input side requires three pieces of information from the user:

- the model has to be selected
- the assumption formula (from FOLTL) has to be given
- the commitment formula (from FOCTL) has to be given

Since the model checker supports a very sophisticated macro mechanism, it is also possible to use names which reference a formula. Moreover, there is a set of socalled *flags* which provide a possibility to influence some internal heuristics of the model checker in order to get the best performance for the specific applications of a user.

The output side of the model checker either delivers the answer *yes* which indicates that the commitment is valid for the model under the assumptions given by the user, or *no* if this is not the case. If the answer is negative a *counter example* is computed as a witness (see section 4.). The reference manual (Th. Filkorn et al. 1994) describes in full detail how to use the model checker.

In the FORMAT framework *Finite State Machines* (FSMs for short) are used to represent behavioural descriptions. A basic data structure which is called the *FSM format* has been defined to establish a uniform interface of the model checker towards the rest of the FORMAT world ((Filkon and Warkentin 1993) contains a fully detailed description of the format). The most remarkable aspect about the format is the use BDDs (binary decision diagrams (R. E. Bryant 1986)) to represent sets, relations and functions. This is the basic data structure used in FORMAT to tackle the well known *state explosion problem*.

The FSM format contains a wide range of possibilities to represent the transition relation of a FSM in a partitioned way. This is a major point for optimizations of the representation, the parallel composition and the model checking process. The modules for composition and model checking are parameterized by a routine to handle the different representations of transition relations. This approach yields the greatest possible flexibility for optimizations and further enhancements of the BDD representation which is a crucial point in the project to get the highest possible performance from the automatic tools.

The space complexity of BDD-based representations is very sensitive to variable orderings. Recently automatic techniques for improving the size of BDD-representations by *reordering of variables* were published (R. Rudell 1993), (E. Felt et al. 1993). This important feature has been integrated into the underlying BDD-package. Based on this the model checker optimizes the representations of FSMs as well as the representations of intermediate results in order to increase performance. By automatic variable reordering the user of the tools gets rid of the problem of determining a suitable variable ordering for the BDD-representations by hand.

2.2 The algorithm

The first step which is performed by the model checker when it has to check a property is the *tableau construction*. It creates from the assumption formulae a *tableau* which is a most general model, i.e. a FSM representing all sequences of behaviours allowed by the assumption formulae and only these. The tableau construction, as it is implemented in the FORMAT model checker, uses BDDs and performs a number of optimizations to reduce the complexity of the tableaux. An description of the full details can be found in (Th. Filkorn 1994).

Thereafter the tableau FSM is composed with the model FSM describing the behaviour of a VHDL body or a state-based specification. The resulting FSM represents those parts of the behaviour of the model FSM which are admitted by the assumptions.

The following step performs BDD-based model checking for FOCTL (as described in (J. R. Burch et al. 1992)) on the resulting FSM. If it turns out that the model does not satisfy the commitment formula the *debugging component* is actived. It generates a *counter example* as an explanation why the formula doen not hold. The counter example is transformed into a VHDL test bench in order to be able to simulate the sequence using some VHDL simulator. This translation is necessary in order to hide the FSMs and BDD-representations from the user of the tools. Interaction takes place only on the level of VHDL and timing diagrams.

3. The checking component

The core part of the model checker (the box labelled *FOCTL Model Checker* in fugire 2.) is an BDD-based implementationbased on the standard model checking algorithms as described e.g., in (J. R. Burch et al. 1992). These techniques are commonly known as *symbolic model checking*.

However, a lot of effort has been spent on improvements and optimizations which make the FORMAT model checker superior to public domain implementations of these algorithms.

4. The debugging component

The purpose of symbolic model checking is to verify whether or not a temporal logic formula holds for a given model. If the formula does hold the model checking is a proof of this formula. If it does not hold the model checker invokes a debugger which constructs a *counter sequence*,[1] a sequence of input vectors which forms a counter example to the temporal logic formula.

---

[1] Whether a counter sequence exists for a particular temporal logic formula depends on the formula. Only formulae with ∀ quantifiers can be proved wrong by a counter sequence. For every formula generated from timing diagrams the existence of a counter example is guaranteed.

The Siemens SVE model checker, developed within the FORMAT project, deals with models extracted from VHDL. Since the models are genuinely represented in VHDL and VHDL simulators are common place where such models are developed, SVE also includes a feature to write a testbench in VHDL which exercises the counter sequence right in the existing VHDL simulator. This section describes the counter sequences generated in VHDL by SVE and illustrates the model checking procedure with an example.

An Example VHDL Design

Our VHDL design of an 8-bit counter looks like this:

```
entity counter is
 port (
   reset       : IN bit;
   clk         : IN bit;
   countout  : OUT natural range 0 to 255);
end counter;

architecture arch of counter is
begin
p: process
    variable i : natural range 0 to 255;
  begin
    wait until clk'event and clk = '1';
    if (reset = '1') then
       i := 0;
    else
       i := (i + 1) MOD 256;
    end if ;
    countout <= i;
  end process ;
end arch;
```

The design is a simple 8-bit counter with a synchronous reset input and it is clocked with the rising edge of input clk.

Model Checking the Design

After the design has been written, an FSM (of name counter(arch)) can be extracted which will be submitted to the model checker. In addition to the model we also need a temporal logic formula to check. As we want to see a counter sequence, we pick a formula which will certainly not hold. We try to prove that the counter can never take the value 10. This formula (in FOCTL ag(countout \= 10)) will certainly not hold and the model checker can be expected to compute a counter sequence which clocks the counter to 10.

We invoke the model checker like this [2] :

---

[2] The first command enables the generation of a VHDL testbench.

```
[user] ?- setFlag(displayMedium,[vhdl]).
[user] ?- mc('counter(arch)', ag(countout \= 10)).
```

M O D E L - C H E C K E R

Copyright (c) 1995 by Siemens AG, ZFE T SE 1. All rights reserved.


```
Model:      counter(arch)
Assumption: tt
Commitment: ag(countout \= 10)
```

C T L   M O D E L - C H E C K E R

```
Commitment: ag(countout \= 10)
evaluating outmost ag (bw):
    step: 1   13 nodes
    step: 2   13 nodes
    step: 3   14 nodes
    step: 4   15 nodes
    step: 5   16 nodes
    step: 6   15 nodes
    step: 7   16 nodes
    step: 8   15 nodes
    step: 9   16 nodes
    step: 10  15 nodes
    step: 11  16 nodes
    step: 12  15 nodes
    step: 13  16 nodes
    step: 14  15 nodes
    step: 15  16 nodes
    step: 16  15 nodes
    step: 17  16 nodes
    step: 18  15 nodes
>>>> time for ctl model checking:          0.566667 sec
Formula is NOT true
```

C T L - D E B U G G E R

```
False in state 18: countout \= 10

Writing VHDL simulation test-bench
 for architecture 'arch' of entity 'counter'
 to file 'cve_tb_counter_arch.vhdl'...
Writing script for Synopsys vhdldbx
 to file 'cve_tb_counter_arch.scr'...

DEBUG FINISHED
>>>> time for debugging:                   0.683333 sec

Model:      counter(arch)
Assumption: tt
```

```
Commitment: ag(countout \= 10)

Formula is NOT true


yes

[user] ?-
```

The model checker has generated a VHDL testbench and a script which invokes the Synopsys VSS simulator. The Synopsys VSS simulator script enters all ports into a waveform display and starts the simulation. The VDHL testbench looks like this. It is valid VHDL which can be used with any VHDL simulator.

```
-- testbench with counter sequence generated by SVE.


entity cve_tb_counter_arch is
end;

architecture TestBench of cve_tb_counter_arch is

signal clk : bit;
signal reset : bit;
signal countout : natural range 0 to 2**8-1;

component counter_uut
                Port (
clk : in bit;
reset : in bit;
countout : out natural range 0 to 2**8-1
);
end component;

begin

UUT : counter_uut
Port Map (
clk,
reset,
countout
);

clk <=
'1',
'0' after 1 us,
'1' after 2 us,
'0' after 3 us,
'1' after 4 us,
'0' after 5 us,
'1' after 6 us,
'0' after 7 us,
'1' after 8 us,
```

```
'0' after 9 us,
'1' after 10 us,
'0' after 11 us,
'1' after 12 us,
'0' after 13 us,
'1' after 14 us,
'0' after 15 us,
'1' after 16 us,
'0' after 17 us,
'1' after 18 us;
reset <=
'0';

end TestBench;


configuration cfg_cve_tb_counter_arch of cve_tb_counter_arch is
for TestBench
for UUT : counter_uut use entity work.counter(arch);
end for;
end for;
end;
```

Simulating the Counter Sequence

The Synopsys VSS simulator can be invoked as described in the script file. Any other VHDL simulator can also be used to simulate the testbench, we just do not generate a script to invoke it. The simulator output is shown in figure 4.1.

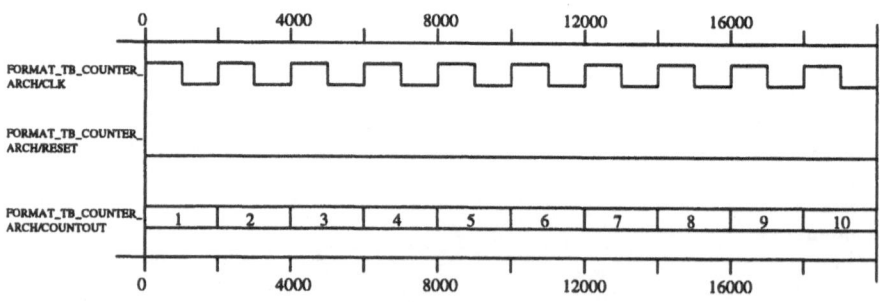

Fig. 4.1. Simulating the counter example

5. The tautology checker

During the interactive verification of a composed system using the LAMBDA theorem prover it has to be checked whether or not a temporal logic formula from FOLTL is a tautology. This task is performed automatically by the *tautology checker* for formulae.

For checking whether a formula f is a tautology, it is sufficient (and also necessary) to check whether $\neg f$ is satisfiable. This problem is equivalent to the problem of determining whether the most general model of $\neg f$ (i.e. the tableau machine $\mathcal{T}(\neg f)$ for $\neg f$) is the empty model. This task is performed by checking whether the CTL formula **EG** true (expressing the existence of a fair path) is true for $\mathcal{T}(\neg f)$.

It should be mentioned that this modular approach makes it also possible to express assumptions by transition systems or a mixture of transition systems and temporal logic formulae. Also, a full FOLTL model checker comes for free and is available for experiments in the model checker. Experiments carried out within the FORMAT project give evidence to the known fact that model checking for the branching time logic FOCTL is more efficient than model checking for FOLTL .

References

R. E. Bryant (1986): Graph-based algorithms for boolean function manipulation. *IEEE Transactions on Computers*, C-35(8):677–691, August.

J. R. Burch, E. M. Clarke, K. L. McMillan, D. L. Dill, and L. J. Hwang (1992): Symbolic model checking: 10^{20} states and beyond. *Information and Computation*, 98(2):142–170, June.

E. Felt, R. Brayton, A. Sangio-Vincentelli, and G. York. Dynamic variable ordering for BDD minimization. In *Proc. of the European Design Automation Conference (EURO-DAC'93)*, September.

Th. Filkorn (1994): Tableau construction for temproal logic formulae using BDDs. Technical Report ZFE BT SE 11/F3, Siemens AG, ZFE BT SE 11, Munich.

Th. Filkorn, H.A. Schneider, A. Scholz, A. Strasser, and P. Warkentin (1994): SVE User's Guide. Technical Report ZFE BT SE 1-SVE-1, Siemens AG, Corporate Research and Development, Munich.

Th. Filkorn and P. Warkentin (1993): Internal representation of transition systems (based on BDDs) V1.1. Technical Report ZFE BT SE 11/F1, Siemens AG, ZFE BT SE 11, Munich, September.

R. Rudell. Dynamic variable ordering for ordered binary decision diagrams. In *Proc. of the 9th Int. Conference on Computer Aided Design (ICCAD'93)*. IEEE Computer Society Press, November.

Reasoning

Nick Chapman, Simon Finn, and Michael P. Fourman

Abstract Hardware Ltd., U.K.

Introduction

Design validation by simulation is well established. However, exhaustive simulation is intractable for most systems. Formal models of behaviour provide an alternative approach to design validation.

For example, a system may be modelled as a finite state machine, represented as a relation between current state and next state. Symbolic model-checking has been used to provide the effect of exhaustive symbolic simulation of such a system.

Symbolic model-checking has proved effective for analysing simple control systems; but again this becomes intractable for complex systems. Complexity may be introduced in parametrised systems consisting of a large number of simple components, or in systems that process data; both features can produce a state explosion.

Validation based on symbolic theorem-proving can apply induction to the treatment of parametrised, and data-dependent systems. Various formalisms have been proposed for modelling and reasoning about system behaviour.

We begin this chapter with an overview of LAMBDA, an integrated suite of software tools for specifying, designing, and proving the correctness of, hardware and software systems. We discuss the design of the LAMBDA specification Logic, L2, and the architecture of the LAMBDA theorem-prover. We then describe how LAMBDA has been used in the FORMAT project to support reasoning about temporal properties of systems described in VHDL.

1. LAMBDA — a behavioural design tool

The LAMBDA system was designed to support the use of higher-order predicate logic as a general-purpose formalism for the formal representation and manipulation of behaviours. The LAMBDA system is implemented in ML, an advanced, general-purpose programming language, which is also used as a command-language for the LAMBDA theorem prover.

The system includes four principal software tools:

1. The Theorem Prover is a proof assistant, designed to conduct proofs about hardware and software systems.
2. The Animator allows the user to animate and experiment with system behaviours.

3. The Browser provides a menu driven, context-sensitive, interface to the Theorem Prover,
4. The DIALOG schematic interface integrates design and proof.

The LAMBDA system makes novel use of verification technology. It has been designed to support Analysis-Driven Design, the development of a system from a specification. LAMBDA is based on a higher-order logic similar to that of the Cambridge HOL system(M. Gordon 1985). The LAMBDA Logic, L2, LAMBDA's specification language, is designed to support specification, animation, and proof. It combines the expressiveness of higher-order logic with polymorphic typing and user-definable types and functions. The theorem-proving technology used in LAMBDA is closely related to Paulson's Isabelle(L. C. Paulson 1994). The DIALOG interface provides a familiar, schematic representation of a partially completed design. It is integrated with the theorem prover, so the user can build up a complex whole by an iterative process of decomposition, refinement, and implementation, while the system keeps track of the correctness of what has been done, and the behavioural requirements for the rest of the design.

1.1 The LAMBDA logic

The LAMBDA Logic, L2, is a general-purpose specification language. Most system description languages are designed to support system description and simulation. L2 is designed to support system specification, refinement, and proof.

In L2 we can specify the behavior of hardware, software, or a combined hardware/software system without necessarily saying how the behavior is to be implemented. The ability of L2 to model behaviour at an abstract level gives a high degree of design freedom.

L2 is based on Higher-Order Predicate Logic, which provides a mathematically expressive formalism, with familiar proof rules. L2 provides (recursive) function declarations and (recursive) type declarations, based on those of the ML programming language.

This provides a familiar syntax for the definition of types and functions, and a powerful framework for the formal modelling of systems. L2 adopts ML syntax for declarations, so that component functions of a specification may be executed directly in ML.

This close correspondence between L2 and ML is feasible because ML types and terms can appear directly as types and terms of the logic. ML declarations can be given a reasonably straight-forward type-theoretic semantics, which is faithful to the operational semantics of ML, and can also be axiomatised in the logic.

1.2 Proof in LAMBDA

The Theorem Prover is the core of the LAMBDA design system. It provides a sound basis for the representation and manipulation of behaviours. A simulation can show that a design behaves as specified for particular input stimuli. However, for many systems, exhaustive simulation, covering all possible input stimuli, is not feasible. A formal proof can validate a design for all possible stimuli. Within LAMBDA, system properties are verified by formal proof.

Some system properties are decidable – an automatic search can check whether the property can be proved. However, in general the search for a proof is an interactive process. The idea behind an interactive theorem prover is that the user should be supported in generating proofs, but absolutely prevented from inadvertently, or optimistically, claiming that a non-theorem has been proved.

LAMBDA adopts the idea, due to Milner(M. Gordon et al. 1979), of using a *safe type* to guarantee correctness. In generating objects of a safe type, the user is restricted to a limited repertoire of operations. Milner's idea was to make **theorem** a safe type, and to provide constructions of new theorems from old corresponding to the proof rules of the logic. LAMBDA uses a variation on this idea.

The primary safe type of the LAMBDA system is **rule**.[1] A rule consists of finitely many premises and a conclusion. If the conclusion follows logically from the premises, we say the rule is *logically valid*. The operations for constructing rules are controlled so that every rule that can be produced is logically valid.

A basic collection of logically valid rules is given as primitive rules of the logic. We use three operations for constructing new valid rules: specialisation, resolution, and rewriting. Specialisation constructs an instance of a rule by substituting particular terms for (meta-)variables in the rule. Resolution of two rules (either fails or) creates a new rule by matching a premise of one rule with the conclusion of another. Rewriting replaces terms in a rule using previously proved equalities.

New valid rules are called derived rules. Derived rules are simply data objects – using a derived rule is no more costly than using a basic rule.

A typical proof begins by creating a 'trivial' rule – one whose premise is identical to its conclusion. Each proof step elaborates the current rule by resolving it with a known rule of the system. The result becomes the new current rule.

For example, suppose our initial rule is:

```
|- out t == not (i1 t && i2 t)
-------------------------------
|- out t == not (i1 t && i2 t)
```

---

[1] This approach follows Paulson's Isabelle.

and we have a 2-input AND gate described by:

```
AND x y z |- P#(z t) /\ x t == a /\ y t == b
---------------------------------------------
AND x y z |- P#(a && b)
```

Resolving[2] the two rules gives the new state:

```
AND x y z |- out t == not (z t1)
            /\ x t1 == i1 t
            /\ y t1 == i2 t
-------------------------------------------
AND x y z |- out t == not (i1 t && i2 t)
```

Simplifying the above rule reduces it to:

```
AND i1 i2 z |- out t == not (z t)
-------------------------------------------
AND i1 i2 z |- out t == not (i1 t && i2 t)
```

Repeating this process with a NOT gate we can synthesise the entire circuit:

```
----------------------------------------------------------
NOT z out, AND i1 i2 z |- out t == not (i1 t && i2 t)
```

Here we used two primitive proof steps. A proof may contain many thousands of such steps. Rather than construct these steps manually, they are generated by procedures called *tactics*. Resolution steps are used to create simple tactics, which are then combined in structured ways: sequence, conditional, repetition, etc., using *tacticals*. Tacticals may be used to program a proof directly, when we know how to do this, or to construct a proof search. The proof terminates when the 'current rule' has the desired form – often, but not invariably, a theorem. Because we use `rule` as our safe type, LAMBDA tactics need no validations; each individual resolution step is self-validating.

The theorem we eventually prove may be a specialisation of the theorem we set out to prove, because the unification implicit in our use of resolution can instantiate one or more variables present in our original goal. This allows parameters to be instantiated appropriately as a proof develops. High-level design decisions are often parameterised. These parameters are instantiated later, to refine the design. The refinement is normally generated by unification. However, this automatic instantiation is sometimes undesirable, so there are ways to prevent it (by making the variables *rigid*).

---

[2] The term P#(a && b) unifies with *any* expression containing an occurrence of a && b; this use of higher-order unification helps produce concise rules.

2. Generating L2 specifications

Within the Format design flow, designers may use VHDL types to specify data, and timing diagrams to specify control. To support reasoning about these specifications, we provide interpretations (or *semantic embeddings*) of these specifications in L2. These embdeddings can be seen as defining the meanings of these other formalisms.

2.1 Modelling VHDL in L2

Reasoning about VHDL using the LAMBDA system is accomplished by embedding VHDL within L2, the formal language of the LAMBDA system. We use the terms *represents* and *translates to* interchangeably: sometimes we say that a particular VHDL object, for example a type or a value, is represented in L2 by some L2 object; at other times we say that the VHDL object is translated into the L2 object.

VHDL is a complex language and we choose a subset which we wish to reason about. The size and scope of the subset are balanced against the complexity of the embedding. Our translation of VHDL into L2 involves the translation of types (section 2.1.1), function definitions (section 2.1.2), statements (section 2.1.3) and expressions (section 2.1.4).

2.1.1 Types. This section describes the translation of VHDL enumeration types, integer types and subtypes of these types – array types are considered separately (see 2.1.5).

VHDL makes a distinction between types and subtypes. For example:

```
type Int is range -1000 to 1000;
type I is range 100 to 200;
subtype J is Int range 100 to 200;
```

The type I is distinct from and incompatible with the type Int, whereas the type J is compatible with the type Int. This means that if we declare variables of each of the three types above called x, y and z respectively, the expression x+y is type incorrect, but x+z is allowed. Checking that we don't mix two incompatible integer types can and must be performed statically by a VHDL compiler or simulator.

This distinction between types[3] and subtypes is not that interesting as far as the translation into L2 is concerned because the static checks are performed by a standard, commercial VHDL analyser. What is interesting is how to translate the range information. This is because it cannot be statically checked that a variable never goes out of its specified range. This checking is handled in the translation of function definitions.

From each VHDL type definition we must generate three definitions in L2:

---

[3] In the remainder of this document the word "type" when used in the context of VHDL will refer to subtypes as well as to types.

1. a type definition;
2. a predicate which tests if an item is an element of that type;
3. a predicate which compares two elements to see if they are ordered.

For example, from the definition of the VHDL type I we generate the following L2 definitions.

```
type t = Universal;
val is_I#(x) = leq_Universal#(+100,x)
               /\ leq_Universal#(x,+200);
val leq_I#(x,y) = leq_Universal#(x,y)
```

These definitions make use of the type Universal and the predicate leq_Universal, which correspond to the VHDL notion of the *universal integer* type. They are predefined as:

```
type Universal = int;
val leq_Universal#(x,y) = x <<= y == true;
```

For enumerated types, the ordering predicate is most easily generated by using an auxiliary function to convert an element of that type into an integer. The two integers generated in this way can then be compared.

For example:

```
type Day = (Mon,Tue,Wed,Thu,Fri,Sat,Sun);
subtype WeekDay = Day range Mon to Fri;
```

would be translated as:

```
datatype Day = Mon | Tue | Wed | Thu | Fri | Sat | Sun;
val is_Day#(x) = TRUE;
fun ord_Day Mon = +1
|   ord_Day Tue = +2
|   ord_Day Wed = +3
|   ord_Day Thu = +4
|   ord_Day Fri = +5
|   ord_Day Sat = +6
|   ord_Day Sun = +7;
val leq_Day#(x,y) = leq_Universal#(x,y);

val is_WeekDay#(x) = is_Day#(x)
                     /\ leq_Day#(ord_Day Mon,x)
                     /\ leq_Day#(x,ord_Day Fri);
val leq_WeekDay#(x,y) = leq_Day#(x,y);
```

In the above example we see how the ordering predicate leq_Day, generated from the type Day is used in the definition of the membership predicate is_WeekDay, generated from the subtype WeekDay. For ease of translation we generate the predicate leq_WeekDay for use by subtypes of WeekDay, although this is not strictly necessary as we could just keep track of the base type of every subtype.

The translation scheme, $\mathcal{TD}$, for type and subtype definitions is:

$\mathcal{TD}[\![$ **type** t **is range** i **to** j; $]\!] =$

```
type t          = Universal;
val is_t#(x)    = leq_Universal#(i,x)
                /\ leq_Universal#(x,j);
val leq_t#(x,y) = leq_Universal#(x,y);
```

$\mathcal{TD}[\![$ **type** t **is range** i **downto** j; $]\!] =$

```
type t          = Universal;
val is_t#(x)    = leq_Universal#(j,x)
                /\ leq_Universal#(x,i);
val leq_t#(x,y) = leq_Universal#(x,y);
```

$\mathcal{TD}[\![$ **type** t **is** $(c_1,\ldots,c_n)$; $]\!] =$

```
datatype t = c₁ | ... | cₙ;
val is_t#(x) = TRUE;
fun ord_t c₁ = 1;
```
$\vdots$
```
|   ord_t cₙ = n;
val leq_t#(x,y) = leq_Universal#(ord_t x,ord_t y);
```

$\mathcal{TD}[\![$ **subtype** s **is** t; $]\!] =$

```
val is_s#(x) = 𝒯[[t]]x;
val leq_s#(x,y) = leq_t#(x,y);
```

The translation scheme, $\mathcal{T}$, for (sub-)type expressions is:

$\mathcal{T}[\![\ t\ ]\!]x = \text{is\_}t\#(x)$

$\mathcal{T}[\![\ t$ **range** l_1 **to** $l_2\ ]\!]x =$
$\qquad \text{is\_}t\#(x)\ /\backslash\ \text{leq\_}t\#(l_1,x)\ /\backslash\ \text{leq\_}t\#(x,l_2)$

2.1.2 Function definitions. The definition of a VHDL function includes explicit type information; the type of each parameter, and the return type must be specified. How is this type information used in the translation of VHDL to L2? We can assume that the VHDL has been type checked by the VHDL compiler and has no static type errors, but we are still left with the problem that the VHDL might contain a (not-statically determinable) type-range error. The translation from VHDL to L2 describes a semantics for VHDL in terms of the semantics for L2. One of the jobs of the semantics is to describe what a type-range error means.

For example, here is the definition of a simple VHDL function:

```
type MyInt is range 1 to 100;
function increment (x:MyInt) return MyInt is
begin
   return x+1;
end;
```

What do the VHDL expressions `increment(200)` and `increment(100)` mean? In the first expression the function increment is applied to an integer value out of the range specified for the formal parameter. In the second expression the function increment will attempt to return a value outside of the range specified for the result.

One way to view the type constraints are as a *pre-condition* and a *post-condition* on the function. The type constraint placed on the formal parameters describes a *pre-condition*. The function only specifies the result for those arguments that fall into the ranges specified. The type constraint placed on the return value is a *post-condition* because it is an assertion about the behaviour of the function.

What we are doing is viewing a VHDL function as a relation. Whereas (total) functions describe many to one relationships, relations are more general and can also describe many to none (partial functions) and many to many relationships. A relation can be modelled in L2 using a predicate[4].

We translate a VHDL function of n arguments into a L2 predicate of $n+1$ arguments. For example the VHDL function `increment` would be translated into the following L2 predicate.

```
val is_MyInt#(x) = leq_Universal#(+1,x)
                /\ leq_Universal#(x,+100);

fun increment (x,ret) =
  is_MyInt#(x) ->>
    is_MyInt#(ret) /\ ret == x ++ +1;
```

The meaning of the VHDL expression `increment(5)` can be described as the set of values of `r` that satisfy the L2 predicate `increment(5,r)`. This turns out to be the singleton set containing just 6, which is what we would have expected.

The meaning of the expression `increment(200)` is described by the set of values that satisfy the L2 predicate `increment(200,r)`: this set contains all integer values. This can be interpreted as saying that when a VHDL function

----

[4] A predicate is just a function that returns a value of Type om.

is applied to an argument outside the range specified that any value could be returned.

The meaning of the expression `increment(100)` is described by the set of values that satisfy the L2 predicate `increment(100,r)`: this is the empty set. We can see how a failed return type is different from a failed argument type. What has happened is that the specified return type is at odds with the specified behaviour of the function. For the particular argument value 100 the function has degenerated to `FALSE`.

The translation scheme, $\mathcal{FD}$, for function definitions is:

$$\mathcal{FD}[\![\quad \texttt{function } f \texttt{ } (p_1:t_1,\ldots,p_n:t_n) \texttt{ return } t_{ret} \texttt{ is}$$
$$\texttt{begin}$$
$$body$$
$$\texttt{end } f;$$
$$]\!] =$$
$$\texttt{fun } f \texttt{ } (p_1,\ldots,p_n,ret) =$$
$$\mathcal{T}[\![t_1]\!]p_1 \ /\backslash \ \cdots \ /\backslash \ \mathcal{T}[\![t_n]\!]p_n \ ->>$$
$$\mathcal{T}[\![t_{ret}]\!]ret \ /\backslash \ \mathcal{ST}[\![body]\!]ret$$

Where ret is a fresh identifier.

2.1.3 Statements. The body of each VHDL function definition will be written in the functional subset of VHDL. The most significant statement that is not in this subset is the assignment statement. The reason that assignment is not in the subset is because of the very complex translation it would entail; reasoning about assignment is notoriously difficult.

The lack of assignment means that we do not need to support local variables or looping constructs. In fact, if the VHDL language had contained an *if-expression*[5] as well as an *if-statement*, the only statement we would need to support would be the *return-statement*.

Because VHDL lacks the *if-expression* we extend the subset of statements supported to include the *if-statement* and the *case-statement*. Every branch of these conditional statements must itself be a single *return-statement* of a further *if-statement* or *case-statement*.

The translation scheme, $\mathcal{ST}$, for statements is:

$$\mathcal{ST}[\![\texttt{ return } e; \texttt{ }]\!]r = \mathcal{E}_0[\![e]\!]r$$

$$\mathcal{ST}[\![\texttt{ if } e \texttt{ then } s_1 \texttt{ else } s_2 \texttt{ end if; }]\!]r =$$
$$\mathcal{E}[\![e]\!]\lambda v\bullet$$
$$\texttt{if } v \texttt{ then } \mathcal{ST}[\![s_1]\!]r$$
$$\texttt{else } \mathcal{ST}[\![s_2]\!]r$$

---

[5] Like, for example the $-?-:-$ construct in the C programming language.

$\mathcal{ST}[\![$

```
case e is
    when e_{1,1} | ... | e_{1,m_1} => s_1
        ⋮
    when e_{n,1} | ... | e_{n,m_n} => s_n
    when others => s
end case;
```

$]\!]r =$

$\mathcal{E}[\![e]\!]\lambda v \bullet$

    if $\mathcal{E}_0[\![e_{1,1}]\!]v \ \backslash / \ \cdots \ \backslash / \mathcal{E}_0[\![e_{1,m_1}]\!]v$

    then $\mathcal{ST}[\![s_1]\!]r$

        ⋮

    else if $\mathcal{E}_0[\![e_{1,n}]\!]v \ \backslash / \ \cdots \ \backslash / \mathcal{E}_0[\![e_{1,m_n}]\!]v$

    then $\mathcal{ST}[\![s_n]\!]r$

    else $\mathcal{ST}[\![s]\!]r$

Often VHDL local variables and assignment are used only in a restricted fashion to simulate the effect of a *let-expression* as found in languages such as LISP and ML. We could extend the statement subset to include local variables and assignment as long as they are only used in this restricted way.

This would enable us to translate function definitions such as:

```
function f (x:Integer) return Integer is
var y,z : Integer;
begin
  y := x * x;
  z := (y+1) * (y+2) + 3;
  return z * z;
end;
```

which currently would have to be expanded out and written as:

```
function f (x:Integer) return Integer is
begin
  return ( ((x*x+1) * (x*x+2) + 3)
         * ((x*x+1) * (x*x+2) + 3));
end;
```

2.1.4 Expressions. Because we translate VHDL functions into L2 predicates, the translation of VHDL expressions is non-trivial. We cannot translate a VHDL expression in isolation, but only in the context of some assertion that is made about it. In the simplest case the expression will be part of a *return-statement*, and so we will assert that the translated expression is equal to ret, the name given to the extra parameter of a translated function definition.

The translation scheme $\mathcal{E}_0$ takes an addition parameter, an L2 expression, and translates the given VHDL expression by asserting it is equal to that parameter. Note that for function applications this equality is contained within the actual predicate translated from that function definition. For example:

$\mathcal{E}_0[\![$x+1$]\!]$ ret $\longrightarrow$ ret == x+1

$\mathcal{E}_0[\![$f(x,1)$]\!]$ ret $\longrightarrow$ f(x,1,ret)

The translation of a nested function application is complicated by the need to give a name to the anonymous result of the inner function application. For example:

$\mathcal{E}_0[\![$f(g(a),b)$]\!]$ ret $\longrightarrow$ exists x1. g(a,x1) $/\backslash$ f(x1,b,ret)

In general a VHDL expression will not be directly contained in a return statement but might be a sub-expression of some outer VHDL expression. The translation scheme $\mathcal{E}$ describes this by taking an additional *continuation* parameter, which says what to do with the L2 expression generated.

The translation scheme, $\mathcal{E}$, for expressions is:

$\mathcal{E}[\![\ a\ ]\!]c = c(a)$
where 'a' is an atomic expression (integer literal or identifer)

$\mathcal{E}[\![\ f(e_1,\ldots,e_n)\ ]\!]c =$
$\qquad \mathcal{E}[\![e_1]\!]\lambda v_1 \bullet\ \cdots\ \mathcal{E}[\![e_n]\!]\lambda v_n \bullet$
$\qquad\qquad$ exists $x.f(v_1,\ldots,v_n,x)$ $/\backslash$ $c(x)$
where 'x' is a fresh identifier

$\mathcal{E}[\![\ e_1 + e_2\ ]\!]c = \mathcal{E}[\![e_1]\!]\lambda v_1 \bullet\ \mathcal{E}[\![e_2]\!]\lambda v_2 \bullet\ c(\ v_1 + v_2\ )$

Atomic VHDL expression such as identifier and literal integers are translated by calling the continuation function directly. To translate a function application we need to generate a fresh name for the additional 'return' parameter. This name is introduced using the **exists** quantifier and represents the result of the function application. The continuation function is called with this name in the scope of the quantifier. Each argument to the function application is a VHDL expression itself, and is translated by $\mathcal{E}$. To describe the continuation functions[6] needed for the argument translations lambda notation is used[7].

If we assume that certain VHDL operators like "+" are total and can operate on an unbounded integer type, then their translation can be simplified.

---

[6] Note: The lambda expression $\lambda v \bullet \cdots$ is at the meta level, part of the translation scheme, whereas the **exists** quantifier is at the object level, part of the generated L2. This distinction is highlighted by using an *italic* font for the meta level and a **typewriter** font for the object level.

[7] The body of each lambda expression extends as far to the right as possible.

Instead of translating them in the same way as function applications, we can use the native L2 "+". For example:

$$\mathcal{E}_0[\![f(1+2,3+4)]\!] \text{ ret} \longrightarrow f(1+2,3+4,\text{ret})$$

This scheme only works because we are assuming that VHDL "+" is a total function. If we want a more complicated semantics for VHDL describing when addition overflows then we will need to complicate the translation process also. For example:

$$\mathcal{E}_0[\![f(1+2,3+4)]\!] \text{ ret} \longrightarrow$$
$$\text{exists x1. ADD(1,2,x1) /\textbackslash\ exists x2. ADD(3,4,x2) /\textbackslash}$$
$$f(x1,x2,\text{ret})$$

The specialised translation scheme $\mathcal{E}_0$ optimises the case of a function application at the outermost level by avoiding the need to generate a new name for the return value and instead using a given L2 expression directly.

The specialised translation scheme for expressions $\mathcal{E}_0$ is:

$$\mathcal{E}_0[\![\ f(e_1,\ldots,e_n)\ ]\!]r = \mathcal{E}[\![e_1]\!]\lambda v_1\bullet\ \cdots\ \mathcal{E}[\![e_n]\!]\lambda v_n\bullet\ f(v_1,\ldots,v_n,r)$$

$$\mathcal{E}_0[\![\ e\ ]\!]\ r = \mathcal{E}[\![e]\!]\lambda v\bullet\ r == v$$
where 'e' is not a function application

Here is a larger example of the expression translation schemes:

$$\mathcal{E}_0[\![f(123,g(a,b+1),h(b,a+1))]\!] \text{ ret} \longrightarrow$$
$$\text{exists x1. g(a,b+1,x1) /\textbackslash}$$
$$\text{exists x2. h(b,a+1,x2) /\textbackslash\ f(123,x1,x2,ret)}$$

2.1.5 Arrays. VHDL has two kinds of composite data type – the Record and the Array. Records are used to group a fixed sized collection of objects with differing types. Arrays are used to group an arbitrary sized collection of objects with the same type. Selection from a record is via a static name. Selection from an array is via a computed index value.

A VHDL array can be indexed with any discrete type, i.e integer types and enumerated types. We will initially consider just arrays indexed by integers, viewing indexing by enumerations as a refinement. VHDL also supports the concept of a multi-dimensional array, but we do not consider these here.

VHDL arrays are not always indexed from a particular fixed offset (i.e. zero or one). Instead arrays can be indexed using any contiguous range of the index type. This index constraint is part of the subtype of the array. In addition VHDL arrays have a direction. This direction is also part of the subtype of the array.

To translate VHDL arrays into L2 we must consider both the translation of array definitions and array operations, and the underlying model of arrays. We have chosen to model VHDL arrays as L2 lists, together with supplementary data.

The following section (2.1.5) considers the translation of array definitions. Section 2.1.6 considers the translation of array operations. Section 2.1.7 compares various models of VHDL arrays. Section 2.1.7 briefly examples some desirable properties of VHDL arrays.

Array Definitions. In VHDL, before we can use any array values, we have to make an array type definition. The pragmatic reason for this is that every array value is at some point either returned from a function, passed to a function or assigned to a variable – VHDL requires us to specify a type at each of these points. An array type definition gives us a name for such an array type. Here is an example of a constrained array definition:

```
type C is array(100 to 200) of Integer range 0 to 255;
```

This definition defines C to be the type of arrays of small integers. The constraint specifies that these arrays will always have exactly 101 elements, indexed from 100 to 200, and that the direction of the arrays is ascending (keyword to).

Arrays become more useful when we consider unconstrained arrays. VHDL functions can be written which take parameters of unconstrained array type. These functions operate by extracting the index range and direction information from the actual array parameters passed in. Here is an example of an unconstrained array definition:

```
type U is array(Integer range <>)
          of Integer range 0 to 255;
```

This definition defines U to be the type of arrays of small integers. These arrays may have an arbitrary number of elements. Their index range and direction are not specified Once we have defined an unconstrained array type, we can define a subtype of it by imposing an index constraint:

```
subtype S is U(100 to 200);
```

In fact, VHDL standard defines constrained array definitions as just syntactic sugar for an unconstrained array definition together with a subtype definition. The translation of array definitions will have this structure also.

The translation will define a L2 predicate is_t for each VHDL definition of array type t. This predicate is used in the translation of the type information of function parameters and function return results.

Translation of unconstrained array definition:

$$\mathcal{TD}[\![\text{ type } a \text{ is array (Integer range <>) of } t; \ ]\!] =$$
$$\text{val is\_}a\#(x) =$$
$$\text{all (map (fn e => } \mathcal{T}[\![t]\!]e) \text{ (elements x));}$$

Translation of subtype definitions:

$\mathcal{TD}[\![$ subtype s is $t;$ $]\!]$ = val is_$s\#(\mathtt{x})$ = $\mathcal{T}[\![t]\!]\mathtt{x};$

Translation of constrained array definitions:

$\mathcal{TD}[\![$ type a is array $(constraint)$ of $t;$ $]\!]$ =

$\qquad\mathcal{TD}[\![$ type a' is array (Integer range <>) of $t;$ $]\!]$
$\qquad\mathcal{TD}[\![$ subtype a is $a'(constraint);$ $]\!]$
$\qquad\qquad\qquad$ where a' is a fresh identifier

Translation of index constraints subtypes:

$\mathcal{T}[\![$ $a(e_1$ $direction$ $e_2)$ $]\!]x$ =

$\qquad$is_$a\#(x)$ $/\backslash$
$\qquad$direction x = $\mathcal{DIR}[\![$ $direction$ $]\!]$ $/\backslash$
$\qquad\mathcal{E}_0[\![e_1]\!](\mathtt{LEFT}$ $x)$ $/\backslash$
$\qquad\mathcal{E}_0[\![e_2]\!](\mathtt{RIGHT}$ $x)$

The translation scheme for directions $\mathcal{DIR}$ is:

$\mathcal{DIR}[\![$ to $]\!]$ = ASCEND
$\mathcal{DIR}[\![$ downto $]\!]$ = DESCEND

The above translation schemes make uses of the functions and values: all, map, elements, direction, LEFT, RIGHT, ASCEND and DESCEND. These are all defined straightforwardly in the array model.

As an example, we give the translation of the array types U and S above:

```
𝒯𝒟 [
   type U is array(Integer range <>)
   of Integer range 0 to 255;
   subtype S is U(100 to 200);
] =
      val is_U#(x) =
            all (map (fn x => is_Integer#(x) /\
                             leq_Integer#(+0,x) /\
                             leq_Integer#(x,+255))
                   (elements x));

      val is_S#(x) =
            is_U#(x) /\
            direction x == ASCEND /\
            LEFT x == +100 /\
            RIGHT x == +200;
```

2.1.6 Array operations. To demonstrate some of the primitive operations available on arrays, consider the following definition of the VHDL function sum, which is used to sum the elements of an arbitrary sized array of Integers (indexed by Integers).

```
type U is array(Integer range <>)
          of Integer range 0 to 255;

function sum (x : U) return Integer is
begin
    if x'length = 0
    then
        return 0;
    else
        return x(x'left) + sum(x(x'left+1 to x'right));
    end if;
end;
```

The example demonstrates array indexing: x(x'left), array slicing: x(x'left+1 to x'right), and various array attributes: length, left and right. array value must carry its bounds. This is important when we consider how to model arrays in L2. Similarly, each array value has a direction, and that direction will affect the results of some operations, so each array value must carry its direction.

In the following sections we provide translation for the array operations that make sense in the functional subset of VHDL. In particular, we do not support selective updating of array elements. The operations available on all arrays are aggregation (creation), indexing and attributes. In addition, 1-dimensional arrays support the operations of slicing and concatenation.

Aggregation (Creation). There are two different notations available for array aggregates: positional and named. The choice of which notation to regard as primitive and which to regard as just syntactic sugar is not obvious.

The problem with named notation is that it allows aggregates to have holes in them. i.e. (5=>1, 6=>2, 8=>3). This is not allowed. The problem with positional notation is that we must consider the context in which the aggregate is to be used before we can discover what array value it represents.

For example if we pass the array aggregate (1,2,3) to a function that takes a parameter of type array, index range 100 to 102, then the aggregate will have that type. If we pass the same aggregate to a function that takes an unconstrained array type, the aggregate value has an index range starting from the leftmost value of the range type used to index the unconstrained array type.

The direction of an array is also determined by the context of its use. This occurs in both named and positional notations. We will sidestep these issues and give only the translation of positional array aggregates. However, named notation will be used in later examples as it is less ambiguous.

$$\mathcal{E}[\![\ (e_1,\dots,e_n)\ ]\!]c =$$
$$\mathcal{E}[\![e_1]\!]\lambda v_1 \bullet \ \cdots\ \mathcal{E}[\![e_n]\!]\lambda v_n \bullet$$
$$c(\ \text{AGGREGATE}\ (left, direction)\ [v_1,\dots,v_n]\ )$$

where left and direction are derived from the context in which the array is used.

Indexing. Indexing into an array is not a total operation; we might attempt to index into an array outside of its index range. We cannot detect these index range 'errors' statically. This means that we cannot model array indexing as a function; it must be modelled as a relation.

Just as VHDL functions were translated into L2 predicates with an extra parameter for the return result, we will add an extra parameter to array indexing for the return result. Indexing into an array outside of its index range will be like failing the subtype precondition of a VHDL function.

The model will contain a predicate INDEX of three parameters. If i is not in the index range of a, the expression INDEX(a,i,v) will be equal to TRUE for all values of v.

Translation of array indexing is similar to the translation of function application. We need to invent a fresh name for the return result.

$$\mathcal{E}[\![\ e_1(e_2)\ ]\!]c =$$
$$\mathcal{E}[\![e_1]\!]\lambda a \bullet\ \mathcal{E}[\![e_2]\!]\lambda i \bullet$$
$$\text{exists }v.\text{INDEX}(a,i,v)\ \wedge\ c(v)$$

where v is a fresh identifier

Attributes. Arrays support the following attributes;

left, right, high, low, range, reverse_range and length.

In general each of these attributes take an optional parameter indicating which dimension of the array they refer to. This defaults to 1. As we are only considering 1-dimensional arrays, we only give the translation for unparameterised attributes.

$$\mathcal{E}[\![\ e'i\ ]\!]c = \mathcal{E}[\![e]\!]\lambda v \bullet\ c(\ i\ v\ )$$

This translation assumes that all attributes operate as total functions.

Slicing. The slice operator returns an array that is a contiguous 'slice' of another array. Slicing could *almost* be defined in VHDL itself rather than being a primitive, except that it is polymorphic.

Like array indexing, array slicing is not a total operation. It must be modelled as a relation.

$$\mathcal{E}[\![\; e_1 (e_2 \; direction \; e_3) \;]\!]c =$$
$$\mathcal{E}[\![e_1]\!]\lambda a \bullet \; \mathcal{E}[\![e_2]\!]\lambda left \bullet \; \mathcal{E}[\![e_3]\!]\lambda right \bullet$$
$$\text{exists } a'.\text{SLICE}(a, (left, \mathcal{DIR}[\![direction]\!], right), a')$$
$$\land \; c(a')$$
where a' is a fresh identifier

Concatenation. Concatenation *is* a total operation. It is translated like any other total binary operator:

$$\mathcal{E}[\![\; e_1 \; \& \; e_2 \;]\!]c \; = \mathcal{E}[\![e_1]\!]\lambda v_1 \bullet \; \mathcal{E}[\![e_2]\!]\lambda v_2 \bullet \; c(\; \text{CONCAT } v_1 \; v_2 \;)$$

As we will see, the operation of concatenation strongly influences how we model arrays.

Example Translation. To clarify the translation of some of the array operations, consider the translation of the VHDL function sum defined above:

```
fun sum (x,ret) =
  is_U#(x) ->>
    is_Integer#(ret) /\
    if LENGTH x = +0
    then ret == +0
    else exists x1.
            INDEX (x,LEFT x,x1) /\
            exists x2.
              SLICE (x,(LEFT x ++ +1,
                        ASCEND,RIGHT x),x2) /\
              exists x3. sum (x2,x3) /\
                  ret == x1 ++ x3;
```

With this translation we can prove useful theorems like:

|- sum (AGGREGATE (n,ASCEND) [1,2,3,4,5], 15)

2.1.7 Array models. The task of modelling VHDL arrays in L2 boils down to defining the following collection of functions/predicates:

AGGREGATE, INDEX, LEFT, RIGHT, HIGH, LOW, RANGE, REVERSE_RANGE, LENGTH, SLICE and CONCAT.

We want the simplest (and most abstract) model that supports the required semantics of these array operations, as defined by the VHDL language standard.

In general the standard, although written in English, is precise. However, the concept of the null array seems ill-defined – Do null arrays have a leftmost index, and what is their length? In other places the semantics, although precise, seem unintuitive. In particular, the interaction of the concept of array direction with the operations of slicing and concatenation is very complex.

We examined four candidate models. We consider just 1-dimensional arrays indexed by integers, but keep in mind that we would eventually like to extend the model to cater for muti-dimensional arrays, and arrays indexed by types other that Integers.

The simplest view of an array is as a mapping from index to value:

```
datatype ('a,'b) ARRAY = Array of 'a -> 'b;
```

However, this would not allow us to recover the INDEX function we require. One solution would be to model the array values themselves as relations: Again, this model will easily extend to arrays indexed by alternative types and multi-dimensional arrays.

```
datatype ('a,'b) ARRAY = Array of 'a * 'b -> om;
```

We also need extra information to define the various attributes. For example, how can we define the function LEFT for these representations?

The solution to the above problems is to have the array value include explicit information about its index range and direction together with the information about the elements. Adding this data allows us to revert to the simpler functional model of arrays:

```
datatype Direction = ASCEND | DESCEND;

datatype ('a,'b) ARRAY = Array of ('a * Direction * 'a)
                                 * ('a -> 'b);
```

This "function + data" model works well until we look at the operation of array concatenation.

The semantics of concatenation specify that if we concatenate two arrays which have index range 10–20 and index range 21–30, we end up with an array with index range 10–30. However, if the second array has index range 25–34 or index range 15–24, the result is exactly the same. The second array must be 'shifted' so that its index range juxtaposes that of the first array. Things become even more complicated when we consider array direction.

It turns out that modelling an array as a list is the most straightforward way of matching the VHDL semantics. Although using lists to model arrays appears to be less abstract than using functions, it supports the required semantics with greater ease.

The explicit data is limited to just the left-bound and the direction (the right-bound can be calculated from the left-bound and the length of the list):

```
datatype ('a,'b) ARRAY = Array of 'a * Direction
                                 * 'b list;
```

Another advantage of this model is that every value of this type represents some VHDL array. Multi-dimensional arrays are different beasts however – they don't support array concatenation, and will probably still be modelled best by the "function + data" model.

Array Properties. When reasoning about VHDL specification involving arrays we don't always want to unfold the definition of arrays in terms of the model. It would be nice if we could perform higher level reasoning about arrays in terms of the properties that they have. In fact, we would like to find a set of array properties that totally axiomatize the operation of VHDL arrays, then the only use for the model would be in the proof of these 'axioms'.

Examples of such properties might include the relationship between attributes LOW, HIGH and LENGTH:

LENGTH a == HIGH a - LOW a + 1

and the associativity of array concatenation:

CONCAT a (CONCAT b c) == CONCAT (CONCAT a b) c

3. Tutorial examples

In this section, we use a couple of simple examples to revisit the ideas and tools discussed earlier, and to show how we can apply them to reason about VHDL. We identify four elements in the reasoning process.

Model This is where we give a meaning to the VHDL constructs in our subset. This model is given in L2. These constructs include such things as: function definitions, type/subtype definitions, expressions, and types.

Translation The translation can be regarded as the *implementation* of the model. The VLT tool constitutes the translator and will produce a collection of L2 definitions from a collection of VHDL definitions.

Proof Obligation This is where we choose what we wish to prove. This might mean we choose ourselves, or perhaps the obligation is generated automatically by some other tool. Three possible forms of obligation include:

Type I Equivalence of two VHDL functions.

Type II Proof that a VHDL function has some property (expressed in L2).

Type III Proof that a VHDL function has some property (expressed in VHDL).

Proof This where we actually carry out the proof using the LAMBDA system.

Each stage will be considered in the following examples.

3.1 Simple reasoning

Here we give a complete example of the overall reasoning process, using a very simple example. We will write two *different* VHDL definitions for the *same* function and then show how to prove they are equivalent. This is an example of a Type-I proof-obligation.

3.1.1 Example: `double`. Both functions take a single integer parameter, and return an integer which is double the argument value. The two functions, named `doubleA` and `doubleB`, use different methods of doubling their integer argument. Although we could make this proof when both functions take an arbitrary range of integers, we will restrict the proof to a particular range of the integers, to show how type/subtype restrictions fit into the reasoning process.

VHDL

```
type Int is range -100 to 100;

function doubleA (x:Int) return Int is
begin
    return x+x;
end;

function doubleB (x:Int) return Int is
begin
    return 2*x;
end;
```

To achieve the proof that these two VHDL functions are equivalent we consider the elements of the reasoning process in order: translation, proof-obligation and proof.

Model First, we briefly recall, from Section 2.1 the L2 model for several VHDL concepts.

Types/subtypes: These are modelled as an L2 type plus an L2 predicate. The predicate is used to capture subtype restrictions such as integer range.

Function definition: A VHDL function is modelled as an L2 relation. The statements and expressions of the body are represented as a truth-valued relationship between the arguments and result.

Subtype restriction: Argument subtype restrictions are modelled as pre-conditions. The return value subtype restriction is modelled as a post-condition.

Primitive operators: Primitive operators such as + and * are represented with the corresponding L2 operators when they exist, otherwise special purpose L2 definitions are written. For example, array indexing in modelled using the L2 function `INDEX`, described earlier.

Translation Running the VLT translator on the above VHDL definitions produces the following L2 definitions. The predicate `is_Int` represents the subtype restriction on the VHDL type `Int`. The L2 predicates named `doubleA` and `doubleB` after the original VHDL definitions each take an additional parameter `ret` which represents the return value of the corresponding VHDL function.

```
val is_Int#(x) =
  leq_Universal#(~ +100,x) /\
  leq_Universal#(x,+100);

fun doubleA (x,ret) =
  is_Int#(x) ->> is_Int#(ret) /\ ret == x ++ x;

fun doubleB (x,ret) =
  is_Int#(x) ->> is_Int#(ret) /\ ret == +2 ** x;
```

Proof obligation The proof obligation which expresses the equivalence of the two functions is written simply as |- doubleA == doubleB. This is known as a sequent and consists of a turnstile followed by a truth-valued expression. In general, a sequent may have a list of hypothesis to the left of the turnstile, but this is not necessary for this example

Proof In LAMBDA reasoning proceeds by means of safe transformations to rules. Rules are a *safe* type in the LAMBDA system; every rule expresses a valid statement in the LAMBDA logic. Each rule is formed from of a collection of premisses together with a conclusion (separated by a horizontal line) and may be read as asserting "if all the premisses are true, then so is the conclusion". Each of the premisses and the conclusion is a sequent.

All rules which have exactly one premiss which is identical to the conclusion are trivially valid. Given the desired sequent to be used for both premiss and conclusion, the system will construct the trivially valid rule. This is the starting point for many proofs in the LAMBDA system, including our example. Because further rules can only be constructed by safe transformations to existing rules, it is impossible to construct an invalid rule.

```
*******   LEVEL 1.1   *******
1: |- doubleA == doubleB
   --------------------
   |- doubleA == doubleB
```

The level number allows us to keep track of the different proof steps. The above rule express the trivially valid statement that:

```
|- doubleA == doubleB
```

may be concluded when

```
|- doubleA == doubleB
```

is assumed as a premiss. Once we have a valid rule we can apply rule transformations. A proof in LAMBDA consists of a sequence of such transformations until the desired rule is created.

It is usual for the desired rule to be a theorem. A theorem is a rule without any premisses. It asserts that its conclusion is true without any assumptions.

For the current example, the desired rule is below. If we manage to construct such a rule within the LAMBDA system, we have completed our proof.

```
----------------------
|- doubleA == doubleB
```

The primitive rules transformations in the LAMBDA system include: unification of rules with existing rules, and rewriting of rules with equivalences expressed by theorems (other rules). Complex combinations of rule transformations (called tactics) can be constructed which capture common patterns of proof.

We will now complete the example proof. We can show that two L2 functions are equivalent by using the rule of function extension. This says that they are equivalent if and only if the return values are equivalent for all possible arguments. When applied to our example we get the following rule. Notice that only the premiss has changed; the conclusion has remained the same. In fact, in this example the conclusion will remain fixed until the end of the proof. All changes will occur *above-the-line*, until finally we reduce the premiss to TRUE and then remove it.

```
*******    LEVEL 1.2    *******
1: |- forall arg,ret. doubleA(arg,ret) == doubleB(arg,ret)
   -------------------------------------------------------
   |- doubleA == doubleB
```

The next stage of the proof is simply to replace the applications of the functions doubleA and doubleB with their respective bodies. This can be done because the system automatically constructs the necessary rewrite rules when the definitions of doubleA and doubleB are entered into the system.

```
*******    LEVEL 1.3    *******
1:
   |- forall arg,ret.
        (is_Int#(arg) ->> is_Int#(ret)
                        /\ ret == arg ++ arg) ==
        (is_Int#(arg) ->> is_Int#(ret)
                        /\ ret == +2 ** arg)
   -------------------------------------------------
   |- doubleA == doubleB
```

One approach now would be to rewrite the subexpression +2 ** arg into the equivalent expression arg ++ arg. Both sides of the equality (==) would then be identical allowing the premiss to be reduced to TRUE. The rewrite that would achieve this aim can be expressed with the following rule.

```
----------------------------
|- +2 ** x == x ++ x
```

This rule is not automatically included in LAMBDA's standard set of integer rewriting rules, but can easily be added once proven. Identification and proof of subgoals is a common proof technique. The proof of this rule is achieved simply by induction on x, followed by rewriting. With the extended rewriting system we can discharge the final step of the example.

```
*******    LEVEL 1.4    *******
------------------------------
|- doubleA == doubleB
```

Although the identification and proof of subgoals like the above is good practice, it is not strictly necessary in this example. We could just as easily have applied induction directly to the variable arg in the rule at level 1.3. The standard LAMBDA rewriting system would then have completed the proof.

3.2 Recursive definitions

One important aspect of the reasoning process is the ability to reason about recursive VHDL functions. The following example demonstrates some of the steps involved.

3.2.1 Example: triangle. Using VHDL we define a simple recursive function which computes the *triangle number* of its argument x, the sum of integers from one upto x.

VHDL

```
subtype ShortInt is Integer range 0 to 255;

function triangle (x : ShortInt) return Integer is
begin
    if x = 0
    then return 0;
    else return x + triangle(x-1);
    end if;
end;
```

The function is defined on a subset of the integers. Although the accepted range could have its upper bound increased arbitrarily the lower bound is necessary because the function is only sensibly defined for positive arguments. We choose to place no restriction on the integer range of the functions result.

Translation

```
val is_ShortInt#(x) =
  is_Integer#(x) /\ leq_Integer#(+0,x) /\
  leq_Integer#(x,+255);
```

```
fun triangle (x,ret) =
  is_ShortInt#(x) ->>
    is_Integer#(ret) /\
    if x = +0
    then ret == +0
    else
      exists x1.
        triangle (x -- +1,x1) /\ ret == x ++ x1;
```

We can see that the generated L2 relation is also recursive. Before looking at any particular proof obligation we might like to proof about **triangle** we need to consider some extra concepts related to recursive definitions in LAMBDA which place an additional burden of the user to show that they are *well defined* before useful rewrite rules can be obtained. In our example the desired rule would be of the form:

|- triangle (x,ret) == *body of triangle definition.*

We explain the reason for the extra restrictions and the form they take with the following pathological example: fun bad x = not (bad x);. This example is not well defined because the recursive call within the body does not reduce the argument x towards any base case; there is in fact no base case given for this function. Any programmer who wrote such a definition would not be surprised when the program entered an infinite loop during execution.

The LAMBDA system also needs to be wary of such ill defined functions. If the system blindly generated the rewrite rule |- bad x == not (bad x), it is only a short proof to conclude |- FALSE and hence destroy the consistency of the entire system. Of course, LAMBDA does *not* produce such a rule. In fact the following two rules are produced.

```
------------------------------------
DOM'bad#(x)   |- bad x == not (bad x)
```

```
------------------------------------
|- DOM'bad#(x) == DOM'bad#(x)
```

The first states that we can replace bad x with not (bad x), but only under the side-condition DOM'bad#(x). This extra predicate is true for those values of x for which bad is well defined, i.e. in the *domain* of bad. The second rule characterise this domain. In this example the domain is empty and the second rule is entirely useless, although in general we would use such a rule to prove that some or all values are within the domain.

Back to the **triangle** example. The system provides us with the conditional rewrite rule: DOM'triangle#((x,ret))|- triangle (x,ret) == *body of triangle.* The first step in any proof which involves the **triangle** function would be to discharge the predicate DOM'triangle for as many values of x and ret as possible. In fact we can discharge the predicate for all possible values, even negative values of x. This is due to the positive sub-type restriction made on the VHDL function's argument. The additional rule which characterises the DOM'triangle predicate is the following.

```
------------------------------------------------------
|- DOM'triangle#((x,ret)) ==
      (is_ShortInt#(x) == TRUE
         ->> is_Integer#(ret) == TRUE
            ->> x = +0 == false
               ->> forall x1. DOM'triangle#((x -- +1,x1)))
```

From this rule we can by a simple inductive proof deduce that triangle is well defined for all argument values:

```
-----------------------
|- DOM'triangle#((x,y))
```

Once we have this rule we can convert the rewrite rule for triangle into the desired *unconditional* rewrite rule.

```
-------------------------------------------------------------
|- triangle (x,ret) ==
      (is_ShortInt#(x)
         ->> is_Integer#(ret)
            /\ if x = +0
               then ret == +0
               else exists x1. triangle (x -- +1,x1)
                              /\ ret == x ++ x1)
```

Proof Obligation We should like to show that the triangle function satisfies the following well known triangle property: $triangle(n) = n(n + 1)/2$. We could specify this property in VHDL, but it is simpler to use L2 directly. This is an example of a Type II proof obligation.

```
|- triangle(natToInt x, natToInt(half ((x + 1) * x)))
```

We have used a couple of standard LAMBDA functions: natToInt and half. The function natToInt converts from a natural number to an integer; this implies that the variable x above is of type natural. This is good because reasoning about naturals is simpler that reasoning about integers. In fact the triangle property is actually expressed entirely at the level of naturals, even though the triangle function operates at the level of integers.

The function half is a natural number function which computes *div* 2 of of it's argument. The advantage of writing half E instead of E div 2 is that we can take easy advantage of the special properties of division by two. We don't even need to know the exact definition of half, but simply need a rule which expresses a critical property of half which we are to depend on whilst proving the triangle property.

```
-------------------------------------
|- half (a + (a + b)) == a + half b
```

Proof As before, we start our proof with the trivial rule containing the same sequent for both premiss and conclusion.

```
*******   LEVEL 1.1   *******
1: |- triangle (natToInt x,natToInt (half ((x + 1) * x)))
   ------------------------------------------------------
   |- triangle (natToInt x,natToInt (half ((x + 1) * x)))
```

The first step is to perform induction on the variable x. Because L2 is a higher order logic, the induction schema for natural numbers is itself expressed as a rule:

```
2: |- forall n. P#(n) ->> P#(1'n)
1: |- P#(0)
   --------------------------------
   |- forall n. P#(n)
```

The best way to read this rule is *bottom-up*: it says that a property P of a natural variable n can be proved by splitting into a base case and an inductive case. The base case says we must prove P when n is zero. The inductive case says we must prove that the property is true for 1'n (one greater than n) under the assumption that the property is true for n.

When we apply this rule to our current proof step, P is automatically instantiated with the correct property.

```
*******   LEVEL 1.2   *******
2: |- forall x.
         triangle (natToInt x,natToInt (half ((x + 1) * x)))
         ->> triangle (natToInt (1'x),
                       natToInt (half ((1'x + 1) * 1'x)))
1: |- triangle (natToInt 0,natToInt (half ((0 + 1) * 0)))
   --------------------------------------------------------
   |- triangle (natToInt x,natToInt (half ((x + 1) * x)))
```

The base case is proved by simply expanding the definition of `triangle` and then rewriting.

```
*******   LEVEL 1.3   *******
1: |- forall x.
         triangle (natToInt x,natToInt (half ((x + 1) * x)))
         ->> triangle (natToInt (1'x),
                       natToInt (half ((1'x + 1) * 1'x)))
   --------------------------------------------------------
   |- triangle (natToInt x,natToInt (half ((x + 1) * x)))
```

For the inductive case, we begin by stripping the **forall** quantifier. The name of the variable is changed from **x** to **n** so that it doesn't clash with the different variable **x** still in the conclusion. If we hadn't performed the renaming the system would have automatically renamed it **x1**, but using **n** is clearer for the example.

Because the proof must continue without making any assumptions about the particular value of **n**, (we say **n** is a restricted variable) the system appends a prime character (') to the identifier **n** to remind us of this fact.

Also in this step we move the the first application of **triangle** (left of the implication (->>)) into the hypothesis and expand the second application into its body.

```
*******    LEVEL 1.4    *******
1: triangle (natToInt n',natToInt (half ((n' + 1) * n')))
   |- is_ShortInt#(natToInt (1'n'))
      ->>
      is_Integer#(natToInt (half ((1'n' + 1) * 1'n')))
   /\ if natToInt (1'n') = +0
      then
         natToInt (half ((1'n' + 1) * 1'n')) == +0
      else
         exists x1.
            triangle (natToInt (1'n') -- +1,x1)
            /\ natToInt (half ((1'n' + 1) * 1'n'))
               == natToInt (1'n') ++ x1
-------------------------------------------------------
|- triangle (natToInt x,natToInt (half ((x + 1) * x)))
```

The current rule is rather messy but can easily be simplified. We can discharge the **is_Integer** predicate which is always true, and also remove the unnecessary assumption **is_ShortInt**.

```
*******    LEVEL 1.5    *******
1: triangle (natToInt n',natToInt (half (n' + n' * n')))
   |- exists x1.
         triangle (natToInt n',x1)
         /\ natToInt (1'(half (n' + (n' + (n' * n' + n')))))
            == natToInt (1'n') ++ x1
-------------------------------------------------------
|- triangle (natToInt x,natToInt (half ((x + 1) * x)))
```

Now we come to the most important steps of the proof. We have to show that there exists a value of **x1** which is the return value of the nested call to **triangle**. The hypothesis (to the left of the turnstile) says that there is such a value for **x1** and even tells us what it is: **natToInt (half (n' + n' * n'))**. By making just this substitution for **x1** we simplify the goal.

```
*******   LEVEL 1.6   *******
1: |- half (n' + (n' + (n' * n' + n')))
      == n' + half (n' + n' * n')
   ----------------------------------------------------
   |- triangle(natToInt x,natToInt (half ((x + 1) * x)))
```

The final step depends on the previously mentioned property of half, together with the fact that addition is commutative.

```
*******   LEVEL 1.7   *******
   ----------------------------------------------------
   |- triangle (natToInt x,natToInt (half ((x + 1) * x)))
```

The triangle property proof is now complete.

3.3 Arrays

In this section it is assumed that VHDL arrays are being used as data objects rather than for simply grouping signals. For example, an array of signals may often be used to wire up a collection of components in a for-generate statement. Such uses of arrays merely as a grouping construct does not entail the need to reason about the arrays as data. The following example is intended to illustrate the use of arrays as data. We concentrate on some examples which use an array of *bits* to represent natural numbers. A good example of an array reading function is array2int which converts such a bit array into the number which it represents. The inverse function int2array, which constructs the bit array from a given natural number would be an array building function.

Bit and BitArray Before we start the example we must decide exactly how an array of bits will represent a natural number. For example, we could choose to have the bit an index n contribute 2^n to the overall value. If this is the case what about the bits at negative indicies? These will represent fractional parts, and so the array would not represent an integer.

One approach might be to state that all negative index positions would simply be ignored, however, the solution we choose is to say that the actual index positions are unimportant and instead take account of the relative index positions, i.e. we just take the bits in sequence from the low-index to the high-index. One implication of this is that both of the following array aggregates represent the same number—4.

```
(0 => '0', 1 => '0', 2 => '1')
(7 => '0', 8 => '0', 9 => '1')
```

What about the array's direction? We shall simply avoid this issue by assuming that all arrays encountered will be ascending. This decision will affect the proof-obligations we must choose.

VHDL definitions. Here are the type definitions for `Bit` and `BitArray`, together with a function which converts from a single `Bit` into the digit which it represents.

```
type Bit is ('1', '0');
subtype Index is Integer;
type BitArray is array (Index range <>) of Bit;

function Bit2Int (b:Bit) return Integer is
begin
    if b = '1' then return 1;
                else return 0;
    end if;
end;
```

Example: `array2int` In the imperative VHDL world an array-reading function like `array2int` would probably be written using some kind of looping construct. Within the functional subset we have found two general styles for specifying array reading functions. The first *looping* style is closer to the imperative style, whilst the second *functional* style is inspired from the functional programming method of list manipulation

For comparison we present the `array2int` in both styles although we have only attempted reasoning with the functional style. It would be interesting to compare the necessary reasoning processes for the looping style.

`array2int` *(looping style).*

```
function array2int_loopFrom (a:BitArray; i:Index)
                            return Integer is
begin
    if i > a'high
    then return 0;
    else return Bit2Int(a(i))
        + 2 * array2int_loopFrom(a,i+1);
    end if;
end;

function array2int_loop (a:BitArray) return Integer is
begin
    return array2int_loopFrom(a,a'low);
end;
```

Note the looping style function is called `array2int_loop` to distinguish it from the functional version defined below. This version works by having the recursive function `array2int_loopFrom` take an extra integer parameter which represents the current array index we are considering. When this passes the highest index value we are done. The second definition simply initialises this with the array's lowest index. Also, notice how the array a is passed unchanged from one recursive call to the next.

array2int *(functional style).*

```
function array2int (a:BitArray) return Integer is
begin
    if IsNull(a)
    then return 0;
    else return Bit2Int(Head(a)) + 2 * array2int(Tail(a));
    end if;
end;
```

The functional style is different in that no additional index parameter is needed. At each recursive call a different array is passed, being the tail of the current array. Strictly, there is no need for the auxiliary functions: IsNull, Head and Tail (they could simply be *in-lined*), but it is cleaner, and makes reasoning easier.

Definitions of functional auxiliaries.

```
function IsNull (a:BitArray) return Boolean is
begin return a'low > a'high;
end;

function Head (a:BitArray) return Bit is
begin return a(a'low);
end;

function Tail (a:BitArray) return BitArray is
begin return a(a'low+1 to a'high);
end;
```

This version of tail only works for ascending arrays. It could be rewritten (with difficulty) to operate on arrays of either direction but since we are assuming all arrays will be ascending this is not necessary.

Proof Obligation One property we might like to prove is the relationship between concatenation of bit arrays, and the numbers which they represent via array2int. To define an obligation in VHDL we need to define an additional function with return type Boolean

```
function proofObligation1 (a,b:BitArray) return Boolean is
begin
    return
        array2int(a&b)
        = array2int (a) + 2 ** a'length * array2int(b);
end;
```

The L2 obligation then has the form: `proofObligation1 (a,b,true)`. This is an example of a Type III obligation. Unfortunately we will not be able to prove such a strong obligation because of the assumptions we have made about all arrays being ascending. This can be fixed by adding some hypotheses. We also have to add some hypotheses which ensure that the argument arrays are within the correct subtype range. Note that multiple hypotheses are separated with the dollar symbol ($).

```
is_BitArray#(a) $ direction a == ASCEND $
is_BitArray#(b) $ direction b == ASCEND
|- proofObligation1 (a,b,true)
```

Reasoning about arrays One of the most difficult tasks during reasoning is the identification of useful sub-goals. These are rules which express some important property which is relied upon at the level above.

Often it is difficult to know the most useful subgoals until an attempt of a proof at the higher level is started. Useful subgoals will be those which apply again and again to higher level proofs. Proof of the lowest level subgoals can often be achieved either directly by rewriting, or by a single induction and then rewriting.

Sometimes the proof of the sub-goal will require even lower level sub-goals. For example, proofs about `array2int` rely on properties of auxiliary functions like `Head` and `Tail`. These in turn rely upon properties of `INDEX` and `SLICE` when used in specific ways, i.e, indexing the low-index element, and slicing from one greater than the low-index element to the high-index element.

Many subgoal will take the form of rewrite rules, which when used at a higher level will simplify expressions. Sometimes the rewrite will only be applicable under certain side-conditions. These are known as *conditional rewrites* and are supported by the LAMBDA system. Here is an example of a conditional rewrite rule called *INDEX'LEFT*.

```
elements a == x::xs |- INDEX (a,LEFT a,ret) == (ret == x)
```

This rewrite allows any subexpression of the form `INDEX (a,LEFT a,ret)` to be reduced to `ret == x` under the assumption that

```
elements a == x::xs
```

This assumption has two purposes: first it ensures that the array **a** is non-null, and secondly it gives the name x to the left-most element of the array which is used in the replacement expression `ret == x`. The identifier `elements` is a function defined on the L2 model of VHDL arrays.

VHDL arrays are modelled as a triple of values. The first component is an integer which represents the left index of the array. The second component is a flag indicating whether the array is ascending or descending. The third component is an L2 list of the elements in left-index to right-index order.

When the **elements** function is applied to an array it simply returns the list component. Lists in L2 are very simple structures. Every list is either the empty list, written [], or is built by *consing* a single element to the head of another list, written **x::xs**. The side-condition in the above rewrite rule uses the *cons* constructor (**::**) to force the list to be non-null and to give a name to the head element.

Another model-based function which is often useful as a hypothesis is the **direction** function. This returns either ASCEND or DECSEND, and is important because many proofs might only be applicable to ascending arrays. The alternative to using model-based functions as side-conditions is to force the user to make proofs completely at the level of the array model. This would mean exposing the triple which represents each VHDL array and making the proof in terms of this triple. The following rule would be used to expose the triple.

```
|- forall left,dir,elems. P#(Array (left,dir,elems))
-----------------------------------------------------
|- forall a. P#(a)
```

This rule says that any property P we wish to prove about all arrays a can be achieved by making the proof for the triple **Array (left,dir,elems)** for all values of **left**, **dir** and **elems**. The intention is that although the proofs of various (reusable) sub-goals (like the *INDEX'LEFT* subgoal above) may have to be made at the level of the model, it would be preferable if the user could work at a higher level.

For example, for recursive VHDL array functions, the user will need some form of induction rule. If the proof was made at the model-level, once the triple had been exposed then the standard list induction rule could be applied. The following induction rule *arrayElements'ind* allows an inductive array proof to be made without resorting to the model.

```
2: |- forall x,xs,b.
       elements b == x :: xs
       /\ (forall a. elements a == xs ->> P#(a))
       ->> P#(b)
1: |- forall a. null a ->> P#(a)
   ------------------------------------------------
   |- forall a. P#(a)
```

This rule says that a property P of arrays a can proved by considering two separate cases. The first case is to prove the property P#(a) under the assumption that a is the null array. The second case is to prove the property P#(b) under the following assumptions: **elements b == x::xs**—which states that the array in non-null and gives a name to the tail-elements **xs**, and **forall a. elements a == xs ->> P#(a)**—that the property is true for all arrays whose elements consist of **xs**, i.e. the tail elements of the array b.

This induction rule has been designed so that when invoked, the assumptions are in just the right form to allow conditional rewrites such as *INDEX'LEFT* to operate.

4. Conclusions

We have introduced the LAMBDA system, and a translation of VHDL into the Lambda Logic, L2. This allows us to reason about VHDL within the LAMBDA system—including reasoning about recursive functions, and reasoning about arrays. We have presented various examples, highlighting four stages in the reasoning process: modelling, translation, formalising proof obligations, and proof. Common proof techniques include induction, rewriting, and the identification and proof of useful subgoals. Proofs in the LAMBDA system proceed by means of safe transformation to rules. Every rule expresses a valid statement in the LAMBDA logic. It is impossible to construct an invalid rule.

Proofs   in   LAMBDA   complement   symbolic model checking (R. E. Bryant 1986). LAMBDA supports data abstraction, the interactive decomposition and refinement of proof obligations, and the use of induction to derive general results; symbolic model checking provides an automated tool that may provide the effect of exhaustive simulation, but symbolic model checking is intractable for complex systems. LAMBDA may be used to decompose the verification task into tractable chunks.

Modelling VHDL in L2 highlights the fact that VHDL was certainly not designed with verification in mind. Many constructs (eg. the notion of direction for an array) introduce superfluous complexity. In addition to the requirements of simulation and synthesis, future behavioural design languages should also take account of the requirements of verification. In particular, simplicity is a good thing!

References

R. E. Bryant (1986): Can a simulator verify a circuit? In G.J. Milne and P.A. Subrahmanyam, editors, *Formal Aspects of VLSI Design*, pages 125–126. North-Holland.

M. J. Gordon, R. Milner, and Ch. P. Wadsworth (1979): A mechanised logic of computation. In *Edinburgh LCF: Lecture Notes in Computer Science—Volume 78*. Springer-Verlag.

M. J. Gordon (1985): HOL: A machine oriented formulation of higher-order logic. Technical Report 68, University of Cambridge.

L. C. Paulson (1994). *Isabelle: A Generic Theorem Prover*. Springer-Verlag LNCS 828.

VHDL Formal Modeling and Analysis

Luis Entrena[1], Serafín Olcoz[2], and Juan Goicolea[2]

[1] Universidad Carlos III de Madrid, Spain
[2] Tecnología y Gestión de la Innovación, Spain

1. Introduction

VHDL, [1-3], has become the standard interface between designers and design automation tools for the exchange of behavioral information about a digital system. A VHDL description simulates the behavior of the described hardware design through its underlying model. This model is composed by a set of processes interconnected by signals, [4].

The process of validating a design by simulation is very time consuming. Inspecting simulation results is the most time consuming part of the validation process, and is prone to errors. The concept of formal verification during the design process is now gaining acceptance, and can be viewed according to various approaches developed within the FORMAT project.

The approach followed by TGI applies formal methods to VHDL in the sense of validating properties of a VHDL description. We start with the use of Petri nets to express the semantics of VHDL, [4]. Then we apply analysis techniques coming from the Petri nets field, based on the structure of the underlying Petri net model. In particular, we are interested in developing a possibilistic analysis because it can offer useful information not directly obtainable from data and timing information given by the designer and also because it implies less computational effort, [5].

All analysis are made in VHDL terms so the designer can get useful information about possible errors, i.e. deadlocks, and about how to fix them. The Petri net model and analysis is hidden to the designer. This approach of applying formal methods to hardware design is not an opposite way to simulation, but rather a complementary solution for the hardware design.

This chapter is organized in two main parts. Section 2 describes the formal model of VHDL developed within the FORMAT project. Section 3 describes how Petri nets analysis techniques are applied to verify properties of VHDL hardware descriptions. Finally, section 4 presents the conclusions.

2. A formal model of VHDL

In order to apply formal methods to VHDL, a formal model of VHDL must be obtained. The formal model developed by TGI within the FORMAT project is based on Coloured Petri Nets [6] and covers all aspects of the language.

This formal model is described in detail in [7] and [8]. In this section we present a summary of this work.

The formal model developed represents the underlying executable model of VHDL. The underlying executable model of VHDL is a set of interactive processes. One of these processes corresponds to an event-driven simulator that manages time and schedules events. The other processes represent the behavior of the system described by the designer. In the underlying executable model, these processes communicate through shared variables that represent the driving, effective and current values of VHDL signals.

Figure 2.1 shows the processing stages we need to perform before a VHDL description can be simulated. First, the design files containing the source code must be analyzed to produce a design library that allows management and reusability of the design information. The language analyzer, however, does not create an executable model. The VHDL executable model is generated by the elaborator, which transforms a design hierarchy into an heterarchy of VHDL processes interconnected by a network of VHDL signals, and their associated information. In a heterarchy of processes there are no processes inside other processes but the model is not flat because processes can use subprograms (functions and procedures). Besides to transforming a network of some library units in the design library into an executable model, the elaboration of the language declarations creates the objects defined by the declarations used in the execution of the model. Finally, the elaborated processes are asynchronously and concurrently executed by the simulator.

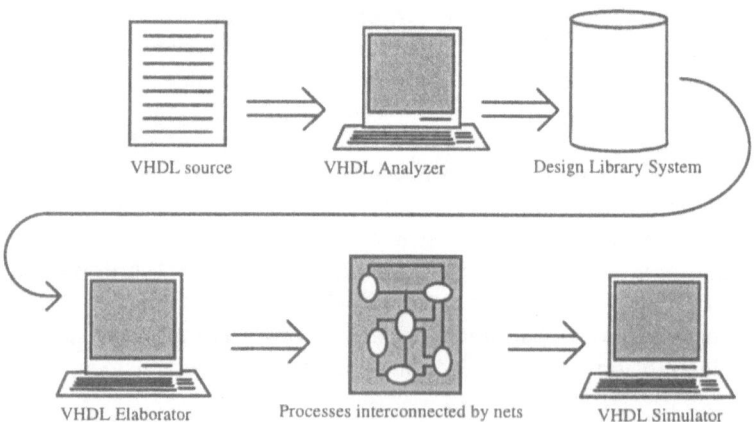

VHDL source   VHDL Analyzer   Design Library System

VHDL Elaborator   Processes interconnected by nets   VHDL Simulator

Fig. 2.1. Analysis, elaboration and execution of a VHDL description

The elaborated model contains the same information that the original description but is described using only a subset of the language which corresponds with the commonly defined as "behavioral" VHDL, the rest of the constructs disappear during their elaboration. The correspondence between this behavioral model and the original description can be recovered by means of the backtracking information produced by the elaborator.

The execution of the VHDL elaborated processes by a simulator creates a software model whose evolution simulates the behavior of the hardware system described by the VHDL description. This software model, the execution model, can be described by means of a network of interactive processes. In this model, there is one process for each VHDL process resulting from the elaboration, and a new process, named kernel process, which represents the VHDL simulator. All these processes consist of sequential statements, that are cyclically executed.

It is possible to obtain a formal description of the software model representing its elements by means of a formal notation, such as Coloured Petri Nets (CPNs), [6]. The rules to translate the software model to CPNs can be summarized as follows:

- Elaborated subtypes are represented through colours. The set of colours of the CPN consists of the set of colours that represent the elaborated subtypes plus a set of colours defined to represent special elements such as transactions, projected output waveforms, index ranges and unconstrained arrays.
- Variables are represented through coloured tokens.
- Elaborated expressions are represented through arc expressions that label the arc from the transition representing the evaluation of the expression and the place representing the result.
- Sequential statements, subprograms and processes are translated as subnets that represent the control flow of the statements. Previously, the statements corresponding to the algorithms of the kernel process have been expressed in a pseudo-VHDL code in order to use the same translation rules for any process of the intermediate model.

The generation of the formal model for a VHDL description is done automatically in three steps. The first step is the analysis of the VHDL description. For this task, TGI chose to utilize an off-the-shelf front-end analyzer and code generator. The chosen front-end was provided by LEDA S.A [11]. The second step is the elaboration of the VHDL description. For this task, TGI has also developed a VHDL Elaborator under the FORMAT project. The VHDL Elaborator carries out an intermediate step that is required for either simulation or verification tools. Finally, the CPN is generated automatically from the elaborated model by the CPN Generator tool.

For analysis purposes, the CPN model is further decoloured to obtain a Place/Transition net (PTN), on which structural analysis techniques can be applied. The decolouring process can produce a PTN with equivalent functionality to the original CPN. However, some of the functionality is eliminated for some analysis because it is not relevant or introduces too much complexity.

3. Petri Nets and VHDL analysis

The definition of a formal model of VHDL in terms of CPNs, which can be further decoloured to obtain a PTN, allows to apply Petri net analysis techniques to detect design errors. There exists a very rich body of knowledge around Petri Nets theory and applications that can be exploited for this purpose. In this section, we describe how these techniques can be applied to verify properties of VHDL hardware descriptions.

Within the FORMAT project, TGI has developed a *Petri Net Analysis Toolkit* (PNAT) that allows to exploit these techniques. This Petri Net Analysis Toolkit consists of a basic core of Petri net analysis tools, on top of which the VHDL analysis tools have been built.

We assume the reader is familiar with the concepts of Petri nets and net systems [9].

3.1 Petri Net analysis

Concurrent and distributed systems are usually difficult to manage and to understand. Thus, misunderstanding and mistakes are frequent during the design cycle. A way of cutting down the cost and duration of the design process is to express in a formalized way properties the system should enjoy and to use formal proof techniques. Errors could be eventually detected close to the moment they are introduced, reducing its propagation to subsequent stages.

Parallel and distributed require to be analyzed from qualitative and quantitative points of view. Qualitative analysis looks for properties like the absence of deadlocks, the absence of (store) overflows, or the presence of certain mutual exclusions in the accesing of shared resources. Its ultimate goal is to proof the correctness of the modeled system. Quantitative analysis looks for performance properties (e.g. throughput), responsiveness properties (e.g. average completion times) or utilization properties (e.g. average queue lengths or utilization rates). In other words, the quantitative analysis concerns the evaluation of the efficiency of the modeled system.

Petri nets can be considered as a graph theoretic tool specially suited to model and analyze Discrete Event Dynamic Systems (DEDS) which exhibit parallel evolutions and whose behaviours are characterized by synchronization and sharing phenomena. Their suitability for modelling this type of systems has led to their application in a wide range of fields.

There exists a very rich body of knowledge around Petri Nets theory and applications. In this work we focus on techniques for qualitative analysis. Techniques for analysing net systems can be divided into the following groups:
1) analysis by enumeration
2) analysis by transformation
3) structural analysis
4) analysis by simulation

The first three groups are called static methods, and their application to nets systems as abstract models leads to exact results. Simulation methods are called dynamic and proceed exercizing the net system model under certain strategies. In this case some bugs can be detected (e.g. some deadlocks), allowing "some confidence on the model", if problems are not manifested during the simulation process.

Enumeration methods are based on the construction of a reachability graph (RG) which represents, individually, the net markings and transition firings. If the net system is bounded, the reachability graph is finite and the different qualitative properties can be verified easily. If the net system is unbounded, the above graph is infinite and it is therefore impossible to construct. In this case, finite graphs known as coverability graphs can be constructed. In spite of its power, enumeration is often difficult to apply, even in nets with few places, because of its computational complexity (it is strongly combinatory).

Analysis by transformation is based on the following idea: given a net system $\langle N, M_0 \rangle$, where N is a Petri net and M_0 its initial marking, in which we wish to verify the set of properties P, we transform it into the net system $\langle N', M_0' \rangle$ such that:

1) $\langle N', M_0' \rangle$ satisfies the properties P iff $\langle N, M_0 \rangle$ satisfies them (i.e. the transformation *preserves* the properties P).

2) It is easier to verify the properties P in $\langle N', M_0' \rangle$ than in $\langle N, M_0 \rangle$.

Reduction methods are a special class of transformation methods in which a sequence of net systems preserving the properties to be studied is constructed. The construction is done in such a way that the net system $\langle N^{i+1}, M_0^{i+1} \rangle$ is "smaller" (i.e. less markings) than the previous in the sequence, $\langle N^i, M_0^i \rangle$.

The applicability of reduction methods is limited by the existence of irreducible net systems. Practically speaking, the reductions obtained are normally considerable, and can allow the desired properties to be verified directly. Because of the existence of irreducible systems, this method must be complemented by some other methods.

Finally, structural analysis techniques carefully consider the net structure (hence their name), while the initial marking acts, basically, as a parameter. Structural analysis techniques investigate the relationships between the behaviour of a net system and the structure of the net.

In this last class of analysis techniques, we can distinguish two subgroups:

1) *Linear algebra / Linear programming based techniques*, which are based on the net state equation. In certain analysis they permit a fast diagnosis without the need of enumeration.

2) *Graph based techniques*, in which the net is seen as a bipartite graph and some "ad hoc" reasonings are applied. These methods are especially effective in analyzing restricted subclasses of ordinary nets.

The four groups of analysis techniques outlined above are by no means exclusive, but rather they are complementary. Normally the designer can use them according to the needs of the ongoing analysis process.

3.2 Motivation of structural analysis techniques

Structural analysis of Petri Nets focuses on the relationship between the net structure and its behaviour. Net structure can be studied using graph theory arguments or through linear algebra based arguments, using the incidence matrices ($Pre = C-$, $Post = C+$, $C = C + -C-$).

The behaviour of a net model is non-linear, nevertheless there exists a nice linear relaxation that allows interesting analytical studies. Let $\langle N, M_0 \rangle$ be a net system, and s a firable sequence of transitions from M_0. The (integer) linear relaxation looks as follows:

$$M_0[s \succ M \Rightarrow M = M_0 + C\sigma \geq 0, \sigma \geq 0$$

where M is reachable from M_0 firing s, σ is the Parikh (or firing count) vector of s and C the incidence matrix of the net N. This equation has been named as the *state* or *fundamental* equation of the net system model.

Unfortunately the reverse of the above implication is not true. More precisely, the state equation has integer solutions, $\langle N, M_0 \rangle$, not reachable on the net system. We call them *spurious* solutions. The existence of spurious solutions leads usually to necessary or sufficient conditions to study classical behavioural properties as boundedness, deadlock freeness, liveness or fairness.

Spurious solutions can be removed using different approaches [10]. A place is said to be implicit if its deletion does not increase the firing possibilities. Adding implicit places, a new net system model with equivalent behaviour is obtained. If the implicit places are chosen carefully, the state equation of the new net system may have no integer spurious solution preventing to conclude on the bound of a place or the deadlock freeness of the system.

3.3 VHDL analysis

Because of the correspondence between a VHDL model and the PTN obtained on the basis of the VHDL semantics, there is also a correspondence between the properties of a VHDL model and the properties of its associated PTN. In this section we describe a set of properties of VHDL models that can be analysed by applying structural analysis techniques to the Petri nets obtained from them.

3.3.1 Analysis of dynamic properties. In this work, we call dynamic properties to those properties related to the dynamic behavior of the PTN model of a VHDL description. The PTN model created for the analysis of dynamic properties could be animated by a Petri Net simulator, and this animation would be related to a possibilistic simulation of the VHDL description. Dynamic properties are intimately related to this possibilistic simulation.

The analysis of dynamic properties is possibilistic due to two main reasons: the PTN model, obtained by decolouring the CPN, and the analysis techniques. Possibilistic analysis causes that the evolution implied by a solution is not guaranteed to happen in real simulation.

The PTN model does not reflect everything of a VHDL description. So, the behavior of the PTN model during a simulation may not be exactly the same as that of the original VHDL description. In particular, conditions cannot be evaluated since data are not modeled. In consequence, the modelling, for instance, of an "If" statement is possibilistic because any branch may be taken every time the "If" statement is executed.

On the other hand, the techniques applied for the analysis are not based on the simulation of the PTN model but on its state equation. The state equation is a linear description of the PTN behavior, so the analysis is also possibilistic because of the inaccuracy of the linear description.

Place-Transition Nets are not able to comprehend all features of the language in a practical way, so some features are partially modeled or not modeled at all. These are the limitations of the translation to PTNs:

1) Data values are not modeled

2) Implicit signals are not modeled

3) Subprogram bodies are not translated

4) Partial association of ports is not allowed

A direct consequence of not modelling data is that conditions of the VHDL descriptions are translated to free choices in the PTN.

TGI has developed tools for the analysis of the following dynamic properties:

1) *leak*, to detect where events or transactions may be lost.

2) *endsim*, to find out conditions producing the end of the simulation.

3) *conservative*, to detect whether the number of transactions may increase or decrease indefinitely.

4) *consistent*, to check whether all statements may be simulated in a repeatable way.

5) *mutex*, to check mutual exclusions

Outputs of these tools are messages that use the names of places or transitions of the PTN. Names indicate in a understandable way the VHDL description element that originates the corresponding place or transition.

The following subsections describe the use and purpose of each tool.

3.3.2 Leak. This tool is intended to detect where events or transactions of the VHDL signals can be lost during simulation.

In PTN terms, this property is equivalent to find a set of transitions that after fired may lose, in a unrecoverable way, tokens from places corresponding to either events or pending transactions in drivers.

More formally, this property is equivalent to find a negative t- semiflow of the PTN, which is equivalent to find two integer vectors σ, M solving the following inequality system:

$$Co + M = 0$$
$$M \geq 0$$
$$\sigma \geq 0$$
$$\sum_{p \in Places} M(p) \geq 1$$

where C is the incidence matrix of the PTN, σ is a column vector with as many elements as transitions in the PTN, and M is a column vector with as many elements as places in the PTN.

If a solution is found, σ shall indicate the transitions included in the t-semiflow, and M shall indicate the places that lose tokens.

3.3.3 Endsim.

Its purpose is to find out if the end of the VHDL simulation can be reached. This property can inform the designer about the presence of a deadlock in the code.

The end of a VHDL simulation is equivalent to a state where every process is suspended and there are neither a signal event nor a pending transaction in any driver.

In PTN terms, this property is equivalent to find two integer vectors σ, M solving the following inequality system:

$$M = M_0 + C\sigma$$
$$M \geq 0$$
$$\sigma \geq 0$$
$$\sum_{d \in Drivers} M(d) = 0$$
$$\sum_{s \in Signals} M(s'event) = 0$$
$$\forall p \in Processes\, M(p'suspend) = 1$$

where C is the incidence matrix of the PTN, M_0 is the initial marking of the PTN, σ is a column vector with as many elements as transitions in the PTN, and M is a column vector with as many elements as places in the PTN. First sum forces that there is no marked driver. Second sum forces that there is no event, so no process can be resumed.

If a solution is found, σ shall indicate the fired transitions to reach the end of the simulation, and M shall indicate the marked places at the end of the simulation..

3.3.4 Conservative. This tool tries to find out the presence in the PTN model of structures allowing a continuous increment/decrement of tokens in the PTN. This situation indicates problems in the VHDL model. When the number of tokens decreases continuously, it indicates the possibility of reaching a deadlock and, in terms of VHDL, the possibility of reaching the end of the simulation of the VHDL description abruptly. When the number of tokens increases, it indicates the possibility of having signal assignments whose transactions may produce no effect in the simulation of the VHDL code.

This property is analyzed searching for a p-semiflow covering every place of the PTN, i.e. solving the following system:

$$Y^T C = 0$$
$$Y \geq 1$$

where C is the incidence matrix of the PTN and Y is a column vector with as many elements as places in the PTN.

3.3.5 Consistent. Its purpose is to check the repetitive behavior of the whole VHDL model.

In PTN terms, this property is equivalent to detect whether all the transitions of the PTN model may be involved in a repeatable behavior. If this property is not verified, it is because there is no structural possibility of a cyclic behavior involving all the PTN and, by extension, the VHDL model.

This property is equivalent to find a t-semiflow, including every transition, that allows to return to the original marking. The property is analyzed finding a solution for the following inequality system:

$$C\sigma = 0$$
$$\sigma \geq 1$$

where C is the incidence matrix of the PTN and σ is a column vector with as many elements as transitions in the PTN.

If a solution is found, σ shall indicate how many times each transition must be fired to return to the original state.

3.3.6 Mutex. The interface of this tool is simple and it limits the property to the checking of mutual exclusions between statements. Internally, the tool tries to find a counter-example for the mutual exclusion of the execution of two VHDL statements.

In PTN terms, the tool finds out the places corresponding to the end of the execution of statements given as inputs. Let p_1, p_2 be the places corresponding to the end of the first and second statement respectively. A solution to the following inequality system shall be a proposal of counter-example:

$$M = M_0 + C\sigma$$
$$M \geq 0$$
$$\sigma \geq 0$$
$$M(p_1) \geq 1$$
$$M(p_2) \geq 1$$

where C is the incidence matrix of the PTN, M_0 is the initial marking of the PTN, σ is a column vector with as many elements as transitions in the PTN, and M is a column vector with as many elements as places in the PTN.

If a solution is found, M will indicate the places marked when the exclusion property is violated, σ will indicate the transitions fired to reach that situation.

3.3.7 Analysis of static properties. Static properties are related to the structure of the model. They are not based on the state equation of the PTN but on the structure of the PTN taken as a graph.

The PTN model created for the analysis of static properties is slightly different from that used for dynamic properties. The differences are intended to reflect some additional features in the structure of the net, mainly those concerning the unfolding of enumerated signals. Although the new PTN model is also possibilistic, the new analysis is not possibilistic because it follows a conservative policy. A message indicating some fact is only reported when the tool identifies that such a fact happens.

The analysis of static properties searches automatically for potential sources of design errors in the VHDL descriptions. This analysis informs about the use of VHDL signals and the synchronization of sequential processes. It has been successfully applied to real life examples without doing any adaptation on the VHDL code.

There is a single tool to do the analysis of static properties. This tool is named *conn*. It takes the underlying graph of the PTN model and gets the strongly connected components of the graph.

The analysis of static properties begins at the generation of the PTN model. First, the PTN is generated reflecting in its inherent graph the anomalous situations that may be detected by conn. Second, some checks are performed directly during the translation.

These are the checks performed during the PTN generation:

- Every port is connected.
- Every writable signal or port is written by a signal assignment or, at least, it has got a port source.

– Every readable signal is read or, at least, it transmits its effective value to some port.

The conn tool gets the list of strongly connected components and filters the list to obtain the places that are alone in a connected component. The VHDL meaning of the appearance of a place in such a list is clearly identified by the name of the place.

These are the typical interpretations of results:

– A value of the driver of a signal that will not be reached. This interpretation corresponds to a place whose prefix indicates that it belongs to a signal and the rest of the name indicates that it is a driver, the process where the driver is allocated and the value.
– A signal whose events will be ignored. This interpretation corresponds to a place whose prefix name indicates that belongs to a signal and the suffix indicates the event feature.
– Processes that will be executed only during the initialization phase, or wait statements that will not resume. This interpretation appears by different possible places. In any case, the places belong to a process and the rest of the name may represent the end of the process or the wait statement.

4. Conclusions

The FORMAT project aims at the development of high-level formal verification and synthesis tools. Among the various techniques developed, TGI has followed a new and promising approach. This approach consists in applying analysis techniques coming from the Petri net field.

In order to apply formal methods to the verification of hardware descriptions, formal models must first be developed. To this purpose, a formal model of VHDL has been developed, which is the formal model of reference of the FORMAT project. This formal model describes the semantics of VHDL in terms of Coloured Petri Nets. It has no restrictions to the VHDL structures used in a design to be analyzed, and it is independent of the abstraction level and description style chosen by the designer. Tools have been developed that produce the CPN model corresponding to any VHDL description and decolour it to obtain a PTN on which the rich body of Petri nets analysis techniques can be applied.

Because of the correspondence between a VHDL model and the Petri net obtained on the basis of the VHDL semantics, the properties of a VHDL model can be analysed by analysing the properties of its associated Petri net. The work carried out by TGI under the FORMAT project has focused on a subset of the Petri nets analysis techniques, called structural analysis techniques. These techniques investigate the relationships between the behaviour of a net system and the structure of the net. For some analysis, these techniques permit a fast diagnosis without the necessity of enumeration. A set of tools has been developed that allows to analyse several general properties of any VHDL description following this approach.

Results obtained with structural analysis techniques have not been as successful as initially expected. The structural analysis of dynamic properties was not very useful for real world designs because of the large number of spurious solutions (i.e., possible sources of error that do not occur in practice) that are usually obtained. On the contrary, the analysis of static properties has proved to be useful even for large industrial examples.

In spite of these limited results, the work carried out by TGI under the FORMAT project has resulted in a very useful environment for the application of Petri Net analysis techniques to the analysis of VHDL descriptions. In the future, we plan to extend the analysis with new properties and apply Petri nets analysis techniques other than the pure structural analysis techniques used so far.

References

IEEE (1988): *IEEE Standard VHDL Language Reference Manual*, IEEE, Inc., New York, N.Y., U.S.A., March.

IEEE (1992): *IEEE Standards Interpretations: IEEE Std 1076-1987*, IEEE VHDL Language Reference Manual", IEEE, Inc., New York, N.Y., U.S.A.

IEEE (1994): *IEEE Standard VHDL Language Reference Manual*, IEEE, Inc., New York, N.Y., U.S.A., June.

S. Olcoz, J. M. Colom (1994): *The Discrete Event Simulation Semantics of VHDL*, Intl. Conf. on Simulation and HDLs, pp. 128–134, January, Tempe (Arizona), U.S.A.

S. Olcoz, J. M. Colom (1993): *A Petri Net Based Analysis of VHDL Descriptions*, CHARME 93, Arles, May, pp 15–26.

K. Jensen (1990): *Coloured Petri Nets: A High Level Language for System Design and Analysis*. In Advances in Petri Nets. Lecture Notes in Computer Science, vol. 483, Springer, Berlin. Heidelberg New York, pp. 342–416.

S. Olcoz, J. M. Colom (1993): *Toward a Formal Semantics of IEEE Std. VHDL-1076*, EuroVHDL'93, Hamburg, pp. 526–531.

S. Olcoz (1995): *A Formal Model of VHDL Using Coloured Petri Nets*, in: *Formal Semantics for VHDL*, Edited by Carlos Delgado Kloos and Peter T. Breuer, pp. 140–169. Kluwer Academic Publishers.

M. Silva (1993): *Introducing Petri Nets*, in: F. DiCesare, G. Harhalakis, J.M. Proth, M. Silva, and F.B. Vernadat, *Practice of Petri Nets in Manufacturing*. Chapman & Hall.

J. M. Colom and M. Silva (1990): *Improving the linearly based characterization of P/T nets*. In: G. Rozenberg, ed., *Advances in Petri Nets 1990*, LNCS 483. Springer-Verlag, pages 113–145.

LEDA (1993): LEDA VHDL System. LEDA S.A.

Synthesis Techniques

Wolf-Dieter Tiedemann[1], Stefan Lenk[1], Christian Grobe[1], Werner Grass[1], Carlos Delgado Kloos[2], Andrés Marín López[2], Tomás de Miguel Moro[3], and Tomás Robles Valladares[3]

[1] Universität Passau, Germany
[2] Universidad Carlos III de Madrid, Spain
[3] Universidad Politécnica de Madrid, Spain

1. Introduction

Synthesis, the activity of constructing implementations from specifications, involves creativeness, design knowledge, refinement, selection of an appropriate alternative from a solution space, etc. Thus, a synthesis process is inherently difficult to automate. Accordingly, automatic (top-down) synthesis approaches have to restrict themselves to predefined architectural models, design styles or technologies if they shall at all produce some practically acceptable results.

An interactive (bottom-up) synthesis approach is not subject to such restrictions. However, it is more an assistance to the user's exploratory action than an automatic tool. This makes interactive synthesis particularly useful just during the early stages of a design (system level synthesis), where the designer has to determine the upper levels of hierarchy for his implementation (P. Michel et al. 1992). On these levels, an implementation mostly consists of a scheme of interacting (communicating) functional blocks.

The design flow of the FORMAT synthesis path supports both ways of synthesis, top-down and bottom-up (c.f. chapter **Synthesis Flow** (beginning p. 79)). According to the FORMAT philosophy, specifications are given on a rather abstract level, namely in terms of timing diagrams. Synthesis output, i.e. an implementation description, is generated in the standard hardware description language VHDL. This opens various possibilities for further processing by commercial synthesis tools in order to complete a comprehensive synthesis process from timing diagram specifications to digital hardware.

An important issue during synthesis is the internal representation of the intermediate descriptions involved. This representation should not only allow a straight-forward modeling of the graphical timing diagrams and an accurate mapping into VHDL code but also provide a formal platform in order to perform synthesis transformations that guarantee the implementation's *correctness-by-construction*. Within the FORMAT synthesis path we use a timed process calculus for giving the formal framework. More specifically, we use a timed extension of the standardized formal description technique LOTOS (ISO 1989), named *T-LOTOS*. As LOTOS, T-LOTOS has the expressive power of a process calculus with value passing. Timing diagrams

can easily be translated into T-LOTOS processes. This supplies a pure behavioural T-LOTOS description of the system.

Starting from a T-LOTOS description, there are two ways to synthesize
VHDL code. First, there is an automatic way, which consists of a direct transformation of the intermediate T-LOTOS code into behavioural VHDL code.
Chapter **Generating VHDL** (beginning p. 265) reports on this approach.
For cases where structural VHDL code is more desirable, we propose a second synthesis approach that is aiming at introducing structure. This is an
interactive bottom-up synthesis approach.

The general synthesis flow has already been introduced in chapter **Synthesis Flow** (beginning p. 79). Here we present the central technical issues
in a more detailed way. The outline of the chapter is as follows. First, we
introduce the formal backbone of the FORMAT synthesis path, i.e. the timed
formal description technique T-LOTOS. The following section explains the
translation of timing diagrams, our graphical specification language, into T-
LOTOS processes. Then, the subsequent two sections concentrate on the
automatic and the interactive transformation of the intermediate T-LOTOS
code, respectively, in order to prepare a suitable representation for translating into either behavioural or structural VHDL code. The finishing section
summarizes some conclusions.

2. T-LOTOS

LOTOS is a formal specification language based on process algebras and equa-
tional specification of abstract data types. It was designed by the ISO (International Organization for Standardization) Formal Description Techniques
group for the formal specification of open distributed systems (ISO 1989),
and in particular for the OSI (Open Systems Interconnection) computer network architecture. T-LOTOS is an extension of LOTOS which includes the
possibility of expressing quantitative time.

LOTOS supports the specification of systems at different levels of abstraction. Specifications needed to capture the requirements and implementation-
oriented specifications are complementary and permitted in LOTOS. Furthermore, there exist tools for supporting the different phases of the specification
like proof-generators, compilers and simulators (J. Quemada et al. 1989),
(C. Miguel et al. 1993),   (J. Tretmans 1989),   (W. van Hulzen 1989),
(J. A. Mañas et al. (1993),   (J. Tretmans and P. van Eijk 1989),
(P. van Eijk and H. Eertink 1990). Further references on the language can
be found in (T. Bolognesi and E. Brinksma 1987).

A history in LOTOS is the sequence of actions that an observer external
to the system takes note in a 'run' of a system. Suppose two actions a and b
occur at the same time, the observer must write down either a;b or b;a, but
can not write both at the same time. Thus, LOTOS does not allow two actions
to take place at the same time, but they can be specified to occur as closed

as desired and in any possible ordering. Interleaving and synchronization are the tools to model concurrency in LOTOS.

The same specification can give rise to different histories, due to the non determinism of the language. LOTOS specifications are composed of concurrent behaviours that communicate via events which take place at shared gates. The events that take place at the external gates are the actions that the external observer notices. Events are instantaneous and atomic, and we remark again that no two events can take place at the same time. The state of a system is determined by the set of events that are allowed to happen in it. This implicit definition of the states of a system is characteristic to Labeled Transition Systems.

Atomic events are called *action denotation* and model different kinds of synchronization. The action g!v denotes a behaviour able to synchronize on gate g and value v. While action g?v:sort-type is able to synchronize on gate g with any value of sort sort-type. The value on which it synchronizes may be later referred to by means of the variable v.

There are also internal actions which are not observable from outside, but whose execution can change the state of the process and therefore its future observable behaviour.

T-LOTOS is a timed extension of the basic behaviour calculus of LOTOS which allows the assignment of precise timing of events of the behaviour. Timed LOTOS provides the minimum extension which allows the formal description of hardware concurrent components and their timing constraints. T-LOTOS is a continuation of some previous works (C. M Nieto et al. 92), (J. Quemada and A. Fernandez 1987). In (J. Quemada and A. Fernandez 1987) quantitative time constraints were introduced. In (C. M Nieto et al. 92) the former model was enhanced with urgency in the execution of internal actions. T-LOTOS introduces urgency in the visible and invisible actions. With T-LOTOS one can, for instance, model VHDL inertial or transport time semantics.

2.1 Syntax of T-LOTOS

This section provides a brief description of the language. A complete definition can be found in (J. Quemada and A. Fernandez 1987).

T-LOTOS allows the assignment of precise timing to the events of a behaviour with respect to a discrete scale of time. In fact the set of natural numbers is used as domain for time, at both the syntactic and the semantic level.

The algebra of finite basic behaviour expressions is defined by the operators in Table 2.1. Each behaviour expression B has an associated gate set $L(B)$, also defined in the table.

Name	syntax	Gate set
Stop	*stop*	$\emptyset$
Termination	*exit*	$\emptyset$
Action Prefix	$a\{t\}; B$	$L(B) \cup \{a|a \neq i\}$
Timed Choice	$a\{t \text{ in } T\}; B$	$L(B) \cup \{a|a \neq i\}$
Choice	$B_1 [] B_2$	$L(B_1) \cup L(B_2)$
Parallelism	$B_1 \| [G] \| B_2$	$L(B_1) \cup L(B_2)$
Process Def.	$P[g_1, .., g_n] := B$	$\{g_1, .., g_n\}$
Process Inst.	$P[g_1, .., g_n]$	$\{g_1, .., g_n\}$
Hiding	$hide\ G\ in\ B$	$L(B) - G$
Enabling	$B_1 >> B_2$	$L(B_1) \cup L(B_2)$
Disabling	$B_1 [> B_2$	$L(B_1) \cup L(B_2)$
Relabeling	$B[g_1/g_1', .., g_n/g_n']$	$(L(B)-\{g_1', .., g_n'\})$ $\cup\{g_1, .., g_n\}$

Table 2.1. Syntax of Timed LOTOS

The basic component of the syntax is the pair formed by an event and a natural number which represents an instant of time. For example, $a\{3\}$ [1] indicates that event a will happen at instant 3. The time attribute of a time event is relative to the instant at which the previous event occurred and on which the action causally depends. For instance, in $a\{1\}; c\{2\}; stop\ ||[\emptyset]||\ b\{2\};$ $stop$, a will occur at instant 1, b at 2 and c at 3; so c occurs 2 instants after the occurrence of a to which it is causally related.

Time attributes of events are non-negative numbers. A null separation between the occurrence of two events is allowed. This has been considered admissible, not only to allow the parallel execution of several actions at the same time, generated for instance by plain interleaving, but also to capture a negligible separation between events. It is clear that in every case, we must be careful to prevent the possible appearance of unbounded sequences of such events. Without this restriction we would have to admit the execution of an infinite number of actions in finite time, against any physical law. But such sequences would only be introduced by specifications including recursive calls without any positive lapse of time, and this can be prevented at the syntax level by an adequate generalization of the concept of guarded definition.

An auxiliary operator *Age*, whose syntax is $Age(t, B)$, is needed to represent the passing of time over a process that does not evolve in any other way. A derived operator *stop* should also be considered as a combination of the original one and the added *Age* operator to represent any deadlocked behaviour.

---

[1] In order to allow compatibility with the available toolset, a time annotation should be used to manage time specifications. The time constraints are used as text comments that will precede the action it constraints. For example, $a\{3\}$ take the form: (* TIME 3 *) a

The data part of T-LOTOS is identical to standard LOTOS. We only must add in the data library the adequate data type to represent time. The time is modeled using the Natural numbers and should have all of its properties.

The introduction of the time as a data type increases the expressiveness of the language by the use of time variables. The expression $a\{t \ in \ 0, 5\}$ means that the event a may occur at any time instant between 0 and 5 and a variable t will record the exact instant the event occurred. This mechanism is very useful when performance measurements or operations with the time variable is needed.

2.2 T-LOTOS operational semantics

The semantics of the calculus is defined using a labeled transition system containing every possible execution path. It is obtained by the application of the following rules:

Stop: The *stop* behaviour does not generate any transition. It can be used to represent deadlock.

Termination (*exit*): The system must accept termination at any instant t.

Action Prefix ($a\{t\}; B$): The system accepts event **a** to take place at time **t**, after that the system will behave like B.

Timed Choice ($a\{t \ in \ T\}; B$): Timed choice is an extension of the simple action prefix operator. It constrains an action to occur at any instant of the given set T. It is a combination of action prefix and choice over time from the semantic point of view. If the set of time instants T is finite, timed choice can be defined in terms of action prefix and choice. In fact, action prefix is a particular case of timed choice, when T has only one element; but due to the frequent use of action prefix, it has been considered convenient to maintain this simpler syntactic form.

Choice ($B_1 [] B_2$):
The system behaves either like B_1 or B_2.

Parallel ($B_1 \ |[G]| \ B_2$):
The definition of the parallel operator includes two conceptually different types of operation: synchronization and interleaving.

Synchronization may occur when both, B_1 and B_2 offer the same event $b \in G$ at the same instant. For instance, ($b\{2\}; stop \ |[b]| \ b\{3\}; stop$) would not synchronize because both b's occur at different instants; whereas ($b\{2\}; stop \ |[b]| \ b\{2\}; stop$) could synchronize, resulting in the event $b\{2\}$. Interleaving may occur when just one B_i ($i = 1, 2$) evolves by performing an action $a \notin G$ and the other remains inactive. In order to describe also the passing of time in the inactive component, an Aging operator $Age(t, B)$ is introduced.

Example: ($b\{2\}; stop \ |[c]| \ b\{4\}; stop$) would interleave. It has the following evolutions:

$$(b\{2\}; stop \,||[c]|\, b\{4\}; stop) \xrightarrow{b\{2\}} (stop \,||[c]|\, Age(2, \, (b\{4\}; stop)))$$

$$(stop \,||[c]|\, Age(2, \, (b\{4\}; stop))) \xrightarrow{b\{2\}} (Age(2, \, stop) \,||[c]|\, stop)$$

Hiding (*hide G in B*): Hiding internalizes actions in B. Example:
$hide\ b\ in\ (b\{1\}; stop) \xrightarrow{i\{1\}} hide\ b\ in\ stop$

Enabling ($B_1 >> B_2$): It allows the activation of a behaviour B_2. Notice that if B_1 does not terminate successfully, B_2 would never be enabled.

Disabling ($B_1 [> B_2$): Behaviour B_1 can be disrupted at any time t, if an event of B_2 occurs. If B_1 terminates successfully, B_2 can no longer take place.

Process: This is the only rule in which the system of equations defining the named processes is made explicit. We systematically try to avoid this cumbersome notation, using it only in those cases in which an explicit reference to the subsumed system of equations is needed. On the other hand, the fact that this system of equations is never modified by the application of the rules justifies the avoidance of explicit references.

2.3 Examples of specifications in T-LOTOS

Due to the high abstraction level of T-LOTOS, it can be used to specify hardware components in a top-down fashion as well as in a bottom-up one. In a top-down methodology the designer begins at high level describing the functionalities of the system and then decomposes the system into several interactive subsystems. In a bottom-up methodology the designer starts with the description of components at very low level, for instance at gate level, and then composes the pieces to obtain more complex structures. The main aspect of both approaches is that it can be assured correctness between design steps.

Here we can see a bottom-up approach starting at gate level to show how to build a set-reset flip-flop. This flip-flop is constructed using two Nor gates, where the output of each gate is used as an input of the other. The component functionality requires that the two outputs, Q and *Qbar*, are complement of each other.

The component diagram is shown in figure 2.1. Each component has a propagation delay, identical for all components we will model in this section. All the specified components are sensible to input changes and also no two subsequent outputs have the same value. We also did not impose restrictions at the inputs of the component (i.e. both, *Set* and *Reset* being 1 at the same time). We consider that the environment will constrain these values.

The actual behaviour of the flip-flop is expressed as a composition of two Nor gates in lines 10-14 below. The Nor gate behaviour is described in lines 18-44 and accepts 3 possible events. It can accept an input event at port *inp1* at any time (TIME t in 0,.00) if the value received is different from

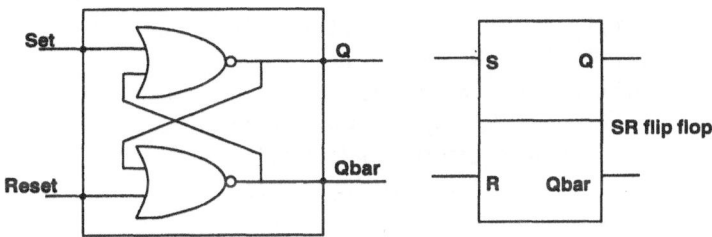

Fig. 2.1. Nor Set-Reset flip-flop

the last received value (line 21). It can also accept an input event at port *inp*2 with the same constraints of port *inp*1 (line 31). Or it may offer an output event *delay* units of time after receiving the input (line 45). Processes representing logical gates should have an infinite behaviour through recursive definition of process. Processes are instantiated with a set of parameters. The values of these parameters are used to represent a state of the component. When there is a change at some of the inputs there is two possible set of instantiated parameters: if the changed input does not project an output change in the future (lines 22 or 32) then the elapsed time must actualize *last* parameter through the operation $(last - t)$. In this expression t represents the time instant when the input has changed and it is assumed that the subtraction between time units, as should be defined in the data part, not shown here, is always no negative ($last - t = last - t$ if $last \geq t$ else 0). If the projected output is different from the actual output value (lines 26 or 36) the propagation delay is initialized with *delay*. The component Norff is instantiated (line 2) with a set of values representing its initial state.

```
 1 norff[s,r,q,qbar]
 2   (false,false,true,false,delay) (* initial conditions *)
 3
 4   where
 5
 6   process norff [s,r,q,qbar]
 7     (sin,rin,qout,qoutbar:bool, delay:time)
 8     :noexit :=
 9
10   Norgate [r,q,qbar]
11     (rin,qout,qoutbar,delay,0 of time)
12   |[q, qbar]|
13   Norgate [s,qbar,q]
14     (sin,qoutbar,qout,delay,0 of time)
15
16   where
17
18   process Norgate [inp1,inp2,outp]
```

```
19    (i1,i2,o1:bool, delay,last:time) :noexit :=
20    (*| TIME t IN  0,.00 |*)
21    inp1?x:bool [x ne i1];
22    ( [(x nor i2) eq (i1 nor i2)]->
23        Norgate [inp1,inp2,outp]
24          (x,i2,o1,delay,(last-t))
25        []
26        [(x nor i2) ne (i1 nor i2)]->
27          Norgate [inp1,inp2,outp]
28            (x,i2,o1,delay,delay) )
29
30    [] (*| TIME t IN  0,.00 |*)
31        inp2?x:bool [x ne i2];
32        ( [(x nor i1) eq (i1 nor i2)]->
33            Norgate [inp1,inp2,outp]
34              (i1,x,o1,delay,(last-t)
35            []
36            [(x nor i1) ne (i1 nor i2)]->
37              Norgate [inp1,inp2,outp]
38                (i1,x,o1,delay,delay) )
39    [] (*| TIME  IN  last |*)
40        [o1 ne (i1 nor i2)] ->
41        outp!i1 nor i2;
42        Norgate [inp1,inp2,outp] (i1,i2,i1 nor i2,delay,0)
43
44    endproc
45
46  endproc
```

T-LOTOS has syntax and semantics formally defined and its time model has an expressive power in describing delays, timeouts and concurrence being well suited to specify real-time distributed systems as well as model hardware systems.

The key point in the use of the language for hardware description is that it allows automatic transformation and verification of the design. The correct generation of various implementations from one specification is highly desirable and possible in the synthesis design path. Moreover, the simulation of the design and the automatic pattern generation are also possible.

2.4 Timed graphs as internal representation

In subsection 2.2 the semantics of T-LOTOS has been introduced on the operational model of a *timed* transitional system. Such notions as equivalence of processes or satisfaction of an implementation relation between a (detailed) implementing process and an (abstract) specifying process are defined directly on the semantical model. Hence, in order to perform the evaluation of these relations automatically, the transitional graphs of the concerning processes have to be built up explicitly. Using the original transitional system from subsection 2.2 would lead to graphs of unmanageable size (for dense time domains even of infinite size), since in each state every possible event would require a dedicated transition arc for every single point in time where this event is allowed to occur and a corresponding successor state that reflects the particular timing situation. In order to condense this representation, a bunch of transitions starting from the same state and labelled with the same event is comprised into a single transition that carries the label (action) denoting the event and a timing label that reflects the time interval of all possible execution points for the associated action.

Such a representation has been introduced as "Timed Graph" or "Timed Automaton" and has been used originally to describe a model for model-checking of real time CTL formulae (R. Alur et al. 1990), (R. Alur et al. 1992). In (X. Nicollin et al. 1992) it has been demonstrated, how timed process algebra expressions can be translated into Timed Graph representations.

2.4.1 Basic concepts. A *timed graph* is mainly a finite state machine graph, which is additionally characterized by a set T of timers. A *timer* can be understood as a stop watch, which always proceeds in time, but can be reset to value 0 at arbitrary instants of time. Hence, a timer contains always the value of time that has elapsed since its last reset. A reset does not affect the continuous flow of time.

The concept of timers is important for the timing annotations at the arcs of a timed graph. Timing annotations consist of

- a predicate on T, which describes a condition that has to hold in order to allow the transition to take place,
- a subset of T, which represents the set of timers, which become reset exactly at that instant when the corresponding transition occurs.

Consider the timed graph of figure 2.2 as an example. On entering the initial state S, timer t_0 is reset. After at least 4 time units have elapsed, an input action a? will be accepted. Simultaneously, timer t_1 will be reset. Next, an output action b! may take place, but only, if t_1 has a value within the interval [1, 5]. This event resets timer t_0 again and takes the timed graph back to state S.

Formally, a *timed graph* is a 6-tuple $(\Sigma, S, s_0, T, T_0, \rightarrow)$, where Σ is a finite alphabet, S is a finite set of states, $s_0 \in S$ is an initial state, T is a finite set of timers, $T_0 \subseteq T$ is an initial resetting, and $\rightarrow$ is a transition relation. Let the set $\Phi(T)$ of permissible predicates ϕ over the set T of timers be defined inductively by

$$\phi ::= t \; op \; c \mid \phi \wedge \phi,$$

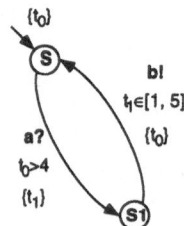

Fig. 2.2. A Timed Graph

$$op ::=< \mid \leq \mid \geq \mid >,$$

where $t \in T$ and $c \in \mathcal{TIME}$. Then $\to \subseteq S \times \Sigma \times \Phi(T) \times \wp(T) \times S$. An element $(s, a, \phi, R, s') \in \to$ represents a state transition ¿from s to s' on event a when predicate ϕ holds. At the occurrence of this transition all timers in R are reset. Instead of $(s, a, \phi, R, s') \in \to$ it is also written

$$s \xrightarrow{a, \phi, R} s'.$$

Note that predicates like "$t = 6$" or "$t \in (0, 25]$" may be used as abbreviations of legal predicates.

2.4.2 Representing timed processes as timed graphs. There is a strong relationship between timed processes and timed graphs that can be exploited to translate them into each other. Such a proposal has been made e.g. in (X. Nicollin et al. 1992). A big advantage of timed graphs is their compact representation, which serves also very well as an internal data structure for software tools.

The translation of timed processes into timed graphs is carried out by defining each operation on processes as an operation on timed graphs. This shall be demonstrated for a selection of some of the most important T-LOTOS operators (c.f. table 2.1), namely Stop, the combination of Action Prefix and Choice (called *Guarded Choice*), Parallelism and Time Passing.

Stop. An inactive process *stop* is modelled by a timed graph

$$(\emptyset, \{stop\}, stop, \emptyset, \emptyset, \emptyset).$$

Guarded choice. Let $P_i = (\Sigma_i, S_i, P_i, T_i, T_{0,i}, \to_i), i \in I$, be timed graphs, then $P \equiv \bigsqcup_{i \in I} a_i\{t_i \ in \ I_i\}; P_i$ describes the timed graph

$$(\bigcup_{i \in I}(\Sigma_i \cup \{a_i\}), \bigcup_{i \in I} S_i \cup \{P\}, P, \bigcup_{i \in I} T_i \cup \{t\}, \{t\}, \to),$$

where $\to := \bigcup_{i \in I}(\to_i \cup \{P \xrightarrow{a_i, t \in I_i, T_{0,i}} P_i\})$ and $t \notin T_i$ for all i.

Parallelism. Let $P_i = (\Sigma_i, S_i, P_i, T_i, T_{0,i}, \rightarrow_i), i = 1, 2$ be timed graphs, then $P_1 \; ||G|| \; P_2$ describes the timed graph

$$(\Sigma_1 \cup \Sigma_2, S, (P_1, P_2), T_1 \cup T_2, T_{0,1} \cup T_{0,2}, \rightarrow),$$

where $S \subseteq S_1 \times S_2$ and $\rightarrow$ is defined by the following inference rules

$$\frac{s_1 \xrightarrow{a, \phi, R}_1 s_1'}{(s_1, s_2) \xrightarrow{a, \phi \wedge intime(s_2), R} (s_1', s_2)} \quad a \notin G$$

$$\frac{s_2 \xrightarrow{a, \psi, Q}_2 s_2'}{(s_1, s_2) \xrightarrow{a, \psi \wedge intime(s_1), Q} (s_1, s_2')} \quad a \notin G$$

$$\frac{s_1 \xrightarrow{a, \phi, R}_1 s_1' \quad s_2 \xrightarrow{a, \psi, Q}_2 s_2'}{(s_1, s_2) \xrightarrow{a, \phi \wedge \psi, R \cup Q} (s_1', s_2')} \quad a \in G$$

S contains all states that can be reached from the initial state (P_1, P_2). The predicate *intime(s)* indicates whether state s is enabled or will be enabled in the future, i.e. whether the process that is modelled by s has reached its timeout or not.

intime can be defined inductively. For instance, we have

$intime(stop) = true$
$intime(\bigsqcup_{i \in I} a_i \{t \text{ in } I_i\}; P_i) = \text{``} t < \max_{i \in I} \{upper\_bound(I_i)\} \text{''}$
$intime(P||G||Q) = intime(P) \wedge intime(Q)$
etc.

Time Passing. The modelling proposed here presupposes that the time variable t_i that keeps the amount of time by which a process $Age(t_i, P_i)$ has to be time-shifted is always bound by the directly preceding prefix. Time passing can thus be handled as a special case of guarded choice.

Time passing means that the time variables that conduct the execution of the prefixed events of process P_i don't have to be reset to 0 on the activation of process $Age(t_i, P_i)$ but to the current value of t_i, i.e. they have to be reset simultaneously with t_i.

Let $P_i = (\Sigma_i, S_i, P_i, T_i, T_{0,i}, \rightarrow_i), i \in I$, and $P_j = (\Sigma_j, S_j, P_j, T_j, T_{0,j}, \rightarrow_j)$, $j \in J$, be timed graphs, then

$$P \equiv (\bigsqcup_{i \in I} a_i \{t_i \text{ in } I_i\}; P_i) \; [] \; (\bigsqcup_{j \in J} a_j \{t_j \text{ in } I_j\}; Age(t_j, P_j))$$

describes the timed graph

$$(\bigcup_{k \in I, J} (\Sigma_k \cup \{a_k\}), \bigcup_{k \in I, J} S_k \cup \{P\}, P, \bigcup_{k \in I, J} T_k \cup \{t\}, \bigcup_{j \in J} T_{0,j} \cup \{t\}, \rightarrow),$$

where $\rightarrow := \bigcup_{i \in I} (\rightarrow_i \cup \{P \xrightarrow{a_i, t \in I_i, T_{0,i}} P_i\}) \cup \bigcup_{j \in J} (\rightarrow_j \cup \{P \xrightarrow{a_j, t \in I_j, \emptyset} P_j\})$ and $t \notin T_k$ for all $k \in I, J$.

2.4.3 Evaluating the enabling predicate. An important issue when comparing two timed graphs A, B is to decide, whether some transition is enabled or not. Here it is crucial to compare the predicates. Assume, for some point in time τ there is a known valuation for all the timers in $T_A \cup T_B$. Then each predicate ϕ denotes an interval of time values relative to τ for which the corresponding transition is enabled. Of course, this interval depends strongly on the actual valuation at τ. For example, assume that at some reference point τ_0 timer t has value 2 and timer u has value 4. Suppose, some transition that is active at τ_0 is labeled with a predicate "$t \geq 3 \wedge u \leq 8$". Clearly, this predicate holds for each point in time later than τ_0, which lies within the interval $[1, 4]$.

In order to generalize this observation, we introduce the notion of *history*. At each time the present value of any timer depends on the point of its last reset. Usually, for different timers this reset point is different. It is the purpose of history to map the differently named timers and the various possibilities of time distances between their resettings into a common scale. A history is basically a list $\Gamma = \langle v_0, e_1, v_1, ..., e_N, v_N \rangle$, where each v_i represents a set of timers that have been reset simultaneously and e_{i+1} denotes an interval that represents the time distance between the resettings of v_i and v_{i+1}. In order to model time dependency, the representation of such intervals may use references to previous intervals. A reference in e_i to the interval e_j is written as π_{j-i}.

Now, by evaluating a predicate with respect to a given history, it is possible to decide, whether the predicate denotes an existing interval or an empty interval. Instead of going too much into detail, we will just show an example.

Example. Let $\Gamma = \langle \{t_2\}, [20, 20] - \pi_1, \{t_1\}, (0, 20), \{t_0\} \rangle$ be a history and $\phi = t_1 \in (30, 40) \wedge t_2 \leq 35 \wedge t_0 > 40$ be a predicate. This situation could arise from a timed graph that has been traversed up to state s along the path shown in figure 2.3. We are interested in finding out whether ϕ is an empty interval or not.

In a first step, we can map the predicate onto the scale given by Γ. If we call this representation $\phi|_\Gamma$, then

$$\phi|_\Gamma = \pi \leq 35 \wedge \pi > 30 - \pi_1 \wedge \pi < 40 - \pi_1 \wedge \pi > 40 - \pi_1 - \pi_2.$$

Correspondingly, the interval that is described by predicate ϕ under history Γ, call it $Int_\Gamma(\phi)$, is given as

$$Int_\Gamma(\phi) = (0, 35] \cap (30, 40) - \pi_1 \cap (40, \infty) - \pi_1 - \pi_2.$$

In order to evaluate this interval, we resolve

$$(30, 40) - \pi_1 = (30, 40) - Int(\textit{smallest-lb}^*(1, \Gamma), \ \textit{largest-ub}^*(1, \Gamma))$$

and

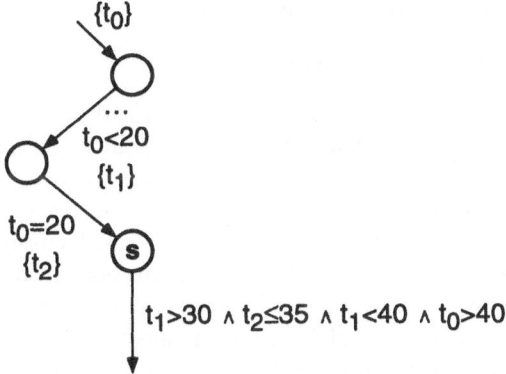

Fig. 2.3. Path in a Timed Graph

$$(40, \infty) - \pi_1 - \pi_2 = (40, \infty) - Int(smallest\text{-}lb^*(2, \Gamma), \ largest\text{-}ub^*(2, \Gamma)).$$

$smallest\text{-}lb^*(n, \Gamma)$ and $largest\text{-}ub^*(n, \Gamma)$ denote the smallest possible value and largest possible value, respectively, for the time span that has elapsed since the last but n-1-th event in history Γ. In this example we obtain for instance $smallest\text{-}lb^*(1, \Gamma) = 20 - (20 - \epsilon) = \epsilon$ and $largest\text{-}ub^*(2, \Gamma) = 20$. In summary, we have

$$Int(smallest\text{-}lb^*(1, \Gamma), largest\text{-}ub^*(1, \Gamma)) = (0, 20)$$

and

$$Int(smallest\text{-}lb^*(2, \Gamma), largest\text{-}ub^*(2, \Gamma)) = [20, 20],$$

so that

$$(30, 40) - \pi_1 = (30, 40) - (0, 20) = (10, 40)$$

and

$$(40, \infty) - \pi_1 - \pi_2 = (40, \infty) - [20, 20] = (20, \infty).$$

Hence, $Int_\Gamma(\phi) = (0, 35] \cap (10, 40) \cap (20, \infty) = (20, 35] \neq \emptyset$ denotes an existing interval.

In summary, timed graphs are a suitable, since *finite*, semantical model for T-LOTOS that allows particularly to perform a comparison of two different T-LOTOS descriptions, for instance w.r.t. consistency, if both descriptions refer to different levels of detail. This property is crucial for providing automatic support of synthesis.

3. Formalizing timing diagrams

3.1 General translation approach

The formal semantics of a timing diagram specification is defined by a transformation into T-LOTOS. A timing diagram specification (see chapter **Specification Languages** (beginning p. 22)) consists of three parts, the system design interface, the formal definition of timing diagrams and a composition expression which combines instances of formal timing diagrams. The transformation of these timing diagram constituents is based on a *compositional approach*. Every (graphical) language element used within a timing diagram specification or any of its parts, respectively, is translated into its corresponding T-LOTOS equivalent. This procedure results in a specification, which mainly consists of a composition of T-LOTOS processes. In the following the translation principle will be briefly presented.

First, in a preprocessing step, the composition expression is syntactically transformed into an equivalent "flat" expression by applying the distribution law for sequential and alternative timing diagram operators. The resulting expression is a purely alternative composition of sequentially composed timing diagrams. Next, each individual timing diagram is translated into a T-LOTOS specification by deriving its semantical model in terms of T-LOTOS.

A single timing diagram is built from combining several graphical elements into a whole. Of course, each graphical element has its very own semantical meaning, which again is defined in terms of a T-LOTOS process. Following the compositional approach, the behaviour of a system (or module) specified by a (single) timing diagram results from a *parallel composition* of the T-LOTOS translations of *each graphical constituent* used within the timing diagram. Such constituents are waveforms, qualtitative constraints, which specify the sequence of events, or quantitative constraints like timing constraints. The constraints imposed by data annotations fall into this category as well.

In summary, a comprehensive timing diagram specification will be translated into a T-LOTOS process *system_behaviour* having a compositional structure as shown in figure 3.1.

The process *system_behaviour* engages not only in observable actions on the system ports, but also in internal actions. Every edge of a waveform in each timing diagram instance corresponds to a uniquely named internal "edge" action which initiates an externally observable input or output action as specified by the edge annotations. Thus, the internal edge actions control the system inputs and outputs taking into account temporal constraints on the edge actions which result from waveforms, qualitative constraints and composition operators.

system_behaviour consists of the folowing processes:

Waveforms is the process which results from the parallel composition of the T-LOTOS process translations of all waveforms in the timing diagram

```
process system_behaviour[<portnames>] :noexit :=

hide <edgenames> in

( ( ( Waveforms[<edgenames>]
      |[<edgenames>]| QualitConstraints[<edgenames>])
    |[<edgenames>]| SeqComposition[<edgenames>])
  |[<edgenames>]| AltComposition[<edgenames>])

|[<edgenames>]|

( TimingConstraints[<edgenames>,<portnames>]
  |[<edgenames>,<portnames>]|
  Data[<edgenames>,<portnames>](<initvalues>) )

endproc
```

Fig. 3.1. T-LOTOS process translation of timing diagrams

instances. Each waveform process specifies the strict sequence of the actions related to the waveform edges.

QualitConstraints is the process which results from the parallel composition of the T-LOTOS process translations of all qualitative constraints in the timing diagram instances. Each qualitative constraint process reflects constraints on actions corresponding to edges of different waveforms.

SeqComposition is the process which reflects the sequential composition of the timing diagrams. These processes reflect the concatenation of waveforms of sequentially composed timing diagrams.

AltComposition is the process which results from the parallel composition of the T-LOTOS process translations of the alternative timing diagram operators. This process permanently selects one of the specified alternative system behaviours (given in terms of sequentially composed timing diagrams) in a nondeterministic way.

Data is the process which results from the translation of the data annotations and the enable conditions related to waveform edges in the timing diagram instances. It initiates the input and output of data values on the system ports controlled by the internal "edge actions". Every such action immediately launches a particular input or output action. In general, this process is parametrized by the data variables declared in the timing diagrams. *initvalues* are the initial values of these data parameters as defined in the timing diagram specification.

TimingConstraints is the process which results from the translation of the timing constraints specified on the waveform edges.

3.2 Translation of graphical primitives

In this section the T-LOTOS process translations of some of the basic graphical primitives of timing diagrams are presented.

First of all we introduce some abbreviating notations used in the formalizations below. The n-ary parallel composition and choice of T-LOTOS processes will be abbreviated as follows:

$$\underset{i=1,\ldots,n}{\overset{|[]|}{}} P_i[act_i] := (\ldots((P_1[act_1] \,|[act_1 \cap act_2]|\, P_2[act_2])$$
$$|[(act_1 \cup act_2) \cap act_3]|\, P_3[act_3])\ldots)|[(act_1 \cup \ldots \cup act_{n-1}) \cap act_n]|\, P_n[act_n]$$

$$\underset{i=1,\ldots,n}{\sum} P_i[act_i] := P_1[act_1]\,[]\ldots[]\,P_n[act_n]$$

The naming convention for actions, which correspond to edges within a waveform is as follows: since every edge is uniquely identified by

1. the name of the system port, where the waveform is specified to be observed,
2. its numeral position in the sequence of edges constituting the waveform, and
3. the name of the timing diagram instance, which specifies the waveform,

a convenient edge name is $portname_{waveform\_position}^{instance\_name}$.

The positional number, moreover, keeps track of the sequential composition of timing diagrams. It accumulates the number of edges specified in waveforms of preceding timing diagrams. Each waveform edge is modelled by a T-LOTOS action having the same name.

3.2.1 Translation of strong constraints. Every strong constraint $SC = (ps_i^{td}, pt_j^{td})$ between a source edge ps_i^{td} and a target edge pt_j^{td} in a timing diagram instance td is translated into a T-LOTOS process SC.

$$\textbf{process } SC[ps_i^{td}, pt_j^{td}, Alt_{ps_i^{td}}] : \textbf{noexit} :=$$

$$ps_i^{td}; pt_j^{td}; SC[ps_i^{td}, pt_j^{td}, Alt_{ps_i^{td}}]$$
$$[]$$
$$(\underset{alt \in Alt_{ps_i^{td}}}{\sum} alt; SC[ps_i^{td}, pt_j^{td}, Alt_{ps_i^{td}}])$$

endproc

where $Alt_{ps_i^{td}}$ denotes the set of actions that are "alternative" to ps_i^{td}, i.e. $Alt_{ps_i^{td}}$ contains every action that corresponds to a waveform edge ps_i^{tdx} in a timing diagram instance $tdx \neq td$ that is related to the same port ps and to the same position i as the action ps_i^{td}.

Informally, the recursive process SC describes the choice either to participate in the triggering source action ps_i^{td} followed by the triggered target action pt_j^{td}, thus excluding any other action defined in alternative waveforms on port ps, *or* to freely engage in any of these alternative actions.

3.2.2 Translation of waveforms. Assume that $WF_p^{td} := \{p_1^{td}, \ldots, p_n^{td}\}$ is the ascending sequence of n edges of a waveform on port p defined in timing diagram instance td.

The semantics of such a waveform ($n > 1$) is defined by a process WF.

$$\textbf{process } WF[p_1^{td}, \ldots, p_n^{td}, Alt_{WF}] \text{ :noexit :=}$$

$$(\ \underset{i=1,\ldots,n-1}{|\square|} SC[p_i^{td}, p_{i+1}^{td}, Alt_{p_i^{td}}]\ )$$

$$|[p_1^{td}, p_n^{td}]|\ SC[p_1^{td}, p_n^{td}, Alt_{p_1^{td}}]$$

$$\textbf{endproc}$$

where Alt_{WF} denotes the set of actions that are alternative to the actions $p_1^{td}, \ldots, p_n^{td}$, which correspond to the waveform's edges.

The translation of waveforms is based on the translation of strong constraints. Every waveform is considered to be equivalent to a sequence of strong constraints among the waveform edges and an "embracing" strong constraint between the first and the last waveform edge. Therefore, the process WF just describes the sequence of actions corresponding to the edges of the waveform.

In order to represent *all* waveforms in a timing diagram specification, each process for any waveform on every system port in any timing diagram instance has to be composed in parallel. This results in a T-LOTOS process $Waveforms$.

$$\textbf{process } Waveforms[Act] \text{ :noexit :=}$$

$$\underset{p\in Ports}{|\square|}\ (\underset{td\in Invoc}{|\square|}\ WF[p_1^{td}, \ldots, p_n^{td}, Alt_{WF}]\ )$$

$$\textbf{endproc}$$

where Act denotes the set of all actions in the specification, n denotes the particular length of each considered waveform and Alt_{WF} represents the actions that are alternative to the actions of each waveform. $Ports$ denotes the set of all system ports and $Invoc$ the set of timing diagram instances used in the timing diagram expression.

3.2.3 Translation of data annotations. The translation of data annotations used within a timing diagram specification (like predicates and computation rules) results in a T-LOTOS process $Data$. This process engages in the internal edge actions as well as in input and output actions on the system ports. Moreover, it is parametrized by data variables.

$$\text{process } Data[\overbrace{p1_1^{td1}, \ldots, pk_n^{tdm}}^{edge\ actions}, \overbrace{P1, \ldots, Pk}^{port\ actions}]$$

$$(\underbrace{v_{p1_1^{td1}} : t_{p1}, .., v_{pk_n^{tdm}} : t_{pk}}_{local\ data\ variables}, \underbrace{pv_1 : t_{p1}, .., pv_k : t_{pk}}_{global\ port\ variables}) \text{ :noexit :=}$$

$$\sum_{inputs} pi_k^{tdj}; Pi?x : t_{pi}[PR_{pi_k^{tdj}}(v_{p1_1^{td1}}, .., pv_k) \text{ and } EC_{pi_k^{tdj}}(v_{p1_1^{td1}}, .., pv_k)];$$

$$Data[p1_1^{td1}, \ldots, Pk](\ldots, x/v_{pi_k^{tdj}}, \ldots, x/pv_i, \ldots)$$

$$[]$$

$$\sum_{outputs} po_k^{tdj}; Po!CR_{po_k^{tdj}}(v_{p1_1^{td1}}, .., pv_k)[EC_{po_k^{tdj}}(v_{p1_1^{td1}}, .., pv_k)];$$

$$Data[p1_1^{td1}, \ldots, Pk](\ldots, CR_{po_k^{tdj}}(v_{p1_1^{td1}}, \ldots, pv_k)/v_{po_k^{tdj}}, \ldots$$

$$\ldots, CR_{p_{i_k}^{tdj}}(v_{p1_1^{td1}}, \ldots, pv_k)/pv_o, \ldots)$$

endproc

where $p1_1^{td1}, \ldots, pk_n^{tdm}$ denote all actions corresponding to waveform edges on k system ports defined in m timing diagram instances. $P1, \ldots, Pk$ denote the actions occurring on the k system ports.

The parameters defined in the declaration $v_{p1_1^{td1}} : t_{p1}, \ldots, v_{pk_n^{tdm}} : t_{pk}$ correspond to the local data variables declared at the waveform edges in the instantiated timing diagrams. Since formal timing diagrams may be instantiated repeatedly, the "formal" data variable names specified there are not unique. Therefore, new variable names have to be created for each timing diagram instance. The type t_{px} of each data parameter is determined by the data type bound to the system port of the related waveform edge.

Each data parameter contains the data value received or transmitted with the particular input or output action that corresponds to the related waveform edge, e.g. $v_{p1_1^{td1}} : t_{p1}$ denotes the parameter related to the data variable defined at the waveform edge $p1_1^{td1}$. The type t_{p1} of the data parameter is the type associated with port $p1$ according to the system design interface.

The parameter declarations $pv_1 : t_{p1}, \ldots, pv_k : t_{pk}$ correspond to the global port variables of a timing diagram specification. They bind always the most recent data value communicated at this port.

Data describes the choice to freely engage in any of the internal waveform actions, and then in the corresponding input or output action on the appropriate system port. Thus, every input or output is guarded by an internal action. Note, that this process does not impose any ordering of inputs and outputs. Their actual sequence will be determined by the ordering of the internal waveform actions.

Every input action $Pi?x : t_{pi}$ is restricted by a *selection predicate* consisting of a conjunction of a data annotation predicate $PR_{pi_k^{tdj}}$ and an optional enable condition $EC_{pi_k^{tdj}}$ that could have been specified for this edge in the underlying timing diagram.

For every output action $Po!CR_{po_k^{tdj}}$ there is specified a computation rule for the data value that will be transmitted on the event of edge po_k^{tdj}. Similar to input actions, an enable condition that could have been specified for this edge is mapped into a selection predicate.

3.3 The operational model

During synthesis it will be necessary to have access to the operational model of the timing diagram specification, i.e. the transitional system that gives the semantics of the T-LOTOS translation.

The generation of this operational model is usually achieved by performing a so-called "expansion", which dissolves the parallel composition operator in a T-LOTOS specification. The result of an expansion is a state-transition model of the specification. A subsequent minimization step reduces the size of the model and a determinization procedure removes nondeterminism.

An example for an operational model of a T-LOTOS specification is shown in figure 3.2. It is obtained from the translation of the timing diagram specification of the Traffic Light Controller as specified in chapter **Specification Languages** (beginning p. 22)). This figure reflects the original view as provided by the FORMAT system.

Each state of the transitional graph is identified by a unique name in terms of an integer number. Further, there is list of formal parameters associated with it. Therefore, a state represents all possible actual configurations of its associated formal parameters. A transition in this graph is labeled with an input or output event of a particular data value within a particular time interval on a system port and determines the actual values for the formal parameters of its target state.

The transitional graph in figure 3.2 consists of 6 states. Each state is represented by a circle, except the initial state, which is represented by a diamond. The formal parameter list is attached in angle brackets, e.g. state "2" has two formal parameters, $p6\_1$ of type *bit* and $p6\_2$ of type *time*. Repeated occurrences of states are represented by a rectangular.

Transitions are labeled with actions. For instance the leftmost edge from state "2" to state "1" describes an output ("!") of a data value *"amber"* on port *FR_LIGHTS* and this must happen within a time interval that is prescribed using a variable t_22 of type *time*. Actually, the output must occur within the interval described by a predicate $t\_22 \in [10\text{-}p6\_2; 10\text{-}p6\_2]$, where $p6\_2$ is a state variable. Finally, the present value of state variable $p6\_1$ is assigned to the formal parameter $p1\_1$ in target state "1".

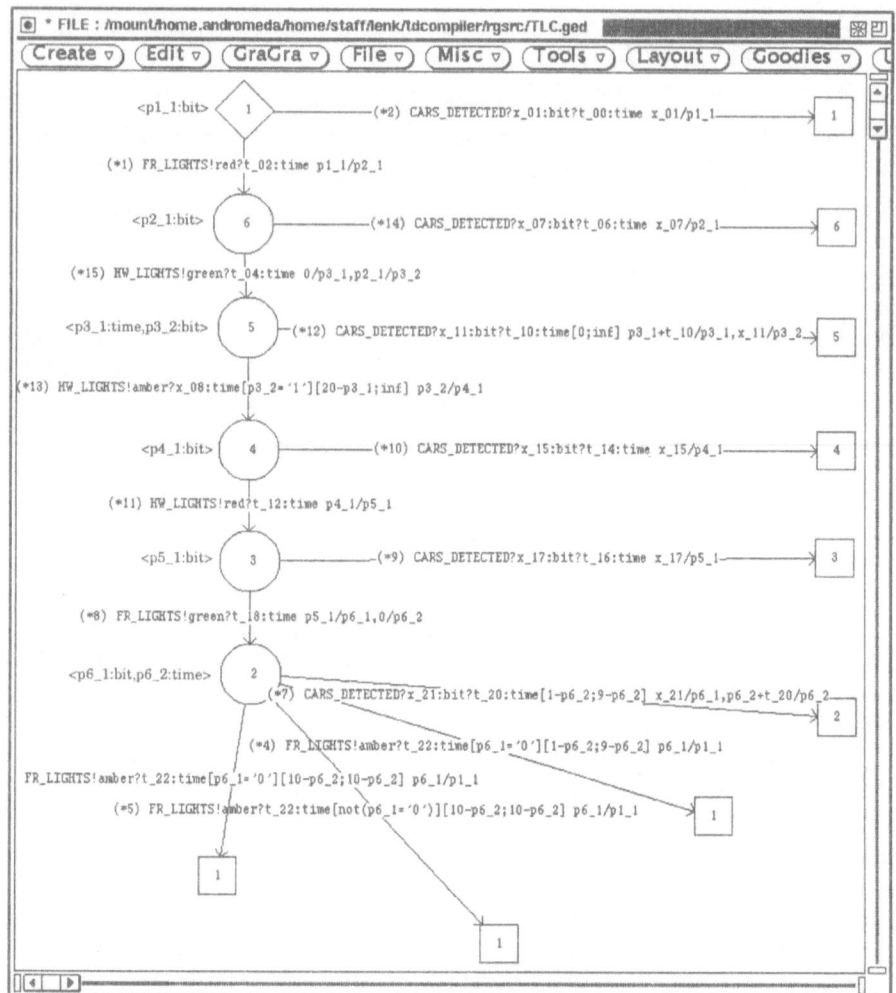

Fig. 3.2. Transitional system semantics of TLC specification

4. Automatic synthesis

As it has been presented in the preceding section, timing diagrams are translated into several T-LOTOS processes, which altogether (i.e. in parallel) describe the behaviour that is visualized by the timing diagrams.

T-LOTOS as a process algebra offers a way to transform each expression that contains arbitrary operators into an equivalent expression using just the action prefix and (timed) choice operators. Conceptually, this can be understood as (1) generating the operational model of a process, i.e. its timed graph representation (c.f. section 2.4), and (2) re-translating the timed graph into a single T-LOTOS process.

As an example for such a translation consider the transition

$$s \xrightarrow{a?,\, t_1 \in (0,6],\, \{t_2\}} s'$$

which translates into the T-LOTOS code

```
process s [a, ...](t1,t2, ... : time) :noexit :=
  let t : time = 0 in
  (* TIME t IN (<(0));(6-t1) *) a?; s'[a, ...](t1+t, ...)
endproc
```

Obviously, such T-LOTOS code reflects just the structure of the timed graph with all of its states and all of its transitions. This finite state machine-like representation is exploited during the translation into VHDL code by adopting a style of modelling FSMs in VHDL (see chapter **Generating VHDL** (beginning p. 265)).

Although such a direct translation results into large and sometimes unwieldy code, it is rather useful for rapid prototyping purposes, or early generation of simulation models.

5. Interactive synthesis

An interactive synthesis procedure is advantageous in case the designer has a vague idea of how his design shall be structured and, hence, is able to allocate at least some of the submodules on the implementation level. The main advantage in contrast to usual formal hardware verification, where specification and implementation are checked for consistency only when the complete implementation is present, is that this approach allows the designer to get fast advice just at that time, when each individual submodule becomes integrated. Therefore, also (potential) partial implementations can be valued. This enables the user to perform a bottom-up style system design, where he first creates small modules using interactively selected, previously defined basic modules from the design library and, in turn, designs more complex modules using the smaller ones. Besides, the bottom-up approach is well-suited to construct a system around one or more off-the-shelf circuits.

The concept of interactive synthesis is connected with the LAMBDA system (S. Finn et al. 1989), in essence a theorem prover basing on the mathematical formalism of higher order logic. Another interactive synthesis system is presented for a Boyer-Moore theorem prover in (F. P. Burns et al. 1994). Within FORMAT we apply this concept in the context of a timed process calculus.

5.1 The synthesis algorithm

Interactive synthesis demands the user to guide the design process by iteratively proposing modules with a known behaviour, either from previous
synthesis sessions or from directly specifying them using timing diagrams.
The synthesis tool verifies automatically, whether each module's behaviour
does not violate any aspect of the design specification.

The key idea to the synthesis procedure comes with the so-called *protocol
viewpoint* that has been outlined in chapter **Synthesis Flow** (beginning
p. 79). Following this viewpoint, a system is specified by its externally visible
I/O behaviour, i.e. its *protocol*. Clearly this premise is strongly related to
our choice taking timing diagrams as specification means. In a similar way
we may consider the behaviour of a partial implementation, i.e. a parallel
composition of all previously selected module behaviours, as being a protocol
description. Now it becomes obvious that the behaviour of the yet unknown
remainder of the implementation, i.e. all those modules that have not been
selected up to the present stage but which are important in order to satisfy
the specification, equal a protocol converter between the design specification
and the current partial implementation.

Formally, this can be expressed with the help of an implementation relation **sat** and the solution of the converter equation. In chapter **Synthesis
Flow** (beginning p. 79) the synthesis algorithm is introduced as follows:

In each iteration i the user selects a prespecified module and interconnects it
with the hitherto existing implementation. This amounts to an instantiation
of a generic process behaviour. Let the instance be called $module_i$. It follows
an automatic verification whether

$$partial\_impl_i \ |[G_i]| \ remainder_i \ \textbf{sat} \ spec_0$$

where

$$partial\_impl_i \ \approx \ partial\_impl_{i-1} \ |[H_i]| \ module_i,$$

$$remainder_i \ \approx \ convert(partial\_impl_i, \ spec_0),$$

and G_i, H_i are appropriate gate sets used for synchronization. Initially, it is
assumed that

$$partial\_impl_0 \ \approx \ stop$$

and

$$remainder_0 \ \approx \ spec_0.$$

Whenever there is an iteration n where

$$partial\_impl_n \ \textbf{sat} \ spec_0,$$

the synthesis is finished and partial_impl$_n$ gives a complete implementation that meets the original specification.

Note, that in general it is *not* true that on completion the remainder is empty, i.e.

$$\text{remainder}_n \approx stop.$$

Actually, the remainder reflects the behavioural difference between the specification and the implementation.

Before we are going to study an example, we shall have a closer look on the implementation relation and the converter generation.

5.2 Implementation relation

A key premise of a formally based synthesis is having a verification method at disposal that allows to decide after each synthesis step whether the synthesized result is a formally correct implementation of the given specification.

Regarding process calculi it is a widespread conception to consider the difference between a specification and a correct implementation just as consisting of the visibility of some additionally interspersed events in the implementation behaviour. Therefore, it is consistent to perform the verification using a *hiding*-operator *"hide* G *in* P", which simply fades out all events in the set G from a process expression P. Whether or not an implementation I satisfies a specification S is checked by verifying "S $\approx$ *hide* G *in* I", where G restricts the gate set of I to the gate set of S. In other words, G contains all implementation-internal events. Unfortunately, this approach is too stringent in practice. The reason is that the different obligations of events in specification and implementation, depending on whether they are input or output events, are not considered. For instance a specification may allow two alternative output actions in either order. Clearly, any correct implementation chooses exactly one ordering for arbitrary reasons and leaves the other out of account. Since neither action may be restricted, the equivalence-checking approach cannot induce the expected result. Conversely, there is no reason to prevent an implementation from participating (potentially) in some actions, which according to the specification won't ever occur. As an example consider a 4-bit register, which can of course go as an implementation for a binary coded digit storage module, even if it accepts a 1 event on its 3rd bit when also the 4th (most significant) bit is set to 1 and, hence, potentially stores a code 11--, which is impossible to occur due to the specification.

Obviously, the relation between a specification and its implementation (even if restricted to the same sort) is not symmetric in general. (K. G. Larsen and B. Thomsen 1991), (K. Cerans et al. 1993) define a *refinement* ordering $\lhd$ on basis of a (timed) modal transitional system that characterizes a process I as a refinement of process S, written I $\lhd$ S. For a simple transitional system a reflexive, transitive relation **sat** that

relates processes I and S, saying "I implements S", can be found in
(W. D. Tiedemann 1992). It is extended to timed transitional systems and
applied to timed graphs in (W. D. Tiedemann 1995). It shall be characterized
only intuitively here.

The general idea behind the implementation relation is to consider a behaviour I as a correct implementation of a specifying behaviour S, when every specified input event is also implemented, and every implemented output
event is also specified.

This simple conception needs to be modified a little for the general case,
where we must expect that the gate set of I is larger than the gate set of
S, i.e. the implementation graph uses a larger alphabet containing all the
implementation-internal events. When comparing I and S, these events can
be ignored w.r.t. their effects on the qualitative behaviour, but they must not
be disregarded w.r.t. to their time effects.

For instance, consider the implementation sequence

$$\xrightarrow{\{t\}} I \xrightarrow{i,\, t = 2,\, \{s\}} I' \xrightarrow{a,\, s < 5,\, \cdot} I''$$

and the specification sequence

$$\xrightarrow{\{u\}} S \xrightarrow{a,\, u < 6,\, \cdot} S'.$$

Let i being an input gate of I and not being in the gate set of S. To answer,
whether I satisfies S or not, we have to check, if the specified input a is
accepted from I, and we see it is not. Instead, I performs first an internal
move and evolves by that to the subsequent behaviour I'. However, it is not
reasonable to consider I directly as a failing implementation, since later I' is
accepting a quite well and still in time. It would be more suitable to make
the result dependent from the comparison of I' and S. But this is still not
completely the right way, since actually we have to take into account that at
the time of comparison, S has already evolved in time by 2 units. What has
to be compared in fact are I' and the time-shifted behaviour $Age(t, S)$, where
$t = 2$. Conceptually, the specification sequence has to be split up into

$$\xrightarrow{\{t,u\}} S \xrightarrow{-,\, t = 2,\, \cdot} Age(t, S) \xrightarrow{a,\, u < 6 - t,\, \cdot} S'.$$

The comparison of I' and $Age(t, S)$ in the context $t = 2$ will reveal, that I
implements S, provided I' implements S'.

In summary, we regard I as implementing S, when each of the following
requirements is satisfied:

(i) If S specifies some input event at a point t in time, then this event must
be accepted from I at the same point in time, or I must have the chance to
"escape" by itself to a subsequent behaviour at a point τ in time before t.
The subsequent behaviour I' has recursively to implement the subsequent
behaviour S' or the time-shifted behaviour $Age(\tau, S)$, respectively.

(ii) If I performs an output event at a point t in time, then this event must be specified in S for this point in time. Recursively, the subsequent behaviour I' has to implement S'.

(iii) If there is any output specified in S at all, then it must be sure that the implementation actually performs some output, or, at least, can "escape" by performing an event under its own control at a point in time earlier than the time limit for the latest possible specified output event.

Requirement *(iii)* shall just ensure that a result can be obtained in cases where only outputs are specified, but only inputs are implemented.

Example. Let the sample timed graph S from figure 2.2 be a specification. It shall be verified, whether the timed graph I that is shown in figure 5.1 is an implementation that satisfies S.

Comparing state I with state S of the graph ¿from figure 2.2, we observe that the interval during which a? is accepted by I is a superset of the corresponding interval for a? in S, since an omitted predicate means "always". Thus, we conjecture that I satisfies S, provided I1 satisfies S1. Checking whether the latter proposition holds, leads to two cases:

– I1 will perform the output action b! exactly 3 time units after being entered; since S1 allows this output within an interval $[1, 5]$, this action is well-timed and it remains to verify that I2 satisfies S;

– I1 can alternatively perform the internal action c as long as state I1 is not older than 3 time units and provided that I3 satisfies $Age(s_1, S1)$ for $s_1 \in (0, 3)$.

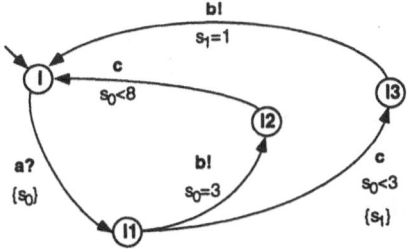

Fig. 5.1. A Timed Graph that implements S

The comparison of I3 and $Age(s_1, S1)$ shows that I3 must perform a b! action exactly 1 time unit after it has been entered. $Age(s_1, S1)$ describes a situation, where S1 holds already for s_1 time units, which is actually a time between 0 and 3. Adding 1 to this interval reveals that b! is implemented at a time larger than 1 and less than 4 time units, which obviously is a specified point in time.

Proceeding in this way, we finally end up with a (finite) verification graph that is depicted in figure 5.2. If such a verification graph can be constructed properly, we say that the timed implementation graph satisfies the timed specification graph.

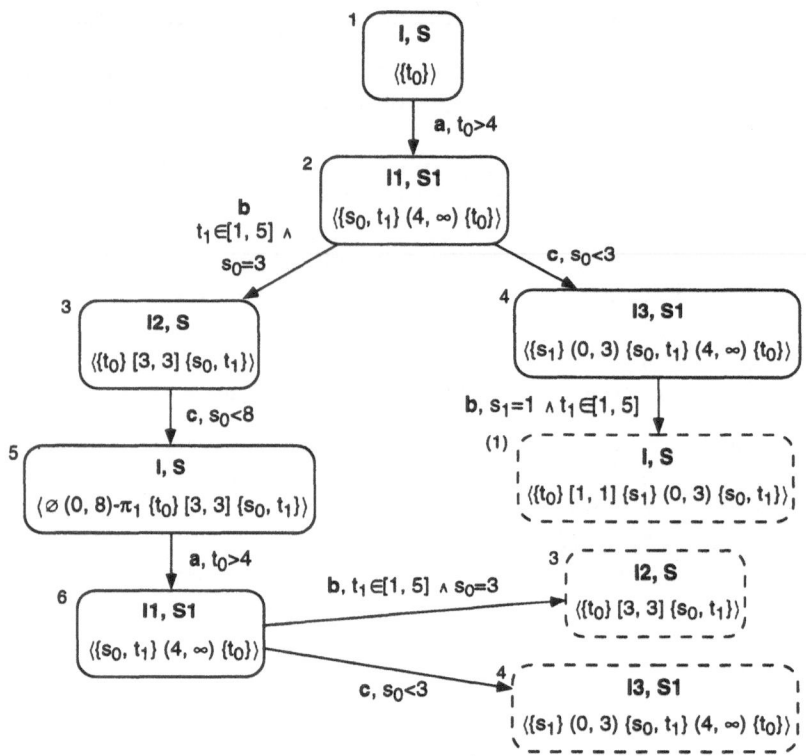

Fig. 5.2. A Verification Graph for I sat S

5.3 Protocol conversion

The task of a protocol converter consists in converting two (different) protocols, or module behaviours, into each other. In our context, two modules follow different protocols, if they do not perform a closed communication with each other or if they mutually violate timing constraints. In terms of T-LOTOS this means that a parallel composition of both equal-sorted module behaviours A and B with their common gate set G hidden, written *hide G in* A|[G]|B, equals a process that is free from deadlocks and produces only internal actions. If they do not communicate in this way, there is the need for a third module, which supplements both modules in such a way, that each module together with the third can perform a closed communication with always the other satisfying all timing constraints. This third module is called *(protocol) converter*. Its description can be derived automatically following a procedure called "equation solving" (J. Parrow 1987), (K. G. Larsen, L. Xinxin 1990).

The principle is illustrated in figure 5.3. Assume two given *deterministic* processes A, B, where A participates in events a and b. This is depicted by gates named a, b. Let B have gates b and c, where b is connected to A, i.e. A and B communicate via gate b. Clearly, the communication of A, B is not closed, since gates a and c are left open. It is the task of a converter, called X, to supplement both process behaviours so that they communicate closed with each other. If X together with B, i.e. $B|[b,c]|X$, will engage in every possible communication of A (and perhaps in further communications without the participation of A in between), we have converted B into A by means of X. In terms of T-LOTOS this can be expressed by an equation

$$A|[a,b]|A' \approx A' \quad \text{where} \quad A' = B|[b,c]|X \tag{5.1}$$

The symmetrical case leads to a similar equation

$$B|[b,c]|B' \approx B' \quad \text{where} \quad B' = A|[a,b]|X \tag{5.2}$$

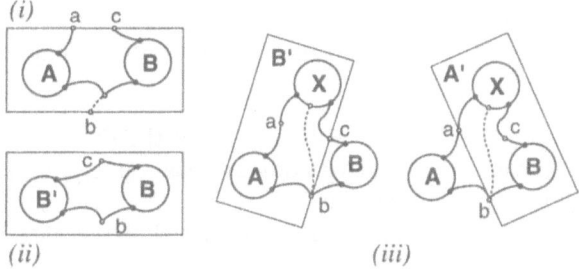

Fig. 5.3. *(i)* open communication, *(ii)* closed communication, *(iii)* converter X supplements processes A and B to establish a closed communication

When combined, equations (1) and (2) result into the single equation

$$A|[a,b]|X \approx X|[b,c]|B. \tag{5.3}$$

Note, that this requirement can be read also as $A' \approx B'$ (c.f. figure 5.3), what underlines the objective of X, notably to act as a two-sided adapter that converts the behaviour of A or B, respectively, in a way that it becomes compatible to its opposite.

However, equation (3) holds also for some undesired X, e.g. an interface that produces an initial deadlock (**stop**) on both sides or that participates in irrelevant communications. To ensure that X neither imposes restrictions on A or B, nor dissipates with superfluous communications, or, in other words, that X neither excludes nor introduces any event sequence that has been possible or impossible without X, respectively, we require the *neutrality* of X. Expressed in terms of LOTOS this leads to an equation

$$AB\|[a, b, c]\|X \approx AB \quad \text{where} \quad AB = A\|[b]\|B. \tag{5.4}$$

All event sequences possible without X are described by $A\|[b]\|B$, all event sequences possible after including X are described by $AB\|[a, b, c]\|X$.

A solution X of equations (3) and (4) can be derived automatically. This has been shown in (W. D. Tiedemann 1995) for a timed calculus without value passing.

5.4 An example: a frequency counter

This chapter describes the design session of a frequency counter board. The task of the frequency counter (FC) consists in counting the events on a particular input port during a fixed period of time beginning with an initialization by a master. After this time period the result of the preceding counting cycle can be requested by the master. The counting cycle period is imprinted and cannot be changed. Each counting result is lost as soon as the subsequent counting cycle starts (no on-board memory). The board is designed to interface with an AT-Bus protocol.

The ports of the FC board are shown in figure 5.4. They are used in the following way:

- The address input port *A0..15* is used to select the FC board for operation. Each of four specific consecutive address data values selects a particular operation mode of the FC board.
- The address enable input port *AEN* indicates that the data at the address port is valid.
- The bidirectional data port *DBUS* is used to transmit data to and to receive data from the AT data bus.
- The input port *IOW* signals the board to receive data on the data port.
- The input port *IOR* signals the board to send data on the data port.
- The input port *CNT* transmits the events to be counted.
- The output port *gate* is a monitoring signal that is asserted during the time period when counting is active.
- The output port *controlreg* is a monitoring signal that reflects the (internal) state of the FC board.

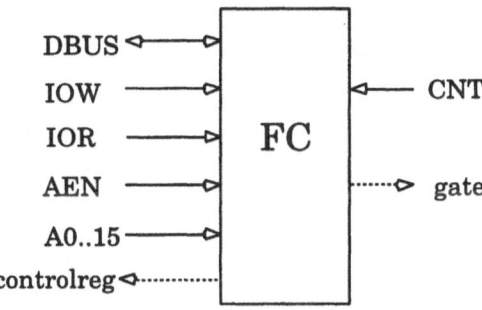

Fig. 5.4. Port configuration of the Frequency Counter

5.4.1 Functional description. The FC board is designed to count events on the *CNT* input port. The board works completely as a slave, i.e. all of its actions are initiated by a master. Its operation can be characterized by two different cycles, which can be addressed separately by the master. These are

– **Count cycle**
  A count cycle performs the counting of events during an imprinted period of time. It is divided into three phases:
  1. First, the board has to be addressed.
  2. The count cycle starts, when a corresponding data value is received on the data port during a write access.
  3. The monitoring *gate* signal is asserted for a fixed time and only during this time all events on port *CNT* are counted. Counting events correspond to a rising edge on this port.

– **Read cycle**
  A read cycle allows to read the counting result back to the master. Note that the master is responsible not to interfere with counting by performing ill-timed read attempts. The read cycle consists of two phases:
  1. The read cycle starts, when the board is initialized for read access.
  2. The result of the most recent counting process is read by the master by performing three consecutive read accesses, each transmitting a part of the counting result to the master.

5.4.2 Specification of the frequency counter. Following the philosophy of the FORMAT synthesis line the frequency counter is specified just by using timing diagrams. In case of the FC board the complete specification can be done within a single timing diagram that specifies the recurring sequence of count and read phases.

An excerpt of this timing diagram is shown in figure 5.5. It describes the initialization of a count cycle and the counting of events during a fixed period of 8 time units.

After a valid addressing of the FC board a falling edge on the *IOW* control port signals a write access by the master. A particular value received on the

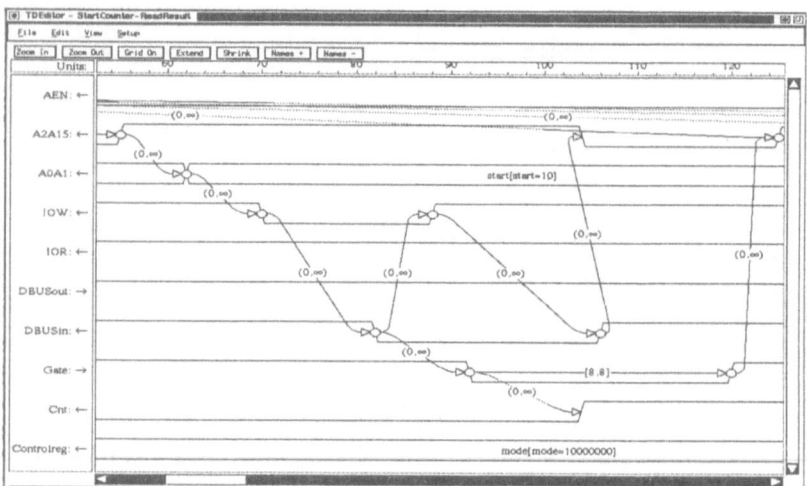

Fig. 5.5. Section of the FC timing diagram specification

data port *DBUS* starts a count cycle. The activation of counting is indicated by a falling edge of the monitor signal *gate*. A weak constraint between a falling edge on the *gate* port and a rising edge on the *CNT* port specifies that only during the low active phase of the *gate* signal counting events, i.e. rising edges of the *CNT* signal, are accepted. As soon as the counting period elapses, i.e. the counting stops, a rising edge on port *gate* will occur. A quantitative timing constraint ([8,8]) on the *gate* signal reflects the fixed time period for counting.

5.4.3 Implementation of the frequency counter . In order to introduce structure into the formal specification derived from the timing diagram translation it is necessary to have a rough idea of how the design shall look like. Such an idea of a block structure for an implementation of the frequency counter board is shown in figure 5.6.

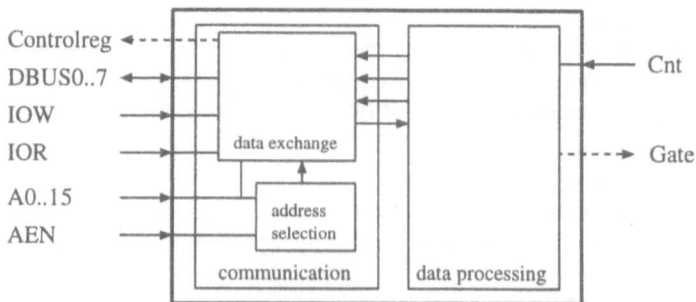

Fig. 5.6. Structure of the Frequency Counter

On the uppermost level, the implementation structure of the FC board can be divided into a communication unit and a data processing unit.

– Communication Unit
The communication unit handles the data exchange between the environment and the data processing unit. To exchange data, the communication unit on the one side has to interact with the master using the master's communication protocol, i.e. the AT-ISA bus protocol. For this interaction the unit uses the data bus $D0..7$, the address bus $A0..15$ and the control ports IOW, IOR, AEN.
On the other side the communication unit has to transfer data from and to the data processing unit. Here, an output port is used to transfer a start signal to the data processing unit, and three different data input ports, which receive each a part of the count result from the data processing unit.
The communication unit is further subdivided into two blocks. The *data exchange block* manages the data transfer between the data bus $D0..7$ and the internal ports of the data processing unit. The *address selection block* evaluates the address value and the enable signal AEN. In case of a valid address detection the address selection block generates a selection signal for the data exchange block.

– Data Processing Unit
The data processing unit performs the event counting. Responding on the start signal the data processing unit starts counting all rising edges of the signal CNT. The duration of the counting period is determined internally. After this period the counting result is available in three parts on three different data ports.

A practical realization of this structure implements the data exchange block directly by an "Intel 8255 programmable peripheral interface", a general purpose I/O component to interface peripheral equipment to a microcomputer system bus. 8-bit-data is transmitted or received across an on-chip buffer between the system bus' data lines and one of 3 parallel ports or an internal control register. The address selection block and the data processing unit are implemented using standard circuits of the 74xxx series.

5.4.4 Specification of the modules . The behaviour of the modules used in the implementation of the frequency counter is also specified in terms of timing diagrams. In the sequel we will give exemplary the specification of the data processing unit. Figure 5.7 shows its timing diagram specification.

A start signal initiates the acceptance of rising edges on the port *Cntin* during the low active period of the *Gate* signal. After this time period the counting result is provided in three parts on the output ports *ResultA..C*. Note that in this module specification the gauging time is fixed to 7 time units, which means a contradiction to the FC specification (see figure 5.5). Therefore, using this module in an implementation should lead to a violation of the specification, which should be detected during interactive synthesis.

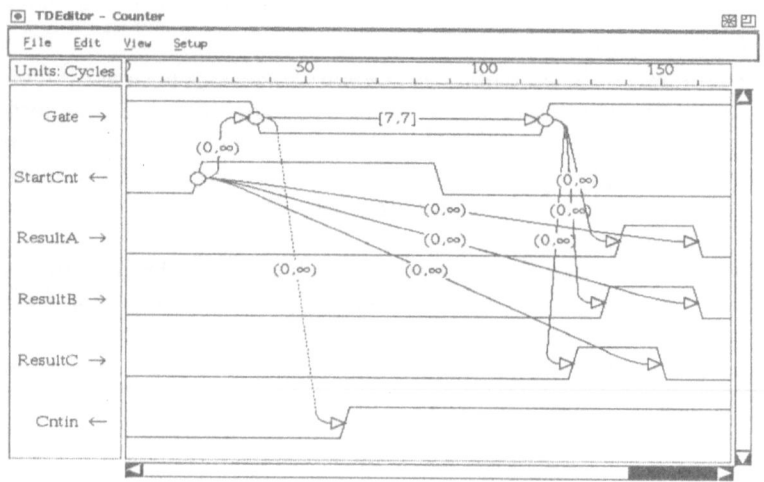

Fig. 5.7. Timing diagram for the Data Processing Block

5.4.5 Interactive design of the frequency counter. This section illustrates some steps of a sample interactive synthesis session that uses the FORMAT Interactive Structurizer in order to design the FC board. According to the "bottom-up" approach, the modules used in the potential implementation from subsection 5.4.3 are assumed to be prespecified and included in some design data base. Their description could originate either directly from a timing diagram specification, or from a previous interactive design session.

When starting a new design, the schematic capture window displays initially just the I/O interface of the specification, i.e. one icon for each port that appears in the set of timing diagrams giving the design specification. These icons serve to connect them to the implementing modules and, thus, establish a link between the port names of the specification and the corresponding implementation.

Next, the user is requested to add a module that he rates as being a partial implementation. A reasonable strategy for the selection of modules is to take those modules first that have as much direct links to the external I/O interface as possible (this reduces the size of the unknown remainder representation and leads to better computation times).

Therefore, in our sample session we use the module I8255T as our first selection. It implements the main part of the communication block (see also figure 5.6). According to the synthesis algorithm outlined in subsection 5.1 the partial implementation, which consists presently of just one module, namely the I8255T module, is first checked for its validity, i.e. it is verified, whether the partial implementation in parallel with the yet unknown remainder (generated by conversion, c.f. subsection 5.3) satisfies the specification. Unless there is a violation, next the partial implementation is checked for completeness, i.e. whether it already satisfies the specification immediately. At this stage of our sample session it is evident that the design is not yet complete, since there are still some unconnected input ports like *AEN* that are required for satisfying the specification.

Figure 5.8 shows the schematic capture window after the first design step. On the left and right margin there are drawn the I/O interface ports. The selected I8255T module is positioned in the middle and connected to the interface ports. A pop-up message informs the user that the design is correct for the present, but still incomplete.

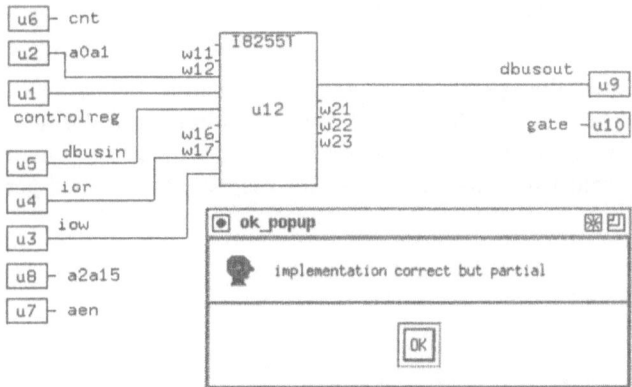

Fig. 5.8. The first design step

In the second step of our sample design a module *COUNTER7NS* is selected. The behaviour of this module shall be the one introduced in figure 5.6. It is intended to implement the data processing unit. The verification of this design choice reveals that the updated partial implementation is not valid. The reason lies in an improper determination of the gauging time. Consequently, the synthesis tool asks to undo the last design step (c.f. figure 5.9).

In order to provide some information about the failure that can help the designer to succeed in doing a better choice, the synthesis tool provides a trace of the verification running into the trouble case (see figure 5.10). This representation shows the trace of actions along which the specification and the implementation meet each other w.r.t. the implementation preorder (see section 5.2) up to the point, where the implementation cannot satisfy the specified behaviour any more. The corresponding node is called *CRASH*. Its successor nodes sum up all possible follow-up actions for both, the specification and the implementation. One can easily figure out that there is a time

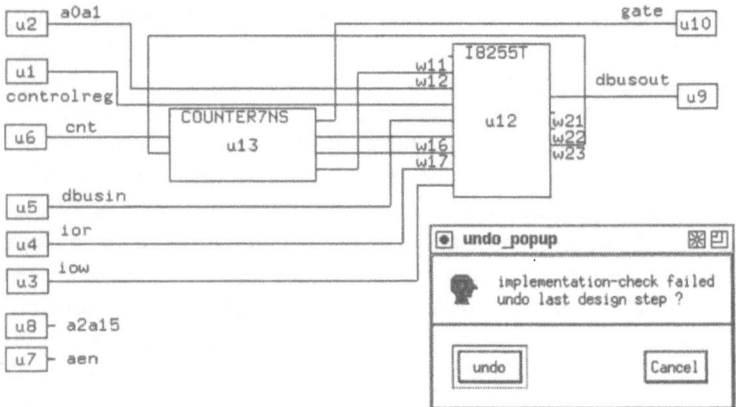

Fig. 5.9. The second design step - a timing violation

conflict between the specified and the implemented behaviour. The module
COUNTER7NS counts the events during a time period that is too short
in comparison with the requirements of the specification. This fault can be
corrected by selecting a new module that respects the proper period of time.

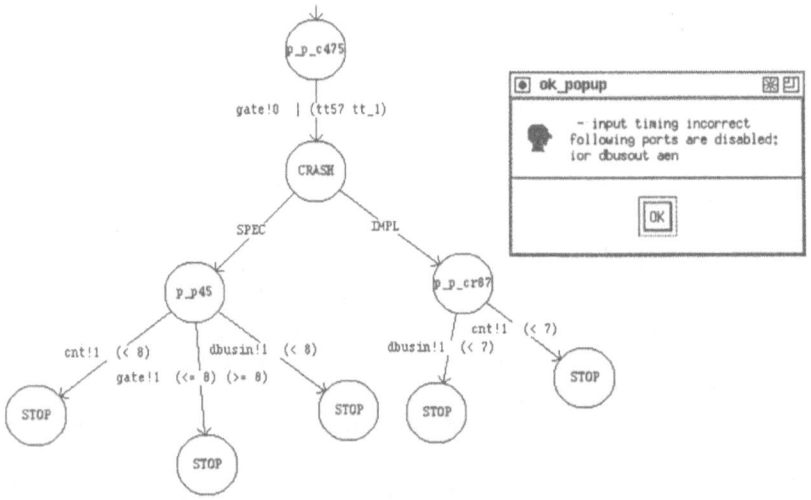

Fig. 5.10. Graph containing the Error Trace

The last design step selects the address module *ADDRESS* and connects
it to its environment. It is not only verified that the present partial implementation satisfies the original specification in parallel with the present
unknown remainder, i.e. the converter between the partial implementation
and the specification, but also that this partial implementation alone satis-

fies the specification. This means that the implementation is complete and correct w.r.t. the implementation relation. The complete design is depicted in figure 5.11.

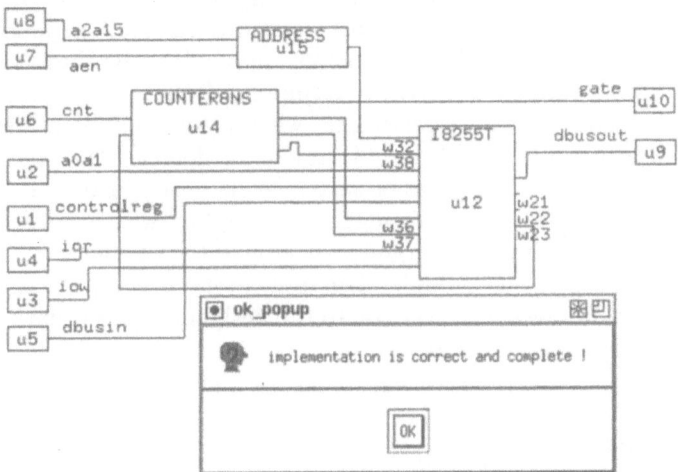

Fig. 5.11. The complete implementation

6. Conclusions

This chapter presented the various techniques used within the FORMAT project in order to synthesize behavioural or structural code from timing diagram specifications. As intermediate representation we use T-LOTOS, a language basing on a timed process calculus. T-LOTOS is not only advantageous for formalizing the visual timing diagrams, but also for performing an interactive bottom-up synthesis approach that allows to transform pure behavioural descriptions, as they are obtained directly ¿from the timing diagram translation, into structural descriptions. Correctness of the transformations is guaranteed with respect to an implementation relation that considers real time constraints. Furthermore, T-LOTOS is qualified to be translated into VHDL. A separate chapter (**Generating VHDL** (beginning p. 265)) is dedicated to this topic.

A CAD toolset developed within FORMAT has been evaluated on selected examples from the telecommunication area. Chapter **Telefónica I+D Industrial Experience** (beginning p. 99) reports on this. Since the tools operate internally on state-transition graphs, they are prone to state explosion and, thus, the size of manageable designs is limited. However, since the synthesis approaches concentrate primarily on the uppermost levels of design, where, thanks to abstraction, the number of ports and observable events is only moderate, it is still possible to deal with medium complexity designs. Furthermore, there are possibilities to alleviate explosion, e.g. by carefully choosing a strategy for expansion of parallel processes or – in case of the bottom-up synthesis procedure – by requesting the user to place his modules in a way that the number of open ports is always as small as possible.

In summary we feel that the FORMAT approach to synthesis is an interesting and convincing contribution to formal hardware synthesis, not at least since it considers real time constraints, what cannot be offered from most of the other formal CAD tools in industry or academia. Moreover, the FORMAT synthesis approach observes in particular its user-friendliness in practice since it rigorously frees the designer from struggling with formal user interfaces: starting with timing diagrams, which give the specification, up to the schematic capture of the module structure, every user interaction is done graphically and in a way that is close to the designers conceptual world. Any formalism is completely hidden.

References

R. Alur, C. Courcoubetis, D. L. Dill (1990): Model Checking for Real-Time Systems; *Proc. 5th IEEE Symposium on Logic in Computer Science LICS'90* 414-425.

R. Alur and D. L. Dill (1992): The Theory of Timed Automata; *Proc. REX'91 Workshop on Real Time: Theory in Practice*, LNCS 600, Springer, 45-73.

F. P. Burns, D. J. Kinniment, A. M. Koelmans (1994): Stride – a tool for formal interactive system synthesis; *IEE Proc. on Computers and Digital Techniques* 141 6, 347-355.

K. Cerans, J. C. Godskesen, K. G. Larsen (1993): Timed Modal Specification – Theory and Tools; *Proc. Int. Workshop on Computer Aided Verification CAV'93* LNCS 697, Springer, 253-267.

S. Finn, M. P. Fourman, M. Francis, R. Harris (1989): Formal System Design – Interactive Synthesis based on Computer-Assisted Formal Reasoning; *Proc. IFIP Int. Workshop on Applied Formal Methods for Correct VLSI Design*, Leuven, 97-110.

K. G. Larsen, B. Thomsen (1991): Partial specifications and compositional verification; *Theoretical Computer Science* 88, 15-32.

K. G. Larsen, L. Xinxin (1990): Equation Solving Using Modal Transition Systems; *Proc. IEEE Symp. on Logic in Computer Science LICS'90* 108-117.

P. Michel, U. Lauther, P. Duzy (eds.) (1992): The Synthesis Approach to Digital System Design; *Int. Series in Eng. and Computer Science; VLSI, computer architecture and DSP*, Kluwer (1992).

C. Miguel Nieto, A. Fernández, L. Vidaller (1992): Extending LOTOS Towards Performance Evaluation; *Formal Description Techniques V*, North Holland.

X. Nicollin, J. Sifakis, S. Yovine (1992): Compiling Real-Time Specifications into Extended Automata; *IEEE Transactions on Software Engineering* 18 9, 794-804.

J. Parrow (1987): Submodule Construction as Equation Solving in CCS; *Proc. Foundations of Software Technology and Theoretical Computer Science*, LNCS 287, Springer, 103-123.

J. Quemada, A. Fernandez (1987): Introduction of Quantitative Relative Time into LOTOS; *IFIP Workshop on Protocol Specification, Testing and Verification VII*, North Holland.

W. D. Tiedemann (1992): An Approach to Multi-paradigm Controller Synthesis from Timing Diagram Specifications; *Proc. EURO-DAC'92*, 522-527.

W. D. Tiedemann (1995): Synthese von Kommunikationsprozessoren aus Spezifikationen in Form von Impulsdiagrammen; *Universität Passau*, Dissertation.

ISO (1989): *Information Processing Systems — Open Systems Interconnection — LOTOS: A Formal Description Technique Based on the Temporal Ordering of Observational Behaviour*. IS-8807. International Standards Organization. Published 15 Feb.

J. Quemada, S. Pavon, A. Fernandez (1989): State Exploration by Transformation with LOLA; *Workshop on Automatic Verification Methods for Finite State Systems*, Grenoble, June.

C. Miguel, A. Fernndez, J. Ortuo, L. Vidaller (1993): A LOTOS based Performance Evaluation Tool; *Computer Networks and ISDN Systems* 25 7, 791-813.

J. Tretmans (1989): Test Case Derivation from LOTOS Specifications; *Proc. FORTE'89*, North-Holland, 345-359.

J. Tretmans, P. van Eijk (1989): *The Formal Description Technique LOTOS*, North-Holland (1989).

P. van Eijk, H. Eertink (1990): Design of the LotoSphere Symbolic LOTOS Simulator; *Proc. FORTE'90*, North-Holland, 577-580.

W. van Hulzen (1989): LOTTE: a LOTOS tool environment; *Proc. Formal Description Techniques FORTE'88*, North-Holland.

J. A. Mañas, T. de Miguel, T. Robles, J. Salvachúa, G. Huecas, and M. Veiga (1993): TOPO: Quick Reference – Front End. Technical report, Dpt. Telematics Engineering Technical Univ. Madrid, Ciudad Universitaria, E-28040 Madrid, Spain, June. Version 3R2.

T. Bolognesi, E. Brinksma (1987): Introduction to the ISO Specification Language LOTOS; *Computer Networks and ISDN Systems* 14 1, 25-59.

J. Quemada, A. Azcorra, D. Frutos (1993): TIC: A TImed Calculus; *Formal Aspects of Computing*, June 1993, Vol.5:224-252.

Generating VHDL Code from LOTOS Descriptions

Andrés Marín López[1], Carlos Delgado Kloos[1], Tomás Robles Valladares[2], and Tomás de Miguel Moro[2]

[1] Universidad Carlos III de Madrid, Spain
[2] Universidad Politécnica de Madrid, Spain

1. Introduction

The aim of this chapter is to describe an automatic technique for obtaining synthesizable VHDL code from a T-LOTOS specification. Although the technique is automated, some guidance from the user is always welcome when a better code is required. There are in principle two ways to perform the translation: translation of the T-LOTOS operators into VHDL code or substitution of T-LOTOS processes by corresponding VHDL blocks from a pre-defined T-LOTOS & VHDL library. Both procedures can could be also combined together. In the present chapter only the first approach is developed.

The chapter is divided into three sections. The present section identifies the problem to be solved by the translator and discusses what it means for the translation to be correct. Section 2. sets out the semantics of elements of LOTOS and VHDL, explains the translation method and the limitations imposed by it. Section 3. gives a practical example of design in LOTOS and translation to VHDL according to the scheme detailed. The example treated is an ethernet bridge. Sections 4. and 5. discuss the testing facilities and the testing methodology provided by the "synthesis path" within the FORMAT project.

LOTOS and VHDL are both standards, LOTOS (ISO 1989) and VHDL (IEEE 1989), (IEEE 1994), and both are useful in describing systems. LOTOS was defined by ISO in terms of a formal semantics. IEEE has not given a formal semantics to VHDL, but recently there have been many individual efforts in this direction and several different semantics are attributable to VHDL as a result (C. Delgado Kloos and P. T. Breuer 1995). The most remarkable difference between the two languages is the level of abstraction: the LOTOS mechanisms to describe systems are more abstract than the ones used in VHDL.

LOTOS specifications describe the observable behavior of systems. The behavior of a system is the set of all possible interaction sequences that can happen. Interactions are represented by events which are atomic, instantaneous and synchronous. Events are associated with gates, and an event will take place at a given gate if and only if every participating behavior expression is ready to interact there and then. When an event takes place all the participating processes synchronize, sharing a common view of the interaction. The behavior expressions describe the system by representing the event sequences allowed.

Both LOTOS and VHDL are languages for the description of concurrent systems. These are the main differences between them:

1. The behavioral specification of systems in VHDL consists of a number of sequential processes that interact concurrently. Within a single process everything is sequential – there is no nesting of concurrent behaviors within a process.
   In T-LOTOS there is more freedom. A process is just an abstraction of a behavior expression and therefore might have concurrently acting subprocesses inside. There are therefore less restrictions in T-LOTOS than in VHDL.
2. The construct for synchronization in T-LOTOS is a multi-way rendezvous (see Table 1.1), whereas in VHDL it is the **wait**-statement, which is a lower-level construct. So it is much simpler to express a complex synchronization among different processes in LOTOS than in VHDL.

Table 1.1. T-LOTOS interactions

B_1	B_2	Condition	Interaction	Effect
$g!E_1$	$g!E_2$	$\mathrm{val}(E_1)=\mathrm{val}(E_2)$	*value matching*	synchronization
$g!E_1$	$g?x:t$	$\mathrm{class}(E_1)=t$	*value passing*	$x=\mathrm{value}(E_1)$
$g?x:t$	$g?y:u$	$t=u$	*value negotiation*	$x=y=v(\mathrm{class}t)$

3. T-LOTOS is a language with an explicit non-deterministic construct, the choice-operator [], whereas in VHDL there exists no such operator.
   T-LOTOS is therefore more general as it allows the expression of families of possible behaviors. There are also other operators that may be used to describe non-deterministic specifications, such as parallelism operators.
4. In T-LOTOS data types are expressed using the algebraic specification language ACT-ONE. Abstract data types are described algebraically by giving a signature and a set of equations between terms generated from the signature.
   In VHDL the definition of data types is given in a concrete way, as in many other programming languages; for example, Ada.

2. Translation of T-LOTOS to VHDL

Many implementation decisions have to be taken when moving from the highly abstract level of T-LOTOS to the more concrete level of a VHDL architecture.

This section describes the procedure for translating T-LOTOS specifications to VHDL. First, a general framework will be described, including a relation between T-LOTOS and VHDL semantics. Practical considerations for translation will then be discussed.

What does it mean to translate from LOTOS to VHDL? In our setting it means:

1. obtaining a concrete implementation in VHDL from an abstract specification in T-LOTOS.

T-LOTOS defines the behavior of a concurrent system, but it does not define any particular implementation. Therefore it is necessary to define a mapping of the abstract elements of T-LOTOS to concrete VHDL structures. This will imply certain limitations. The generated code will not be optimal VHDL, for example.

To continue, a further aspect of the translation task is:

2. to define the interaction with the environment.

An interface layer is required between the generated VHDL code and its environment. It supplies a view of the environment to the VHDL code that is compatible with the LOTOS model. The interface fixes certain implementation details that are not determined by the LOTOS abstraction, but the abstraction holds as a description of it.

Finally, translation has to:

3. interpret the time expressions of T-LOTOS.

The generated VHDL code must implement not only standard LOTOS, but also T-LOTOS, the annotated extension defined within the FORMAT project.

These are the theoretical elements, but we have one more, from the practical point of view. Translation must:

4. provide a useful VHDL implementation, i.e. one that is useful in the design process.

We must ensure that the generated VHDL code is synthesizable, at least for some synthesis tool. Testability is also an important issue that should be taken into consideration.

These are the requirements if we want to combine the advantages of using T-LOTOS with the generation of useful VHDL code. In the next section we will analyze the relation between LOTOS and VHDL to be able to ensure that we comply with these requirements. From this study a set of mandatory guidelines on T-LOTOS code will be derived, and the resulting model for translation will be described.

2.1 Relation between LOTOS and VHDL semantic elements

LOTOS specifications consist of a behavior and a data part. These parts will require different treatments in the translation procedure.

Data. The data part will be translated using a mapping (based on a naming mechanism) from LOTOS data types to VHDL data types.

The definition of such a mapping is limited by:

1. VHDL types;
2. types and definitions supported by the simulators and synthesizers.

The mapping defines the types that may be used in LOTOS specifications.

The equations of LOTOS will later be used in the verification/validation process. But after translation to VHDL, the semantics is provided by the VHDL data types. It is important, therefore, that the semantics of the target VHDL data types and the semantics of the LOTOS originals be consistent.

The exploration of this issue will be deferred until after the semantics of the behavior part has been set out, below.

Behavior. The T-LOTOS behavior part is defined as a set of processes combined by binary operators. The synchronization is realized by a multi-way rendezvous with value negotiation.

The processes evolve independently when they do not have to synchronize. Processes synchronize through parallel operators.

We can identify three semantic elements to translate:

1. events;
2. processes;
3. other operators.

Events. The basic element in T-LOTOS is the *event*. It is a combination of a gate and several experiments, that may be seen as event parameters. Events are important because they are the level of granularity of the specification. Two or more events can occur simultaneously, but one event cannot occur partially. Therefore, one event is an indivisible unit of behavior. Thus a T-LOTOS specification is devoted to clearly state when each event may occur, and how events are ordered along time.

The role of gates in T-LOTOS may be compared with the use of *variant record* variables in traditional procedural languages: there are many ways to organize collections of data into structures, but the right selection will permit easy exchange of information among different program blocks. Therefore, the meaningful information is the combination of a gate and its parameters in the *event*. Different real actions may occur at the same gate, in a similar manner to conventional multiplexing of communication lines. Nevertheless, multiplexing implies a complex overloading of single events and therefore makes it necessary to perform a deep analysis of the specification in order to define the correct type of the VHDL signals.

LOTOS synchronization is performed by a multi-way rendezvous and this implies:

1. More than one action may be involved in the occurrence of one event.
2. When the resulting event happens, all the involved actions occur simultaneously.
3. Value negotiation, matching and passing are performed in the rendezvous.
4. There is no limit to the number of values to be negotiated.

VHDL performs synchronization by the use of signals. Therefore, we have to decompose the sophisticated LOTOS rendezvous in terms of the much more simple VHDL signal interchanging.

Processes. A run of a T-LOTOS process may be seen as a sequence of actions, some of which require synchronization with the environment. A process evolves concurrently with other processes and cooperates with them where necessary. Its internal code may also run in several concurrent threads of control.

It is important to note that the behavior of a process is independent of the context. The only way to influence a process is by the synchronization. The gates involved in the external synchronization are defined in the header of the process.

This is quite similar to entities in VHDL. Each entity is defined by means of a declaration and an architecture definition. VHDL processes execute their internal code sequentially in a single thread of control, concurrently with other processes.

Operators. The *basic operators* are: inaction (stop), successful termination (exit), action prefix (;) and choice ([]). Every LOTOS expression may be reduced to combinations of these operators. It is important to provide an efficient translation for those operators. Due to their simplicity, they can be mapped into simple VHDL constructs, as we will see later.

The most powerful T-LOTOS operators are the *parallel operators*:

|| Full synchronization. The two processes must synchronize at every gate of the interface.
||| Interleaving. The two processes evolve independently.
|[S]| Partial synchronization. The processes only synchronize at the gates listed in the set S.

There are no equivalent explicit constructs in VHDL. In the general case, we will implement them via an extra VHDL entity communicating with the two processes, in order to take care of the multi-way information flow. When the synchronization scheme is simple, the additional entity may be suppressed.

Other operators provide mechanisms that allow one to compose complex functionalities from simple sub-processes. These operators are: hiding (hide) sequential composition (>>), and the inhibition composition operator ([>).

The hiding operator can be translated via hierarchy in VHDL, as it allows us to hide the signals used in the lower-level components of the system.

Enabling and disabling operators may be handled in several ways. The simplest one is to substitute them by an equivalent expression in basic operators. This may be done using tools like LOLA (J. Quemada et al. 1989). This approach simplifies the LOTOS subset to translate, but the main drawback is the size of the resulting specification. Another drawback is the consequent loss of modularity.

The second option is to use intermediate VHDL signals to implement each LOTOS operator. This allows advantage to be taken of the LOTOS structure of sub-processes, reducing the size of the VHDL code. The main drawback is the communication load imposed by coordination between the sub-processes.

2.2 Restrictions imposed by the translation

In the previous sections we have analyzed the relation between T-LOTOS and VHDL semantic elements. But we do not intend to translate full T-LOTOS specifications. Partially because it will not be possible, and partially because it will not result in useful VHDL specifications. Furthermore, it will not be necessary, because from a timing diagram specification not every variety of T-LOTOS specification is obtainable.

In this section we identify the restrictions on the source code imposed by the translation technology. These restrictions are checked at compilation time. The checks impose no extra execution loading. The following is the complete list of restrictions grouped by type:

1. Dynamic creation of processes
   T-LOTOS permits the dynamic creation of processes. It does not seem reasonable to use dynamic architectures, when hardware is defined. A static architecture is required.
   Within the constraints of this static architecture, recursive processes are allowed.
   The types of recursion allowed are:
   a) Tail-recursion (self-recursion): always allowed.
   b) Parallel operators: only used to compose processes.
   c) Mutual recursion: cannot involve an unbounded number of instances of a process, i.e. the situation: `P:= P <parallel_opn> Q` is not allowed.

2. Value negotiation
   Value negotiation is very powerful, but also very complex. In real situations it is possible to avoid this structure. It is not a hard limitation when modeling hardware, where value negotiation does not seem natural.
   In our model we restrict value negotiation to value passing. This implies:
   a) the direction of the values has to be defined;
   b) selection predicates are only allowed in the events that receive data;

   c) all partners involved in a synchronization must offer/accept the same number of parameters. This implies the typing of gates – inside a process, one gate always offers the same number and type of parameters.

3. Rendezvous

Applying the previous limitations, it is immediate to conclude that multiway rendezvous is not necessary.

Using the value passing convention, one of the partners puts one or more data values and the other partners must accept them.

Then the synchronization is reduced to: 1 to N ($N \geq 0$) value passing.

The allowed synchronization is summarized in the Table 2.1,

Table 2.1. Allowed synchronizations

offer	$g!E_1$
accept_1	$g?x : t$ with class$(E_1) = t$
. . .	. . .
accept_N	$g?x : t[t = E_1]$ with class$(E_1) = t$

In the table a value offer and N variable offers are shown. The type of the value must be the same as the variables offered. Selection predicates are used in the variable offers. Synchronization will only take place if the value offered complies with the selection predicates.

4. Data Types

A library of VHDL data types has to be provided. Every T-LOTOS data type must be directly mapped to one of those data types. To use extra data types, the corresponding VHDL library has to be provided.

2.3 Translation scheme

From the considerations of the previous sections we derive the following general translation scheme:

1. T-LOTOS processes are implemented as VHDL entities. The LOTOS gates are implemented as VHDL ports. The implementation of these entities is defined by a VHDL architecture.

   The architecture contains a VHDL process described as a finite state machine. This allows for user-provided VHDL architectures, but they must match the entity declaration.

   A T-LOTOS process may be either atomic or compound. To translate a compound process to VHDL, we translate its components and provide a VHDL architecture that combines them appropriately. There is one such architecture provided for each constructor of T-LOTOS.

2. Recursion, without process creation, is implemented by combining a VHDL process with local variables. The local variables are updated with the new values provided by the actual parameters. Mutual recursion of processes is translated by mutual activation of the finite state machines.

3. The translation of the basic operators of LOTOS uses one or more of the states of the finite state machine:
   a) Inaction (stop) is translated by an idle final state which can only transit by occurrence of a global reset.
   b) Action prefix (;) which allows an event to precede a behavior expression, is translated by consecutive states of the finite state machine machine.
   c) Choice ([]) between two behavior expressions is translated with the if statement. We do not allow non-determinism that cannot be resolved by the environment.
4. Synchronization: value negotiation is restricted to value passing. It is straightforward to implement it using signals with the proper signal declaration and mapping.

Let us study an abstract synchronization between two LOTOS processes: one process offering a variable and the other offering a value. For the interaction to take place, three requirements are necessary:

   a) the two processes must be ready to interact, i.e.: both of them will wait for the other in case one is ready to synchronize before the other;
   b) the value must be of the same class of the variable (this is guaranteed by imposing on LOTOS gates a given direction and type);
   c) both of them will continue their behavior after the synchronization simultaneously.

The first and third conditions refer to delaying the execution of one VHDL process until the other is ready to synchronize or accepts the value.

The wait statement is used for this task, but a simple protocol to perform LOTOS rendezvous is needed. The behavior protocol shown in Table 2.2 behaves strictly as the LOTOS synchronization does.

Table 2.2. Rendezvous protocol

Phase	Sender	Receivers
Meet	send sender ready wait receiver ready	wait sender ready send receiver ready
Exchange	send value send sender ack	wait sender ack process value
Leave	wait receiver ack send prot finished	send receiver ack wait prot finished

This protocol can be extended to any number of processes. The processes offering values have all the same code corresponding to the receiver shown in Table 2.2. The advantages of this approach are:

   a) the circuits described have a distributed behavior, instead of depending on the decision of a centralized device;

b) the VHDL specification maintains a closer link with the LOTOS specification because it is intended to maintain a syntactical link;

c) the code obtained is efficient in length, signals and speed.

We translate the three different phases (meet, exchange and leave) to three different states of the finite state machine. Then we define a separate entity which handles most of the protocol.

5. Selection predicates in LOTOS are conditions on data that decide if a certain synchronization is feasible. In our implementation model, those conditions are evaluated during the exchange phase of the protocol.

6. Guards in LOTOS are expressions associated with events. Only if the guard expression is satisfied is the corresponding event offered for synchronization. In our implementation model, those conditions are evaluated during the meet phase of the protocol.

7. The use of timing constraints in a T-LOTOS specification prunes the synchronization tree: the constraints reduce the number of synchronizations that are feasible at any time. Moreover, when an annotation specifies that an offer is to occur within a certain time interval, then we can usually do without the synchronization protocol. Our implementation uses a counter to control whether timing constraints are met or not.

Let us see an example of how such annotated offers are translated. The following T-LOTOS behavior:

```
a?x:integer (* time tx in 0;5 *); B
```

is translated as:

```
WHEN 0=> reset_cnt <= 1; -- Counter is reset
         next_state<=1;
WHEN 1=> if cnt_cnt = 5 then
         -- Count is checked wrt UB.
            x:=a;
            next_state<=2;
         end if;
WHEN 2=> -- Translation of B
```

The offer can be enriched with a guard an a selection predicate:

```
[guard(var)]->a?x:integer (* time tx in 0;5 *)[pred(x)]; B
```

where guard(var), pred(x) are predicates on LOTOS variables. This offer is translated as:

```
WHEN 0=> if guard(var) then
            reset_cnt <= 1;
            next_state<=1;
         end if;
WHEN 1=> if (cnt_cnt=<5) and (pred(a)) then
```

```
        -- substitution of x by a
           x:=a;
           next_state<=2;
        end if;
  WHEN 2=> -- Translation of B
```

The VHDL code thus obtained is much more compact than the one in which no timing information is present.

2.4 Optimizing the code

To summarize, the design methodology in the FORMAT project starts with a timing diagram specification which is translated to T-LOTOS. This T-LOTOS specification is subjected to several refinements and transformations and after that it is finally translated to VHDL. We have made some optimizations based on the specifications produced by this synthesis method. We present some of them below:

1. the variables not used within the specification are not translated into the VHDL code.

This is quite a common optimization in compilers. A variation is:

2. saving on variables that are used only within predicates of external offers. We use the value of the equivalent VHDL signal to check the predicate instead.

The most important optimization we have incorporated in the tool is the following:

3. reduction of the number of states in the T-LOTOS specification.

This optimization can be applied whenever there is an initial state where several actions are possible, a final one where all of them have occurred, and all the intermediate states needed to allow every possible ordering of the actions. This set of traces is simplified to a subset, where all the output events are ordered into a single execution trace, while the inputs are allowed to happen at any time. This optimization is very notable in examples with a large number of gates. The optimization is illustrated in figure 2.1.

3. Design of an ethernet bridge

In this section we describe the design in LOTOS of a system and its translation to VHDL by the technique described in the previous section.

The system is a *bridge* connecting three *ethernet* LANs, as shown in figure 3.1. It allows transparent communication between the ethernets, and incorporates a learning mechanism. The design is not optimal in the sense

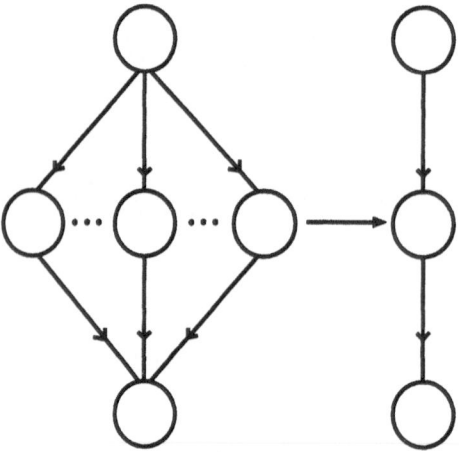

Fig. 2.1. Reduction of traces in Harpo

that it could be improved by incorporating a "spanning tree algorithm" or similar, but it is appropriate for the purposes of illustration.

Each attachment of the bridge to a LAN is a *port*. The bridge listens promiscuously and stores the address in each packet's source address field in a cache, together with the identity of the port at which the packet was received. For each packet received, it looks through its cache for the address listed in the packet's destination address field:

1. if the address is not found in the cache, the bridge forwards the packet to all ports except the one from which it was received;
2. if the address is found in the cache, the bridge forwards the packet to the port specified in the table. If it is the same as that from which the packet was received, the packet is dropped (filtered).

The bridge ages each entry in the cache and deletes it after a certain period of time in which no packet has been received with that address in the source address.

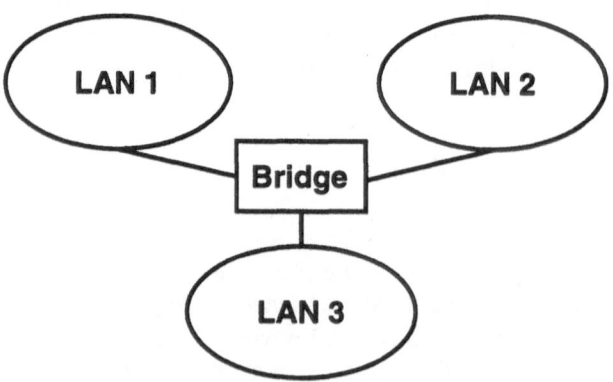

Fig. 3.1. Ethernet bridge

We follow a *bottom-up* approach to the specification of the ports. LOTOS *gates* are both

1. channels of information, and
2. points of synchronization.

These two aspects are represented by separate concepts in VHDL, where communication is through **ports** and synchronization is by means of implicit or explicit signals and **waits**. To translate a LOTOS gate into VHDL, therefore, we define a protocol in which VHDL **ports** and **waits** are the primitives.

Packets received have to be accepted at the Ethernet port of the bridge. We model reception with an offer in LOTOS to gate **in**. Next, the packets are passed through to the interior of the bridge (through gate **income**), and the behavior is repeatable:

```
B1:= in?f1:frame; income!f1; B1
```

LOTOS names are translated to the VHDL name-space with the prefix V_, so the VHDL code generated for the above sequence is:

```
when 1 => -- Activate V_in
            if Ok_in then
            V_fr <= V_in;
            -- End V_in
            next_state <= 2;
            end if;
when 2 => -- Activate V_income
            V_income <= V_fr;
            if Ok_income then
            -- End V_income
            next_state <= 3;
            end if;
```

The bridge passes processed frames to the Ethernet ports through the **outcome** gate. The ports then put them onto the Ethernets. This aspect of the behavior of the Ethernet port is modelled in LOTOS as follows:

```
B2:= outcome?f2:frame; out!f2; B2
```

Both behaviors are possible for a given Ethernet port. So the ports overall behavior is the non-deterministic choice between B1 and B2:

```
B  =   (in?f1:frame; income!f1; B)
   []  (outcome?f2:frame; out!f2; B)
```

VHDL is deterministic and so we have to use the **if then else** to translate the choice of behaviors. We use the boolean variables **Ok_in** and **Ok_outcome** to determine which way to branch. Recall that a separate library module is responsible for resolving the synchronization. Signals V_in and V_outcome activate two instances of the library module, one controlling each alternate branch.

```
when 1 => -- Activate V_in
           -- Activate V_outcome
           if Ok_in then
             V_fr <= V_in;
             -- End V_in
             next_state <= 2;
           elsif Ok_outcome then
             V_fr <= V_outcome;
             -- End V_outcome
             next_state <= 3;
           end if;
```

We need to encapsulate the behavior we have defined in order to use it in the three ports of the design. LOTOS *processes* provide such an encapsulation, and can be parameterized on gates and variables that allow several instantiations of the same behavior. Processes are also the mechanism to define recursive behaviors. These two facts are needed in the ports of the bridge (see Figure 3.2).

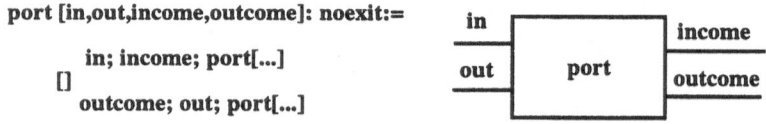

port [in,out,income,outcome]: noexit:=

　　　in; income; port[...]
[]
　　　outcome; out; port[...]

Fig. 3.2. LOTOS code and diagram of the port

VHDL processes are implicitly tail recursive, but they do not allow for mutual recursion. That has to be built into the translation with a signal activation mechanism. This implies that LOTOS processes are translated to VHDL entities, which concurrently instantiate components (references to entities).

The three ports we have specified have to communicate with the bridge. There are three types of *parallel operators* in LOTOS, which allow *synchronization* and *interleaving* of behaviors. The ports will behave independently (*pure interleaving*) at gates in, out and income and will synchronize at gate outcome. The situation is depicted in Figure 3.3.

Concurrent execution of processes is natural in VHDL. Nevertheless, additional mechanisms are needed to translate LOTOS synchronizations. If there are more than two processes involved then library components are needed in the translation.

In the previous specifications, little has been said about the data types, but only some variables fr of type frame have been used. LOTOS has algebraic data types based on ACT ONE (H. Ehrig et al. 1983). Data types include both the definition of sets of values (sorts) and the operations defined on these sets. The definition of sorts and operations is called the *signature* of

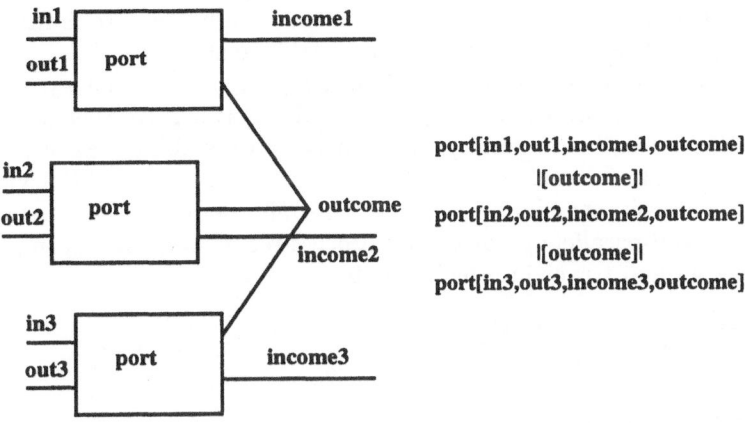

Fig. 3.3. Connection of the ports

the data type, and the relations that govern the operations of the data type
are called *equations*. The translation of LOTOS data types is based on the existence of a library where the basic data types (bit, boolean, bit_vector,
std_logic, std_logic_vector, integer, lists, queues and memories)
are defined. The user can create new data types with a VHDL package and
then translation will be based on a renaming mechanism.

Two lists have been used in the specification of the ethernet bridge to
implement some buffering in the ports for the incoming and for the outcoming
frames. Checking the lists can be done using LOTOS *guards*:

```
process port[inp,outp,income,outcome]
             (id: nat,ibuf,obuf: queue):noexit:=
 [notEmpty(obuf)]->(*send first to ethernet*)
 []
 [not(IsEmpty(ibuf))]->(*send first to bridge control*)
 []
   inp? f: frame; port[...](id,Append(f,ibuf),obuf)
 []
   outcome? f:frame;
   ([Dest(f) eq id]->
     port[...](id,ibuf,Append(f,obuf))
   []
   [Dest(f) ne id]-> (*flooding*)
     port[...](id,ibuf,obuf))
endproc
```

The translation of the guards to VHDL is done with the if then else statement. There is a branching to a different state depending on the evaluation
of the test. With the use of lists, the ports can store frames that will be sent

to the bridge as soon as it can process them. The buffers are limited to N positions, and the $N + 1$th frame the port tries to store is lost.

In the design of the bridge we follow a *top-down* methodology. We have considered it as a whole when specifying the ports. Nevertheless, we will split it into parts for reusability, modularity and testability reasons. But to maintain the interface defined with the ports, we keep the monolithic view but hide the composition and internal gates. The *hide* operator allows the designer to do this, and parallel operators and process recursion allow decomposition of the design and traversing the hierarchy:

```
process control_table_add
        [i1,i2,i3,out]: noexit:=
hide
  req_in,ans_out,req,ans in (
   memory [req,ans] (<>)
   |[req,ans]|
   (control [req,ans,req_in,ans_out]
   |[req_in,ans_out]|
   mux [i1,i2,i3,out,req_in,ans_out])
  )
```

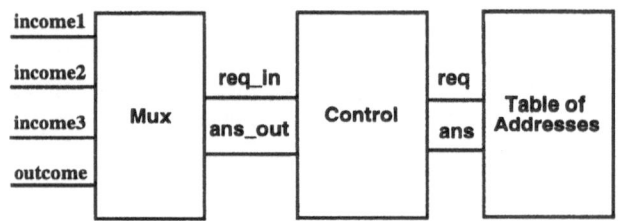

Fig. 3.4. Processes composing the bridge

The specification of processes *memory*, *control* and *mux* involves the LO-TOS elements already introduced. Behavior of process *memory* follows the sequence:

1. acceptance of an address at a source port;
2. update of the memory with source address and incoming port;
3. return of the result of the lookup in the memory for the port of the destination address.

The *control* removes the data of the frames and passes the source and destination addresses to the *memory*, restoring the data and attaching the result of the lookup. *mux* adds the port identifier to the incoming frames and delivers them back to the ports once they have being processed by the *control*. The connection of the three processes is shown in figure 3.4.

The resulting VHDL specification has a main entity *bridge* which instantiates the translation of the three *ports*, the *mux*, the *control* and the *table of addresses.* The signals corresponding to gate *outcome* are connected to a special library module needed to rule out the synchronization. All of the components have to be initialized at the same time, in order to cooperate as stated in the LOTOS description. Let us present the VHDL code of one of these components, for example the *control.*

```
ENTITY P_Control IS
   PORT(
           clk:       IN std_logic;
           CSP_Control:    IN std_logic;
           Reset:  IN std_logic;
           req_a:  IN  std_logic_vector(1 downto 0);
           req:     OUT t_table_info;
           req_r:  OUT std_logic_vector(1 downto 0);
           ans_a:  OUT std_logic_vector(1 downto 0);
           ans:    IN  natural;
           ans_r:  IN  std_logic_vector(1 downto 0);
           a_a:    OUT std_logic_vector(1 downto 0);
           a:      IN  t_bridge_info;
           a_r:    IN  std_logic_vector(1 downto 0);
           b_a:    IN  std_logic_vector(1 downto 0);
           b:      OUT t_bridge_info;
           b_r:    OUT std_logic_vector(1 downto 0));
END P_Control;
ARCHITECTURE beh OF P_Control IS
SIGNAL state: Integer range 0 to 9;
SIGNAL next_state: Integer range 0 to 9;
SIGNAL CS: std_logic;
-- auxiliary signals declaration deleted

BEGIN
  Gate_Val_1: Synch_Val_s
  PORT MAP(
          clk => clk, Reset => Reset_b,
          tin => tin_b,   gt_a => b_a, Ok => Ok_b,
 gt_r => b_r, nack => Nack_b, ack => Ack_b);
-- instantiation of library components
-- that perform the protocol
SEQ: PROCESS(clk, Reset)
BEGIN
IF last_state = '1' OR Reset = '0' THEN
  CS <= '0';
ELSIF CSP_Control = '1' THEN
  CS <= '1';
  state <= 0;
ELSIF clk'event and clk = '0' THEN
  state <= next_state;
END
COM: PROCESS(state,Ack_a,Nack_a,a,Ack_ans,Nack_ans,ans)
VARIABLE vlast_state: std_logic;
-- auxiliary variables declaration deleted
BEGIN
 vlast_state:= '0';
 vReset_b:= '1';
```

```
 -- default variables setting deleted
IF CS = '1' and clk = '1' THEN
CASE state IS
WHEN 0 => vReset_a:= '0';
          next_state <= 1;
WHEN 1 => IF Ack_a='1' THEN
             vOk_a:= '1';
             next_state<=2;
          END IF;
WHEN 2 => IF Ack_a='1' THEN
             vOk_a:= '1';
              brinf_t_bridge_info:=a;
             next_state<=3;
          ELSIF Nack_a='1' THEN
             next_state<=0;
             vReset_a:='0';
          END IF;
WHEN 3 => vReset_req:= '0';
          vVal_req:=
          Table_info(Get_src(Get_Fr(brinf_t_bridge_info)),
                     Get_dest(Get_Fr(brinf_t_bridge_info)),
                     Get_Port(brinf_t_bridge_info));
          next_state <= 4;
WHEN 4 => IF Ack_req='1' THEN
             vOk_req:= '1';
             next_state<=5;
          END IF;
WHEN 5 => vReset_ans:= '0';
          next_state <= 6;
WHEN 6 => IF Ack_ans='1' THEN
             vOk_ans:= '1';
             next_state<=7;
          END IF;
WHEN 7 => IF Ack_ans='1' THEN
             vOk_ans:= '1';
             outp_nat:=ans;
             next_state<=8;
          ELSIF Nack_ans='1' THEN
             next_state<=5;
             vReset_ans:='0';
          END IF;
WHEN 8 => IF (outp_nat=Get_Port(brinf_t_bridge_info)) THEN
             next_state <= 0;
          END IF;
          IF ((outp_nat=0)or
              (outp_nat/=Get_Port(brinf_t_bridge_info)))
          THEN
            next_state<=9;
            vReset_b:= '0';
            vVal_b:=
            Bridge_inf(Get_Fr(brinf_t_bridge_info),
                       outp_nat);
          END IF;
```

```
WHEN 9 => IF Ack_b='1' THEN
               vOk_b:= '1';
               IF ((outp_nat=0)or
                   (outp_nat/=Get_Port(brinf_t_bridge_info)))
               THEN
                  next_state<=0;
               ELSE  vOk_b:= '0';
               END IF;
            END IF;
END CASE;
END IF;
 last_state <= vlast_state;
 -- auxiliary signals are assigned
 -- auxiliary variables contents
END PROCESS;

END beh;
```

The interface presents the VHDL signals translating LOTOS gates, plus a clock, a chip select, and a global asynchronous reset. This description of a finite state machine has two processes: a sequential and a combinatorial one. Several library components are instantiated in the protocol that implements the LOTOS synchronization. The combinatorial process contains the logic for the sequential flow of the *control* process.

4. System testing

One of the principal applications of formal description techniques is testing. Their use improves the quality of the process of the system design significantly, and reduces the consumption of resources.

Generation and application of tests requires great effort for any implementation under test (IUT). Usually this work is done manually by experts who have to provide an implementation dependent test suite. The approach has three main drawbacks:

1. hand generation of a bulk of test cases is very expensive;
2. the risk of introducing errors in the test cases is very high and validation of the test cases is needed;
3. it is difficult to reuse and maintain test cases because low level details are contained in them;
4. test application is a time consuming task;
5. decisions about results is under human interpretation.

Methodologies based on formal description techniques (FDTs) benefit from automatic generation and tool support in the test application phase.

Formal support is provided by the use of LOTOS as an intermediate language. Some advantages of using LOTOS are: existence of transformation tools, verification and validation tools. LOTOS formal support provides links with formal notions of tests validation, test generation and test execution formalization. Section 5. will describe the application of this methodology using an example.

4.1 Derivation and validation of test cases

Figure 4.1 describes a methodology for tests generation using the formal support provided by FDTs.

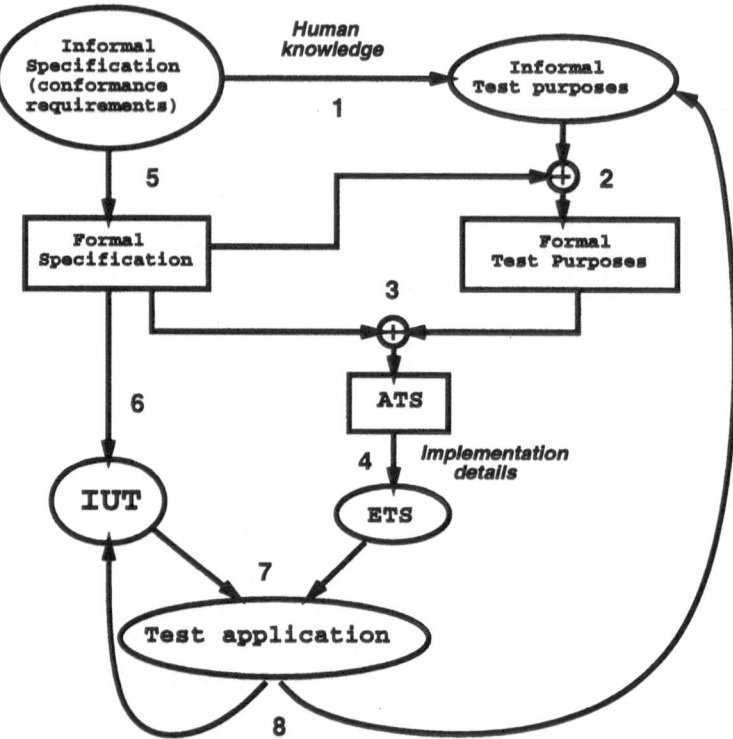

Fig. 4.1. Methodology for test suite derivation

The relevant steps are:

1. the testing requirements are captured in an informal specification – a human expert, taking personal experience and environment restrictions into account produces the informal test requirements document;
2. the informal test requirements are formalized – for consistency between the formal specification of the protocol and the test suite, the same abstractions must be used in both formal and informal versions (e.g. same symbols, level of granularity, ...);

3. the formalized test requirements are combined with the formal specification in order to produce (formally specified) test suites;
4. this test suite is converted into an executable test suite (ETS) by adding implementation details;
5. the formal specification is derived from the same informal specification;
6. the IUT is derived by any means from its formal specification – usually this derivation is performed manually in order to optimize performance, to add non-standard features, to enhance robustness, and so on. This process may introduce errors, therefore conformance to the original specification has to be demonstrated;
7. conformance may be demonstrated by combining the IUT and the ETS, that is, by execution of the conformance test suite;
8. after execution of the test suite, both the IUT and the informal test requirements may be modified – the IUT needs to be modified if it does not conform to the requirements. More test requirements may be added for specific behaviors.

In the FORMAT framework the implementation language is VHDL, and the specification language may be TD or LOTOS. Tests may be produced either by hand or automatically. A test run will apply the tests to the IUT in order to determine if the implementation behaves as defined by the specification. Test cases may be derived by hand but must satisfy the following constraints:

1. Complementarity: when the implementation expects a datum, the test case must provide it.
   When the implementation sends a value, the test case must handle it properly.
2. Completeness: the test case must react to any valid behavior of the implementation.
3. Fixed result: the test must provide a deterministic result for any valid behavior of the implementation.
4. Fault detection: the test must detect wrong behaviors of the implementation, according to the requirements specification for the test case.

4.2 Test suite application

The last step in the testing of a product is the test execution. In this section we describe the architecture of the test execution tool. The requirements, functionality and result are explained. The tool inputs are test cases; and its outputs the corresponding verdicts. Test classification, results of test execution and verdicts are described.

We assume the existence of a specification of the product and some implementations of it. The purpose is to verify the correctness of the implementations with respect to the specification.

The test execution requires the application of tests to the IUT. The interaction is accomplished through the interface of the implementation. When

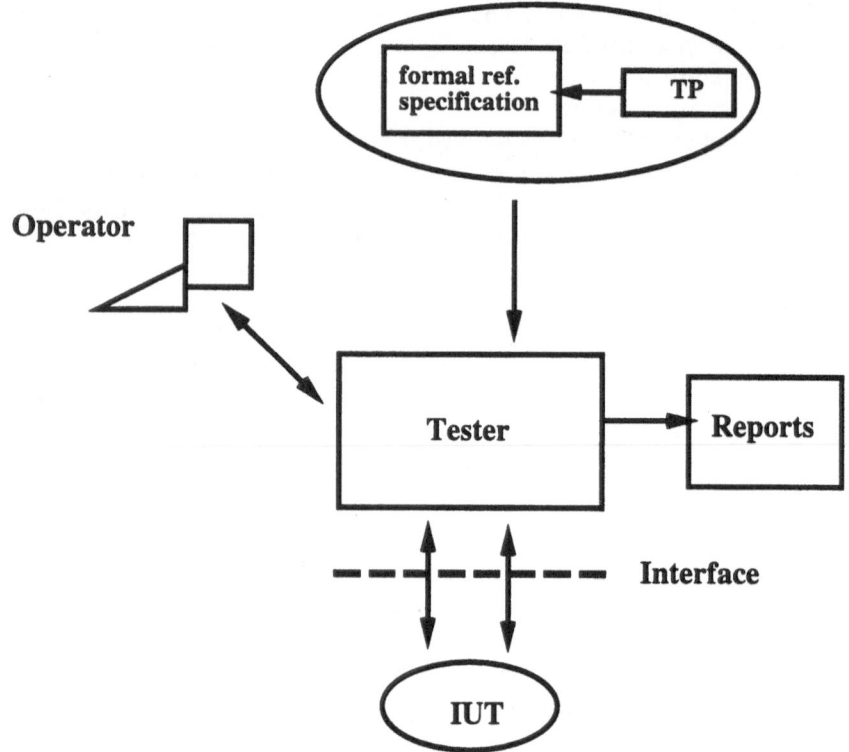

Fig. 4.2. Test execution framework

the application has been performed, the *informal* result has to be formalized and interpreted in terms of the formal framework (LOTOS+Testing), in order to complete the test execution.

The proposed tester gives:

1. formal support for the testing process;
2. operational aspects of the execution.

Formal support. The formal support is based on LOTOS as FDT, but the language itself does not provide support for testing concepts.

1. Verdict assignation: the verdicts are defined according to ISO9646 defined in (ISO DP 9646-1 1988). It states that we must provide a verdict for each possible termination of the test. It is important to notice that due to correct, but non desired behaviors of the IUT, some executions of tests do not provide information about the correctness of the IUT. The verdict assigned to each possible termination provides the basis to decide whether the implementation behaves correctly or not. The outcome and the result analysis are used to classify the test.

The *observed outcome* is the trace of events which occurred during the execution of a test case; it includes every input and output from the IUT at the points of control and observation.

The *foreseen outcome* is identified and defined by the abstract test case specification taken in conjunction with the protocol standard.

The next step is the production of **verdicts**: "is a statement of pass, fail or inconclusive to be associated with every foreseen outcome".

The result analysis is performed comparing the observed outcome with the foreseen outcome. the possible verdict will be:

a) **pass**: this means that the observed outcome satisfies the test purpose and is valid with respect to the relevant standard;

b) **fail**: this means that the observed outcome is syntactically invalid or inopportune with respect to the relevant standard;

c) **inconclusive**: this means that the relevant outcome is valid with respect to the relevant standard but prevents the test purpose from being accomplished.

2. Deadlock definition: the deadlock definition is necessary to define the result of the execution of a test case. The formal definition of deadlock requires the enrichment of LOTOS with a time model. The formal time model combined with the test case provides an operational definition to decide deadlock when a *real* timer expires.

3. Testing composition: application of test cases to the implementation implies the combination of each case with the IUT under certain rules. These rules may be summarized with the concept of imposition: the test must be able to receive any valid output of the IUT, and must send (when corresponding) valid inputs to the IUT.

Operational aspects. When test cases are derived using formal specifications in LOTOS as support, automation of the testing process is increased. The operational aspects may be summarized as:

1. test processing in an automatic, semiautomatic or by hand mode;

2. chaining of test cases;

3. verdicts assignment to each test execution;

4. recording for report generation.

5. Testing environment

In the previous section the use of the FORMAT tools for defining and implementing hardware systems has been described. A crucial part of the systems development is the testing part. Testing shares a lot of elements with systems design; we must think about the structure of the code, define the interfaces, code the behavior of the process, and so on.

Nevertheless, design and implementation of tests and systems differs on a number of important concepts. Most of the differences are derived from the fact that tests are executed some number of times in a very controlled environment. This reduces the performance requirements of tests. Thus, it is not so important the efficiency on surface or speed of the produced VHDL when doing testing. On the other hand, instead of having a single system implementation, we will need to define thousands or hundreds of different tests.

The support for managing, modifying, executing and interpreting test cases is more important than efficiency or performance when working with tests. We must concentrate on improving the quality of the process.

In this section we will show the use of FORMAT tools for defining, implementing and executing tests. The front end of the environment is the Time Diagram Editor (TDE). The core of the system is the compiler from TD to VHDL, and some extra features have been added to configure a Testing Environment.

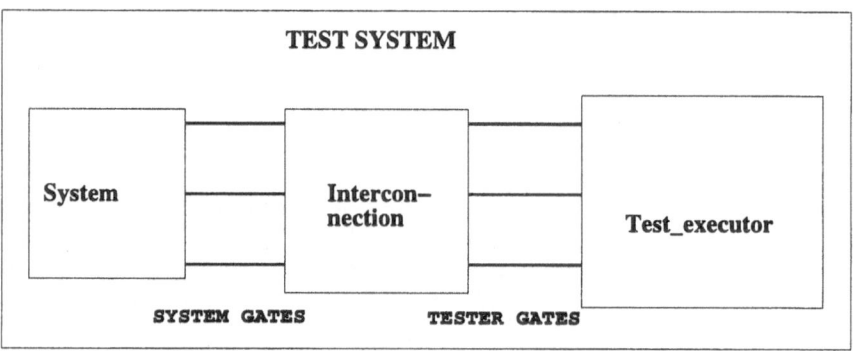

Fig. 5.1. Testing environment

Figure 5.1 describes the Validation Environment (VE) of FORMAT. It takes as input two pieces of informations: a description of the test in the TDE, and a system definition in VHDL. The result of this process is a verdict on the compliance of the implementation according to the test, and a detailed log of the test run. The process is automatic after the human operator has entered the information into the TDE.

The VE splits the testing process into three sequential steps:

1. test case production;
2. test case implementation;
3. test case execution and report generation.

The rest of this chapter describes by means of an example, the characteristics of each step, and how the different tools work together.

5.1 Test case production

The Timing Diagrams Editor (TDE) is the front end of the testing environment. The operator must read carefully the document describing the informal testing and implementation requirements of the system, and produce an informal definition for each test case. The informal definition is formalized using the TDE.

By its nature, tests are simpler than systems. In fact they are a representation of the behavior of a subset of the system behavior we are testing. However we must have in mind a different point of view when working with tests. We may summarize the difference in a single word: *complementarity*. Complementarity between system and test means:

1. when the system produces a signal, the test must capture it and perform the appropriate action;
2. when the system is waiting for one or more signals, the test must provide with a correct value.

The operator must take into account these considerations when designing tests. There are tools and methodologies for generating test cases. We will focus on supporting the generation of test cases by hand. Future works will afford other generation techniques.

The use of TDE as a front end for the production and maintenance of test cases offers several advantages:

1. the definition of new test cases and the modification of the old ones take place within a much more friendly environment in which the operator does not need to worry about low level details of the implementation language (VHDL);
2. the complexity is reduced because the operator does not need to learn new languages, tools or environments and systems and test cases can be specified using the same TDE.

Figure 5.2 shows a test case defined using the TDE. The Control block of Initialization (CI) is defined as a state machine. This machine changes the state during the initialization phase of DEPTH. When this phase finishes, the CI machine is in waiting state.

The CI is ruled by a state machine which holds the reset line of the system down until the initialization finishes. The CI waits for signal ARR, then issues a request access (ic_acc_ped) to the control of the interface of the Motorola bus (IABM). When access is granted (ic_acc_com), the contents of the table of initialization are loaded in registers a, b, c and d.

The starting address of the table is loaded in ic_ai register. The contents of the following four addresses are loaded in registers a, b, c and d. All are 32 bits wide.

The address in ic_ai and a two bits internal counter (di[1:0]) are used as base+offset for writing the configuration registers a, b, c and d.

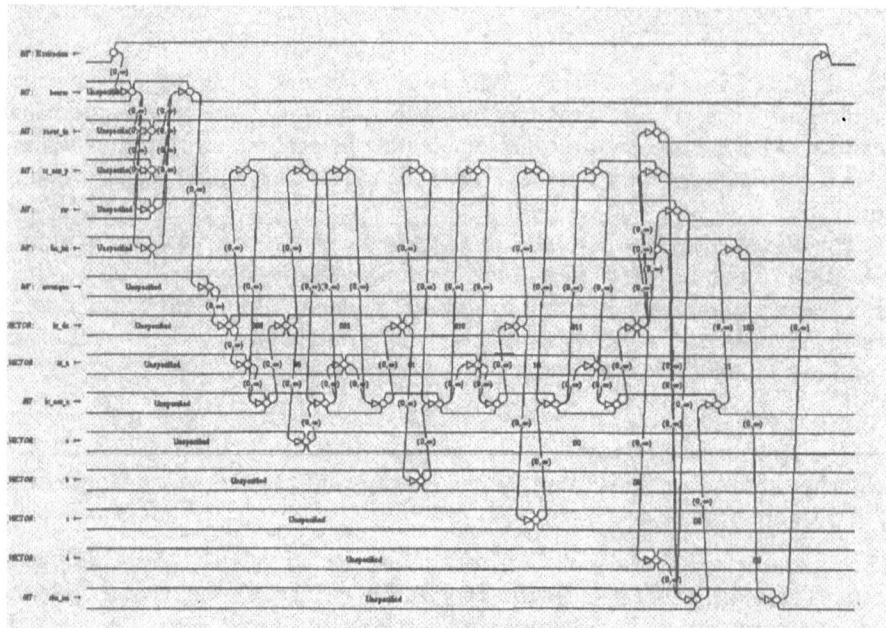

Fig. 5.2. Time diagram of a test case

When the last position of the table is accessed, the control releases the internal reset line and signals the end of the initialization phase on fin_ini. The latter remains high until a return signal r_fin_ini is detected.

The test cases are intended to test the behavior described above. They should cover the following phases of activity:

1. detection of the starting signal (excitacion='1');
2. generation of internal reset;
3. load of the starting address;
4. detection of fin_ini changing from '0' to '1' signaling the end of the initialization phase.

5.2 Test cases implementation

Test cases are translated automatically from TD to VHDL. The translation uses LOTOS as intermediate language. It offers two important advantages:

1. the operator is not overloaded with the tedious work of producing a large number of low level VHDL lines of code. Instead more abstract work is required and the testing process is speeded up;
2. the use of automatic coding avoids many minor errors that manual coding could introduce. That increases confidence in the testing process, because the number of sources of error upstream of the test is reduced.

The architecture of the code produced for our example is summarized on figure 5.3.

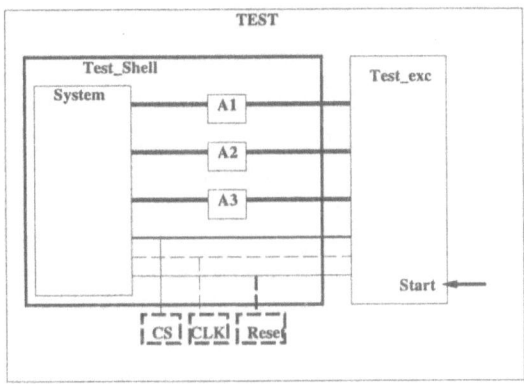

Fig. 5.3. VHDL architecture of a test bench

In the figure, **System** is the IUT implemented using VHDL, **Test** is the tester process implemented on VHDL using the compile from TD to VHDL. Note that the Testing environment adds some new components: the interface adapters (**A1, A2, ...**), **Test_Shell** and **Test Environment** itself.

The interface adapters provide protocol adaptation for each port of the system. They provide wire and protocol compatibility between **System** and **Test**. This is required because the wire and protocol interface of the latter is fixed by the compiler, whereas the interface of the real system may change.

Test_shell offers extra information with which to execute the test:

RESET: this is used to restart **Test** and **System**;
CS: this is used to start **Test** and **System**;
CLK: this is a global clock for **Test** and **System**;
Start: this is the gate used to signal the start of execution of the test.

5.3 Test case execution and report production

The final objective of the test process is the production of a report about the compliance of the system with the testing and system requirements. It is necessary to run the test to produce such a report.

In this phase the test system gets the VHDL code of both the system and the test and combines them. The test system is simulated and a report is obtained for each test case.

The results are represented graphically by the waveform produced by the simulator (see figure 5.4). The text log contains an exhaustive description of the changes of the signals in the interface between the **test_shell** and the test case. This information may be examined when detailed information about the test run is needed.

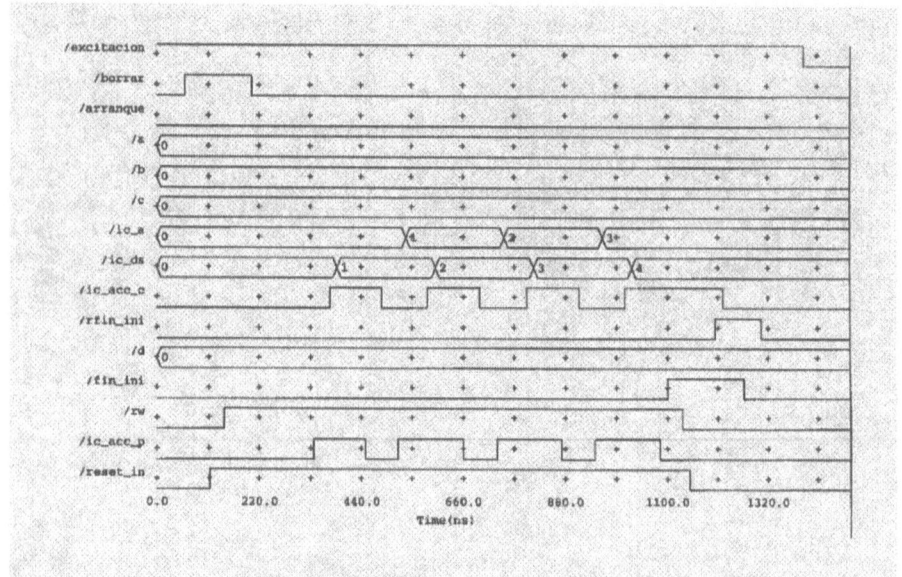

Fig. 5.4. Execution waves

The verdict is produced when signal *rfin_ini* drops to 0:

1. if this signal goes back to 0 ⇒ success;
2. if the signal does not go back to 0 ⇒ fail.

6. Conclusion

We have described the use of LOTOS as a formal language basis for the generation and testing of VHDL code. The specification, design and implementation of a three-way Ethernet bridge has been presented as an illustrative example of the application of the FORMAT VHDL-generation toolset. The testing methodology and tools have been illustrated through application to a circuit initializer.

References

C. Delgado Kloos and P. T. Breuer, (eds.) (1995): *Formal Semantics for VHDL*. Kluwer.

H. Ehrig, W. Fey, and H. Hansen (1983): ACT ONE: An Algebraic Language with two Levels of Semantics. Technical Report Bericht Nr. 83.103, Tech. Universität Berlin, 1983.

IEEE (1989): IEEE Standard VHDL: Language Reference Manual. IS Std 1076–
   1987, The Institute of Electrical and Electronics Engineers, April. 2nd printing.
IEEE (1994): IEEE Standard VHDL: Language Reference Manual. IS Std 1076–
   1993, The Institute of Electrical and Electronics Engineers.
ISO DP 9646-1 (1988): Information Processing System - Open Systems Interconnection - OSI Conformance testing methodology and framework - Part 1: General
   concepts. DIS ISO/TC97/SC21/WG1 DP 9646-1, ISO.
ISO (1989): *Information Processing Systems — Open Systems Interconnection —
   LOTOS: A Formal Description Technique Based on the Temporal Ordering of
   Observational Behaviour.* IS-8807. International Standards Organization, 1989.
   published 15 Feb.
J. A. Mañas, T. de Miguel, T. Robles, J. Salvachúa, G. Huecas, and M. Veiga
   (1993): TOPO: Quick Reference – Front End. Technical report, Dpt. Telematics
   Engineering, Technical Univ. Madrid, Ciudad Universitaria, E-28040 Madrid,
   Spain, June. Version 3R2.
J. Quemada, S. Pavón, A. Fernández (1989): State Exploration by Transforma-
   tion with LOLA; *Workshop on Automatic Verification Methods for Finite State
   Systems*, Grenoble, June.